PERSONAL DIARY OF
ADMIRAL THE LORD LOUIS MOUNTBATTEN
1943–1946

PERSONAL DIARY OF

ADMIRAL THE LORD
LOUIS MOUNTBATTEN

Supreme Allied Commander,
South-East Asia,
1943–1946

Edited by
PHILIP ZIEGLER

COLLINS
8 Grafton Street, London W1
1988

William Collins Sons & Co. Ltd
London · Glasgow · Sydney · Auckland
Toronto · Johannesburg

British Library Cataloguing in Publication Data

The Diaries of Admiral the Lord Louis
    Mountbatten Supreme Allied Commander
    South-East Asia, 1943–1946.
    1. Mountbatten, Louis Mountbatten, *Earl*
    2. Great Britain, *Royal Navy* – Biography
    3. Viceroy – India – Biography
    I. Ziegler, Philip
    941.082'092'4   DA89.1.M59

ISBN 0-00-217607-6

First published 1988
Text © Emberdove Ltd 1988
Selection, Preface and editorial matter
© P. S. & M. C. Ziegler & Co. 1988

Photoset in Linotron Sabon by
Rowland Phototypesetting Ltd
Bury St Edmunds, Suffolk
Printed in Great Britain by
William Collins Sons & Co. Ltd, Glasgow

CONTENTS

LIST OF ILLUSTRATIONS

(Unless otherwise stated, all photographs come from the Broadlands Archives.)

EDITOR'S NOTE

Lord Louis Mountbatten, as he then was, kept this diary partly as a personal record for his own use, and partly to inform a very short list of people to whom a copy was sent – the King among them. The diary was not therefore 'Top Secret' since it did not contain details of operational movements that would have been of major benefit to the Japanese. The names of Allied military units were often added in manuscript at a later date. It was, on the other hand, highly confidential, in that it discussed personalities and organizational problems with a frankness that would have caused considerable embarrassment if it had become more widely read.

I have shortened it by a little over a third. Mountbatten used the diary as an *aide memoire*, and I have frequently removed details of reception committees, guards of honour, and so on, that would have been of no interest to the general reader. I have also removed many of the accounts of routine inspections that add no fresh material, or of dinners, interviews or meetings where little is recorded beyond a list of names. These exercises inevitably distort the picture of Mountbatten's daily life. If a diary entry begins 'Left Palam airfield 1100' the reader can be reasonably sure that the Supreme Commander had already inspected three or four units and conducted at least one meeting. His pace of work was furious and his sustained energy phenomenal. The effect of my cutting is also to make the text sometimes scrappy: the reader will leave Mountbatten in Singapore and rejoin him in New Delhi. This is to be regretted, but the alternative was to swell an already long narrative with much tedious detail. Nothing has been removed on grounds of secrecy or because it might have been embarrassing to those concerned.

I have confined footnotes to those places where the reader would otherwise be unable to identify a name in the text or where I felt additional information would be interesting or entertaining. Mountbatten's meticulousness as a diarist ensures that examples of the former description are relatively rare. Once one begins to add supplementary information in footnotes there is no stopping. I hope I have exercised enough but not too much restraint. Rather than explain the significance of abbreviations in a footnote and risk the reader having forgotten what they mean when they recur, I have listed the less familiar of them in appendix I on page 344. I have also listed in appendix II those Christian and nicknames which regularly appear in the text.

PREFACE

By the late summer of 1943 the tide of war in South-East Asia was on the point of turning. It called for considerable faith to accept that this was so. Earlier that year a premature and ill-conceived counter-offensive in the Arakan peninsula in North Burma had failed ignominiously. 'The very limited operations carried out this year', wrote the corps commander, General Irwin, in mid-April, 'have disclosed the lamentable fact that the Army is not yet sufficiently trained or efficiently led to take on the Japanese on even superior terms in numbers or material.' Patiently General Slim had been building up his new 14th Army to resume the attack on Burma but there was still a long way to go. Numerically the six divisions in India and the three American-Chinese in the north slightly outnumbered the five or six Japanese divisions then in Burma, but the latter had the advantage of interior lines of communications and superiority in the techniques of jungle warfare. The Japanese still had the better aircraft and their fleet dominated the Bay of Bengal. The balance of power was shifting, but it would be well into 1944 before this became apparent.

The idea of appointing a Supreme Commander to take control of all the allied forces in South-East Asia had been mooted in May 1943. Mountbatten was far from being the first choice. Leo Amery, the Secretary of State for India, had put forward his name early on but Churchill had pooh-poohed the idea. It was only after some half dozen more senior officers had been considered and, for one reason or another, rejected, that Mountbatten's candidature was revived. Churchill quickly convinced himself that this had been his intention from the start, and that a young and dashing admiral with a background in Combined Operations was the obvious choice to breathe life into the tired old military machine and rescue the British armies from a long-drawn-out and painful slog through the Burmese jungle. On 24 August 1943 he sent telegrams to the Prime Ministers of South Africa, Australia and New Zealand announcing the new appointment:

Mountbatten has unique qualifications in that he is intimately acquainted with all three branches of the Services, and also with amphibious operations. He has served for nearly a year and a half on the Chiefs of Staff Committee, and thus knows the whole of our war story from the centre. I regard this of great importance on account of the extremely varied character of the South-East Asia front by land and sea. Mountbatten is a fine organizer, and a man of great energy and daring. His appointment has been cordially welcomed by the President, and the American Chiefs of Staff, and was hailed with delight by Soong, on behalf of the Generalissimo.

Mountbatten, at the age of forty-three, now found himself full Admiral, promoted above the heads of all his contemporaries and many far senior officers. The resentment that this transmogrification inspired was not to make things any easier for him over the next two years. The organization of the new South-East Asia Command was complex and cumbersome. As Supreme Allied Commander Mountbatten was responsible to the British Chiefs of Staff, but also, to an extent which was never satisfactorily defined, to the Combined Chiefs of Staff of Britain and the United States. His deputy was the American Lieutenant General Stilwell, 'Vinegar Joe' by nickname and temperament, who was also commander of the Chinese troops in Burma and Assam and Chief of Staff to Generalissimo Chiang Kai-shek – a position in which he was independent of Mountbatten.

Mountbatten's Chief of Staff was Lieutenant General Pownall, whose role was envisaged by Alan Brooke, the Chief of the Imperial General Staff, as being that of a nanny who would ensure that his headstrong and exuberant charge did not stray too far off the rails. This view of Pownall's functions was not shared by the Supreme Commander. The Deputy Chief of Staff was an American, Lieutenant General Wedemeyer. His role was seen by the American Chiefs of Staff as being that of a watchdog who would ensure that Mountbatten did not divert the allied war effort in pursuit of purely imperial objectives. This view of Wedemeyer's functions was not shared by the Supreme Commander.

Then came the three Commanders-in-Chief, all far older than Mountbatten. The Commander-in-Chief Eastern Fleet was Admiral Somerville, eighteen years Mountbatten's senior and an officer whose courage, charm and distinction were only matched by a sense of hierarchy and propriety. General Giffard, the Commander-in-Chief Allied Land Forces, was an honourable and kindly gentleman; competent, prudent, conservative, and resolved to defend his prerogatives against the incursions of an inexperienced naval overlord. Air Marshal Peirse was the Commander-in-Chief least likely to cause Mountbatten trouble, but the air element of the Command was confused by the fact that at the outset the 10th American Air Force under General Stratemeyer was responsible not to Peirse but to General Stilwell.

Mountbatten's instructions were to defend India, to drive the Japanese from Burma, Malaya and the rest of South-East Asia and to reopen land communications with China across the north of Burma. His various masters had differing priorities among these objectives. To Churchill the recovery of Britain's Asian Empire, above all Singapore, was of paramount importance. The Americans had scant sympathy for such imperial ambitions. To their mind the principal if not only reason for Mountbatten's activities was to reopen the road to China. This fundamental divergence was to plague the Supreme Commander until the end of the war.

Another recurrent problem was the failure properly to define the role of a Supreme Commander. Was Mountbatten a true commander with his own planning staff, imposing his decisions on inferior Commanders-in-Chief, or a chairman of committee whose function was to harmonize and occasionally to arbitrate between largely autonomous Commanders? Mountbatten not surprisingly felt the former, though professing that this had been imposed on him somewhat against his will by the Chiefs of Staff in London and, still more, Washington. The Commanders-in-Chief were equally convinced that the latter was correct. Mountbatten's time in South-East Asia was marked by a series of compromises between these two points of view; sometimes to the advantage of the Supreme Commander, sometimes of the Commanders-in-Chief, but involving much embittered wrangling that was never to the advantage of the allied cause.

Another problem for the Supreme Commander was the relatively low priority given in London and Washington to the war in South-East Asia. Mountbatten had been sent out to practise a bold amphibious strategy, avoiding war in the jungle by striking far behind the Japanese lines. To this end he prepared innumerable plans for landings by sea in Burma, Malaya, Sumatra and elsewhere. All were confounded because the tools were denied him; the promised landing craft time and again disappeared for use in the Mediterranean or on the Normandy coast. It was the final irony that Mountbatten's one major maritime enterprise, Operation ZIPPER, took place only after the Japanese surrender.

It was therefore with inadequate material, ill-defined powers and uncertain objectives that Mountbatten set forth in October 1943 to take command of what he knew was likely to prove a turbulent crew. It was typical of the man that he was wholly undaunted; his ebullience waxing as the difficulties grew more oppressive. He was going to need all his ebullience over the next three years.

THE DIARY

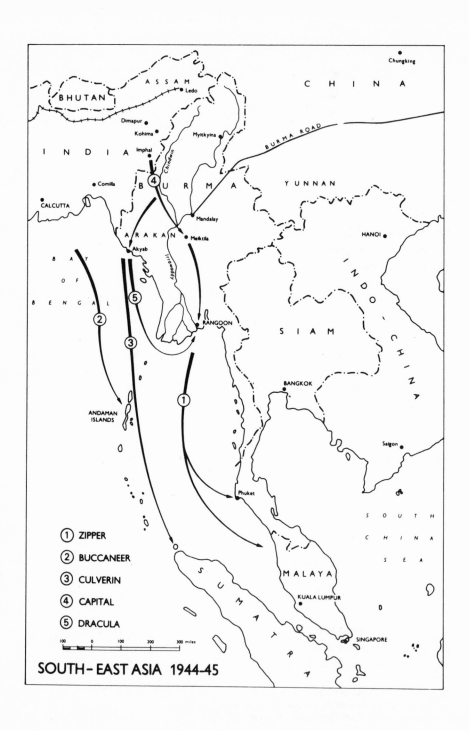

① ZIPPER

② BUCCANEER

③ CULVERIN

④ CAPITAL

⑤ DRACULA

SOUTH-EAST ASIA 1944-45

SATURDAY, 2 OCTOBER 1943   The Air Ministry asked me to be at Northolt by 2310. In spite of my little 10 Horse Power Ford giving out for the first time in two years when I was going home to catch the Admiralty car at Chester Street, we reached the aerodrome by 2307. The Chief of the Air Staff[1] had paid me the very high compliment of coming down in person to see me off. His staff, however, had told him that I was leaving at 2200. He therefore arrived one hour and ten minutes too early and, very sensibly, left messages of good luck and returned wearily in the blackout.

The party which left in the York included John Keswick, my Political Liaison Officer,[2] Micky Hodges, my Signal Officer-in-Chief and Arthur Leveson, my Flag Lieutenant.

Patricia[3] came down to see us off and was shown over the magnificent York aircraft called Ascalon, which had been built to take the King to North Africa and is shared by the Prime Minister. I had His Majesty's lovely cabin with a large and lovely bed, writing desk and chair, and a nice little bathroom attached. We took off at 2330.

SUNDAY, 3 OCTOBER   We landed at Gibraltar at 0800, and went to the Mount, where Vice Admiral Sir Harold Burrough provided bath and breakfast. The Governor, Sir Noel Mason-MacFarlane, was still away in Italy.

Noel Coward turned up and kept me company while I was having my bath!

Incidentally I heard both in the Middle East and Iraq how much his tour had been appreciated, and how popular it had been among the troops. He tells me that Mr Beddington, the Ministry of Information

---

[1]   Air Chief Marshal Sir Charles Portal, later Viscount Portal of Hungerford.
[2]   Director of Jardine Matheson and authority on Chinese affairs.
[3]   Mountbatten's elder daughter, now herself Countess Mountbatten of Burma.

cinema expert, who did everything in his power to prevent *In Which We Serve* being made, and who warned both Noel and me that if we persisted in our efforts to make this film he would have a ban put on it in America and neutral countries to prevent their seeing bad propaganda, has been honoured by His Majesty with the CBE!!![1]

We took off from Gibraltar at 1130. I had received a signal from General Eisenhower asking me to arrive at the El Aouina Aerodrome, but the pilot of the Ascalon knew better. He said El Aouina had too short a runway for a York class aircraft and that he landed the King at Sibala No.1. I was unable to shake him in his decision and we sent a most immediate telegram to give our change of destination. We landed punctually at 1545 at Sibala No.1. There were no cars to meet us, but we eventually got some up from the local air station. The pilot had to go to Algiers to pick up Field Marshal Smuts. I suggested it might be better to wait and see if he was at Tunis, but as the pilot had written instructions to be at Algiers before nightfall he thought he had better leave without delay and went.

No one had heard of General Eisenhower in Tunis and after one hour and a half we gave up looking for his headquarters, and made for the North African Air Force Headquarters which I had visited in July. Here I found Tedder[2] who gave me a great welcome.

Eisenhower eventually turned up very upset because he had waited two hours for me at El Aouina Aerodrome. The runway had been extended during the last three months to take an aircraft of the York class, and Sibala No.1 two days before had had mud patches which would have wrecked the York, so that the pilot's decision could not have been worse. To cap it all Field Marshal Smuts had changed his itinerary on account of engine trouble and landed at El Aouina just after the York had left Sibala!! This left Eisenhower the problem of trying to accommodate both the Smuts party and my party at short notice!

I had a valuable hour's talk with Smuts. After dinner Eisenhower, Tedder and I had a really good and helpful talk about my own job.

MONDAY, 4 OCTOBER   We left at 0900 in the Liberator Marco Polo which was to take us on. We landed at Cairo West at 1830.

[1] *In Which We Serve* was Noel Coward's film based on the exploits of Mountbatten's destroyer HMS *Kelly*. The Ministry of Information had doubts, because in the end the destroyer was sunk.

[2] Air Chief Marshal Sir Arthur Tedder (later Baron Tedder) was Commander-in-Chief of the Mediterranean Allied Air Force.

Dick Casey,[1] the Minister of State, kindly put me up in his lovely house at Mena opposite the Pyramids. He had asked the three Commanders-in-Chief to dinner, Admiral Sir John Cunningham, General Sir Maitland Wilson and Air Marshal Sir John Linnell (representing Sholto Douglas who had gone home). After dinner he held a proper Defence Committee with the Secretary present, and we discussed what help the Middle East could be to South-East Asia in the war against Japan.

TUESDAY, 5 OCTOBER   We left Cairo West at 1145 and reached Habbaniya at 1545. Stewart Perowne[2] having let me in to call on the King of Iraq, the Regent, the Prime Minister and Chief of the Army Staff, the Ambassador, Sir Kinahan Cornwallis, had telegraphed to Cairo saying that he had arranged a dinner party for me to meet them. Casey had cabled back that I could not stay for dinner as we had to leave Habbaniya at daylight the next morning 50 miles away from Baghdad. When we arrived at Baghdad in the Hudson it was 1635, and to get back before dark meant leaving at 1730.

My staff went off to the Embassy and thus had a chance of seeing Baghdad, but I was driven back by the Ambassador in the opposite direction to the Regent's house in the country. It then transpired that the Foreign Office had so worded their telegram that the Ambassador was sure I had an urgent and important message for the Regent. The Regent and King Feisal II were staying at Jerusalem and when the Ambassador asked the Regent to come back, he naturally refused. The Ambassador insisted that he must come back to receive my urgent message and attend the dinner party he was giving for me. The Regent then flew back leaving King Feisal in Jerusalem. I told the Ambassador I had nothing to say to the Regent, Prime Minister or anybody else, and that I was only seeing them to oblige the Foreign Office and at the personal sacrifice of not seeing Baghdad at all.

The Ambassador implored me to deliver some message to the Regent to avoid an awkward situation for him. I thereupon took it upon myself to give the Regent a warm message of welcome from the King and glibly informed him that the King was counting the days to the Regent's visit to Buckingham Palace! The Regent was much touched by this special mark of attention from His Majesty and asked me to convey

---

[1] Later Baron Casey, Australian politician and proconsul.
[2] Arabist, old friend of Mountbatten and currently Public Relations Attaché at the British Embassy in Baghdad.

his profound thanks to His Majesty and say how much he was looking forward to the visit.

Meanwhile my faithful Flag Lieutenant arrived bearing an enormous box of chocolates as a gift for the King of Iraq. Since His Majesty is only 8 years old this appears to be the most popular form of gift, but I was very angry that it was brought in after we had discovered that the King was in Jerusalem, as I had naturally begun to hope to be able to eat the chocolates myself!

At the end of the interview the Prime Minister, Nuri,[1] drew me aside and said in a hoarse whisper, 'Have you brought your driver with you?' This took me aback and I replied, 'Which driver?', being uncertain whether he was referring to a brassie[2] or a chauffeur. Nuri replied, 'The famous one, of course', and as I was now completely out of my depth I brought the conversation to an end by saying 'No'.

Discussing the matter later, we came to the conclusion that the Prime Minister must have seen the film *In Which We Serve* and that Stewart Perowne, who was an old friend of Able Seaman Lawlor, must have pointed him out in the film as my driver. The only other alternative is that, having been soundly beaten at golf by me, he had explained away his defeat to the Prime Minister by putting his failure down to my golf clubs.

WEDNESDAY, 6 OCTOBER   We took off at 0630, first light of dawn, and landed at 0645 with a burnt-out solenoid in the variable pitch gear of one of our propellers. It took 2 hours to mend and when we left at 0900 we realized we were due to land in Karachi in the dark.

I could not help getting a certain thrill at the moment when we crossed the coast of India, to feel that it had fallen to me to be the outward and visible symbol of the British Empire's intention to return to the attack in Asia and regain our lost Empire.

We landed in the dark at 2030 and were met by a vast concourse of officers. The whole party was put up in the brand new Governor's House at Karachi, where our host was Sir Hugh Dow, Governor of the newly created Sind Province.

THURSDAY, 7 OCTOBER   We took off again at 0900. An overwhelming crowd of high officials and newspaper men met us at New

---

[1] Nuri Es-Sa'id, who survived as Prime Minister until murdered in July 1958.
[2] A now disused term for some sort of wooden golf club.

Delhi. They included the Commanders-in-Chief, India, Eastern Fleet, Air Force, South-East Asia Army Group, as well as an incredible number of Admirals, Generals and Air Marshals commanding various portions of the fleet, air and ground forces, not to mention all the American generals, and last but by no means least, my old friend General Wingate and some Chinese officers.

General Auchinleck drove me to his magnificent house, where I and the Commanders-in-Chief are staying with him.[1]

MONDAY, 11 OCTOBER On October 11th I moved into my new house, lent me by the Raja of Faridkot. This house merits some description, as I must confess it is the last word in millionaire luxury.

It has about a dozen absolutely first-class bedrooms, each with a dressing room and bathroom, a large dining room, a small dining room, a drawing room and billiard room, which is for general use, and upstairs I have a small sitting room for myself.

It was only finished a short while ago and is furnished with all the latest and most modern fittings and I must confess we are living in the lap of luxury.

I had intended to use it as a big Senior Officers' Mess for all officers of Brigadier's rank and above, which would have entailed putting up lots of tents in the grounds, but the Raja struck at this, so I am confining the party to the senior members of my staff and the ADCs, who live in an RAF Mess just opposite, except for Flags, who has got himself into the pantry of the second dining room and is turning it into a beautiful bedroom!

There was a bit of misunderstanding about my Headquarters when I first arrived. I had been given three floors of a complete block of the new Secretariat for the South-East Asia Command Headquarters. Since the naval, military and air Commanders-in-Chief form part of the South-East Asia Command and only the air staff were already accommodated in New Delhi, it followed that the Eastern Fleet and Army Group Staffs had to find accommodation in New Delhi at the same time as my staff. Admiral Somerville and the Naval Staff thereupon moved into the ground floor of my new block, and General Giffard and the Army Group Staff selected the second floor, leaving me and my staff to try and get into a single floor in the middle. It took a lot of tact persuading the

[1] Subsequently Jawaharlal Nehru's official residence and now the Nehru Museum.

Admiral and the General to move their parties out into other, but unfortunately less salubrious blocks, which have now been turned over to them, but I felt it really was essential that I and my sixteen officers of Major General's rank (!) should also be housed in one block with the rest of my staff.

On the first day that I moved into Faridkot House the Air ADC, Squadron Leader Wilson, said to me, 'Have you got a book?', to which I replied, 'Why? Have you run out of detective stories?' and then discovered that he meant a Visitors' Book as no less than twelve people had asked to put their names in it on the first day. I told him that I had not got a book, that this was an operational Headquarters, and that no social callers were received. He then asked me what he was to do about the people who left visiting cards, and I told him not to accept them for the same reason. So I shall be unpopular with the Delhi community, but I hope not with those who want to get on with the war.

On Sunday, the 10th, I drove over with Flags to see the old Viceregal Lodge and showed him Mrs Ronnie Greville's sitting room in which I got engaged twenty-two years ago next February. It is now used as a University.

THURSDAY, 14 OCTOBER   Meeting with Commanders-in-Chief, General Wedemeyer and General Browning[1] about Airborne Troops. Took Generals Giffard and Wedemeyer to see General Wingate, who is unfortunately in hospital with enteric. He has had it for about ten days but refused to report sick in his mad desire to see me personally on my arrival, as he wished to get certain things cleared up. Now he is out of action for some weeks at a most unfortunate moment.

General Pownall arrived with some more staff in time for dinner and we had discussions all the evening.

FRIDAY, 15 OCTOBER   Left Palam airfield 1100. We went in our Liberator, the Marco Polo, whose name had meanwhile been written up in Chinese characters.

I took two sailors, two soldiers, one airman and one political officer with me. The party included Micky Hodges, Flags, Lieutenant Colonel

[1] Major General Frederick 'Boy' Browning, then in command of the 1st Airborne Division.

Dobson (the great Chinese scholar), and last, but on a trip like this, by no means least, John Keswick. We landed at Chabua airfield in Upper Assam at 1700. Here I was met by various American Generals, headed by Stratemeyer, and many other senior officers. We dined in the mess on the old polo ground and later visited a remarkable collection of snakes which a US Medical Orderly at the hospital has collected. In peacetime he is the curator of the Reptile House at Long Beach California. In the same cage as a rock python was a pathetic looking duck which had been sitting there for two days waiting to be eaten. When we arrived they were just feeding a white rat to half a dozen cobras. The cobras kept missing the rat, while our 'curator' kept saying in a pansy voice, 'My, my, their aim is very bad tonight!' I asked him to release the rat, but no sooner had I made my request than one of the cobras got it and proceeded to swallow it.

The Americans are taking the most abnormal precautions for my safety. Armoured cars, and men with tommy guns in jeeps drove with us everywhere and outside my room four men stood with tommy guns loaded and at the ready. I hinted that it was unnecessary to take such precautions, but they absolutely insisted.

When I finally turned in it was extremely awkward. My room was brightly lit, the windows were only covered with wire screens and had no curtains or blinds. The four tommy gunners were thus able to follow my every movement whilst undressing.

I should perhaps explain at this point that Dr T. V. Soong[1] had told me that the news of my impending visit had leaked through to the Japanese and it was probably known that I would be flying through on the day of the 14th. He begged me to change my itinerary and take a fighter escort. I had just changed the day of my departure, as it happened, to fit in with General Somervell's[2] movements, but I did not want to take a fighter escort as it means that extra petrol has to be flown over the 'Hump' to get the fighters back and, in any case, I am no great believer in fighter escorts. We therefore changed our time so as to cross the 'Hump' by night.

Dr Soong was only too tragically correct. The Japanese put out a terrific fighter sweep on the day of the 14th for the first time for many months and shot down three wretched transport aircraft, as well as damaging others.

---

[1] Chinese Foreign Minister and brother-in-law of the Generalissimo Chiang Kai-shek.
[2] Lieutenant General Brehon Somervell. Commanding General, Services of Supply.

SATURDAY, 16 OCTOBER We left Chabua at 0300 by the light of a lovely full moon. I must confess to feeling a slight thrill at taking off on what must be one of the most dramatic flights over the so-called 'Hump' of the mountains. Hot as it was on the ground, we had to get into thick flying clothes and put on oxygen masks, as we went up to 18,000 feet to get over these grim and forbidding mountains into China.

Although we could not see much at night, there was a glorious sunrise and soon we could see the mountains below us and by 0600 we slid into Kunming airfield.

I should have explained that General Stratemeyer refused to let me go without any escort and escorted me himself in a fully armed B.17 (i.e., an American Liberator).[1]

On our arrival we were met by the Chief of Staff to General Chennault, who commands the 14th US Army Air Force in China. We were taken to the charming little house which the Generalissimo has built for General Chennault, where we had bath and breakfast and changed into blue uniform, which we had been told was what was being worn in Chungking.

We had unfortunately to leave our Marco Polo here (the Chinese name being much admired by all the local inhabitants) because the field at Chungking is not big enough to take a four-engined aircraft, so General Stratemeyer took us on in the C.47 belonging to General Chennault and we reached Chungking at 1135.

The landing there was certainly one of the most nerve-racking in the world, because Chungking is built on the steeply sloping sides of two great rivers, the Yangtse-Kiang and the Chialing, at the point of their confluence. There are only two flat places within thirty miles. One is an island in the Yangtse which is used by the China National Aircraft Corporation, and the other a small plateau on the mainland at a bend in the river. To approach the latter, one has to fly very low over the hills, get between the towering banks of the Yangtse and land on this very small strip. Very exciting!

I have never seen such a crowd as was there to receive us, led by the Minister of War, General Ho Ying Chin. A Guard of Honour of 300 very smart Chinese soldiers was drawn up and a band played 'God Save the King'.

I learnt later that the news of my change of plan had not got through

---

[1] Mountbatten presumably meant B.24. The B.17 was the Fortress, which would not have been used for this mission.

to the Chinese authorities for some reason or another, although it transpires that the British authorities realized that they need not expect me until they had a further message giving the precise time of my arrival. The Ambassador told me that he advised the War Minister not to go down until this final message was received, but in fact the Minister, and all the Chinese Generals, trooped down on the 14th and stayed for hours on the airfield. The Guard and Band, I gather, camped on the airfield for three days, to be quite certain not to miss the moment of my arrival!

I was highly distressed at this unintentional discourtesy, but John Keswick tells me that this was the best thing that could have happened for 'face'. In fact, it appears that the Generalissimo frequently postpones visits at the last moment for this very reason.

At General Ho Ying Chin's I found myself in an adjacent room to my old friend General Somervell, USA, and we shared the only bath in the house. Though, when we turned on the hot water tap in the basin there was always a splendid rush of hot water, the hot water tap for the bath appeared to have a fitting on it like an American ice cream soda fountain, so that a pathetic, thin stream came out, with the result that it took about an hour to fill the bath.

Major General Grimsdale, who, as Head of the Military Mission, will come under my orders in future (as well as acting as Military Attaché), gave a fork luncheon for me to meet all the Chinese Generals and Admirals, as well as all the foreign Attachés.

Immediately after the lunch I called a meeting in his bedroom (the only room available), which was attended by the American Generals, as well as Grimsdale and Micky. We discussed plans in the light of our most recent knowledge, in readiness for discussions with the Chinese.

Lieutenant Colonel Dobson is acting as my ADC and living in the house with me – or rather in a bungalow outside. He is a fluent Chinese scholar and has lived a lot in China, and his presence is most helpful. For instance on coming into dinner I was invited to go first. After a considerable battle, I persuaded the ladies of the party to go in before me. Fatigued after this battle, I readily gave in to General Ho Ying Chin's pressure to precede him into dinner. Dobson pointed out to me that I had not battled nearly hard enough with General Ho Ying Chin and for the rest of the visit we had the most wonderful and strenuous battles as to whether my host should precede me into meals or not, and I only gave in just before we reached the point of physical violence. This, evidently, is the height of good manners!

The food on this occasion was European, but a hot, sticky, yellow wine made from rice was poured out of kettles into glasses the size of a big thimble. Everybody at dinner toasts each other every three or four minutes. The word they used is *Gombay*, upon which one has to drink one's glass and then tilt it forward to show it is empty to the man whose health you have drunk. It is then instantly refilled. After I had drunk some twenty *Gombays* and was beginning to feel a bit 'woozy' I discovered the magic password *Saybiyang*, which allows one to drink a sip only and has an overriding priority over *Gombay* so that one cannot be forced to do a *Gombay* if you insist on making it a *Saybiyang*.

After dinner I wanted to read some papers, but as they had put in an expensive porcelain light bowl which obscured the light to such a degree that one could not read, I asked Dobson to remove the shade. He held up his hands in horror and said that it would be considered as having drawn attention to their lack of hospitality in not having produced an efficient light, so we stayed in semi-darkness all the evening, feeling frightfully polite.

SUNDAY, 17 OCTOBER   I went first to the Military Mission Head-quarters and then paid my official call on the Minister of War.

Wherever we go every ten minutes boiling hot tea is brought in. At the smartest houses this tea is made with green leaves which produce an almost colourless liquid to which it is sacrilege to add either sugar or milk so that I personally did not find it very appetizing.

At 1230 I called on Dr T. V. Soong when we discussed the removal of General Stilwell.[1] Dr Soong said the Generalissimo had made up his mind absolutely to remove Stilwell and indeed I had heard from General Somervell that the Generalissimo had made it quite clear that Stilwell no longer had his confidence or the confidence of any of the Chinese he was working with, and that he was in effect *persona non grata* with whom he never wished to have any more dealings.

After lunch I went with our Ambassador, Sir Horace Seymour, to call on the US Ambassador, Mr Gauss. I then went to call on General Stilwell at his house and was photographed with him afterwards, which gave him great pleasure for certain special reasons. [2] I went up for tea to

---

[1] In the original version of the diary this appeared as 'X'. Mountbatten later wrote in the name of Stilwell.

[2] Presumably because he thought it would strengthen his credit with Chiang Kai-shek.

the Seymours' house on top of one of the hills. It had originally been built for the Generalissimo but was too small for him. Here I met the Chinese, British and US Press representatives at a social 'off-the-record' gathering. From there I went on to General Chennault's house and had a long and interesting talk with him.

At 8 o'clock that night we had a large official dinner in the Ministry of War during which the Minister himself, General Ho Ying Chin, was sent for by the Generalissimo.

Later on Somervell was sent for and about midnight he came into my room and said, 'This is the gosh darndest country I have ever had any dealings with. Would you believe it? After the Gissimo had told me categorically that Stilwell was out he sent for Stilwell this evening, kissed him on both cheeks and said he loved him more than ever and said he was right in again.'

MONDAY, 18 OCTOBER   After lunch T. V. Soong called for me in his car. We drove down to the Yangtse and crossed in a ferry to the other side.

On the south bank we found some more cars waiting for us as well as those that had been taken over in the ferry and drove out along the beautiful winding mountain road to the 'Chequers' of China, Huang Shan, the Generalissimo's country residence. This consists of a series of modern villas built on the peaks of hillocks in the heart of the mountains amidst indescribably beautiful scenery. General Somervell and I shared a very modern guest house, with live trees growing through the verandah, whilst the Generalissimo and Madame Chiang Kai-shek lived on the highest peak.

We were received by J. C. Huang, the biggest and fattest Chinese I have ever seen in my life. He was the secretary of the YMCA and is in charge of the New Life Movement. In order that he should be able to be paid he has been made an honorary Lieutenant General.

T. V., Huang, the Naval ADC, and I sat round in my little sitting room waiting to be summoned to the presence.

Every three minutes one of the Chinese jumped up and telephoned volubly, presumably to find out if the Generalissimo were disengaged. After a quarter of an hour the great news came that he would see me. All the Chinese sprang to their feet and rushed to throw the door open. Meanwhile I went slowly into my bedroom to find the letters that the King and the Prime Minister had given me to deliver. T.V. followed me into the bedroom and said, 'Won't you please come at once, the Generalissimo is waiting?' I replied that I had these letters to find and would not go without them. I went on slowly looking for the letters while T.V.'s anguish became more and more extreme. Finally he begged me to leave the letters until another time as he said it was so important not to keep the Generalissimo waiting. I replied, 'He has kept me waiting a quarter of an hour, why shouldn't he now wait for me?'

We then walked slowly up the hill to the Generalissimo's house although the Chinese were secretly anxious to break into a run! I have never come across such awesome reverence as they show towards the Generalissimo. I very much doubt whether devout Christians could show any more reverence for 'Our Lord' if he were to appear on earth again.

On arrival at the house on the peak we were shown in a small but comfortably furnished sitting room where Madame Chiang Kai-shek joined us almost immediately. I must say she is most striking looking and extremely handsome. She has a beautiful figure and the most lovely legs and feet imaginable. She has very great charm of manner and is more than fluent in English, speaking the language better than the average educated American or English woman.

After welcoming me she started a rapid sotto voce conversation in Chinese with T.V. I had suspected he was out of favour after Stilwell, whom he had evidently been trying to kick out, had returned to favour. It was not difficult to understand the Chinese conversation on this occasion, I imagine it went something like this:

> 'What the hell are you doing here trying to muscle in with our visitor?'
>
> 'Not at all, he is a great friend of mine and the least I could do was to bring him here.'
>
> 'Well, you can clear out quick before my husband comes in and kicks you out.'
>
> 'I cannot just go out like this. What am I going to say?'
>
> 'You will excuse yourself by saying that you are feeling ill and that you must go home.'
>
> 'Very well, if you insist.'

Whereupon T.V. took out his handkerchief and started mopping his brow and saying, 'I am afraid I don't feel well. I wonder if you will forgive me if I go.' He rose and left the room, his sister explaining he was much too ill to come and he must certainly go back to Chungking to recover. I discovered afterwards he was sent straight back to Chungking to his house.

Meanwhile the Generalissimo arrived and sat between Madame Chiang Kai-shek and myself. He is a most arresting person – far the most impressive Chinese I have ever seen. When shaking hands or being polite to foreigners he uses the Chinese word for 'good' (*ha*) constantly; rather as Sam Hoare used to say 'Yes' the whole time.

I had a two-hour interview with Madame doing the translation and she is so good at it that one does not feel one is talking through an interpreter.

I first presented my letters and it was only later in the visit that I discovered how much store had been set by them. After the Generalissimo said at the end of the visit that he was proposing to inform the King and the Prime Minister how much he had appreciated my visit I asked him to include the President as well, since I pointed out I was now 'half American'. He refused by saying that General Somervell had come out without any letter from the President!

I began my remarks to the Generalissimo by telling him that I had come straight on out without even waiting for my staff to arrive in Delhi, in order to make his acquaintance, and in particular to seek his advice. I pointed out what a young and inexperienced officer I was to have been given such a high post, but that if I could lean on the wisdom and experience of the best and most renowned soldier of our generation I should face the future with far greater confidence. I made a few more complimentary remarks of this type which, had they been made to me, would have made me squirm, but they went down like a dish of hot, green tea with the Gissimo.

We ironed out most of the difficulties which I thought would confront us at the following day's conference. After two hours he got up and left and Madame invited me to stay for a *tête-à-tête* with her. I told her that I realized the success of my mission depended upon whether she was prepared to help me or not and she replied that if there was one thing she prided herself on it was being a fine judge of human character and that she had already made up her mind to become my firm friend and I could rely on her to help me in every way possible in the future. I must say the old girl was as good as her word and helped me in every conceivable way during the rest of my stay.

The Generalissimo and Madame came down to our bungalow for dinner. I had been told by Dobson that to create the greatest possible effect with the lovely Cartier Chinese vanity case which Edwina was giving to Madame I should select a moment when there was a large gathering of people to see the presentation. I must admit that this method had worked very well with Madame Ho Ying Chin, to whom I had given the customary present on leaving, and who had shown it, with delighted pride, to all the guests.

However, Dobson did not realize that Madame's reactions in this matter are American, and not Chinese. She did not open the case at all but took it in to dinner with her and put it down by her side. She then leant over to me and said in a confidential whisper, 'I cannot tell you how tantalizing it is not to be able to open and look at my present.' I replied, 'But why don't you open it now?' She said, 'My mother taught me that it was not good manners to open a present in the presence of guests.' This is, in effect, correct American etiquette, a point which I had overlooked, or, to be more honest, had not even known until Al Wedemeyer confirmed this. However, the next day she expressed her great delight with the gift, and gave me two beautiful Chinese seals with carved lions on the top and with a chop carved on the underside, one for Edwina and one for me.

TUESDAY, 19 OCTOBER   A conference was held in the dining room of our house starting at 10 a.m. and continuing until 6.30 p.m., with two intermissions, including a long one for lunch. The Generalissimo took the chair, Madame sat on his left, and I at his right.

The meeting could hardly have gone better, as every point over which I had expected to struggle he gave way on, thanks to my having talked it over with him in private beforehand, received his reactions and then got Madame's advice how to tackle that point at the official conference, so that he would not lose 'face' in front of his Generals.

They gave us an excellent Chinese lunch in the dining room of the staff villa and I had a separate meeting with Madame and the Generalissimo after lunch, at which we cleared away certain knotty problems that were left.

I was worried by the security aspect and refused, when servants came into the room with green tea, to talk, until finally they banished all the servants from coming in at all. At the end of the conference I asked the Generalissimo to make all the Generals burn the notes which they had been improperly taking of all the secret proceedings. He readily agreed and made them tear up their notes and place them in a big bowl on the table and they were then ceremoniously burnt.

That evening there was a state banquet in the dining room of the staff villa, to which some forty or fifty people had been bidden from Chungking, including the rest of my staff.

A radiogramophone played Chinese music throughout the dinner and when the Generalissimo stood up and proposed my health in a few well-chosen words the gramophone was playing at its loudest and Hollington Tong who did the interpreting could hardly hear what the Generalissimo said. My reply had equally to be shouted, to try and drown the effects of the gramophone, and no sooner were the speeches over than the gramophone was shut off altogether and we all sat down amidst stony silence.

That evening the Generalissimo paid me the compliment of asking whether he might come to my room to discuss certain knotty problems which General Somervell had really been sent over to discuss and which I made quite clear were not my responsibility. He made some very nice remarks saying that he had formed such a high opinion of me and had such great faith in my judgement and trustworthiness that he wanted the benefit of my views and advice. As I am never at a loss for advice to give others it may be imagined that I did not hesitate to tell him what I thought, and to my great surprise he accepted all my suggestions and a certain special difficulty appears now to have been resolved as a result of this conversation.[1]

As I had to leave early in the morning we had to take leave that night before going to bed and I must say I left the Chiang Kai-sheks with a real feeling of affection and regard and I am sure that this is reciprocated, since I was told on my return that he had been ringing up constantly to make certain that I had arrived back safely.

He has asked if he may return my call as soon as I get to Ceylon as he does not want to come to Delhi!

WEDNESDAY, 20 OCTOBER   Our party left Huang Shan in a scotch mist at 0800. We went down the greasy road skidding round hairpin bends over the precipices in a most alarming manner. I went to take leave of the Ambassador and he and Lady Seymour accompanied me to the airfield. It had been raining and although the road appeared excellent in dry weather it had a slimy surface on which we skidded all over the place, and it took us half an hour to get past two lorries which had also skidded all over the road.

---

[1] This cryptic comment probably relates to Chiang Kai-shek's agreement to the British carrying out covert operations in Siam and Indochina.

At the airfield General Ho Ying Chin and party were drawn up as usual and General Stratemeyer was waiting to take me in his C.47.

The arrival may have been rather frightening but it was nothing compared with the departure. We took off in a mist so thick that we could not see the opposite bank of the Yangtse towering above us. The moment the aircraft left the runway we had to bank sharply and fly up the vale of the Yangtse bending and twisting while we were gaining height. We had to fly blind most of the way to Kunming and arrived safely in fine weather at 1245 having taken off at 1030. We had intended to transfer immediately to the Marco Polo and return over the 'Hump' by daylight but unfortunately Wilson, the Air ADC, had somewhat lightheartedly sent a message to have some lunch put in the Marco Polo for us. This had spread all round Kunming and the news of the Marco Polo's impending departure had become known. General Stratemeyer was most averse to my going unless I took an escort of 6 fighters but as this would have meant sending the petrol they used back by air over the 'Hump', I did not feel this was justified and so decided to postpone my departure until dusk to fly back over the dangerous part in the dark.

We arrived in Chabua in the dark.

THURSDAY, 21 OCTOBER   At 0900 we visited the airfield and installations in the Dinjan and Chabua districts. They have all been installed by the Americans and development is going ahead very satisfactorily. At 1200 we were back at Chabua airfield, where Air Vice Marshal Williams, the British AOC, Bengal and Assam met me with a Lockheed and we flew off. The Americans had again taken fantastic precautions with armoured cars and tommy gunners for my safety and this time the British insisted on a fighter escort. There has been quite a lot of Japanese activity in the district over which I was to fly and as petrol supply is not the same problem on this side of the 'Hump' as on the other, I agreed.

It really seems funny suddenly to find oneself the object of such intense precautions when the early part of the war was spent in disregarding personal safety.

We flew down to Manipur Road at a height of about 600 feet and then turned and followed the wonderful new Imphal road which has been recently cut into the heart of the mountains, rising to a height of about 6000 feet. We got an excellent view, flying along the road. I was

Mountbatten arrives in Delhi to be met by (left to right) General Giffard,
Air Chief Marshal Peirse and General Auchinleck. 7 October 1943.

Faridkot House.

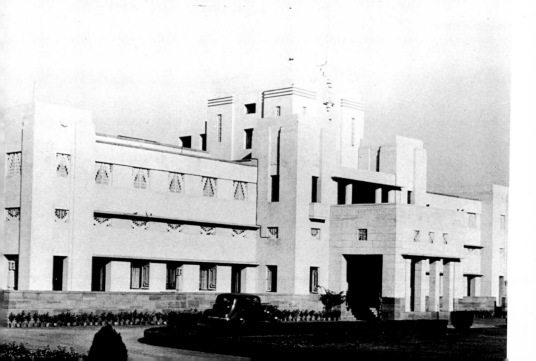

Mountbatten in Chungking, flanked by the Generalissimo and Madame Chiang Kai-shek. To the left in the front row are Generals Ho Ying Chin, Somervell and Liu. Captain Hodges is to be seen behind Mountbatten's left shoulder and General Stilwell is on the far right. 19 October 1943.

Rikki Tikki, the baby mongoose, browses on Mountbatten's epaulettes.

interested to see the large double lines of traffic going up and down the road, keeping the forward troops supplied. We landed at Imphal at 1400, where I was met by Lieutenant General Scoones, Commander of the Fourth Corps, who gave me lunch with his AOC in his Headquarters. After lunch I inspected and addressed the RAF at Imphal and at 1530 we flew on to Chittagong with our usual fighter escort. Chittagong is a port at the mouth of the Karnaphuli River, with reasonable modern installations. The Japanese had come over the day before with nineteen heavy bombers and twenty-one fighters, forty in all, and had been met by an equal number of our Hurricanes, who had forced the Japanese bombers to drop their bombs clear of the dock area. I was surprised to see what very small craters the Japanese bombs had made.

The natives, contrary to their usual custom, did not panic and run away, but I cannot help suspecting that this is partly due to famine conditions, which are bad in Chittagong, and the feeling that if they go away they won't get any food.

FRIDAY, 22 OCTOBER   I left at 0710 and drove to the Chittagong airfield where I visited and inspected the RAF. We took off at 0830 in the Lockheed and flew to Comilla, a big air station, and new headquarters about 80 miles north northwest from Chittagong. Here I again inspected and addressed the RAF and looked at the new Combined Headquarters. I transferred to the C.47 aircraft which General Stratemeyer has given me and flew it myself for most of the way to Jessore, one of our night bomber stations, where I again inspected and addressed the RAF. From there we flew in the C.47 to Barrackpore, having first flown over Calcutta. Here I was met by Lieutenant General Slim, commanding the 14th Army. He drove me to his Headquarters in the old country Viceregal Lodge at Barrackpore, where he introduced me to all the Generals, Brigadiers, Air Commodores and Group Captains of the Combined Staff and then shattered me by saying, 'And now I hope that you will address my staff.'

I had not thought of anything special to say, so I talked about the war in Europe, which I found they knew nothing about. I then staggered them by saying that I understood that it was the custom to stop fighting during the monsoon in Burma, but that I was against this custom and hoped that they would support me and keep the battle going to the best of their ability, whatever the weather conditions were. I hope that this policy, spoken on the spur of the moment, may perhaps yield great results later on, but that remains to be seen.

After lunch we transferred once more to the Marco Polo and flew back to Delhi, where we arrived at 1830, most of the high-ups being there to meet me. Coming back to Faridkot House seemed like coming back home after all our adventures and I was glad to see that a new contingent of my staff had arrived out from England.

After dining I went straight to see General Auchinleck to tell him what had been happening. I found him in a most difficult mood, very put out by the proposals that General Somervell had been making and which I had already in my heart of hearts decided to back![1]

SATURDAY, 23 OCTOBER to FRIDAY, 29 OCTOBER This period has been occupied in many meetings with my own Commanders-in-Chief and also the Commanders-in-Chief, India, to discuss plans. The Staff are gradually moving into the building, but we are still very weak, particularly on the secretarial and signal side, until the next convoy arrives.

On Sunday I lunched with the new Viceroy, Lord Wavell,[2] and had a very long and valuable talk with him afterwards on the help I want him to afford me on the lines of communication.[3] I am glad to hear from him that he intends to tackle the famine problem personally and is going to tour the famine areas at once.[4]

I caught a green praying mantis in the drawing room after dinner one night and put it in a large box. Next day my steward, Moore, caught a yellow praying mantis and put it in the same box. By the evening there was only the head, forearms and wings of the green praying mantis left. Presumably the yellow one had been a female and had, in accordance with the custom of the species, eaten the male.

One day the gardener found a three-week-old baby mongoose in the garden which I bought for three rupees. It lives in my dressing room and hisses and squawks alternately most of the day. Naturally it has been christened Rikki Tikki.[5]

---

[1] These probably related to Somervell's view that the reconstruction of the Assam railways should be handed over to American engineers.
[2] Wavell had been appointed Viceroy in June 1943.
[3] In particular to Assam, to supply the Chinese armies.
[4] Bengal was in the grip of famine, believed to have cost two million lives.
[5] After the eponymous hero of Kipling's short story about a mongoose, Rikki Tikki Tavi.

In my capacity as a military officer I have claimed the right to a charger and the QMG has produced a 15-year-old white polo pony called Pipli. It goes along very lazily and quietly for most of the ride but on two occasions bucked more violently than any pony I can remember within recent years. It was only by great luck that I landed back in the saddle. There are some lovely rides round here along the golf course and round the old fort, etc. I usually go from 0715 to about 0815 and get to the office about 0915.

On Thursday night I went with Flags for a drive in a jeep and for a look at Humayun's Tomb. I had not seen it for 22 years and it made me feel very sentimental seeing it again as I had last visited it by moonlight with Edwina.

I cannot get over the complete tameness of all the animals here; birds, squirrels, monkeys, all seem to let one walk almost on top of them before they move and show not the least fright. The only monkeys that are a little bit nervous are the mothers with babies slung under their tummies.

I find that Vinegar Joe (General Stilwell) is a movie fan like me and so we have been to the pictures together in Delhi.

I have discovered that I am known by all my staff and, incidentally, throughout Delhi, as the 'Supremo'.

SATURDAY, 30 OCTOBER, to FRIDAY, 5 NOVEMBER 1943   I had expected to take over the South-East Asia Command officially on the 1st November, but when I proposed this to the Viceroy he pointed out that he could not yet legally entrust the defence of India to me, since it was at present constitutionally the responsibility of General Auchinleck, as Commander-in-Chief in India. This necessitated various council meetings and telegrams between the Government of India and the India Office and finally, yesterday, they said that the necessary legal steps had been taken and I am to take over next Monday. Incidentally, I become responsible for the defence of India against the Japanese, but not of course against attacks by tribesmen on the North-West Frontier.

Until I take over I go over to the Daily Intelligence Meeting at 1000 at GHQ and then at 1030 bring my Commanders-in-Chief back for a daily meeting here, which usually lasts until twelve.

We are still desperately struggling with plans and, without giving away any secrets, I think I can explain the position.

India has been a country that has been starved, not actually of food, as in Bengal, where a famine is rife, but pretty well of all war essentials. Up till now whatever has been available has gone, somewhat naturally, to the existing battle fronts in the European and North African theatres of war, and now that much more is likely to become available they find it hard to adjust themselves to the prospect. They all feel rather like Bob Laycock[1] must have felt when, after 41 days in the wilderness, he came into Shepheard's and had a large menu put in front of him, and hardly knew what to order, having been starved for so long.

There is also no doubt that the climate and the antiquated and slow methods used in India have their effect on the keenness of officers after a year or two, and so I have found that the plans made by the India Staff are somewhat pessimistic and unenterprising. My team of British and American planners, who have come in bursting with enthusiasm and desperately keen for aggressive plans, find that the lines of communication which run up the Bengal and Assam railway and the Brahmaputra River are not capable of carrying supplies for the type of operation which they would like to carry out.

My next problem has therefore been to try and increase the carrying capacity of this rickety old narrow gauge railway and its many ferry crossings over the Brahmaputra. This is by no means easy for me to do as I have no direct authority over it. It has required immense tact, patience and firmness to get some rapid action taken, but if I can win the first victory with the Government of India over this question it will undoubtedly improve the prospects of victory over the Japanese later on.

Hardly a day passes without some new bottleneck making its appearance which requires great ingenuity and tact to overcome. All my staff, however, have complete faith that whatever we intend to have done will get done by some means or another, and so I am not pessimistic about the future, though God knows it looks black enough on paper.

On Monday I was allowed to take General Sir George Giffard with me to visit General Wingate in hospital. He has been terribly ill with typhoid and is still very weak, but he is now well on the road to recovery. This he owes to the fortunate fact that his wife, hearing he was ill, informed someone at COHQ that the only person who could manage him in these circumstances was Sister McGeary, the matron of the Imphal hospital, who had looked after him the last time he came out

---

[1] Major General Sir Robert Laycock, Mountbatten's successor as Chief of Combined Operations.

of Burma. This they telegraphed to me in Chungking and I arranged to have her flown down. From the time she arrived, Wingate took a turn for the better and this week has been able to sit up in bed and take an interest in his important work.

Lieutenant-General Carton de Wiart, VC, arrived out from England on 30th October and is staying with me at Faridkot House. He is going to Chungking as a member of my staff and also as a personal representative of the Prime Minister. We all like him a lot and I am attaching Lieutenant-Colonel Dobson (our Chinese scholar) to his staff.

I have also seen Lieutenant-General Lumsden, who is here on his way out to Australia as the Prime Minister's representative on General MacArthur's staff, and who is going to arrange for the necessary exchange of liaison officers between MacArthur and myself. I spent a lot of time composing a beautiful letter to MacArthur which Lumsden is going to deliver to him. I have also sent MacArthur a telegram of congratulations on his great victory at Rabaul, which I hope will please him.

Vice Admiral Helfrich, Commander-in-Chief of the Netherlands East Indies Fleet, which is now under my command, has come up from Colombo to see me and is staying at Faridkot House. He is a most charming old boy and I am sure we shall get along well together.

General Hurley,[1] who is one of the President's personal representatives, has come to India and China to write a report. I gave him lunch on his way to Chungking and have invited him to come and see me on his way back. He belongs to the Opposition Party and was Secretary for War in the previous Administration, but he appears to enjoy the personal confidence of the President. He talks an awful lot (even more than I do!) but he is a very pleasant old gentleman.

The Maharaja of Jaipur invited me to come and see his magnificent palace here. It must be about twice the size of Faridkot House and rather pompous. It appears that he had wanted it to be a much simpler house, but that Lady Willingdon[2] had come down one day with him when the walls were already 6ft high and had insisted on altering the whole design to fit in a large and pompous hall with a dome. This meant tearing down most of the foundations and starting again. Jai was still complaining bitterly about this, but had said that she was so masterful when she was Vicereine that no one could stand against her when she

---

[1] Major General Patrick Hurley was to become US Ambassador to Chungking.

[2] Lord Willingdon was Viceroy, and perhaps more noticeably his wife was Vicereine from 1931 to 1936.

decided on something. He is very anxious for me to move out of Faridkot into his own house which he has offered me, but of course it is too late to move and it really is a lot more comfortable at Faridkot.

The Raja of Faridkot collects motor bicycles. He has 37 different varieties. I have given him a parachutist's motor bicycle which collapses and fits into a cylindrical container only fifteen inches in diameter. He is absolutely delighted with this toy and since he has allowed the Government of India to have the house rent free for me, it is a very cheap gesture on the part of the Government.

After a considerable struggle I have succeeded in getting Lieutenant General Slim appointed in command of the 14th Army.[1] I met him at Barrackpore and like him immensely and he has been up to Delhi to see me.

The particular part of the Secretariat we are in now used to house a Civil Department of the Government of India previously. The result is that we have taken over hoards of Indian chaprasis, etc, who sit about in large droves and do nothing except give the place an air of complete indolence. I have told Admiral Jerram[2] I want the whole lot to clear out and we are going to try and replace them with European other ranks, male and female. I am anxious to try and get an alert air of bustle about my Headquarters, the same as we had at COHQ and we certainly will never succeed with all these Indian loafers sitting and lying about all the corridors.

The security arrangements at the present moment are lamentable. A small Indian boy about 4 foot high (whom I suspect of being a Japanese spy in disguise) comes into my office every day to try and sell me chocolates and cigarettes. I had given the ADCs orders that he was not to be allowed in, but he has been too smart for them on six occasions! I therefore took the matter into my own hands and on the last occasion he visited me I made him unpack the whole of his tray of wares, etc. outside in the passage and then left him to pack them all up again. I thought that this would cool off his desire to sell me anything and he has not been near me again!

SATURDAY, 6 NOVEMBER, to THURSDAY, 11 NOVEMBER The whole of this week we have been feverishly engaged in planning, as

---

[1] Hitherton Slim had been commanding XV Corps, the two British–Indian divisions which had retreated from Burma.

[2] Rear Admiral Sir Rowland Jerram was Comptroller of Administration.

enough of my staff have now arrived out to be able to go into all the facts and figures prepared by GHQ, India. Many of the planners worked the last 36 hours without any sleep. I was interested to find that the Commanders-in-Chief and the senior staff officers who attended the meetings subconsciously produced the usual effect of enlarging on all the difficulties of every plan and very rarely enthusing about the merits of any of them. At the end of three hours at our final meeting when things looked very black all round, I made up my mind which course I wanted to follow, drew the meeting's attention to the well-known adage 'Councils of War don't fight' and that I now knew why a Supreme Commander had been appointed. We would adopt plan 'C' and I would now point out its merits. I began by putting myself in the place of the Japanese Commander-in-Chief and showed how horrifying it would be for him to be faced with what we intended to do. The whole meeting immediately cheered up and we all ended up intensely enthusiastic about the plan which I had chosen.

This is a funny country. At one moment it proceeds at the pace of a bullock cart, at the next minute Sir Malcolm Campbell's Bluebird is not in it. I arrived on October 7th and looked round the Headquarters on October 8th. I settled that I wanted to have a large War Room built from which Navy, Army and Air Operations could be controlled. As there was no room big enough inside the Secretariat I placed an immediate order for one to be built. On October 12th I selected the exact site. When I got back from Chungking nothing had been done. I made a row. Every three or four days I made another row. Finally I sent for the head man of all and made such a fiendish row and pointed out that there had been more than three weeks' delay in starting that he undertook to get the work started the next morning. 150 Indians arrived the following morning and in three days they had built a colossal room about 120ft × 35ft with thick walls about 20ft high. They were ready to put the roof on after three days. I have never seen such industry; all the bricks were thrown up by hand and looking out of my window I could see never less than 30 or 40 bricks flying through the air, an altogether remarkable sight which I had never seen in England. On the fourth day part of one of the walls collapsed amidst much 'zobbing'.

I told Admiral Helfrich that he could use Faridkot House as a hotel. He took me at my word and immediately asked if he might invite the Dutch Ambassador from Chungking to stay with him! Luckily Dr Lovink turned out to be the most charming and interesting man imaginable. In fact I took a great liking to both Helfrich and Lovink and had many useful talks with them. Admiral Helfrich was the Allied Naval C.-in-C. of the British, American and Dutch fleet during the battles against the Japanese in the first half of 1942.

Admiral Helfrich has presented me with a Dutch flag to fly, to add to my collection of Chinese, American and British. When we get them all the house will look like Selfridges, and the car like a carnival party.

Actually I have worn out my only Union Jack on the car and have been going around without any flag which apparently is considered very bad form. When I threatened to go to my office in a jeep Admiral Somerville was deputed by the remainder to tell me that this simply could not be done!

As mentioned in the last report I require an immediate and vital increase in the tonnage of the Bengal and Assam Railway, and so I got the American Railway experts from Persia over and they have put forward suggestions which will, I feel confident, solve my difficulties. The chief expert, Colonel Yount, lunched with me and gave me a most encouraging account.

One night I dined with the Auchinlecks to meet all the Army Commanders. I was most encouraged to find them very friendly and all only too anxious that I should go into their Commands and inspect any of the troops which are due to join the South-East Asia Command.

General Wetherall, the Army Commander in Ceylon, lunched with me as next week he and his troops come under my command. The difficulty I mentioned last week about my taking over the defence of India has been resolved by my receiving a beautiful letter beginning, 'The Governor General in Council has been pleased to invite you to take over the defence of certain parts of India', or words to that effect.

FRIDAY, 12 NOVEMBER to SATURDAY, 20 NOVEMBER   The planning has become more and more feverish all this week because I constantly find that figures I had been given are challenged by other officers from the very departments which produced them. The complete lack of co-ordination inseparable from the original set-up out here has made it very difficult to pull the whole thing together quickly. As fast as I deal with one bottleneck another one seems to appear. However, I have no doubt we shall get over all difficulties in time.

The two Assistant Deputy Chiefs of Staff, Commodore Langley and Air Vice Marshal Whitworth Jones, arrived this week. Within a few hours of their arrival both had disappeared head and shoulders in the planning morass and both are beginning to look pale and wan from the strain. If the effort put into planning could win the war the Japanese would already have been beaten!

Admiral Jerram's adopted god-daughter, Mrs Bols, acted as a guide to the Sunday afternoon party.[1] I dropped the party off at my Head-quarters and drove Mrs Bols a distance of 400 yards down to the Commander-in-Chief's residence, where she is living, in order to go in and have a cocktail with the Auchinlecks. During that one drive of 400 yards on a Sunday afternoon with the roads practically deserted, someone must have seen us, and I gather that all Delhi is agog with the fact that I should have been seen with a blonde in a jeep!

Micky came back with the reconnaissance party I sent down to Ceylon. I have decided to move my main Headquarters to the ancient capital of Kandy, which is at a height of about 2000 feet and so the temperature never rises above 85°, whereas in Delhi it reaches 115°. In any case I want to keep my Headquarters mobile and do one move from Delhi before moving to Singapore, or wherever our next stopping place may turn out to be, because at present we are almost entirely dependent upon GHQ India for our Intelligence, Public Relations, Administration, etc., and I want to make sure that my staff can stand on their own feet. I shall, of course, have to keep a rear Headquarters in Delhi the whole time for liaison with GHQ India and the Government of India, but I think it will be a good thing to get away from the social and political atmosphere of a large capital, even though Delhi itself is certainly a most beautiful city. I do not think I have ever seen a garden city so well and attractively laid out as Delhi.

I have asked my four Commanders-in-Chief, Somerville, Peirse, Giffard and Stilwell, to keep their staffs that they bring with them down to a smallest possible number, and I find that the minimum total with which we can move to Kandy is 4100! I must admit that this includes officers, other ranks, male and female, Navy, Army and Air Force, British, American, Chinese and Dutch. In case anyone should think that this number is excessive I am told that when Eisenhower moves to Rome the party will be something like 26,000!

General Wingate has been very ill indeed with typhoid. In fact, he was on the dangerously ill list when I was in Chungking. The doctors said he would not be fit until January and he could certainly not attend

[1] A sightseeing expedition to the Qutb Minar.

to any form of business until well on in December. With his indomitable will power he has made a most miraculous recovery and is now living with me at Faridkot House. He has been gaining close on two pounds a day and will be shortly back with his troops. He was the man who did that wonderful exploit in taking the Long Range Penetration Group into the heart of Burma this year. Previously he made his name in Abyssinia and Palestine as a sort of second Lawrence of Arabia, who is, as a matter of fact, a cousin of his.

Our great excitement this week has been the passage of the Generalissimo and Madame Chiang Kai-shek through India.[1] Their movement was so terrifically secret that I alone was told about it and the Viceroy, the Government of India and the C.-in-C. India only heard of it indirectly through me. I sent down Lieutenant General Carton de Wiart and Lieutenant Colonel Dobson to sit and wait for them on the American airfield at Agra. Here nothing was known of their impending arrival, but Dobson went round the various hotels and finally found six very sheepish-looking Chinese generals who had registered under false names. De Wiart and the six generals spent 48 hours sitting on the airfield as the arrival of the Generalissimo was kept so secret that even the Chinese did not know within 48 hours when he would come.

Finally a rumour came through that they were likely to arrive shortly and so I flew down and was received on the airfield by all the Generals. I was told that it was bad for 'face' for me to hang about on the airfield for the Generalissimo lest by doing so the Chinese should think that I was not a person of almost equal importance! So I went off and visited the Fort of Agra, which I found absolutely fascinating. I particularly liked the lovely pearl mosque. We were shown the pathetic little room and private mosque where Aurangzeb shut up his father, Shah Jehan, when he seized the throne.

From here we went on to see the Taj Mahal. Its beauty is greatly impaired by the fact that the whole of the dome is covered with scaffolding which was put up in 1939 when they wished to repair the dome. The work was stopped on the outbreak of the war but the scaffolding has been left there ever since because people are too busy now to do the repairs. Nevertheless, there is no doubt that it is one of the most thrilling, impressive and beautiful sights in the world. The moment when one comes through the gateway and looks down the little formal gardens with their fountains and sees the marble dome with its

[1] On their way to a summit conference at Cairo.

four marble towers is a great thrill.

I realized more than ever what a great gesture of devotion it had been to my fiancée when in 1922 I left the Prince of Wales's party during their visit to Agra in order to snatch a few more hours with Edwina. As a result I had never before seen the Taj Mahal.

We then returned to the airfield and found the Generals still sitting disconsolately around. As it was half past eight I decided to fly back to Delhi. I must say the city looked very beautiful by night; in particular the tomb of Saftar Jang, which lies alongside the Willingdon airfield, looks quite lovely, floodlit in red lights to indicate its position to approaching aircraft.

The next morning Carton de Wiart rang up to say the Generalissimo had arrived just before midnight and so I told de Wiart to return. He was extremely well received by the Generalissimo.

The Viceroy, for the first time I believe in history, collected all the twelve Governors together at the Viceroy's House for a series of conferences. I am told he treats the Governors like an Army Commander treats his Corps and Divisional Commanders, and the conference consists of a series of lectures in which he tells them how he thinks they ought to run their provinces. I am all for this, as I am quite sure there is plenty of room for improvement! He gave a dinner party more or less in my honour to meet all the Governors. I must say a state banquet in Delhi is a most impressive sight. The Lutyens staterooms are quite fairy-like lit up at night. There were fifty khitmagars and chaprasis in scarlet and gold livery, one behind each chair, who salaamed with both hands as the guests came in. I was amazed to find that I had been allotted an exact niche in the order of precedence, and found that I ranked after the Governors of Bombay, Madras and Bengal, but before all the remaining Governors! Why I should rank before any I cannot make out, but if one does rank before any, why I should rank after three of them is a great mystery.[1]

I couldn't help laughing at the fantastic degree of pomp and circumstance which is kept up out here compared with the simple life that the King and Queen lead at Buck House. I do not know how many servants they have got left at Buck House, but there are 270 in the Viceroy's House. The amazing thing is that I am told that Lord Wavell has reduced the degree of pomp and ceremony to considerably below

---

[1] The Warrants of Precedence ranked the Governors of Bombay, Madras and Bengal directly after the Viceroy. The Commander-in-Chief, India, followed, and then the other Governors. Mountbatten was presumably equated with Auchinleck.

what it had been in Lord Linlithgow's days so we are gradually moving in the right direction.

On Friday a further three hundred officers and other ranks arrived by convoy to fill up the Secretariat, the Signal Department and junior staff appointments in my own Headquarters. Now at last we have got more stenographers than Generals! The difficulty has been that whereas the senior officers can easily obtain air passages from the United Kingdom or the United States, the junior officers and stenographers have to come by sea.

SUNDAY, 21 NOVEMBER   By now the secret is out that a further meeting of the President, Prime Minister and the Combined Chiefs of Staff, this time including the Generalissimo and Chinese staff, is to be held at Cairo.

The South-East Asia party left in three aeroplanes. The first one contained an all-American party – my Deputy Commander, Lieutenant General Joseph Stilwell, Major General Stratemeyer, Major General Chennault and two Staff Officers. The next aircraft, which left at noon on Saturday, contained Lieutenant General Carton de Wiart, Lieutenant Colonel Dobson, my Chief Political Adviser, Mr Dening,[1] and three of my Planning Staff.

The third aircraft to leave was the Air Commander-in-Chief's own, which he lent me for the trip. In this I took my Secretary, Paymaster Captain Brockman,[2] and Major Generals Wedemeyer and Wheeler, USA.[3] This aircraft was a C.47 converted to take bunks, so we were able to get some sleep. We flew direct from Delhi to Basra in one hop of thirteen hours, leaving just after midnight on Saturday.

I was met at Cairo West airport by Air Chief Marshal Sir Sholto Douglas, the Air Commander-in-Chief.

The scene at Cairo West was really extraordinary, as Admirals, Generals and Air Marshals and high political figures, both British and American, were arriving every five or ten minutes, zero hour being Sunday evening.

I was whisked away at once to the Minister of State's villa, and

---

[1] Esler Dening, a Foreign Office official.
[2] Formerly Secretary to the First Sea Lord, Dudley Pound, and to remain closely associated with Mountbatten until the latter's death.
[3] General Wheeler was Principal Administrative Officer and, wrote Mountbatten, 'one of the nicest men I have ever met'.

taken in straight away to see the Prime Minister. After half an hour's talk with him, the Generalissimo called and I sat with the Prime Minister and Generalissimo and their interpreter and listened to the two great men holding forth. Unfortunately Madame Chiang was still suffering from conjunctivitis and the fatigue of the journey and so did not come.

The interpreter, Doctor Wang Chung Hui, was not nearly as good as she is, and I am certain that he mistranslated some of the things that were said.

For instance, the Prime Minister said, 'Tell His Excellency that I will return his call tomorrow at noon.' The interpreter in due course replied, 'The Generalissimo is delighted and says when will you call?' The Prime Minister replied, 'Tell His Excellency that when the sun is at its zenith I will come to make my report.' Dr Wang had to ask the Prime Minister to repeat this twice and must have translated, 'The Prime Minister says he will come at "tennish" to make his report', because the Generalissimo replied, 'About ten o'clock will suit very well.' The Prime Minister was horrified and said, 'I never get up as early as that. Please explain that the sun does not reach its zenith until twelve o'clock', and so it was fixed for twelve.

I arranged for the Prime Minister to take Colonel Dobson with him as an interpreter in future, to avoid such misunderstandings.

I then had another interview with the Prime Minister and remained to dinner. Besides Dick Casey (the Minister of State) and the Prime Minister, the Chief of the Air Staff (Portal) and Air Commander-in-Chief (Sholto Douglas) and the CIGS (Brooke) and Military Commander-in-Chief (Wilson), and the PM's Chief of Staff (Pug Ismay) were there.

Believe it or not, but we sat around the dinner table for over five hours. I must admit, however, that we discussed business the whole time. I finally got to my villa at 2 a.m. It is on the outskirts of Cairo and the whole of the South-East Asia party are accommodated in it, including the Chinese Liaison Officer. It is known as 'Villa 30'.

MONDAY, 22 NOVEMBER   Bob Laycock (my successor as CCO) and Antony Head (who succeeded Macleod as COJP) called to see me at my villa in the morning. They were followed by the Chinese delegation, headed by General Shang Chen.

I gave the latter an inscribed copy of my *Introduction to Polo* as he is a great polo fan. He has promised to give me the book he has written on polo in Chinese in return.

I then drove out to Mena House. The whole of the hotel has been converted into offices and conference rooms. All the various delegations are in some thirty-five different villas. This arrangement is not nearly so good as at Quebec where all eight hundred delegates lived and worked together in the Château Frontenac. Not only does it take anything up to twenty minutes to get from one villa to another but they are very difficult to find, and Al Wedemeyer spent two hours in trying to find Villa 30 after having dined with friends last night.

I settled down to work in my office going through all the points I wished to raise at the conference.

I had lunch with Pug who was in great form and was able to advise me on several of my more knotty problems.

I had been having trouble with the Admiralty and the Eastern Fleet. The Admiralty began by making a signal to the Commander-in-Chief, Eastern Fleet, that they did not propose accrediting any naval war correspondents to me and furthermore implied that the Eastern Fleet was not under my command. Pug advised me to see Charles Lambe[1] about this which I did immediately. Needless to say, Charles was able to fix up matters to my satisfaction with the First Sea Lord and a signal clearing up the position has now been approved by the Prime Minister.[2]

I dined with the President who was living in Ambassador Kirk's villa. There were only five of us, the other three being the Prime Minister, Harry Hopkins, and the President's Chief of Staff, Admiral Leahy.

After dinner an informal Plenary conference was called to discuss what we were to say to the Chinese on the following day. The party included the Combined Chiefs of Staff as well as Generals Stilwell, Stratemeyer and Chennault.

TUESDAY, 23 NOVEMBER   This conference is going all haywire. I had expected to put my proposals before the British Chiefs of Staff, at the same time as my Deputy Chief of Staff, Al Wedemeyer, put the same

---

[1] Charles Lambe was currently Captain of the aircraft carrier *Illustrious*. He was Mountbatten's oldest friend and was eventually to succeed him as First Sea Lord.

[2] The clarification was not as satisfactory as Mountbatten imagined. Somerville was equally convinced that he had prevailed at Cairo, and the dispute grumbled on for many months.

plans before the American Chiefs of Staff. I had then naturally supposed that the plans would be considered in my presence by the Combined Chiefs of Staff.

Having worked out that all the resources I was asking for could be made available I then presumed there would be a meeting among the Combined Chiefs of Staff and the Chinese military Staff.

Fourthly and finally I presumed the matter would be dealt with on the highest level at a Plenary meeting between the President, Prime Minister and the Generalissimo and the Combined Chiefs of Staff.

Believe it or not but these four meetings were held in the reverse order since it was considered of the utmost importance that the Generalissimo should not be kept waiting to join in the discussion.

The result was that the first official meeting at 1100 on Tuesday was a full Plenary session between the President, Prime Minister and Generalissimo, the Combined Chiefs of Staff, the Chinese staff (headed I am glad to say by Madame), and the South-East Asia staff.

At this meeting I put forward all my plans in detail, though God knows I was nervous of doing it as I know how insecure the Chinese are about secret plans, or at least how efficient the Japanese secret service in Chungking is. Everyone was very polite about the plans and they appear to have been received gracefully.

I had done my best to persuade the Generalissimo to come in person, pointing out that he was not only the head of State like the President, but also a professional soldier, and thus corresponded to our Chiefs of Staff, but all my flattery failed to convince him that he would not lose face by coming to a Combined Chiefs of Staff meeting. The result was that all the Chinese generals, headed by General Shang Chen, came and were unable to express any views whatever since they had not had time to be briefed by the Generalissimo.

WEDNESDAY, 24 NOVEMBER Had South-East Asia Command meetings most of the morning. Field Marshal Sir John Dill (Head of the British Joint Staff Mission in Washington) invited me to lunch at the British Chiefs of Staff villa where I found Portal, Brooke and Cunningham.[1] We had a very satisfactory gossip. I have been particularly touched by the warmth of the welcome I have received from my late colleagues on the Chiefs of Staff Committee.

---

[1] Andrew Cunningham had recently replaced Dudley Pound as First Sea Lord.

I went over to the Generalissimo to see if I could clear up the difficulties which his Staff had raised. I told the Generalissimo that the counter proposals which he had put up were on the very lines I had been working on, until we found that logistic difficulties prevented us from carrying this plan out. To prove that we had worked it out in great detail I showed him a marked map and full technical details. The old boy's eyes glistened. He said, 'I like this plan, we will carry it out.' I repeated very patiently that the plan was not possible and gave exact reasons. However, he defeated me by saying, 'Never mind, we will carry it out all the same.'

I may say that he made several more illogical suggestions and I cannot help wondering how much he knows about soldiering. My position, incidentally, is really extraordinary, a sailor having to deal in great detail with military and air matters and argue with various generals. A. B. Cunningham hit the nail on the head when at the end of the first conference he said, 'The Admirals are on land – and the Generals are all at sea.'

I finally defeated the Generalissimo by saying that I would carry out the particular plan concerned if he was able to get the extra resources out of the President and Prime Minister, knowing full well that was quite out of the question. However, it served the purpose of keeping him friendly with me and transferring his wrath to quarters more suitably equipped to take it.

My British interpreter, Dobson, told me that throughout the interview Madame was on my side, and in addition to translating what I said, reinforced my arguments with some of her own. She even looked over at Dobson and shrugged her shoulders when the 'Gimo' was being particularly obstinate and dense.

THURSDAY, 25 NOVEMBER   I accompanied the Prime Minister and Anthony Eden to an interview with the Generalissimo and Madame to try and clear up some of the points which had been raised the night before. After this the Prime Minister drove me to the President's villa where we all had a series of photographs taken. After the photographs I gather that the President and Generalissimo had a satisfactory meeting at which the latter agreed to all our points.

I had a very satisfactory lunch with the American Army Chief of Staff, General Marshall, who was most helpful. Indeed, in some ways, the Americans appear even more determined to back me than the

Mountbatten addresses an RAF unit, an enterprise rendered more difficult by the noise of aircraft landing and taking off. 16 December 1943.

Trying a new carbine, under the instruction of Brigadier Merrill.

Mountbatten with General 'Vinegar Joe' Stilwell.

British. Admiral King, the Commander-in-Chief of the US Fleet, also went out of his way to say that he agreed with everything I put up and I had his wholehearted backing.

We all attended the American Thanksgiving Service in the Cairo Cathedral. Up to that moment the existence of the conference had been kept as a total secret but this gave the whole show away in the most spectacular manner possible.

I dined with Bob and Antony[1] at Shepheard's Hotel, which was crammed full and very gay. The restaurant had an excellent band and the scene reminded me of a pre-war London season.

FRIDAY, 26 NOVEMBER I had a meeting with Hap Arnold[2] and General Marshall to study the directives to give effect to the reorganization of our air forces. Marshall told me that in the evening the Generalissimo had had another meeting with the President, at which he had gone back on every single point which he had agreed to before lunch. I therefore dashed round to see Harry Hopkins, who gave me the low-down.

From there I went to the British Chiefs of Staff meeting at which I reported the reversal of policy by the Generalissimo and was duly despatched by them to try and restore the situation.

I found the Generalissimo very difficult, although he kept on assuring me of his personal regard and told me he was protecting my interests as much as his own.

I lunched with the Prime Minister, the only others there being Pug Ismay, Jumbo Wilson (C.-in-C., Middle East) and Sarah Oliver.[3] After lunch I had a long and satisfactory talk with the Prime Minister and persuaded him to have a Plenary meeting called at once at which all the difficulties of Chiang Kai-shek could be discussed. This he did and at 4.15 the President, Prime Minister, Generalissimo and Madame met.

Unfortunately they had no secretary present and no comments or conclusions were written down, but I was told by the Prime Minister that the Generalissimo had agreed once more to all the points he had rejected the day before.

When I attended the Chiang Kai-shek tea party Madame told me

---

[1] Presumably Laycock and Head respectively.
[2] General Arnold was Chief of the United States Army Air Force.
[3] The Prime Minister's daughter, married to the comedian Vic Oliver.

that I should be a very happy man as the Plenary meeting had agreed to everything I wanted. I stayed there after the tea party to see the Generalissimo to thank him for having come round once more on every point. I asked his assurance that he really meant to support me to the full and received it. I asked his concurrence to the reorganization of the British and American Air Forces and obtained it.

He told me he was going to visit the Chinese forces in India and I offered to accompany him, which appeared to please him very much.

I dined at the Embassy with Lord and Lady Killearn. The guests were the Prime Minister, Sarah, Bob, Anthony[1] and Alec Cadogan.[2] The Prime Minister was in great form and we stayed at dinner until 0015. Although he was due to fly off at dawn the following morning for the meeting at Teheran with Stalin, he did not leave the Embassy until 0130.

The Prime Minister did his very level best to make me stay another week to wait the return of the main party from Teheran, but I pointed out that I had a war on my hands and really must get back.

SATURDAY, 27 NOVEMBER All the high-ups having left for Teheran, there were no Chiefs of Staff meetings and so I called a South-East Asia Command meeting to clear off outstanding points.

Joe Stilwell absolutely staggered me by coming in and saying that the Generalissimo had that morning rejected all the points which he had agreed to at the last Plenary meeting the previous evening, and had instructed Stilwell to try and obtain a complete reversal of every point.

I told Joe, 'I am rather hard of hearing. I am afraid I was unable to catch what you said. Please be good enough to send me a telegram at Delhi and also send one to the Chiefs of Staff.' I really could not face staying another week and in any case my best hope will be in getting the Generalissimo to myself as he passes through India.

I am delighted that the Prime Minister and President and Combined Chiefs of Staff are at last being given first-hand experience of how impossible the Chinese are to deal with. They have been driven absolutely mad and I shall certainly get far more sympathy from the former in the future.

---

[1] Presumably Eden rather than Head (Mountbatten habitually spelt both Anthony, though the latter in fact lacked the '*h*').
[2] Sir Alexander Cadogan was Permanent Under Secretary at the Foreign Office.

MONDAY, 29 NOVEMBER [New Delhi]   At my daily meeting with the Commanders-in-Chief I gave them a full account of the Cairo Conference and went through further operational plans during the morning. I did not much like the new plans and so instructed the Force Commanders to revise them and to meet me at 1800. I still did not like their plans at 1800 and so left Henry Pownall to go through them again the next day along certain lines, as I had to go off to meet the Generalissimo to try and settle up all the points which appear to have gone astray with him.

TUESDAY, 30 NOVEMBER   Shortly after midnight I went with Carton de Wiart to Willingdon airport, where we turned in in the C.47. Unfortunately this type of aircraft has a definite slope when on the ground and so we found ourselves sleeping at a considerable angle.

I must confess that for the first time since I have been out here I was really in a distressed state of mind, all my plans for all operations appear to be going astray. However, my sense of humour returned to me when I read Wilson Brand's[1] *aide memoire* on whom I should see at Ramgarh the next day. After referring to the Generalissimo and his staff this typewritten document said I would be accompanied by the British 'Staffilissimo', which I thought a peculiarly happy description of my own staff! It turned out that Wilson Brand's handwriting was so bad that the poor Wren who had typed it out had misread British Staff Mission as 'British Staffilissimo'!

We went to the hotel at Ramgarh for breakfast and had hardly sat down when we heard the hum of a large transport aircraft, and hastily left our breakfast to go and meet the Generalissimo who arrived with Madame and a large staff of generals by air from Karachi. I took them to breakfast at the hotel and so was able to complete my own interrupted meal. Afterwards we drove in a colossal procession preceded by British and American motor cycles, armed jeeps, etc., and followed by about 20 cars to Ramgarh. I sat between the 'Gimo' and Madame and had an hour and a quarter's very good talk.

At Ramgarh we saw the Chinese 20th New Division and elements of the 38th and 22nd New Divisions in training. We saw their tank driving school and artillery practice and went around their quarters. We attended an enormous lunch party given in the American Mess.

[1]   Brigadier Brand, of the British Military Mission in Chungking.

I should explain that Ramgarh, which was built as a Prisoners' of War camp, was turned over by Lord Wavell to General Stilwell to train Chinese troops which had come out of Burma into India. Additional Chinese are flocking in from China and they receive first-class training and are well equipped. The only criticism which I could note was that the American instructors actually commanded the Chinese troops during their exercises so that they may not do quite so well when they are commanded by their own Chinese officers in battle.

After lunch we went to an enormous parade where 12,000 Chinese troops were drawn up. The Generalissimo and I drove round in a jeep inspecting the troops.

After the Generalissimo addressed them through a microphone, raising his voice to a high-pitched scream and gesticulating wildly. I heard my name mentioned several times and gathered from Madame that he was informing the Chinese troops that he was formally placing them under my command and that they were to obey me faithfully. He then called upon me to address the troops, which I did, my address being translated sentence by sentence by General Huang, the enormous fat Master of the Household.

Finally, I drove back between the 'Gimo' and Madame to Ranchi. From my point of view the day was the greatest possible success, because every point on which the 'Gimo' appeared to have gone back on the last day at Cairo he conceded again to me. Indeed, I went much further and got a number of other knotty problems settled.

We really had a most delightful gossip and the old boy was nice enough to say, 'I hoped when I met you at Huang Shan that we were going to become friends, but after our many meetings in Cairo and after this delightful day together I feel we have now actually become friends.'

Madame told me that in China friendship was rarely given, and when given was regarded as sacred and that she was particularly delighted that the 'Gimo' now regarded me as a friend, as it would be such a help in our coming campaign.

Madame gave me a lot of excellent advice and even helped me prepare future addresses to Chinese troops, as she of course knows their mentality and the right thing to say to them.

WEDNESDAY, 1 DECEMBER to FRIDAY, 3 DECEMBER 1943 This period has been taken up in further feverish planning. Admiral Somerville has come up in person to take part in these discussions and I feel that on the whole we are making reasonable progress.

I must say that this job is enough to turn my few remaining hairs completely grey. I could not have believed so difficult a job could have been invented for anybody and those who envy me my job (if there are any) must be mad.

Rikki Tikki has grown beyond all recognition. She is at least twice the size she was when I went away and embarrassingly friendly. She does not like to be left alone by night and squeaks and grunts and scrabbles at my bed until I let her in. When I kick her out she complains bitterly and goes on squeaking lamentably most of the night.

I dined one night with the Anglo-American Dining Club, about a dozen British and a dozen American officers from Lieutenant to Colonel. I had a very good gossip with most of the Americans, which I hope will do some good, as my American Public Relations Officer, Colonel Bellah, tells me that most of the Americans he has met are fed up that Stilwell has been put under me and loyally feel it should have been the other way round.

SATURDAY, 4 DECEMBER to FRIDAY, 10 DECEMBER   I have only just heard that the heavy tiled roof of the new Officers' Mess in which the Generalissimo, Madame and the rest of our party had lunch at Ramgarh fell in with a resounding crash shortly after we had left. Most of the debris landed on the spot where the Generalissimo, Madame and myself had been sitting!

At 0200 on Monday Micky called me with a most immediate signal from the Combined Chiefs of Staff in Cairo, demanding my views on some very important operational matters.[1] I had the Chief of Staff and his Planning Staff and the three Commanders-in-Chief and their Planning Staffs called and the Planners spent the rest of the night up preparing a draft answer which we considered in the morning. I heard afterwards from General Wedemeyer that he and the rest of my staff and representatives in Cairo were asked the same questions and put in a paper to the Combined Chiefs of Staff which was almost identical with the long telegram which I sent off. I feel it is satisfactory to know that the

---

[1] The meeting with Stalin at Teheran had led the Chiefs of Staff to rethink their approval of Mountbatten's projected offensive, the necessary resources being needed in Europe.

South-East Asia party think along the same lines even if separated by 3000 miles.

We had our first meeting in the new War Room on Monday. It certainly is a great success.

On Tuesday I dined with the Viceroy to see the famous film *Casablanca* again. I wanted to get a military concession out of the Viceroy and waited until after the cinema when I thought he would be in a good mood. I then started off by saying: 'I hope you enjoyed the film', to which Lord Wavell replied: 'No, I didn't. It was a rotten film, I couldn't understand it, it all went much too fast. I never go to the cinema if I can avoid it and unfortunately I cannot avoid it here as there is a theatre in the Viceroy's House.'[1]

It can be imagined that this did not make my approach to the military proposal any easier.

On Wednesday most of the South-East Asia party came back from Cairo. The first party came with Major General Sutherland, Chief of Staff to General MacArthur, who has come to stay with me at Faridkot House. I have made good friends with him and like him, and he tells me that General MacArthur is very friendlily disposed towards me and is sure we will get on well together when I go to see him.

SATURDAY, 11 DECEMBER   I addressed my staff at 0845 in the new War Room. Some 250 officers came, including the Commanders-in-Chief's Planners, and afterwards I encouraged them to ask questions about policy, etc. So far as I was concerned, today was a historic day, because after trying to get general agreement both at Cairo and at Delhi on the unification of the British and American Air Forces in the South-East Asia Theatre, I decided the time had come when I must act. I saw Generals Stilwell and Stratemeyer who had just come back from Cairo and told them I intended to issue a directive myself and they lodged a protest. In fact, they wanted to cable their objections direct to Washington, but I would not agree to this, and insisted that they should submit their comments to me and that I would telegraph them to the American Chiefs of Staff.

I passed on their protest by telegram, adding that since I was unable

---

[1] In his diary Wavell described *Casablanca* as 'a typical film story of the sentimental-thriller type'. He marvelled at Mountbatten's insatiable appetite for the cinema and commented: 'He is still youthful and I am afraid received the impression that I was a cheerless killjoy.'

to accept a state of affairs where a subordinate Commander in my theatre had independent responsibilities for combat air operations I was overriding the objections and publishing a directive that day integrating the British and American Air Forces under the command of my Air Commander-in-Chief, Air Chief Marshal Sir Richard Peirse.

I am forming the Bengal Command of the RAF and the 10th US Army Air Force into one integrated striking force to be known as the Eastern Air Command, which I am placing under Major General Stratemeyer, USA, whom I am also appointing as second in command of all British and American Air Forces in South-East Asia under Peirse. Under Stratemeyer I am forming an Anglo-American Tactical Air Force under Air Marshal Sir John Baldwin, and an Anglo-American Strategic Air Force under Brigadier General Davidson, USA.

This is the big test, because although I am supported up to the hilt by the whole of the RAF and my American Generals, Wedemeyer and Wheeler, it is a serious step to override the protests of the two American Commanding Generals, Stilwell and Stratemeyer. It is time we had a showdown in this theatre as to who is in command of this party and I do not believe the US Chiefs of Staff will reverse my decision. I know it is really essential for the future conduct of war. I had General Stratemeyer to lunch and to show the strained state of feelings today he went to Wedemeyer privately and asked: 'Why has the Supremo asked me to lunch today? I have already been once in October'! The idea of sociability evidently did not enter his mind!

SUNDAY, 12 DECEMBER Troubles never come singly. The Commanders-in-Chief (led, I am sorry to say, by James Somerville) had staged a communal protest about the organization of our respective Planning Staffs and so I had them all down to an informal meeting at Faridkot House this morning. I pointed out that this was not a British set-up, but an Anglo-American one and that we had to accept some of the Americans' ideas on planning. They wanted the right to hold separate meetings without me, so I asked Giffard:

'Did you ever have meetings of your Corps Commanders in the 14th Army?'

'Yes,' he replied, 'from time to time, when I wanted their views.'

'What would you have said if they held meetings without you and sent you joint resolutions signed by each of them?'

Giffard unhesitatingly replied: 'I should never have allowed that. That would be mutiny.'

I finished up with: 'Thank you for pointing out so clearly what you three Commanders-in-Chief are doing to me.'

Afterwards Giffard and Peirse both came into line and agreed to carry on with the present planning set-up for a further period of trial, but I fear James Somerville, although he agreed, was not satisfied.[1]

The real trouble is that the various Commanders-in-Chief and the Americans were having a very happy time without anyone to integrate their efforts; each going their own way, and they very naturally resent a Supreme Commander being put over them, and naturally resist efforts of integration and unification; and, unless I am firm, I might as well throw up the job. Luckily Pownall and Wedemeyer are completely on my side over this, and I feel that in a few months' time we shall be laughing over our early difficulties, but if some fortune teller had prophesied, while I was in the *Illustrious* two years ago, that, before the end of 1943, I should have to override the views of four Commanders-in-Chief, knowing in my heart of hearts that I was right, I would never have dreamed it possible.

MONDAY, 13 DECEMBER We took off at 0100 and arrived at Chittagong at 0800. In spite of elaborate precautions to ensure that the people knew the time of arrival as 0800, some busy-body took off half an hour just for luck and told everybody I was arriving at 0730, with the result that all the important people, such as Air Marshal Sir John Baldwin, were left hanging about on the airfield, and all the airmen and soldiers who had been drawn up for me to inspect were also kept waiting half an hour through no fault of mine.

I inspected the 6th Squadron of the Indian Air Force, and also the RAF personnel of the station. After this I inspected the men of the Heavy and Light A.A. Regiments stationed in the neighbourhood. I think it is well at this point that I should explain my system of inspection to avoid giving details later. I have arranged that I always shake hands with all the officers, British and Indian, first, then I go over and talk individually to one or two dozen selected English-speaking NCOs and

---

[1] The problem arose over the unresolved question as to whether Mountbatten was a true Supreme Commander with his own planning staff or presided over three semi-independent Commanders-in-Chief, each with their own staffs. The issue was never finally settled but the practice adopted was in the end much closer to the view of the Commanders-in-Chief than this entry suggests.

men. If the unit is British I have all the soldiers or airmen gathered round me and stand on a soap box and talk to them for twenty minutes about the war. If the unit is an Indian unit, they are fallen in on parade, and I walk round and say a few words in my broken Urdu to about every twentieth man.

Incidentally, I was absolutely shattered by one man who was unable to understand what I thought was my faultless '*Tumhare naukri khitni hi?*' I repeated it twice and finally he said in an Oxford accent, 'Oh, you want to know how many years' service I have. I have twelve years' service, Sahib.'

TUESDAY, 14 DECEMBER   I was called shortly after sunrise and tripped out into the jungle in my pyjamas. A smart British sentry who had been put outside my hut insisted on presenting arms, which I found most incongruous. The jungle was alive with movement; various brightly coloured birds flew about and a mongoose came and had a look at me. After breakfast I talked to the officers of the Headquarters Staff of 15th Corps and later inspected all the other ranks attached to this Headquarters.

After lunch we drove down to Ponnaz, where Jack Winterton, who commands the 123rd Indian Infantry Brigade, met me. I inspected his Brigade and talked to the Suffolks. We then went up to the front line.

It was so different to what the front line looked like in France when I visited it in 1918 that I could hardly believe that I had reached the front. I climbed a hillock to an observation post, and there between the British and Japanese outposts was a wonderfully peaceful scene. Water buffaloes were browsing in the paddy fields, the herd guarded by cheerful brown children. White paddy birds were unconcernedly taking the ticks off the backs of the buffaloes. It was sunset, and the villagers who had been working on the roads on our side of the line were passing over into enemy territory for the night, as their homes were in Japanese occupation.

It seemed almost a shame that the tranquillity of this scene should be disturbed by the evening barrage, but they assured me that they usually fired off some rounds at this time of day. So two batteries of Field Artillery opened fire on the Japanese positions. We heard the shells screaming overhead, and then saw the bursts. But the interesting part was that the children, the workpeople and the cattle took not the least bit of notice.

I am told that the Japanese do not fire on the Burmese unless they wander too close to one of their bunkers or strong points, and then they machine gun them, whether there are women and children among them or not, so that by now the local inhabitants have learned to avoid the strong points.

After this we had tea just below the observation post and within easy range of the Japanese. We then got into our jeeps and returned.

I got back just after sunset to the Headquarters of the 5th Indian Division. Briggs[1] himself has a little caravan rather like Monty's in the desert. He picked up the idea when he was serving in the desert. The remainder of us are in tents. My camping outfit includes a collapsible wash basin and a tiny collapsible canvas bath which enabled me to wash off the dust of the day. I am getting gloriously sunburnt. There is a little electric light generating set attached to the Headquarters, and electric light leads are led to each tent.

WEDNESDAY, 15 DECEMBER   I left at 0800 with General Briggs in his open desert car. We drove to the foot of the Mayu Range and there transferred into jeeps to drive across the Ngakyedauk Pass. A road has been constructed across this Pass in three weeks; a truly miraculous feat. We have only recently captured this territory from the Japanese, and there is no other lateral road in our hands that crosses the Mayu Range since the Japanese hold the Buthidaung–Maungdaw Road.

Our sappers (mostly Indian troops, who, when their enthusiasm is aroused, work much harder than British sappers) have constructed a road which leaves the Corniche standing. At present only jeeps can use it but it is going to be improved for heavier traffic. At places there is a sheer drop of several hundred feet where the road has been blasted out of the soft rock. I insisted on driving myself, mostly in double low gear 4-wheel drive. Going up hill was all right but going down hill was really rather terrifying as if one failed to take a corner correctly one would go for six.

One of the difficulties in the Arakan is that there is practically no stone except in a few places where there is a very soft local stone which breaks up too easily. The result is that most of the stone for metalling the roads has to be imported into the country. Another alternative is to import coal and bake bricks which are used to metal the roads. Unless roads are metalled they become impassable during the monsoon.

[1] Major General Briggs was Divisional Commander.

As we climbed to the top of the Mayu Range the wild nature of the jungle became more and more apparent; although very beautiful and full of wonderful coloured birds it is a hell of a country to have to fight over. Personally I cannot imagine more difficult terrain and all the soldiers admit that it is the most difficult country for fighting in the world. Japanese snipers can sit up in the dense trees and pick off our men as they advance. The Japanese have also constructed a series of strong positions known as bunkers in which they have machine guns. The bunkers are so arranged that they cover each other and there is no case on record of British troops having at any time successfully captured a Japanese strong position. It is true that during the last 2 months they have pushed the Japanese back in the Arakan some 7 miles in very successful outpost fighting but this is largely because they had not constructed really formidable strongpoints in this district.

Wingate pointed out to me that it was equally true to say that the Japanese had never captured a British strongpoint in the jungle. When I replied: 'Well that's encouraging anyway', he said: 'Not at all, the only reason they have not captured any strongpoints is that the British have never succeeded in building any strongpoints!'

An interesting point is that plenty of hessian canvas has been hung over the road to prevent the Japanese observing the quantity of transport being used on the Pass. Hessian has also been used to prevent nervous drivers from seeing the sheer drop where the road passes over a precipice. This is considered to have minimised serious accidents on this difficult road.

At the top of the Pass I was met by Major General Messervy commanding 7th Indian Division. I had not seen him since 1922 when he was one of Lord Reading's ADCs and a distant admirer of Edwina's.[1] He accompanied me down to the valley on the west side of the Mayu Range where representatives of his division were drawn up for me to meet and speak to. My talk was punctuated by the sound of firing as the Japanese were counterattacking the positions we had recently captured. I saw the only unwounded officer of Queen's Patrol who with only 7 killed and 18 wounded had killed 30 Japanese and wounded 50 in a recent engagement. It is only during the last month that the casualty rate has turned in our favour, the Japanese used to kill two or three British to one Japanese and now we kill nearly two Japanese to one British.

---

[1] On that occasion he told Mountbatten that the proper way to mount a polo pony was to run up from behind, take a flying leap and vault into the saddle. Mountbatten's experiments with this technique proved painful.

I must say the whole morale of our troops in the Arakan is definitely better than I had been led to expect but this has been brought about by a complete change of Commanders all the way through, in the last two months. I found the men in great heart, bursting with enthusiasm and keen to get at the Japanese. If we can only make a really good plan I feel confident of victory in this part of the front.[1]

We drove back over the Pass and I inspected the 136th Field Regiment of the Royal Artillery. While I was addressing the men Vengeance dive bombers flew overhead and peeled off as they dived down on to the Japanese counterattack which was still in progress.

When we got back to 5th Division's Headquarters the Corps Commander, Christison, had got back and I had to talk with him and the two Divisional Commanders about future plans. We worked each other up to a fever heat of enthusiasm and I then decided to take the Corps Commander and Army Commander back to Delhi with me to re-vitalize our plans and sent off the necessary signals.

We all had lunch at the Headquarters and then drove off in jeeps to the head of the Naaf River. Coming down that way the day before I had had to cross in a ferry but today the bridge over the arm of the river at Bawli Bazaar had been completed and I performed the opening ceremony by walking across it.

It has been built by Indian sappers in under six weeks from timber felled in the district and will take the heaviest vehicles. Considering that the stream runs at speeds up to 7 knots and must be several hundred feet wide at this point it is a grand feat and typical of all the splendid engineering feats which have taken place within the last few weeks. I inspected the men who had built the bridge and congratulated them.

At 1515 I visited the 4th Field Regiment and 56th Anti-Aircraft Regiment. After this the officers entertained me at tea while the band of the North Staffordshire Regiment played for the troops. The bandmaster told me that he was expecting his band to be disbanded at the end of this tour so I gave orders countermanding this as I consider bands to be essential at the Front to keep up the spirits of the troops. I enquired what concert parties they had and was introduced to the man who was running the local concert party. He told me that his troupe consisted of men only because the Insurance Company would not insure girls up in the forward areas. I was unable to make out whether the risks for which

---

[1] 'Louis Mountbatten came round to see us and did us all the power of good,' General Lomax told his mother. 'He spoke amazingly well to the men, who were delighted to see him. He has a great personality.'

they could not be insured came from the British or Japanese troops! I must follow up the question of entertainment and films for the men at the Front.

THURSDAY, 16 DECEMBER   I left at 0900 having inspected and talked to my personal Guard consisting of some 20 British gunners. We reached Ramu at 0935 ten minutes ahead of time and had to wait until 0945, the programme time, for me to inspect the Detachment of the 81st West African Division. They are magnificent-looking men.

My talk to them was somewhat interrupted by the arrival of a Squadron of Lightning fighters which had come in to refuel. I went over and talked to the American pilots, I then went on to talk to the officers and men of 607 Squadron, RAF.

I was continually interrupted by aircraft coming in to refuel and taking off again and was quite unable to get through my normal talk. Finally I said, 'It is no good carrying on with this talk. I was only trying to convince you that we will eventually have enough resources to ensure our ultimate victory over the Japs and the sight we see today on this airfield is better proof of that than anything I could tell you.' This went down very well and I got out of having to complete my talk amidst cheers, though whether the cheers were because they were escaping the rest of my talk or not, I should not like to say.

Incidentally, in almost every case where there has not been some loud-voiced Sergeant Major to call the men to attention when I have finished speaking, they have clapped most enthusiastically. I mention this not because I believe it to be a personal matter, but merely to show the intense enthusiasm there is for getting on with the war in this Front. I certainly promised them nothing that would account for undue enthusiasm, as I told them that we could not begin to crush the Japanese until Germany was defeated and that they would have to fight on by themselves until the additional resources arrived, and that they would then have to stay out until the war was completed. Actually, this is going to be a very serious problem, but I believe more serious among the troops that are in India than those that are in the fighting lines.

I had decided to fly over the Japanese positions and the country behind them to see for myself what the conditions were like and ordered a Mosquito to be made available. I had asked that it should be supplied with bombs, since we knew where the Japanese Headquarters were, and I felt that it would save petrol if we were to drop a bomb on them at the same time as I was doing my reconnaissance flight. Unfortunately they had no bombs to fit Mosquitoes at Ramu. My Mosquito, however, had a good supply of machine guns and so we decided to shoot up any craft we found on the Kaladan River. From Ramu (which is on a level with Cox's Bazaar) we flew inland for some 50 miles until we hit the Kaladan River. We then flew down the river following its course for another 50 miles. This river comes out south of Akyab, and we turned off just north of Akyab, flying across the Mayu River to Donbaik, which is on the coast just north of Akyab. We then flew up the coastline of the Mayu Peninsula, looked at St Martin's Island and then flew back up the Naaf River and on to Dohazari, where we landed at 1150. Although we had flown over the Japanese positions we had not seen anything of them, so dense is the jungle in most places. It was a very thrilling experience flying a Mosquito, which is the fastest aircraft in the world, having a top speed in excess of 400 miles an hour. In places we flew under 1000 feet and the sensation of speed is quite fantastic.

I was rather glad when we got back, as it would have been a somewhat unpleasant situation to have made a forced landing behind the Japanese lines.

We flew on in my American C.47 to Comilla, where we landed at 1410. I was met by the Commander of the 14th Army, Lieutenant General Slim, and the new Commander of the Tactical Air Force, Air Marshal Baldwin, and was taken to see 171 Wing, 681 and 684 Squadrons and the 3rd Indian Light A.A. and 6th Indian Heavy A.A. Regiments, who had been waiting on parade for one and a half hours. I was very angry to think that the programme had been so badly organized, and that I had been invited to start one hour later than usual at a time when I should have started half an hour earlier than usual. I offered to forego lunch but the Army Commander pressed me to have it and so I gave way, realizing that unless I did so he, the Air Marshal and all the other officers would have to give up their lunch too. After lunch I talked to the British and American officers of the Army and Air Headquarters. There were too many for me to shake hands with them all this time. I then addressed the other ranks. This time it was not aircraft that interfered with my talk, but an incredibly persistent cawing on the part of a colony of crows in a tree nearby.

I refused to go on until the crows had been dispersed, which was done by throwing stones at them. Every time that the volley of stones ceased the crows came back, cawing louder than ever. Finally a team consisting of two Lieutenant-Generals, one Air Marshal, one Major

General, one Air Commodore and three ADCs kept up a constant bombardment at the tree and under this somewhat disturbing influence I continued my speech.

I went on to No.74 Indian General Hospital and addressed the doctors and nurses. I found they had 1000 beds and 1800 cases. Many of the men were lying on the floor and in other places additional beds had been shoved in, thus overcrowding the wards.

I then went on to No.92 Indian General Hospital, and said to the Colonel in charge, 'How many beds have you got?' He replied, '750.' I thought that I would be very clever and said, 'And I suppose you have got over 1000 cases in the hospital,' and he replied, 'Oh no, we have only 500 cases here.' I offered to introduce him to the Colonel commanding No.74 Hospital so that they might even out their beds a bit better!

I must say that the medical situation on the Arakan front is a scandal and I have telegraphed for Major General Thompson, my chief military doctor, to come down at once and investigate the matter thoroughly for me.

They are over 700 nurses short in the 14th Army alone, and I am told that they have a higher allocation of nurses than the rest of India. They say it is quite impossible to get any more trained nurses out here, so I offered to telegraph home to Edwina to see if she can produce a few hundred volunteers from St John's to come out and help nurse the wounded which we shall inevitably have in the coming battles. Everybody received this suggestion with great enthusiasm, but I agreed not to do anything about it until the matter has been gone into officially after General Thompson's visit and inspection.

I cut out dinner in order to have an urgent planning meeting with Slim and Christison. At 2200 I flew back to Delhi taking them with me in my own aeroplane.

FRIDAY, 17 DECEMBER to MONDAY, 20 DECEMBER   We landed at Willingdon airport at 0350 on Friday and spent the next two days planning with the various Commanders concerned. I had called in the various other Commanders including the Americans and we had a most profitable planning meeting. I felt that the enthusiasm of the men in contact with the enemy would be infectious to all of us who had been sitting in Delhi too long and I have never seen a series of meetings go so smoothly, so swiftly and so satisfactorily. From having felt really in despair about the stickiness of the whole situation, I am back on the crest of the wave and think we can achieve something fairly good.

I called Wingate in to the discussions and had him to stay with me. He, too, is full of optimism.

TUESDAY, 21 DECEMBER to MONDAY, 27 DECEMBER   On Tuesday I held my first meeting with my own staff without the Commanders-in-Chief being present. It was a great success and I gather it pleased my staff. In future I am going to have three meetings a week with them in the morning and three with the Commanders-in-Chief.

This week I signed the most unusual document which has so far fallen to my lot to sign. This was a proclamation by which I am taking over on the 1st January the Government of unoccupied Burma from the Governor of Burma. Apparently I am empowered to do this without even consulting the Governor, merely by signing a proclamation. This proclamation also places this part of Burma under martial law.

The question of public relations and photographic coverage in the South-East Asia Command is giving me nearly as much of a headache as the military plans. First the Admiralty would not play and wanted the naval correspondents to be accredited to Admiral Somerville instead of myself. I fought the battle at Cairo with the First Sea Lord and the Prime Minister and won it.

Then, simultaneously, the Americans under General Stilwell and the GHQ India Public Relations Directorate refused to play with us. Sir Philip Joubert[1] was in despair, as their refusal to co-operate or help us was reaffirmed at each meeting he had.

I arranged to hold meetings myself, but realized that it was essential that they should succeed, as I did not want to go into meetings and have my wishes turned down and then have to start to fight.

The man who was making all the trouble on the American side was Brigadier General King, the American Chief Signal Officer. After Wedemeyer and Joubert had failed to obtain any co-operation out of him as far as photographic coverage units went, I drafted a signal to General Marshall telling him that I was getting no co-operation from General King. I sent for Micky Hodges to find out whether King was co-operating on the signal side and he told me he was co-operating very

---

[1] Air Chief Marshal (retired) Sir Philip Joubert de la Ferté was the Deputy Chief of Staff in charge of information and civil affairs.

well. I showed Micky my draft signal to Marshall, which worried him, as he thought it would have repercussions on the good feelings between him and King. I offered to hold up the signal long enough for him to go and see King, and sent a message inviting King to dinner before our movie show that night. Micky succeeded in frightening him so much at the prospect of being reported by name to General Marshall that he broke out into a cold sweat and thanked him profusely for having persuaded me to hold up the signal. He sat next to me at dinner and the cinema, evidently getting more and more worried and making advances to me, but I refused to talk shop. After everyone else had gone I asked Joubert, Wedemeyer and Pownall to join us and said that I understood that he had refused to co-operate in any way, but now that I had met him I felt there must be some mistake as he had been so co-operative with Micky and such a very friendly guest this evening. He hastily assured me that he would do anything I wished and we then and there arranged provisional terms which satisfied Joubert.

The next day I had to meet the notorious Jehu. A curious character; he is a small-time Indian journalist of Welsh origin who has risen from Second Lieutenant to Brigadier entirely in the Public Relations world.[1] He is certainly competent, but quite phenomenally unpopular with everyone I have come across. It appeared he had hoped to transfer to my staff as a Major General, or, at all events, to be allowed to run both my public relations and Auchinleck's.

While he still thought this and just before I arrived out, he apparently issued a directive that I was to be played up in the various pamphlets and papers which he issues to the troops. After I refused to accept his help for more than the first few weeks he must have changed his mind, because a pamphlet entitled 'How Strong is Japan' consisting of 14 pages was held up by him after 20,000 copies had been printed because it had contained a photograph of my arrival and a paragraph saying that I was going to lead the British to victory. He apparently gave as his reason that Auchinleck would not like this. Luckily this got to my ears a day before our meeting with Auchinleck and Jehu and so I was able to tell Auchinleck the whole story the day before. He investigated it and found that over a quarter of a million pages had been destroyed on the grounds of 'inaccuracy and undesirable items'. As the entire pamphlet, except the last page, was a reprint from *Life* the only undesirable

---

[1] More Scottish than Welsh, on both sides. His father had been Regius Professor of Geology at Edinburgh.

item from Jehu's point of view could have been the photo and write-up I got on the last page. Of course the Auk himself had never seen the pamphlet before, as indeed I was quite sure, but I think that this revelation so shattered Jehu's morale that we had a relatively easy meeting the following day.

I only mention this to show the lengths one has to go to try and get people to co-operate without actually having to refer the matter to higher authority after open disagreement.

On Xmas Eve Bunnie[1] and I drove to Meerut in my wonderful new 1943 Cadillac, which is a gift from General Marshall, and has appropriately arrived about Christmas time. It has an automatic gear shift which is quite fascinating, as there are no gear leavers at all, only an accelerator and a foot brake. It has a radio telephone from which I can talk to General Wedemeyer's 'Command' car and to Headquarters. After having driven round so long in a 10 Horse Power Ford, the luxury of this car is unbelievable. Among other things it has a remote-control partition which can be operated from the back seat when one wants to talk to the driver.

I have been given silk flags for my office (which is really an American custom) by General Marshall, the Generalissimo and the Dutch Commander-in-Chief which will be put up, together with my Union Jack. Eisenhower has all his allied flags on top of the bonnet of his car, but I have succeeded in making them look less ridiculous by putting two on each side of the mudguard. It was quite a job preventing Faridkot House from looking like Selfridges, but we have avoided this by putting up four flag staffs in the garden about fifty yards apart.

They put the sheave about six inches from the top of the mast, so that the flags flew permanently at half mast. I told them to put the sheave into the truck so that the flags could be hoisted 'close-up' as in a warship. Then the trouble started. It was found that the masts were not strong enough to support the weight of the lightest carpenter they could find; nor would it support the weight of a ladder without cracking. They therefore started to dig up the foundations of the mast only to find of course that the cement had set so hard that they were unable to get the flag staff out. Finally they got a sort of fire escape ladder which did not have to rest against the mast.

---

[1] Lieutenant Colonel H. H. 'Bunnie' Phillips, an old friend whom Mountbatten had brought out to concern himself with various covert operations.

CHRISTMAS DAY   On the afternoon of Christmas Day the State Agent and all the State servants and our own servants presented us with the customary Christmas gifts or 'dollis'.

The scene was very like the feast in *Chu Chin Chow*. At least twelve magnificent trays were carried in filled with every form of fruit and flower, and nuts and fish, including one fierce looking 40lb fish.

Two live turkeys were also carried in. One of them immediately made a mess on the carpet, so we put them on to the marble floor, which successfully anchored them, as they were too frightened that they would skid if they moved. Meanwhile consternation reigned while a sufficiently low-caste sweeper was sought who could remove the mess. Lady Linlithgow told me that when she first arrived out here at the Viceroy's House she had a pet dog that made a mess in her boudoir. Although they had 270 servants it took so long to find a man of sufficiently low caste to be able to clean up the mess that she had done so herself before they found him.

MONDAY, 27 DECEMBER   A terrible tragedy happened today. My little mongoose, Rikki Tikki, was killed by being accidently stepped on by my steward, Moore. She had become so incredibly tame that I feared sooner or later that this might happen, since her main object was never to leave Moore's feet. Wherever he walked she would run in and out in a sort of figure of eight round his feet the whole time, and whenever he tried to sit down she would run up his trousers. She would follow him, or me (if he wasn't about!) down the stairs or up the stairs, or anywhere about the house or garden, and if she wandered off would always come if her name was called.

Luckily he was walking very fast, almost running, and his heavy boot killed her instantaneously. She had grown from being only six inches from her nose to her tail to over eighteen inches and was the tamest little pet imaginable. Poor Moore was quite white from the shock of having been the cause of her death.

TUESDAY, 28 DECEMBER to MONDAY, 3 JANUARY 1944   I mentioned last week that General Marshall had sent me a Cadillac which arrived at Christmas time. General Arnold has sent me an aeroplane fitted up exactly like his own, which arrived a couple of days after Christmas, so that the American Chiefs of Staff are doing me proud! It has ten very comfortable seats, a knee-hole writing desk, pantry and cupboard, etc., and is fitted like a very luxurious yacht.[1]

The integration of the Air Forces out here is doing extremely well, and the arrival of the new Spitfire Squadrons is making the whole difference. On New Year's Day 14 Japanese bombers, escorted by 15 fighters, came over to attack our coastal forces off the Arakan. A single squadron of 12 Spitfires took off and shot down 13 and damaged, or probably destroyed, another 10. Only one Spitfire was damaged and this had to do a forced landing on enemy territory. However, the pilot got out of his machine unhurt, set fire to it, and made his way back to our lines. To sum up, 12 British machines destroyed or damaged 23 out of 29 Japanese for the loss of one. This is the first air victory of this nature that I have heard of in this part of the world since the war started.

I had a typical passage of arms with General Stilwell at a meeting on New Year's Day. We were arguing about when certain American Units, which were attached to and training with British forces, should be moved into Burma. General Stilwell said, 'I should like it placed on record that I am responsible for the training of all American forces in this theatre and I am the person to decide when they are adequately trained and can move forward.'

I replied: 'I accept that in principle, but would remind you that these troops are being trained under British officers. I am responsible for operations and will decide when Units move into the fighting lines. In other words, General, I should like to place on record that I am the Supreme Commander out here and that what I say goes.' He took it very good-naturedly and laughed and said, 'We none of us dispute that.'[2]

MONDAY, 10 JANUARY [Dhukwan] On this day I visited 5 Columns and the staff of the Training Wing, the Royal Engineers Group and the Burma Rifles and a US Air Commando.

I will not describe all the visits in detail since I always follow the same routine. To begin with I have all the officers of the Unit introduced to me and usually have a few moments' conversation with each one of

---

[1] The aircraft was always referred to as the Hapgift, since 'Hap' was General Arnold's nickname.
[2] Mountbatten was always convinced that Stilwell at bottom liked and admired him. Vinegar Joe's diary entry a few days after this meeting read: 'The Glamour Boy is just that. He doesn't wear well and I begin to wonder if he knows his stuff.' Soon Mountbatten became a 'fatuous ass' and a 'pisspot'.

them. After that I move over to a group of selected NCOs and men and talk with each of them in turn, usually about their homes as they are all terribly homesick.

If the Unit is an Indian or Ghurka Unit then I inspect them and stop and talk in my very broken Urdu or Ghurkali and to any man who had medals or looks in any way distinguished.

I had a tea with Burma Rifles and I must say I was very moved by the quiet courage of these officers and men, many of whom have seen their homes burnt and destroyed and know that their wives and families have been killed. None expects to find any of his earthly possessions when we do re-conquer Burma.

In the evening we got to Lalitpur airfield and here I talked to the US Air Commando under the command of Colonel Cochran, whose second-in-command is Lieutenant Colonel Alison. They are the most enthusiastic couple I have ever met. All the officers and enlisted men appear quite unusually young and they refer to the 33-year-old Cochran as 'the old man'. Among the pilots is Sergeant Jackie Coogan with whom Edwina and I made a film on our honeymoon in Hollywood in 1922 when he was about 5 years old! He made his name in *The Kid* with Charlie Chaplin a year before. His parents stole all his money from him, I believe.

After this we arranged to fly over to Malhone in light aeroplanes. Cochran offered to take me in his little Stinson. It looked such a simple aircraft to fly that I thought I would strike a high note by suggesting that I should fly it. Cochran readily agreed and got into the back seat while I got into the pilot's cockpit. Everything seemed quite simple until I started off, when I found that the rudder bars had brake pedals attached and with my long legs I could not avoid pressing the wheel brakes every time I moved the rudder bar. Furthermore I was not used to taking off across wind as one has to do with a landing strip and as the aeroplane got blown about I tried to correct it by using the rudder, which jammed first on one and then the other wheel brake. The first time I jammed on the wheel brake accidentally the aeroplane turned completely round, the next time I put it on more gently we tipped up and the wing nearly hit the ground. By this time I was getting very frightened, so I opened the throttle full out and by the mercy of God we took off without hitting anything. I imagine it must have been a very funny sight to the crowd that was watching us take off, but poor General Wingate was very worried as he felt himself responsible!

Once we were in the air Cochran leant over and strapped the belt round, saying, 'I suppose you realize that if you touch the brakes on landing we shall certainly turn over.'

I was rather horrified to find that we were not landing on an airfield at all, but in a clearing in the jungle, which was to be used for an exercise that night. I put the tops of my toes on the rudder bar in such a way that I could not accidentally touch the brakes and landed on the uphill part of the clearing. It was fortunately a perfect landing, although the part I selected to land on had a number of rocks which caused an accident later that night!!

I had not flown solo since 1937, but do not believe I should have had any difficulty if it had not been for those infernal brakes.

WEDNESDAY, 12 JANUARY [Lalitpur]   At 1215 I drove off in a jeep with the General.[1] We stopped on the way and had a luncheon off one of the American 'K' rations which are issued to this Unit. It was excellent. I found the Americans had, as usual, sent a large armed guard of 20 men with tommy guns who took up defensive positions round our picnic party, though God knows who they thought was going to attack us in the heart of India. After lunch I persuaded them to go back to their own camp and we went on unescorted to Gona.

Here I visited 6 columns of a West African Brigade. I had expected to follow the routine that I had followed with the Ghurkas, that is that I would inspect the troops and not address them. However, the Brigadier assured me that they would understand if I spoke to them in simple language. Modelling myself on Edgar Wallace's hero, Sanders of the River, I addressed these Hausas in simple language, ending up with an exhortation to go into the jungle and kill all the Japanese. Upon this they went wild with excitement, screamed and yelled and cheered, and waved their knives and rifles in the air. I have never known such a reception. It appears they were getting bored with their training and had thought that I had come to send them off the next day to the jungle, which, unfortunately, was far from being the case. However, I had nearly as great a success with each of these African Columns, all of whom screamed with delight whenever I had finished speaking.

The only tiring part about the West Africans was that I had to do an additional talk to the white officers and NCOs, since they could hardly be expected to be satisfied with the baby talk I had given their black

[1] General Wingate.

troops. Thus I gave a talk to the officers and NCOs of every two Columns together after I had talked separately to their Columns.

I was told a delightful story that had occurred in Calcutta when one of the West Africans from the 14th Army had gone on leave. He was seen entering a shop, the doorway of which was blocked by a very pale-faced Bengali. Whereupon the coal black West African turned haughtily to the civilian and said: 'Out o' my way, black man!'

We finally drove on to Saugor where I was met by Brigadier Bernard Fergusson. He is a remarkably young officer to be a Brigadier. He used to be in the Black Watch, he wears an eye glass, has a large moustache and looks the typical stage Englishman. He has proved himself one of the most brilliant and courageous jungle fighters we have in the British Army.[1]

THURSDAY, 13 JANUARY   Today I visited and talked to 8 Columns and the Brigade Headquarters. We then drove to an open clearing where light aircraft met us and flew us to Lalitpur where we transferred to the Hapgift and flew on to Gwalior. Here I stopped and inspected No.84 Squadron of Vengeance dive bombers and then flew on to Willingdon airport at Delhi in time for dinner and a movie show.

During these four days I had given the following number of talks: Monday – 7; Tuesday – 10; Wednesday – 16; Thursday – 10. A total of 43 talks in 4 days, equivalent of 14 hours talking!

FRIDAY, 14 JANUARY to MONDAY, 17 JANUARY   I found a tremendous lot of work to catch up with on return. I also found that the Air and Army Group Commanders-in-Chief had put in official papers protesting that the move to Kandy was going to be difficult. However, I overrode them as I do not like the idea of constantly chopping and changing plans. We have had enough of that for reasons outside my control in any case.

I found the first three editions of our new daily paper *SEAC* (pronounced See-Ack) on my return. Frank Owen[2] has done a magnificent job. General Giffard, who is down on the Burma front, tells me the soldiers are absolutely delighted with it. Considering he has only got

---

[1] Fergusson's two books *Beyond the Chindwin* and *The Wild Green Earth* provide an admirable picture of Wingate's campaigns behind the Japanese lines.

[2] Former editor of the *Evening Standard* whom Mountbatten had appointed to this function against the strong protests of P. J. Grigg, the Secretary of State for War.

one Marine Subaltern, two ORs from the Army and two ORs from the Air Force and a naval telegraphist to help him, and produces seven days a week, it really is a wonderful show.

THURSDAY, 20 JANUARY   The Hapgift took off with a full load at Willingdon airport at 0350. We arrived at 0800 at Santa Cruz airfield, where we were met by the senior naval, military and RAF officers and escorted to Government House, where we all had bath and breakfast and changed from blue uniform into white tropical uniform. Sir John Colville[1] was most helpful in putting up with such an invasion.

I had not of course been to Bombay since November 1921 and the only two parts I remembered were the famous Gateway of India, where the Prince of Wales was landed, and Government House on the Malibar Hill, where we stayed with George Lloyd. It was from here that the Prince of Wales wrote to his father to say he had not known what real pompous, regal court life was like until he had stayed with the Lloyds!

I went to inspect HMS *Highway*, one of the new LSTs. As COHQ were responsible for inventing and designing this type of ship and as this was the first of the type I had had a chance to see I was absolutely thrilled by all I saw.

We took off from Santa Cruz at 1230 in the Hapgift and we arrived at Poona at 1300.

FRIDAY, 21 JANUARY   At 0900 I left by car for Ahmednagar which we reached at 1110. Throughout my trip I was accompanied by two jeeps fitted with wireless sets and a signal officer so that we remained in touch with Corps and Divisional Headquarters throughout the trip. This was lucky as I had to change the programme half way through.

SATURDAY, 22 JANUARY   I only discovered this evening that we are close neighbours of Nehru's here as he and his colleagues are confined in the fort. I enquired if it was possible to see him but found that visitors were not allowed without the Viceroy's permission.

MONDAY, 31 JANUARY [New Delhi]   Today I had a full dress meeting of all the Commanders-in-Chief, including Admiral Somerville and General Stilwell, to discuss a very important paper.[2]

[1] Governor of Bombay.
[2] Almost certainly the revised CULVERIN, a plan for an attack on Sumatra.

General Festing is staying at Faridkot as my guest.

In the evening I gave a large dinner party for the Viceroy and General Auchinleck to meet the senior officers of the South-East Asia Command. We only had officers of Major General's rank upwards.

SATURDAY, 5 FEBRUARY to MONDAY, 7 FEBRUARY 1944 This morning over a hundred of our staff, British and American, male and female, Army, Navy, Air Force and Political Officers, went to Willingdon airport at 0745 to say goodbye to Generals Wedemeyer, Macleod[1] and twelve other officers, British and American, who were going home to present my views on South-East Asia strategy to the Prime Minister and Combined Chiefs of Staff.[2]

Nothing could have shown more clearly the splendid Anglo-American family feeling that exists than that so many hard-worked officers should voluntarily have gone to the airport at this early hour to see the party off. It was rather like saying goodbye to a football team with metaphorical cries of 'Don't come back without the cup!'

Half an hour later the Hapgift left for Bombay with Admiral Jerram and some staff officers. One naval officer who was supposed to take passage back to Bombay in the Hapgift arrived early and tried to get into the C.54. Luckily Flags bowled out the error, otherwise he would have been taken as far as Cairo non-stop!

A great battle has started in the Arakan; General Tanabashi has come round behind our front-line troops with a great number of Japanese and is attacking our lines in the rear. I am keeping close touch with the situation, which is certainly very anxious for us.[3]

TUESDAY, 8 FEBRUARY I left at 0100 in the Hapgift. We flew to Comilla which we reached at 0700 and were met by General Giffard, General Slim and Air Marshal Baldwin. I immediately went up to Army Headquarters and had a long discussion on the present battle.

The AOC at Imphal had telephoned to say that the weather was too bad to fly over the mountains and I therefore flew to Kumbhirgam where I addressed the personnel of the RAF Station as well as 110 Squadron and 168 Wing.

[1] Brigadier General Macleod, Head of Combined Operations in SEAC.
[2] The AXIOM mission – a doomed attempt to sell CULVERIN to the British and American Chiefs of Staff.
[3] This assault, powerful though it was, was mainly a deception operation to divert attention from the main Japanese thrust to come shortly on the Imphal Plain.

The weather had picked up a lot at Kumbhirgam and so I said I would try the flight to Imphal unless the weather was really too bad. Imphal agreed that it was worth trying the flight and so I took off at 1330 under fighter cover.

Although it was cloudy over the mountains Imphal was quite clear and sunny. On arrival I was met by Lieutenant General Geoffrey Scoones, Commanding 4th Corps. The Mercury (my flying wireless and cypher station) had already arrived and so we were in direct communication with my Headquarters in Delhi throughout my trip. This was the aircraft which Micky Hodges invented for my trips.

I found great excitement going on because the AOC had failed to inform the Corps Commander that he had cancelled my arrival and, furthermore, the Corps Commander was of the opinion that the flight need not have been cancelled as it appeared that Imphal had been in sunshine all the morning.

The 23rd Division particularly had hurt feelings, as my visit to most of their units had to be cancelled and I therefore had to undertake to remain another day at the end of my trip to visit the aggrieved battalions.

WEDNESDAY, 9 FEBRUARY   At 0640 I left with the Corps Commander by car for Tamu. In the last few months our engineers have driven this 80-mile road through virgin jungle over the mountains and have made it a double track road with an all-weather Tarmac surface. It resembles the Corniche in the South of France and is an amazing engineering feat.

We arrived at 1030 at Tamu, where I was met by Major General Gracey, commanding the 20th Division. He had collected officers and representatives from the 80th Brigade in one group and from the 100th Brigade in another group, whom I met and addressed. The most interesting person was Lieutenant Colonel Williams, the Corps Elephant Adviser.[1] He introduced me to the Chief Mahout, who was wearing his national Burmese costume and carried an ivory and silver-hilted dah, which is the traditional insignia of this appointment.

I should have mentioned that, whereas Imphal is in Assam, Tamu is of course well inside Burma. I must admit I got quite a kick out of crossing the frontier from India into Burma, since it is the first time I

[1] The celebrated J. H. Williams, usually known as 'Elephant Bill' and later the author of a book of that name.

have been inside Burma since I took over the government of British-occupied Burma.

I must admit I have never visualized being a Governor of any place and least of all the tenuous mountain jungle of Northern Burma!

The Corps Commander told me an amusing story about my PAO, General Wheeler's, first visit to this part of Burma. He enquired from 'Elephant' Williams how long the period was before a baby elephant was born and was told 'Two years'. A little later he saw a teak forest on the slopes of a mountain above a river and said, 'Anyway, it is easy to get the teak away here, as it rolls into the river automatically and floats down the stream.' He was informed that this was not the case, because teak has to be dried for three years before it would float. That evening he said to the Corps Commander, 'If it takes two years to produce a baby elephant and three years for teak to float, I have a feeling things are not going to happen very rapidly on this front!'

The Hapgift had come down to the Tamu airstrip and we had a picnic lunch on board on the way back.

THURSDAY, 10 FEBRUARY We left at 0700 for Tiddim. This involved a drive of 167 miles along a road built within the last few weeks under even more remarkable conditions than the road to Tamu, since it goes up through mountains up to 9000 feet in height and crosses roaring torrents at several places. It has been built entirely by the Corps engineers and is a really outstanding achievement. The scenery is indescribably beautiful and although it takes on an average ten solid hours of driving to get from Imphal to Tiddim every moment of it was really thrilling.

Pioneer battalions were working along the road. I noticed that most of them who were wielding a shovel had a mate who worked with them by pulling on a lanyard attached to the shovel to help lift it when it was full of earth. The Corps Commander told me that the first time he met this arrangement he asked an Indian Officer what the object was and received the following charming reply: 'Sahib! It is a device whereby two men can do the work of one'! Bulldozers and graders and even steam-rollers were at work on this road, though it is not an all-weather one and frequently has to be closed after rain.

It is at the end of these tenuous lines of communication that the gallant 17th Division are fighting. They have been fighting solidly in Burma ever since the Japanese invaded two years ago and I found their spirits very high and their morale unimpaired, in spite of all they had been through.

We arrived at 1800 at Tiddim, which is 6000 feet above sea level amongst pine trees and tall rhododendrons. I was met by Major General Cowan, who commands the 17th Division. They had built a special little hut of thatched grass for me with a brick fireplace which was very welcome, as it is bitterly cold at night.

FRIDAY, 11 FEBRUARY   I spent this day visiting the various units of the 17th Division. First of all I drove a jeep up to Kennedy Peak. This proved an even more hair-raising drive than yesterday's, since the road rises to about 9000 feet with in many cases sheer precipices of 1000 feet or more.

The day before they had brought up for the first time in history some medium artillery. The 5.5″ guns' axle width is only about 2″ less than the width of the road and at one point the wheel of one of the guns went over the precipice, but somehow they succeeded in hoisting the gun back into the road and getting it up into position, and when I arrived the Japanese on Milestone 22 were under fire from 5.5″ and 25-pounder guns.

I addressed the various units at Kennedy Peak and was shown all the Japanese positions. They did not cease their bombardment during my visit as the Japanese are now kept under a permanent bombardment by artillery. In one place they have wired in a Japanese strongpoint, that is to say, our troops have put a wire fence round the outside of the Japanese defensive positions so that they cannot get out, nor can relieving troops get in without having to cut the wire in the face of our investing troops.

The view from Kennedy Peak beggars description. I saw a town lying at the bend of the river, clearly visible to the naked eye and could hardly believe it when I was told that this was Kalemyo, which is some 37 miles inside Japanese-held territory.

I should have said that the last 100 miles of the Tiddim Road is all inside Burma and this is the furthest I have ever penetrated into the country.

The men on the bulldozers are really most remarkable. They will take them anywhere. Two of them went over the edge recently. One succeeded in regaining control after the first 600 feet of wild rush and managed to pull up the bulldozer before he reached the river. Another young driver was not so lucky. The bulldozer turned over on him so that his arm had to be amputated in spite of his entreaties not to be separated from his 'dozer'. When I went to talk to the men of the Medium Battery who were on a precipitous ledge the Divisional Commander noticed two bulldozers nearby. He called up to one of the men and said, 'Bring your party down here', pointing to the ledge on which I was standing. The driver immediately said, 'My dozer hasn't got a blade. Will it do if I bring the other one down?' The idea that he might be wanted without his 'dozer', or that the precipice was really too much to ask him to negotiate, apparently never entered his head.

Later I visited representative units of the 63rd Brigade and then I inspected some of the Burmese local irregular troops, the Tiddim Scouts, the Chin Levies and the Chin Guerillas. Some of these were young boys whose service rifles were as high as themselves and whose uniforms consisted of any cast-off clothing that could be spared by officers and men of the regular forces. Others were staid old fighters. Several were wearing red flashes pinned to their hats, each flash indicating that the man had killed a Jap.

A wonderful hospital has been erected within the last few weeks at Tiddim. It is all under canvas of course, but contains X-ray rooms, operating theatres and every modern convenience. It has 500 beds which is a remarkable achievement for a Field Ambulance Unit. In fact, next month it is to be taken over as a Casualty Clearing Station and the Field Ambulance will become mobile again and move further forward.

I spoke to a number of wounded officers and men who had just been brought in from the previous day's fighting; all in wonderful good heart. I wonder if people at home realize how constant the fighting is on the Burma front and how regular is the stream of wounded passing through our Casualty Clearing Stations and Hospitals.

When you think that men wounded at Milestone 22 have to be carried for the first six hours in a bamboo stretcher through precipitous jungle before they can even get to a jeep trail one realizes what they have to undergo. The jeep trail is horribly bumpy and rough and the trip from Kennedy Peak to Tiddim with wounded takes another four hours.

American Voluntary Ambulance Units operate on the Tiddim Road. They drive with admirable care, but it takes them over 24 hours' continuous driving to get the wounded from Tiddim to Imphal and at Imphal they are still many, many miles from the nearest railway or port. How different is the fate of a man wounded on the Central Burma front from one of our men wounded in Italy or North Africa, and yet this is the front where the medical arrangements have been most neglected and where we are still 700 nurses short.

After the hospital I met the Divisional Headquarters staff and addressed them. At every Brigade I visited on this front I have been presenting medals and decorations to men who had earned them recently. I felt really very proud pinning the ribbon of the DSO on to that gallant and famous fighter, General 'Punch' Cowan, in front of all his staff.

SATURDAY, 12 FEBRUARY   At 0900 I inspected the 1st Battalion West Yorks at Tangzan.

We stopped for lunch at Milestone 87. By this time several of the cars in the convoy were giving trouble owing to the bad road and to a large percentage of water in the petrol which had been drawn at Milestone 109. Later on more serious trouble occurred and two cars had to be left behind. I noticed no less than three newly overturned lorries which had fallen off the road since our trip south.

At 1600 we reached Milestone 36 and visited No.88 Indian General Hospital, where Miss McGeary is now the matron. It was she who saved General Wingate's life twice, once when he came out of Burma severely ill and once when he had such bad typhoid last November. She is one of the most remarkable people I have ever met. All who serve under her adore her and she is a great go-getter. Having been transferred from the 4th Corps Casualty Clearing Station at Imphal to this General Hospital she no longer comes under General Scoones, but under a new General, whom she mistrusts! A new CO had just been sent to her hospital with instructions to see that she does not try to short-circuit official procedure or to apply to highly placed officers direct for help to get her hospital properly equipped. I soon dealt with that situation and enjoyed doing so!

By the time we reached Imphal at 2000 two more of our cars had fallen by the roadside. This gives an idea of the tremendous strain under which transport works on this part of the Burma front.

SUNDAY, 13 FEBRUARY   At 0800 I left 4th Corps Headquarters and drove to Milestone 131 on the Kohima Road, where I visited and addressed the Corps Artillery. After this we drove back through Imphal to the South where some 1700 officers and men of the 37th Brigade were drawn up on parade. This included one of the Maharaja of Patiala's Infantry Battalions. Most of the Sikhs were over six feet in height and of quite magnificent appearance with their tied-up beards. I pinned the ribbon of the CBE to Colonel Balwan Singh, who remembered my coming to Patiala with the Prince of Wales 22 years ago. On conclusion the Mountain Battery gave a demonstration of going into action which rivalled the Naval Field Gun competitions at Olympia. What struck me most was the docile discipline of the mules who allowed a 200lb gun carriage to be thrown on to their backs without flinching.

I was told an amusing story concerning a lecture which had been given to this brigade on the South-East Asia Command. One of the Gurkhas was asked if he remembered the name of the Supreme Allied Commander and replied: 'Yes, Sahib! Lord Mountain Battery!'

I lunched with the Corps Commander and at 1400 General Wingate came up for a final conference. At 1515 we left Imphal air strip reaching Comilla at 1635, where I immediately went into an urgent conference on the situation in the Arakan.

This seems a good point at which to give an account of the Arakan fighting, most of which has by now been released to the press.

On Friday, 4th February General Tanabashi made a very skilful outflanking movement with a large force of Japanese estimated at about half a division. He threaded his way through the dense jungle as far as Taung Bazaar unobserved. This is not really surprising, because the tactical air reconnaissance cannot see through the dense jungle and although we have many patrols out it is not possible to patrol the whole jungle. Taung Bazaar is well in the rear of the Eastern end of our Front line, so this force immediately constituted a very serious threat to our lines of communication and to the rear of our Front. In similar circumstances last year Tanabashi caused the withdrawal in considerable disorder of the whole of the British forces, not only on account of the actual superior fighting morale of the Japanese, but because the British were afraid of having their lines of communication irretrievably cut. General Irwin, who commanded the British forces at that time, told me on his return to London that the morale of all forces had been very low and their outlook completely defeatist.

I have been doing everything in my power to improve the morale, particularly on the Arakan Front, and with a new set of commanders on all levels down to most Brigadiers the same troops are fighting quite differently this year.

This battle, which is now at its height, is of the utmost importance to us in South-East Asia, as it is a battle of morale. In importance it will rank with El Alamein. The same troops that were so badly defeated by Rommel rallied themselves together under Alexander and Montgomery and inflicted a crushing defeat on him. The same troops that ran before Tanabashi last year have stood firm to the last man this year and I feel confident of ultimate victory.

Just one small indication of the difference in morale may be given. Last year British County Regiments, on hearing of the presence of Japanese in a certain district, would withdraw. This year the first British unit to get the news of the Japanese arrival in force at Taung Bazaar was an Indian mule company under the command of a subaltern who were on their way between Goppe Bazaar and Taung Bazaar. Instead of turning tail he formed his mules into a circle and put half his muleteers around them, to protect them. The remaining half he formed into battle patrols and went forward to engage the Japanese!

Poor old Frank Messervy has had his Divisional Headquarters overrun for the third time this war. He had to fight in his pyjamas with revolver and grenades. His batmen, cooks, clerks and orderlies and some gunners from a Medium regiment have formed a strongpoint and have already turned out the Japanese in hand-to-hand engagements on no less than three occasions. In this area alone Messervy has counted over 700 dead Japanese bodies, so the total casualties inflicted must be much greater.[1] The only failure to be recorded to date is that of poor Jack Winterton, who allowed his brigade to be pushed off Hill 1070 contrary to orders and has had to be relieved. One Japanese battalion put down road blocks on the road between Bawli Bazaar and Maungdaw but has now been driven off the road and is fighting desperately in the foothills.

The air battle has been very fierce as the Japanese have, of course, been trying to prevent our supplying these forces by air which are cut off by road. After two sorties had been turned back Brigadier General Old, commanding the Integrated Troop Carrier Command, led a British squadron in person in a third attempt and got through magnificently. What better proof of Anglo-American co-operation and leadership could be asked for?

Fierce fighting is going on in the Ngakyedauk Pass, which I visited so

[1] 'Hold on and you will make history' was Mountbatten's message to the defenders. They did both.

recently and which Tanabashi's forces, I regret to say, still hold, having taken the Pass from the rear across precipitous jungle where we had no troops. They have thus cut off Messervy's Division, which still has to rely on air supply.

Whatever the outcome of this battle, the high morale and grand fighting that has been put up by every officer and man of the 15th Corps fills me with overflowing pride at being associated with such men who could rally themselves together in such a remarkable manner after last year's débâcle.

I left Comilla at 2000 and we had supper on board the aircraft, arriving back at Delhi at 0210.

MONDAY, 14 FEBRUARY to SUNDAY, 20 FEBRUARY   This week I have been very busy dealing with all the various problems and requirements raised by the battle in the Arakan and the points raised by Al Wedemeyer's party in London.[1]

Simon Elwes has been sent out as the official portrait painter in India and is painting the Viceroy, Auchinleck and the Commanders-in-Chief. His secretary is the beautiful Ulrica Murray Smith (née Thynne). It is his intention to brutalize my face and he has so far succeeded admirably, as it consists of a series of mauve, purple, green and yellow splodges with a couple of large poached eggs where the eyes should be. After having sat no less than four times he wished to destroy the canvas, but I told him I would sooner go down to posterity as a gorilla than have to do all the sittings again. Ulrica poses in my cap to save me time. Simon tells me that a beautiful Belgian countess posed in 17th Hussars boots to enable him to finish off the King's portrait so that it is evident that the extremities of his portraits are posed by the opposite sex!

MONDAY, 21 FEBRUARY to FRIDAY, 25 FEBRUARY   Peter Murphy[2] and Bunnie Phillips returned from Ceylon on Monday. Needless to say Peter had had his usual fantastic adventures. To begin with, he ran out of money and only borrowed enough from Bunnie to pay for his night's lodging at Bangalore. The next day, while Bunnie and

---

[1]   Where they were presenting CULVERIN to Churchill and the Chiefs of Staff.
[2]   Peter Murphy was probably Mountbatten's closest confidant, a talented man of great charm and left-wing views. He was in SEA Command as intellectual odd-job-man to the Supreme Commander.

another staff officer went off to have lunch at Bombay, Peter stayed outside because he had not enough money to buy lunch and did not like to borrow more money from Bunnie. On coming out of the lunch room Bunnie and his friend asked Peter why he had not been to lunch, thus, in Peter's eyes, adding insult to injury.

However, whilst walking about outside the lunch room Peter observed an Indian woman and child being smuggled on board. After lunch they tried to turn off a Colonel who was going to a meeting at GHQ Delhi, claiming that additional mail taken on at Bombay necessitated this. Peter discovered the Indians were relations of the Second Officer of the aircraft (an Indian National Airways one) and led a 'strike' of the passengers, which resulted in the woman and child being turned off and Peter being 'run in' to me by Indian National Airways.

I sent Peter to see Frank Owen, who prints the *SEAC* in Calcutta. He went in the Sister Anne (a new aircraft with six bunks and four armchairs and long range tanks which has been given me by the Air Commander-in-Chief). Peter had breakfast with me before going. I had been dictating to my Petty Officer Writer and asked him to wait outside a moment while I gave Peter his instructions for Calcutta. Peter, to my surprise, suddenly started talking to me in French as follows:

'*Tu sais, mon vieux, ton sécretaire m'a prêté le dactylo qui vient de sortir. C'est un épatant type. Il travaille à merveille et, du reste, il comprend le français très bien!*'

I must confess I burst out laughing and said, 'Well what the Hell is the point of telling me all this in French then?'

On Friday Paulette Goddard came to lunch. She is on her way through to entertain the US troops in China. I had the senior British and American officers to meet her and got little Sally Dean, our youngest Signal Officer in. Someone had told me that she had had a very dramatic escape from Paris and subsequently from the Channel Isles and again from Paris a second time, and I started asking her about it. As she unfolded her riveting tale everyone stopped talking and for most of lunch she completely held the floor; so a young 22-year-old girl completely wiped the eye of one of America's most famous film stars.

SATURDAY, 26 FEBRUARY I have had pressing invitations to stay from Jaipur, Bhopal, Bikaner, Gwalior, Bharatpur, Nepal, Kashmir, Patiala and Jodhpur as I knew all the rulers of these States, or their fathers, very well.

Funnily enough the only invitation I have accepted has been to Rampur whose ruler, the present Nawab, was only fifteen when I met him in Lucknow many years ago and whom I cannot claim to know particularly well. However, I got to know him and the Begum through their son, Bachan, who is the ADC to the Auchinlecks and as they promised me a completely restful and quiet weekend with no sort of arrangements or programme I thought I would accept on condition the visit was kept out of the Press. Therefore, after lunch I motored down with Bunnie and Flags to Rampur. The run takes nearly four hours and is rather tedious because the main roads in India have only a single width of tarmac but a wide width of dust (or in this case dried mud) on either side, which is intended for bullock carts. Actually the bullock carts always remain on the tarmac until the last moment and one spends one's time dodging them by going on to the rough sides of the road.

I should explain that Flags, who has become a great friend of the family, had gone down the week before to ensure that 'no arrangements' were made. It required a committee consisting of the Nawab, his brother, his Prime Minister, his senior British Staff Officer, and Flags to decide how to implement the condition that there should be 'no arrangements'.

I said I would come in plain clothes and so the Nawab for the first time since the war started said he would also put on plain clothes.

Rampur is one of the model states of India. The outskirts of the city are beautifully planned with very dashing really modern houses designed by the local architect. The Palace from the outside is less gaudy than usual, inside the taste is appalling.

There were 70 other guests staying in the house over the weekend but, in virtue of the 'no arrangements', the Nawab saw to it that I did not meet any of them. The Palace is so vast that it is perfectly possible to live in an entirely separate wing without knowing of the presence of the others.

In our wing we each had a colossal bedroom, a large dressing room and a large bathroom as well as a private dining room and enormous sitting room, etc. It was with difficulty that Flags had persuaded him not to have an Indian ADC and retinue living permanently outside my bedroom door and he had twelve chaprasis removed from our corridor just before I went upstairs. Flags also persuaded them to cancel the proposal that two khitmagars, one with a silver cigar box and the other with a salver of drinks, should follow me wherever I went.

The part of the Palace we lived in was built about forty years ago but for dinner we went to the modern wing which was completed by Messrs Waring and Gillow in 1933 at a cost of half a million pounds for the present Nawab. As one passes between the old and the new wings the entire atmosphere changes from mid-Victorian mock-baronial splendour to a super-luxurious New York hotel atmosphere laden with incense.

The main entrance hall has a large marble staircase, gilt statues and modern pictures. Leading off from this is a very garish night-club where members of the Nawab's immediate family and entourage were gathered together drinking cocktails. A first-class jazz band was 'swinging it' on the stage. Leading off the night-club there was a frightfully modern billiard room, all of which, including the cloth of the billiard table, was light blue. Beyond one saw a vista of the Mogul garden. This really was absolutely lovely. It is a very large sunk and walled garden with fountains playing all down the centre, the whole being floodlit from the top of the Palace. The Nawab explained that neither the flood-lighting nor the fountains were ever on in wartime but that this was an exceptional occasion.

We dined in the very dashing modern dining room, done up in the most expensive Rue Charles-Laffitte style.[1] The menus were printed and bound in little cardboard folders with the arms of the State in colours and tied with ribbons, just like a Lord Mayor's Banquet in peacetime!

The food was much too good and there was much too much of it, nor could one observe the elsewhere prevailing shortage of wines (though His Highness may well have been opening his last bottle for this occasion!).

After dinner we sat around at the little tables in the night-club while His Highness played the trap drums in his band, and finally forced me to do the same though I had not played the drums for over 20 years!

The Begum is rather a nice creature, only fourteen years older than her twenty-year-old son.

His Highness assured me that there were 'no arrangements' for me next day and that I could have a complete day's rest.

SUNDAY, 27 FEBRUARY Bunnie and I, who were in adjoining rooms, woke late next morning and could see from our window the

---

[1] Mountbatten's old friend Yola Letellier lived in the Rue Charles-Laffitte in an elegant *haute-bourgeoise* mansion.

most gorgeously caparisoned elephants. After we had got dressed we naturally went down to see these elephants and their wonderful State trappings. They had had their faces, chests and front legs painted with the most beautiful patterns and did various tricks at the bidding of their mahouts.

Drawn up outside the Palace were a dozen of the most modern motor cars headed by a Bentley. The Nawab said: 'Would it amuse you to come and see my cottage industries and select some materials for Lady Louis and your children?' With this inducement I got into the Bentley and we drove to the old Artillery Lines which he has just converted into first-class cottage industries. Here the local people are taught spinning, weaving, hand-printing, mechanical knitting, etc. Their products sell very well and the Nawab is gradually buying looms and mechanical knitters to put into the homes of those of his subjects who are not already employed in the many factories he has been putting up.

He insisted on driving me round all his factories but thank God let me off going in to inspect them. He has succeeded, within the ten years since he succeeded his odious and hated father, in erecting a whole series of really modern first-class factories, including the second biggest and certainly the most modern power house in India. There is now no unemployment whatever in the State.

He also showed me the large experimental farm and laboratories where seeds are produced by his Department of Agriculture for free issue to his subjects. Every ten miles or so there is a Branch Office at which the peasants can obtain seeds and free lessons in the latest art of husbandry.

One cannot help being impressed by all one saw and by his intense enthusiasm. In the town itself he has had loudspeakers put up at regular intervals where the people can collect to hear the latest war news. A very dashing modern cinema is just being completed and the town planning is really first class.

Considering that the late Nawab refused to give his son a proper education and is reputed to have had him beaten by his sweepers on the slightest pretext, it is really amazing that the son should have developed into such a wise and public-spirited ruler.

He is obviously really respected by his subjects who welcomed him respectfully but enthusiastically everywhere, and he is one of the few rulers who can go around without police escort.

On our return we wandered through some of the State apartments, large banqueting hall, ballroom, drawing rooms, etc., and were finally led through to the jewel house. Here Their Highnesses offered to show me some of their jewels. Flags warned me that this was the supreme honour, since normally they were only shown to the Viceroy, and never to any other guests.

I must say it was fascinating. The approaches were guarded by State Police who unlocked and opened an iron door leading to a very large inner hall, in the centre of which was a strong room. The passage between the inner strong room and the outer walls of the hall was patrolled by Gurkhas.

Rampur, I learnt, is the only Indian State allowed to have a Gurkha Regiment among the State Troops, a privilege arising from their loyalty and alliance with the Nepalese in the Indian Mutiny of 1857.

The Nawab and his brother then each produced a different key from their pockets and together opened the double locks of the outer steel door of the jewel house. Meantime a strong box was brought up which again had to be opened by double keys and inside there rested more keys which opened the inner doors of the jewel house and the safes inside. In addition to keys the inner Chubb's safes each had double combination locks which only the Nawab and the Keeper of the jewel house knew.

Special tables with white table cloths and chairs around them were erected in the courtyard outside the jewel house. Officers of the household struggled out with heavy caskets which were opened in turn and spread before us. I can never describe the Arabian Night effect of this unbelievable quantity of jewellery.

The Nawab's State necklace contains four of the best-known diamonds in the world – the Empress of India, the Klondyke, and the Twins. The Empress of India is reputed to be the third finest diamond after the Kohinoor and Hope diamonds and I can well believe it as it is not only colossal but quite magnificently cut and set.

I have never seen such a collection of pearls. There were three necklaces in which each pearl was the size of my thumb nail, besides rows and rows of pearls of slightly lesser size. There was a complete sash to be worn over the shoulder and falling below the hip, made up of about thirty strings of pearls. One could put one's hand into a casket and bring out handfuls and handfuls of pearls, nearly all of very good quality. I asked how many there were and he replied: 'Just over ten thousand!' But the really fascinating things were the parures of diamonds, emeralds, rubies, etc., including coronets, tiaras, necklaces, bracelets, rings, ear-rings, 'epaulettes', and puggaree ornaments.

One emerald necklace really had exceptionally fine coloured stones fairly free from flaws, but I think the finest stone in the collection was a solitaire ring with an emerald of very deep green and entirely flawless which his grandfather had bought sixty years ago for a quarter of a million rupees.

The Nawab claimed to have heard of Edwina's emeralds and pearls and asked to be allowed to come and see them in England after the war!

At three o'clock the Nawab released us (on condition that we came to see his massed bands at 5 o'clock). We staggered off to bed as we were so tired. At 5 o'clock we had tea on the aerodrome in a gorgeous State shamiana, whilst in front of us the Massed Bands of the Nawab's State force beat the retreat. They were wearing their pre-war full dress and had been drilled under a British Director of Music and were incredibly smart. In addition to the brass bands of the Infantry Regiments there was a Gurkha Pipe Band and an Indian Pipe Band, who at one stage of the proceedings played reels and strathspeys!

After this performance we were driven through the streets of the capital to the fort. On the way the Nawab saw a man beating his bullock and stopped the whole procession while he cursed him roundly. As everyone beats bullocks in India I was quite surprised.

Inside the outer walls of the fort there are two other palaces, one for the children and one used by the Nawab and the Begum. Apart from this there is a State Durbar Hall which really is magnificent. One thousand people can be seated at the Durbars and we were shown the golden throne and golden State Hookah which looked like Hollywood stage props for the Arabian Nights. We were then taken to the Nawab's library which has the third finest collection of original Persian and early Indian manuscripts in the world.

We then went to the Nawab's private palace and were shown his collection of 250 radio sets. Not only has he a standing order for the latest types of sets to be sent to him but he has a private workshop where he assembles radiogramophones, etc. On the top of the palace there are some thirty aerial arrays and down below there is an aerial exchange so that suitable aerials can be plugged on to any of the sets.

I said to the Nawab: 'Have you any other collections like this?', and he replied: 'Lots, what would you like to see?' I said: 'Well, what do you recommend?' to which he replied: 'Would you like to see some cigarette cases?' On saying I would he clapped his hands and khitmagars walked in with trays, each holding about forty cigarette cases. Most of them were gold, jewelled, or enamelled and there were all types of shapes and sizes. After about twenty or thirty trays had been brought in he held up his hands to indicate that enough had been brought.

Meaning to flatter I said: 'I see you have nearly a thousand cigarette cases', but this was evidently the wrong thing to say as he corrected me and said, 'I have just over 18,000 but I thought the other 17,000 would bore you.'

We were then taken to the nursery and shown his collection of children, which seems to be nearly as large as the other collections. They varied in age from his twenty-year-old heir apparent, who is in the Army, to a six-month-old baby. I had to sign their birthday books and autograph books. I asked if any of his girls were engaged to be married and he said: 'Alas, only this one', pointing to the five-year-old daughter!

The Begum's bangle woman was present in the nursery, with at least a thousand glass bangles which the Begum and the children were trying on.

We arrived back exhausted to find that the British colony had been asked to supper in the night-club and a small dance afterwards! Half way through the dance the Nawab took me round some of the modern rooms of the Palace. Waring and Gillow had certainly crammed everything that money could sell into these rooms.

The Nawab's own bedroom and sitting room were built one above the other with a private lift connecting them.

The bathroom had a sunken Roman bath cut out of a solid block of marble in which twelve people could have swum. It was surrounded by marble banisters on which one could sit and presumably watch people swimming. He had his own private barber's shop adjoining the bathroom and the lulus were weird and wonderful to behold. Behind them there was a private gymnasium. We wandered through his wardrobe room where two or three hundred vivid-coloured suits were hung up and thousands of ties, shirts and socks. His French valet walked behind with Bunnie and kept making sotto voce remarks, such as: 'Can you beat it? He never wears one of these suits! What a waste of money!'

We wandered through room after room, each more fantastically luxurious than the last. The Indian music room has no furniture at all, as everyone, including the band, sits on the floor.

Bogus balconies were carved into the walls, behind which were painted panoramas which could be lit by various green, mauve and blue spotlights to reproduce various conditions of moonlight or sunset.

MONDAY, 28 FEBRUARY   I had worn plain clothes up to this moment but on Monday morning I had to put on uniform so as to go straight into a meeting on arrival in Delhi. This was the moment the Nawab had been waiting for.

He said: 'I hear you will be leaving in uniform, so I shall turn out the guard.' I assumed that this would give him pleasure and accepted the situation. However, I might have guessed that turning out the guard was going to be something unusual. The Guard of Honour consisted of over a hundred of his First Regiment of Infantry, and the band consisted of eighty! I was, very correctly, received with 'Rule Britannia'.[1] Between each rank of the guard a red carpet had been laid and we were preceded and followed by ADCs. I was made to inspect every rank of the band, which I found an unusual proceeding!

The Nawab and his brother and all his staff were all wearing uniform and after the guard had marched past we were garlanded with colossal gilt garlands and had itr and paan distributed to us.

On parting the Nawab announced that he and the Begum would return my visit in Kandy and he hoped that I would take his son on my staff. I have told Flags to deal with this situation since it was really he who led me into the visit!

When we finally left we were quite bewildered. The weekend had been no rest but it had certainly been a change.

TUESDAY, 29 FEBRUARY to FRIDAY, 3 MARCH 1944   The battle in Arakan has now been brought to a victorious conclusion. As most of the details have been released to the press there can be no harm in recapitulating some of them here. On the 4th February General Tanabashi,[2] who last year inflicted so severe a defeat on the British and Indian Forces in Arakan, brought a column of Japanese estimated to be 10,000 strong, through the jungle and got into Taung Bazaar behind our lines.

Their object, of course, was not only to cut our lines of communication but to encircle our front-line troops.

This year every man stood and fought to the end so that not only was the Japanese plan completely foiled but Tanabashi's force was doomed from the moment the British refused to retire.

[1] Appropriate to a Naval Commander-in-Chief.
[2] Mountbatten discovered a little later he was really called Tanahashi.

We immediately flew in transport aircraft to keep the encircled troops supplied. The Japanese put up fighter sweeps of over 100 fighters to try and prevent this but failed, thanks to the gallantry of our air force.

Meanwhile we threw in 2 reserve Divisions under Lomax and Frankie Festing,[1] who between them cleared up the Japanese road blocks across the main Bawli Bazaar–Maungdaw lines of communication, and took Tanabashi's force in the rear.

Briggs's Division fought with the utmost gallantry and, in conjunction with Lomax, have opened the Ngakyedauk Pass after it had been cut off for 17 days.

During all this time our wounded lay on the ground attended only by supplies dropped from the air.

I am told that copies of our newspaper *SEAC* which were dropped did a great deal to keep up morale, and we even dropped razor blades so that the troops were able to shave to the end!

At the end of the battle a conservative estimate shows that we had killed or seriously wounded more than 4500 Japanese and that of the remainder at least half are believed to have been wounded. Not many of them will have been able to struggle back through the jungles to rejoin their main force, and the attack which the main force put in was simultaneously repulsed.

SATURDAY, 4 MARCH   I entertained His Highness of Rampur and his son the Nawabzada, Bachan, at lunch today at Faridkot. I turned out the guard for him, which I thought served him right!

He told us the most amusing tale at luncheon about the Maharaja of Benares, who is such a severe orthodox Hindu that he cannot eat in the same room as a Mahomedan.

Nevertheless, the Maharaja always insists that the Nawab should stop and have luncheon with him when he passes through Benares. The two rulers meet together and then the Maharaja goes off to have his luncheon alone. After that he endeavours to go and sit with the Nawab while he is eating his lunch, but the Nawab (who has a great sense of humour) refuses as an unorthodox Mahomedan to eat his meals in front of an orthodox Hindu and so he goes to another room to eat his luncheon.

Recently the Maharaja came to stay at Rampur. The Comptroller of

[1]   Major General Festing, commanding the 36th Division.

the Household, who arrived in advance to prepare the way, insisted that arrangements must be made for the Maharaja to see a cow on first waking up, as this was part of his religion. It appears that at Benares there is a Princely Cow Shed alongside His Highness's bedroom and that before he is called the door is opened, a cow is led in sufficiently far for His Highness's eyes to alight on the cow when first waking up.

At Rampur the royal suite is on the first floor. The Nawab therefore arranged for one of his factories to transport a crane on to the balcony of the royal suite and each morning a cow was hoisted up on the crane and swung in at the Maharaja's bedroom in time for his eyes to alight on it when first they opened in the morning!

MONDAY, 6 MARCH   Took off in Sister Anne at 0600. During the flight we saw to our north the Himalayas rising up through the clouds, the sun-capped peaks of which made a lovely and impressive scene. Mount Everest was very clearly visible although over 100 miles away. We had a following wind and so reached Chabua at 1300. The Americans provided a fighter escort of 16 P.51 Mustangs which I must say I thought very excessive and am having followed up. We landed at a very rough strip which had just been cleared in the jungle at Taihpa Ga at 1440. I was met by General Stilwell who took me along to address some of his officers and men, although they could hardly hear what I said as the 16 fighters insisted on circling overhead, after which we had a meeting to discuss a number of very vital outstanding points.

I noticed that my programme did not include a visit to the Front and complained to General Stilwell about this. He explained that he did not feel it possible to include a visit to the Front, as it was so fluid in this part of Burma that they had not succeeded in mopping up all the Japanese forces as they advanced and that the road up to the Front was under fire from snipers.

I said to him: 'Well, you are going up to the Front again, aren't you?' – to which he replied: 'But I am an old man and it does not matter about me whereas I am responsible for your safety.' I soon made it clear to him that the only person responsible for my safety was myself and unless he could prove to me that there were other reasons why I should not go up to the Front I intended to go. He then countered by saying he had not got a proper Headquarters and would not have room for my staff, so I told him I would leave my staff behind and go entirely alone without any luggage and that we could leave the driver of his jeep behind and I would drive it.

At this he gave way and made a very pleasant host. We drove on up to the Corps Headquarters of the Chinese American Combat Force some 11 miles south of Taihpa Ga through the most appalling jungle track imaginable. I found they had no tents or normal arrangements but had made up large umbrellas by sticking 'supply dropping' parachutes on top of bamboo poles and under these we ate and slept.

Stilwell introduced me to General Liao who commands the 22nd Chinese New Division. He received his military education in Saumur and has only recently picked up English which he talks with a strong French accent! We could hear the sound of gunfire all round our Headquarters during the night and twice had to douse all our lights when a Japanese aircraft flew over. I slept under the same 'umbrella' as Stilwell.

TUESDAY, 7 MARCH to TUESDAY, 14 MARCH We left at 0600 daybreak, in a jeep which I drove, and were preceded by General Liao. Every few hundred yards he would stop and ponderously clamber out and walk towards us. Stilwell used to mutter: 'Ur-ur! Here comes another lecture!' General Liao would then explain exactly where the Japanese positions had been and how his troops had taken them. He started by saying: 'Three days ago we had a big fight here.' The next time we stopped it was: 'Two days ago we took these positions.' As we passed through the remnants of Maingkwan village he proudly announced: 'We took this yesterday.'

I have never taken kindly to the few fresh battlefields I have visited, chiefly because the smell is so appalling, but this was particularly unpleasant. At one place I saw at least fifty Japanese bodies and half a dozen horses which had been killed the day before. Already the maggots were running all over their faces, which looked puffed and blown out, and it was with the greatest of difficulty that I overcame a wave of nausea and avoided being sick. I was relieved to notice that the Chinese escort with us had all got their handkerchiefs out. They had them tied round their mouth and nose like a respirator. Ahead of us we could hear the crackle of rifle fire and the explosion of mortar bombs as the Chinese continued to advance.

I must confess I was not sorry when we turned back and made for Stilwell's Headquarters, where he left me.

I drove on back in his jeep through the jungle, where Pioneers were still busy clearing the way. We came to one place where they had been felling some bamboos, and as we forced our way over them a most amazing accident occurred. A bamboo which had been lopped off must have got bent out by the front wheel and then released violently so that it snapped forward and hit me in the left eyeball, missing both my helmet and the bony structure round the eye. I was knocked out of my seat and the jeep rushed forward, momentarily out of control. I switched off the motor and got out.

It took a certain amount of moral courage to feel and see if my left eyeball was still in its socket, as I could not believe after such a blow that it could still remain there. My relief at finding it still in place was tempered by my finding that I was completely blind in the left eye. I put a first-aid dressing on and drove on. Further along the trail I came across a medical dressing station run by Seagrave, the well-known American medical missionary who has spent many years in Burma and has now joined the American Army and runs this dressing station with the help of a number of Burmese volunteer nurses.

He took the dressing off and I was disturbed to find that I could still see nothing out of the left eye. He washed it out and dressed it for me and told me to go and see Doctor Scheie at Ledo. I replied: 'That will be easy because I have arranged to drive up the Ledo Road today and I shall be there within about ten hours.' He replied: 'Young man, this is plenty serious. You must fly there and as quick as you can.'

When I got to Taipa Ga I found the Sister Anne and the whole of my party waiting on the airfield, where I had left them the night before, and so I abandoned my Ledo Road drive and flew up to Ledo itself. On arrival I was taken to No.20 General Hospital of the US Army where their famous opthalmic specialist, Captain Scheie, had a look at my eye.

He said: 'You must cancel your tour and go straight to bed.' I suggested that as Sister Anne had a bed I could fly back in her to Delhi, but he would not hear of it and had me in bed within five minutes with both my eyes firmly bandaged.

I never realized before that if you injure one eye the only way you can rest it is to put atropine in and bandage both eyes, as otherwise the good eye causes the bad eye to move and gives it no rest. Shortly after I had been put to bed they moved me in an ambulance to a new basha hut which had only been completed a day or two before.

I now found myself in bed amid surroundings I couldn't even picture.

I spent five days in this state of complete blindness, not only not allowed to leave the bed but with instructions to try and avoid lying over on my side, or moving too much. They were the longest 120 hours I can remember. Three nurses did eight hours each per day, and were feeding me like a baby, washing me, reading to me and attending to all my other wants. I got to know their voices and their touch extremely well.

It was a unique experience, getting to know people extremely well from long conversations and not knowing in the least what they looked like, and it was really quite a thrill seeing my surroundings and each of them for the first time when the bandages were taken off on Sunday. The US Army Signal Corps very kindly provided a radio set so that I could listen to the Anglo-American All Forces programme which Mr Eade got going at my request so as to give our troops in Burma something to listen to besides the enemy propaganda from Saigon. Although it is only an hour a day (1830 to 1930) it really is excellent and tremendously popular and a much-needed innovation. We must try and extend the hours as soon as we can.

I understand when the Chinese were first admitted to this hospital they were very grateful for the attention they received and gladly helped out when convalescent in sweeping out the wards and keeping the place tidy. Since their recent victory over the Japanese the wounded now consider themselves as national heroes and will not at any price touch a broom, claiming that the Americans should sweep out for them! The day before I left Colonel Ravdin had issued an order that anyone on convalescent duty who failed to carry out his share was not to receive any food until he had done so – in fact 'no sweepee no eatee'!

The Mercury has proved her great worth, as I don't know how I could have kept control of the situation without having her nearby and Micky can well be proud of her.

I was much touched that old Joe Stilwell should have flown up from the Front on Sunday to come and pay me a visit in hospital. He and I always get along very well personally.

One of the difficulties has been attending to business, because during the first day or two they would only allow me a few minutes each day to dictate signals. Although they would normally have wished to keep me another ten days in bed I finally persuaded them to let me fly back on Tuesday, the 14th, on condition that I took Captain Scheie to look after me. As he has been working for a whole year without any rest I accept the offer, as I intend him to have a much-deserved holiday in

Delhi. He tells me that the blindness was caused by bad internal haemorrhage but although it is too early to say anything definite he is hopeful of no permanent injury now that the haemorrhage has cleared up.

We took off at 0700 and got to Comilla at 1000. Here I had an emergency meeting with General Slim and Air Marshal Baldwin and their staffs. At 1230 we flew on, reaching Delhi at 1845 in a storm.

It was nice to be back at Faridkot, though maddening not being allowed to read. It means that all my signals and papers have to be read to me.

WEDNESDAY, 15 MARCH to WEDNESDAY, 22 MARCH   Although I never allowed myself to be put on the sick list officially I was virtually put on the sick list unofficially throughout this week.

I wasn't allowed to read or write, and Doctor Scheie only allowed me to come up to the office for the meetings in the morning. In theory I was supposed to spend the afternoons resting, but in point of fact there was so much to catch up with that people came to do business with me most afternoons, and when I hadn't got visitors with me my secretary was reading papers to me.

I find it takes nearly twice as long to work when everything has to be read to one and one's own dictation has to be read back.

Doctor Scheie left on the Sunday, having pronounced my eye as completely out of danger and having stopped the atropine drops. He wanted me to go away on sick leave but there was too much going on, and as the Chief of Staff left on Friday evening for a tour of the Front, I decided I could only go away for twenty-four hours.

SATURDAY, 25 MARCH to WEDNESDAY, 29 MARCH   During this period I was allowed to read a gradually increasing amount each day but I found difficulty in focusing so work wasn't easy.

My time has been very fully occupied with all the excitements of the Japanese attack on the Imphal plain, etc.[1]

THURSDAY, 30 MARCH to SUNDAY, 2 APRIL 1944   During this period I went back to full duty and also allowed Simon Elwes to have

---

[1] The Battle of Imphal, decisive engagement of the Burmese War, began with a Japanese attack on 7 March, while Mountbatten was blinded in hospital.

another crack at the portrait he is painting of me. Usually he has a remarkable knack for getting likenesses but this time he has failed. Finally in despair he asked me whether I could tell him what was wrong with it. I took a good look at it and realized that he had muddled me up with the Viceroy, whom he is also painting, as he had painted my left eye drooping much lower than the right. He raised this eye a quarter of an inch, opened the eyelid an eighth of an inch and the result is now a recognizable, if not very good likeness.

MONDAY, 3 APRIL   I took off from Willingdon airport at 0630 in the Sister Anne. We arrived at Jorhat at 1330 and I was met by Brigadier Wilson-Haffenden, on behalf of General Stopford, who has just moved the Headquarters of the 33rd Corps to Jorhat. I knew Wilson-Haffenden well from the old Combined Operations days as Largs. I must admit he shook me severely by saying that the Corps Commander and the senior members of his staff were more than four hours overdue by air, so I had horrible visions of another Wingate crash.[1] However, Monty Stopford luckily turned up a few minutes later, having been delayed four hours in taking off as his airfield had been flooded.

We had lunch in the American mess and then I had a conference at which Lieutenant Generals Stilwell, Slim and Stopford, Air Vice Marshal Baldwin, Major Generals Lushington[2] and Lentaigne,[3] as well as numerous Brigadiers and Colonels were present. We discussed the coming battles on all the Burma fronts. At 1700 I flew to Chabua which we reached at 1740.

TUESDAY, 4 APRIL   At 1200 I was turned over to the Americans. After lunch I first went and visited No.758 Railway Shop Battalion, who have taken over the engine repair shops at Dibrugarh. I found them bubbling over with enthusiasm having repaired more than three times the number of locomotives and waggons in their first month as had ever been achieved by the Bengal and Assam Railway Company. As I had been responsible for the militarization of this railway and bringing over the American Railway Engineers, which include this Unit, I was

[1] General Wingate had been killed in an air crash in North Assam on 24 March.
[2] Major General G. E. Wildman-Lushington was Assistant Chief of Staff.
[3] Major General Walter Lentaigne succeeded Wingate in command of the Special Forces.

With Generals Stilwell and Wingate in January 1944.

The King's Pavilion, Kandy.

Addressing the crew aboard the French battleship *Richelieu*.

Mountbatten in March 1944 on his way to hospital at Ledo after being almost blinded by a bamboo branch. His companion is Colonel Wilson.

particularly thrilled to meet them. They gave my address a very friendly reception and I have great hopes for the future from them.

After this I went round further American Units. In one or two cases rain interfered with the proceedings but we managed to get everyone into huts. Every now and then I found the audience very heavy in hand to begin with. It seemed to be my fate in several Groups to find some Middle Westerner chewing and spitting almost straight in front of me. But in the end even the worst of audiences cheered up and laughed at some of my jokes and without exception they all clapped at the end (though I suspect that this is largely due to the innate good manners of the average American).

472 Quartermaster Truck Group told me that they had operated over 3,000,000 truck miles with less than 10 vehicles out of 7000 requiring major repairs; an amazing feat even for Americans.

WEDNESDAY, 5 APRIL   At 1045 I took off from Dinjan airfield in the Sister Anne and arrived at Maingkwan with the usual fighter escort at 1145. Here I was met by Lieutenant General L. J. Sun who commands the 38th Chinese Division and whom I had got to know quite well in Chungking. It is interesting landing at Maingkwan where there is now a full-size airstrip capable of taking transport aircraft when last time I was there it was a stinking battlefield. Indeed, I understand that the strip was built within one day.

Sun drove us down to his Headquarters at Uga-ga which is just beyond Wallabum. The road is pretty shocking because it is only a temporary supply road since the main Ledo road is being built well to the eastward of the supply road and only joins it south of Wallabum.

I was received at his Headquarters with a Guard of 140 and 16 buglers. Considering that these men had only recently been in action I was astounded at their smart turn out. As at Chungking the Chinese soldiers of the Guard all stare one straight in the face throughout one's inspection which really makes the inspection much easier since there is no difficulty in catching the eye of every man in turn. When one inspects Indian troops not one of them looks you in the eyes intentionally and if you occasionally catch a soldier's eye by mistake he immediately turns them away. There can be no question that the Chinese way is infinitely superior if one wishes to establish contact with the men in the ranks during one's inspection.

Lushington and I had a conference with Lieutenant General Sun at which we were able to deal with all his little troubles and then he gave us the most magnificent Chinese lunch imaginable. How he managed it was a mystery to me but I suppose he had been saving up for some time for my visit, as I missed him on the last occasion through the accident to my eye. The chopsticks were cut out of local bamboo.

After lunch we looked at some guns which the 38th Division had captured intact with their ammunition; a hitherto almost unknown event in this theatre. General Sun also showed me the chop (seal) of the Commander of the Japanese 15th Division which his men had captured. I believe it is without precedent for a Japanese Divisional Commander to lose his chop since he loses face if he cannot put his chop on his orders.

On our way back it started to rain heavily and the road, which had been difficult enough when dry, became almost impassable since slippery mud formed immediately. It was not long before the road became completely blocked with lorries that had got themselves hopelessly bogged. At my insistence we left our convoy, walked with great difficulty past the whole of the traffic jam, entered jeeps that had got stuck in the far end of the traffic jam, turned them round and drove in them to Maingkwan.

Here I was thrilled to see men of the 50th Chinese Division who had been flown in from China that morning. Many of them were still wearing their enormous hats which look quite incongruous alongside their new American equipment. The Generalissimo has certainly answered the appeal which Carton de Wiart and Stilwell put in on my behalf for these troops very quickly.

I was met at Maingkwan by Brigadier General Pick, the creator of the Ledo road and the Commanding General for this district. He flew back to Ledo in the Sister Anne with me. I took over the pilot's seat and flew Sister Anne along the Ledo road as I found it was impossible to keep this winding road in sight in among the jungle covered mountains if I was not flying it myself. The others complained that I had made them feel very sick by jinking the aircraft about to follow the road but I pointed out that it had been a very bumpy day and they would have been sick anyhow over the mountains. After an hour's flight we arrived at Ledo and proceeded straight to General Pick's bungalow.

THURSDAY, 6 APRIL I addressed the American officers and NCOs attached to the Chinese Army and as many of the Chinese as understood

English. I was struck dumb by the Field Laundry Unit because it is a far more up-to-date mechanized laundry than I have ever seen anywhere in the world. Not only had the Americans put up the most colossal wooden sheds covering I imagine at least 100ft × 50ft × 30ft high but they had all the latest machinery and were washing, ironing and pressing the suits of all the American soldiers fighting on this front! I said to the officer in charge: 'I suppose you were the manager of a big laundry in the United States?' to which he replied: 'No, I was a stockbroker, I've never done this before!'

Colonel Ravdin[1] shattered me by collecting all his doctors, nurses, medical Corps men and patients in their large chapel which they have specially built out of wood. I found it very difficult to address a mixed audience sitting in pews with myself standing on the altar steps, and had to cut out all my vulgar jokes.

When I went through the hospital I was amazed to find how really modern it all is. The main operating theatre has eight operating tables each in groups of two so that each senior surgical specialist can take charge of 2 operations simultaneously carried out by junior surgical teams. They carry out on an average 1000 operations a month and I went in and saw a gas gangrene wound being treated which thoroughly revolted me. I went through all the Chinese wards as well as the American ones and was astounded to find what absolute children some of the Chinese soldiers appear to be. One emaciated young sergeant who had been badly wounded looked about 15 to me but proudly said his age was 19.

I arranged later on to see the Japanese prisoners, who of course were behind barbed wire under guard. Only one of them could speak English but he was very polite and kept bowing in bed. He told me he had learnt his English in Tokyo Middle School. He answered all questions readily and was anxious to volunteer more information than we asked for.

This new system by which wounds are dressed in plaster and the dressing is not changed for days and even weeks at a time may be very advanced but produces the most ghastly stench which nearly made me sick; particularly in the Japanese ward.

That night General Pick gave a dinner party to all the senior Chinese, American and British officers, over 20 of us in all. With practically no warning they called upon me for a speech. I had drunk about 4 'old-fashioneds' being very thirsty and not realizing how strong

---

[1] In command of the 20th General Hospital.

they were and felt somewhat light-headed. I have no recollection of what I said in my speech but I was told afterwards that I was very eloquent and it went down very well. (Memo: Get drunk before making a speech.)

FRIDAY, 7 APRIL   I was informed for the first time today that it was Good Friday. I had no idea that we were anywhere near Easter which shows how out of touch one can get.

At 0800 I visited the various British Units in the area including No.44 Indian General Hospital. I must say that the general equipment and standard of our hospital was pathetic when compared to the US Hospital but of course it is on a smaller scale.

I saw the first lot of wounded from one of Wingate's Brigades and found them all very cheery and very delighted with the way the air evacuation scheme was working from the centre of Burma.

I found that neither the Medical Officer nor the Administrative Commandant had been prepared to pay Wingate's men because the latter had had their pay books removed before entering Central Burma for security reasons. It appears the Army will not pay a man without a pay book. I must say I was extremely angry and am arranging to have the Administrative Commandant sacked.

At 1050 we left in a jeep convoy for a trip down the famous Ledo Road. I drove the leading jeep accompanied by Brigadier General Pick, who arrived in this theatre the same week as myself, and who has made the most striking difference to the Ledo Road construction. I should perhaps explain that Ledo is the extreme rail head in the north-east of India and that the Americans are constructing a road from Ledo through a range of mountains to the Hukaung Valley.

The road has already got as far as a point just south of Wallabum, a distance of some 120 miles as the crow flies and much further as the road winds. The road surface has been 'rocked' (as General Pick calls 'metalling') for a width of 22 feet and the unrocked part extends about 14 feet on either side, making a total width of 50 feet. They have over a hundred bulldozers at work already and on an average build about a mile of road a day. When one considers that the jungle in this part of the world is so dense that a reconnaissance party can rarely hack its way through more than a mile and a half of jungle a day without enemy opposition it should be realized what a fine feat this is.

In each successive part of the Burma front that I have visited the jungle appears to get worse. Here the tree tops are so close together that flying over them at a considerable height the surface of the jungle looks like tightly packed, but rather uneven moss. Inside the jungle one can hardly see daylight. This is the notorious creeper country where thick creepers abound between the tree tops and the tangled undergrowth; altogether a hell of a country to fight in!

Although this is the 'dry' season we had heavy rain showers every night so that the unrocked part of the road became impassable. The road is being rocked from Ledo to the south and from Shingbwiyang to the north but an unrocked gap of six miles exists between these two points which has now become completely impassable as vehicles get bogged in the mud over their axles.

The original designer of this road (another United States Engineer Officer) selected a bad track and General Pick is very proud of the fact that he had already shortened the first 35 miles of road by no less than six miles, by cutting off unnecessary loops and bends.

The Indian State Labour Units from Cochin and Travancore working on the road are not supposed to leave the borders of India so General Pick has very conveniently moved the boundary of Burma many miles to the south as far as officers of these units are concerned. I do not altogether like this form of deception and have since obtained the Government of India's approval for them to work in Burma.

My footsteps have been dogged all over Ledo by a very cheeky little American photographer. He insisted on pushing us all into the operating theatre to be photographed with a coloured soldier who was just coming round from the anaesthetic. We all gathered round the head of the unconscious man, including the operating room orderly. As the photograph was about to be taken the negro woke up, and seeing the orderly standing unpleasantly near him, yelled out, 'Stand back, soldier, or I shall be obliged to strike you.'

We continued on our way at 1330. Up to this point the road had been fairly level and dusty but as we entered the mountains a tropical downpour started. We were soon soaking in our jeeps and took shelter in a basha in one of the American transport lines.

Eventually we climbed to the top of the Pangsau Pass which we reached at 1445. This is the highest point of this stretch of the road, and is, incidentally, the frontier between India and Burma. We all left the jeeps and climbed up to the highest point and as we did so the rain stopped and the sun burst out, giving us a truly remarkable view of India to the north and Burma to the south.

We grouped around General Pick who was explaining the layout of the road, when the cheeky photographer arrived. He picked up General Pick's hand and said: 'Point right down that road, General.' He pushed Lushington back a couple of feet and said: 'You're not going to like this', and seized my chin and turned my head around. I thought the time had come to remonstrate and said in my best American: 'What goes on here?', to which the photographer replied: 'I am going to take a photograph, that was what we came here for, wasn't it?' He then held up his hand and said: 'Hold it', stepped back six paces and fell over backwards. After we had recovered sufficiently to be able to talk I turned to General Pick and said: 'Well, General, you have certainly got a prize buffoon as a photographer', to which the General replied: 'My photographer? I thought he was yours, otherwise I should have stopped him ages ago.'

We then drove on into Burma but could not go very far owing to the unrocked portion of the road, so had to turn around and drive back, arriving back at General Pick's bungalow for a late tea.

SATURDAY, 8 APRIL At 0800 we took off from Ledo airstrip in the Sister Anne. After we were in the air my staff produced a Japanese battle flag which had recently been captured at Maingkwan, and which General Pick had instructed my staff not to hand to me until we were in the air, as he thought I might have refused to accept it. I must say that the Americans are extremely thoughtful people.

After three-quarters of an hour we arrived at Jorhat airfield, where Lieutenant General Stopford and staff met me. We drove out for about forty minutes to the place where the 23rd Brigade of the Special Force was being concentrated.

I spoke to five of their columns, the other three having already moved on. I tried to cheer them up over the loss of their gallant leader, Wingate, and told them what an excellent fellow Lentaigne, their new General, was. At 1230 I got back to Jorhat airfield where I had been given to understand there would be about 200 Americans to talk to. It turned out that there were 150 officers and 2000 men, whom they expected me to address through a loudspeaker. I did away with the microphone and found that the whole party could hear me quite well. They were mostly American Air Force and quite childishly enthusiastic.

The moment I have finished talking to any Americans they always besiege me with short snorter bills[1] that they want signed, and produce their own little cameras to take photographs. I must have been following Paulette Goddard around as her signature always seems to be the last one on the short snorter bills, and I begin to suspect that my tour is becoming like hers!

At 1300 we took off for Imphal. Wherever I have flown in Burma I have been plagued by fighter escorts of from four to sixteen fighters but today, when we were flying over the battle areas, there was a misunderstanding between the British and American fighters and neither turned up. When we landed at Imphal we found the airstrip deserted except for a burnt-out aircraft and two jeeps. No one was there to receive us because it afterwards transpired that there had been a misunderstanding as to the day on which I was coming.

I asked why the airfield looked so deserted and was told the leading Japanese column was within four or five miles. I drove on down to the new Headquarters of the 4th Corps where I found the Corps Commander, Geoffrey Scoones. He was in great form although very surprised to see me. He ran me through the whole position and expressed great gratitude for the timely help I had provided in flying in the 5th Indian Division into the Imphal Plain in time to meet the Japanese attack.[2] He was full of bounding optimism and told me that in every encounter there with the Japanese we were getting the better of them. He is delighted that they have ventured so far because they would be easy to kill and few would get back.

He produced the first unwounded Japanese prisoner I have yet seen, in fact a deserter who was fed up with the Japanese Army. I asked him what sort of treatment he expected to receive from British hands and he had the nerve to reply: 'Good treatment, the same as your prisoners receive from the Japanese!' When I think what they have been doing to our prisoners it makes me sick. The other day they captured a mule train of the West Yorks. Twenty-three of the wretched muleteers were caught. They were tied up by their hands to trees and flogged until they were insensible. They waited until they recovered consciousness and then a Japanese officer went round and killed all except one with a bayonet. The one who did not die and eventually recovered had twenty-one bayonet thrusts in him. This is only a sample of the many

---

[1] A 'short snorter bill' was a dollar bill on which the autographs of VIPs were collected.
[2] Mountbatten's decision to take American aircraft off the flight over the Hump to China and divert them to the supply of the Imphal battle front was one of the crucial factors in turning possible defeat into decisive victory.

atrocity stories I am beginning to collect. One day I hope to catch some of the Japanese responsible and put them on trial.

Punch Cowan came up to Corps Headquarters to meet me and I went with him over to see his Division (17th). I had last seen them at Tiddim and found them there in great heart. I knew they would fight well and they certainly have. They have fought their way back along 170 miles of road, almost yard by yard. They were opposed by an entire Japanese Division which had cut the road at several places. They brought back practically the whole of their 2000 lorries, together with all their wounded and vital stores. To fight their way along the road they had to hold the mountain ranges on each side of the road. They estimate they inflicted over 1800 casualties on the Japanese and their own losses were 180 killed, 220 missing and about 800 wounded. They had only got back the evening before and had all slept like logs. I went round and had a very informal talk with the Devons and some of the officers of the Ghurkas, and found them all with their tails vertical, rubbing their hands and saying, 'Where are the next lot of Japs?' I was delighted to be able to tell Cowan that he had been awarded a bar to his DSO.

We were an hour flying over from Imphal to Sylhet where General Wingate was flying when his aeroplane crashed and he was killed. We looked out for the wreckage of his aircraft but couldn't see it through the dense jungle, as I believe he crashed in a valley, and we, of course, had to fly over the mountain tops. We landed at Sylhet after an hour's flight and were met by Wingate's successor, Major General Walter Lentaigne, and various other officers.

I was driven to what I imagined was to be the place I was to spend the night but on the door being opened an American voice shouted out: 'Officers, 'shun', and I found at least a hundred British and American officers together expecting an address. I was shattered as no one had told me about this and apparently the programme had failed to reach us. However, I pulled myself together and talked to them. I was then taken over to the open air cinema where I was called upon to address some two thousand men, including Troop Carrier Squadrons of the US Army Air Force, and RAF as well as many soldiers.

At 2030 we had dinner at Lentaigne's Headquarters where I found Miss McGeary, who had just been evacuated with the 91st Indian General Hospital from the Tiddim Road to Sylhet. She was furious at being taken away from the fighting area but delighted at being able to open up the hospital for the troops of her beloved General Wingate.

After dinner I was invited to hold a technical discussion on the future of the Special Force with the Headquarters Staff Officers and was horrified to find two war correspondents hidden among them.

EASTER SUNDAY, 9 APRIL   At 0740 I started my usual round, visiting the 91st Indian General Hospital. The hospital was interesting. Matron McGeary had already got busy and things were improving in the way that they always do with her. I talked to dozens of Wingate's men of every Brigade and found them uniformly happy and contented and well looked after. It is a curious psychological fact that however badly a man of the Special Force has been wounded, be he English, Gurkha or West African, the tremendous relief of having been successfully evacuated by air from 100 miles behind the Japanese lines makes them full of good cheer and feeling that they are lucky to be out again.

It is clear that they are having a tougher time than last year, since they are being attacked by the Japanese in much greater numbers and are fighting more fiercely. Against that must be stated the fact that they have better equipment and far better air facilities. I was even shown a Japanese wounded prisoner who had been flown out by air for questioning.

At 1115 I attended a drumhead memorial service for Wingate with officers and men of his own Headquarters. The Padre said in his address that Wingate was a very fine Bible scholar and knew more about the Bible than most clergymen.

At 1200 I took off from Sylhet, accompanied by Lentaigne, and after 40 minutes arrived at Hailakandi where Colonel Cochran met me. He drove us straight to his Mess where we were each given an entire half chicken for our Easter luncheon! After lunch I met the whole of the personnel of No.1 Air Commando, having previously only seen a few representatives at Lalitpur when I first visited Wingate's forces.

This party has the highest morale of any unit I have seen in this theatre and it is entirely due to the inspiring personal leadership of Phil Cochran and John Alison, and their enthusiastic co-operation with Wingate. All their men were friendly and eager, laughed and clapped and generally reacted in the most enthusiastic and human way.

Phil Cochran is an extremely good-looking, dashing young leader who has got more decorations for gallantry this war than any other American ace. He is the prototype of the famous 'Flip Corkin', the Air Force Colonel in the strip cartoon 'Terry and the Pirates' and the speech which he made to young Terry on getting his pilot's wings in this trip was recorded in Congress as expressing most nearly the ideal for which young Americans were fighting. When I told Phil Cochran's men that I had achieved the highest honour open to an Englishman by appearing in the strip cartoon with their Colonel it brought the house down.

The following incident illustrates what a born leader of men he is. As is now generally known, the two first Brigades were to be flown in to two separate airfields known as Broadway and Piccadilly. For the last four days before the fly-in no reconnaissance was carried out over them so as not to draw attention to them. At 1700 on D-Day all the soldiers were in the gliders and the gliders were lined up behind their tugs. The air Armada was awaiting Cochran's word 'Go'; but Cochran was waiting the results of last-minute photographic reconnaissance. The prints were brought to the airfield still wet and showed that Piccadilly airfield had been hopelessly blocked by the Japanese during the last four days, whereas Broadway appeared still to be open.

Wingate felt that their plans might have leaked out and that there might be an ambush at Broadway. He and Cochran however unhesitatingly took the risk and switched both Brigades to Broadway at five minutes' notice. This in itself was a sufficiently daring decision, but Cochran's method of telling his Piccadilly tug and glider pilots of this last-minute and possibly disastrous change was an inspiration in itself. He called them round him and said: 'Look, boys, we have found a better place to go to – Broadway!'

MONDAY, 10 APRIL [Arakan]   I was driven to the Headquarters of the 36th Division near Maunghnama, where Frankie Festing met me. At 1100 Frankie took me for the most dangerous drive of my life in a jeep. We went up a recently constructed jeep trail just south of the Ngakyedauk Pass. It was excessively steep, winding and on very loose soil. Frankie's idea of driving was going as fast as he could in double low ratio with the four wheel drive in. We came out of a dense bit of the jungle full tilt at an open corner where the road hangs over a precipice. The far side front wheel went clean over the precipice, but the speed at which we were cornering was such that the car turned on back into the road before the wheel fell over the edge.

The noise made by the peculiar variety of crickets in this jungle was like a high-speed buzz saw and deafening above the noise of the jeep engine.

At Point 1619 I was met by Hugh Stockwell, commanding the 29th

Brigade, whose troops are holding this part of the line. From this point, the last part of which rises sheer for over 500 feet, one gets a very magnificent view of all the Japanese positions. A heavy artillery barrage was going on all round of medium and field artillery. As I watched, a squadron of Vengeance dive bombers came over and bombed the Japanese positions which were to be stormed that day. Immediately in front of us lay the famous tunnels for which we had had to fight so hard and which were still not completely and securely in our hands at that date.

We drove back to the Headquarters of the 29th Brigade where I talked to representatives from this Brigade, whom I had last seen near Poona. I also met 'Stainless Stephen' of BBC fame,[1] who had been amusing the troops and who wanted me to sign his short snorter bill. I lunched with Hugh Stockwell at his Headquarters. What a nice chap he is, almost a second Bob Laycock.

We drove to the famous Razabil Fortress and climbed to a vantage point at the top of Razabil, where I was given a description by an officer who took part in the attack of how the Fortress was taken. This was the natural Fortress for which the Japanese Commander is credited to have thanked his gods, and once one has seen it one realizes that he had every reason to do so. It had been prepared for a siege, like the Rock of Gibraltar, with deep bunkers and fox-holes and tunnels and might have withstood for a much longer time if our troops had not succeeded in completely encircling it. Before the artillery and heavy tanks could complete the encirclement the last remnants of the Japanese garrison fled by night.

There seems to be a misapprehension that the fighting in the Arakan has completely died down. The battle that was going on in front of my eyes that day resulted in over 220 Japanese bodies being counted, so that the total casualties must have been considerably higher.

We had tea at the Headquarters of the 25th Division and then drove from Maungdaw to the neighbouring little village of Kappagaung, where our engineers had been constructing a new wharf. I met and talked to representatives of the port parties, etc., before embarking in a dear old Landing Craft, Personnel. We shoved off at 1800 and sat on the canopy of the LCP drinking in the cool sea breeze. I for one felt terribly homesick for Combined Ops and life at sea.

---

[1] A radio comedian of considerable reputation.

TUESDAY, 11 APRIL   At 0940 I took off from a small airstrip nearby in a Moth. We flew low over the Ngakyedauk Pass and landed east of the Mayu Range at Laungyaung.

Here I was met by Major General Lomax who commands the 26th Indian Division. The Corps Commander and our staffs had already arrived by jeep. We drove on to Wings Hill. Brigadier Lowther, who commands the 4th Brigade, and two of his Battalion Commanders described the battle of Point 315, when the Lincolns and Wiltshires made their gallant advance to clear the Japanese off the east side of Sinzweya during the recent battle.

We lunched in Lomax's Headquarters. The mess furniture was very simple. It consisted of a rectangular pit with some planks put across the middle. One sat on the edge of the pit and used the planks as a table.

At 1400, after lunch, we met Frank Messervy at Sinzweya, which was where his administrative Headquarters were encircled for 17 days. It will surely go down in history as one of the most outstanding and odd battles fought by the Indian Army. Frank took an hour describing it and it was a most interesting hour. He began as usual by leading us up the highest 'feature' in the centre of the 'box'. The prelude to every description of a battle I have had during the last two days has been a scramble up the highest 'feature' in the heat and dust of the day.

The Japanese Commander was called Tanabashi, although I now hear his proper name is Tanahashi. (Incidentally, a poor joke but one which made the troops laugh in my recent addresses was to the effect that his name had been changed because whereas last year he bashed us, this year he made a hash of it.) Tanahashi overran Frank Messervy's Divisional Headquarters so that his Headquarters staff had to fight their way back through the Administrative Headquarters of his Division which were about a mile to the south, set in a small plain. This plain was oval in shape with an average diameter of about a mile, and with a steep little range of hillocks (on which we were now standing) in the middle. All round the plain were the high hills of the Mayu Range, overlooking it as the sides of a bowl overlooking the bottom.

In this 'box' there were about 10,000 men of whom less than 2000 were combatant soldiers, the remainder being cooks, clerks, medical orderlies, mechanics, Pioneers, and administrative personnel generally. There were insufficient numbers to hold the high range of hills all round the bowl so that only certain 'features' at the edge of the 'box' were held by us. Our men were repeatedly driven off by the Japanese and recaptured their vital positions by heroic counterattacks.

On no less than three occasions all the ammunition, which had been buried in the central range of hillocks, was blown up by Japanese artillery fire. The whole of the 'box' was under almost continual artillery bombardment for seventeen days and nights.

Food and ammunition and medical supplies were dropped to them from the air, otherwise of course they could not have carried on. The Medical Dressing Station had been put on one of the edges of the bowl to avoid being shelled as the whole of the little plain was under constant fire. There was a deep nullah between the rest of the 'box' and the Medical Dressing Station. One night the Medical Dressing Station was overrun by the Japanese. We could not fire on them indiscriminately since they were all among our wounded. Frank Messervy is an unemotional man but he says that he will never forget, as long as he lives, the shrieks of our wounded as the Japanese went from bed to bed butchering them. When they had murdered all the wounded they took the six doctors and shot them one by one through the ear. The last one (an Indian doctor) was not killed by his shot, which somehow glanced off his skull, but thinking he had been killed fell down in a dead faint. When he came to he realized what had happened and smothered himself in blood from the others and was left for dead. It is to him we owe the account of what the Japanese did. The deep nullah and the blackness of the night prevented reinforcements reaching the Medical Dressing Station in time to prevent slaughter.

Another curious incident is that the Japanese never touched any of our motor transport, which had been left in No Man's Land, presumably because they were hoping to make use of them in their advance northwards later on. In order to avoid the rest of our lorries from being shelled, Messervy had them pushed out into No Man's Land, whence we recovered them untouched at the end of the battle. Luckily Christison had sent some tanks into the 'box' a few hours before it was surrounded and they were invaluable in blasting a way open for the relieving troops.

The whole story is so thrilling that I am trying to get one of the MOI writers from home to write it up in popular pamphlet form.

After this I met representative officers and men who had fought in the 'box' and told them that their battle would go down into history as one of the hardest and most gallant and unusual ones ever fought. I then saw some more men of the 72nd Brigade and talked to them.

At 1645 I took off from Maunghnama airstrip.

THURSDAY, 13 APRIL to FRIDAY, 14 APRIL [New Delhi]   These were two very hectic days as I not only had to implement action on every sort of matter I had discussed during my 10 days' tour but a major question of policy had arisen in my absence.[1] I found that considerable differences of opinion that existed had produced a somewhat negative result and had the old business of trying to instil enough enthusiasm and optimism to produce the necessary positive result.

Why is it that in Delhi there always appears to be a somewhat negative atmosphere whereas at the Front everybody is full of dash and go? I do hope that when we move to Kandy we shall take the Front atmosphere with us and leave the Delhi atmosphere in Delhi.

On Friday I had a farewell luncheon with the Auchinlecks and a farewell dinner with the Viceroy.[2] On both occasions I had extremely satisfactory conversations with them at which we vied in paying each other compliments. These were certainly sincere on my part as I do think that both Wavell and Auchinleck have given me every possible support and been most helpful and friendly.

On Friday evening came the devastating news of the Bombay disaster.[3] As if we hadn't enough troubles already without having a large part of the facilities of the only good port in India destroyed. However, we shall no doubt rise above it and get the port going again very soon.

A curious side-light of this show is that my Chinese staff were visiting Bombay and the Chinese Naval Captain was killed by the explosion whilst the Chinese General and his staff were severely shaken. I could never make out why the Chinese wanted to send a Naval Officer to me since they no longer have a Navy of their own so that his loss can hardly be said to be a disadvantage though he was a nice fellow who had served for two years in the *Resolution* and spoke good English, unlike the General whose English is very weak.

SATURDAY, 15 APRIL   I was really very sad at leaving Faridkot House. After seven months I had come to look upon it as a second home.

I had asked the Raja what he would like to commemorate my use of his house and he asked for:

[1] Mountbatten wanted a vigorous follow-up to Slim's now inevitable victory at Imphal; General Giffard maintained that nothing could be done until the monsoon was over.
[2] 'Farewell' before SEAC Headquarters moved to Kandy in Ceylon.
[3] An ammunition ship had exploded in the harbour, doing immense damage.

(a) A photograph;
(b) The Phoenix shield which was put in the house to be left there
     with a suitable tablet;
(c) A jeep.

I agreed to (a) and (b) but told him he couldn't have a jeep as we were short of them at the Front. I have already given him a parachutist's motor bicycle which we had no use for here and he collects motor bicycles, and felt that this should have been enough.

The Raja has also asked me if I would recommend him for promotion to the rank of Maharaja but this I refused to do as I felt it had nothing to do with me. These Indian rulers are extremely friendly and hospitable and generous but they always seem to want something out of one at the end.

I said goodbye to the 55 servants, gardeners, etc., at Faridkot House and caused consternation by shaking hands with the sweepers, as these belong to the depressed classes. I inspected the Guard for the last time and then drove down to Palam airfield which I reached at 0730 to find that all three Commanders-in-Chief – Auchinleck, Giffard and Peirse – had taken the trouble to get up at that early hour and motor out all the way to Palam to see me off. I really did feel very touched at this unexpected gesture.

The new York aircraft which has been sent out for me and which I share with the Air Commander-in-Chief (and incidentally the other Commanders-in-Chief also) had just arrived a few days ago and I used her for the flight to Colombo.

This York differs from the King's and the Prime Minister's in that there is no separate sleeping cabin for me, but the space gained makes the whole aircraft much more roomy and comfortable. The galley is actually put at the tail and then there is a large compartment with enormous armchairs, there is excessively adequate lavatory accommodation; a large sleeping cabin with four enormous bunks which can be converted to a dining saloon by day; an office with a desk and typewriter at which Stobbart was able to type the letters I dictated in flight; and all the most up-to-date navigational gadgets imaginable. The whole is upholstered in two shades of grey leather and could not possibly be more comfortable or indeed luxurious.

We did not take off until 0800 and then flew at 12,000ft straight to Colombo arriving punctually as forecast at 1445. When one realizes that the distance between Delhi and Colombo is exactly the same as that between London and Athens one realizes more than ever what a tremendous difference air transport has made. I believe our average speed was in the neighbourhood of 220 miles per hour.

On entering the South-East Asia Command territory I was met by six Spitfires who escorted us down to Ratmalana airfield. Here a vast concourse was awaiting us, headed by the Commander-in-Chief, Ceylon, Admiral Sir Geoffrey Layton, and the Commander-in-Chief, Eastern Fleet, Admiral Sir James Somerville.

After a meeting with Layton and Somerville at which various outstanding points were discussed the former dragged me off to a football match. This was the final of the Inter-Services League to be played between Ceylon Civil Defence Services and the Royal Air Force.

These two teams had already met twice previously and on each occasion the match had resulted in a draw after extra time. Excitement was therefore at fever heat. Although my arrival was supposed to have been kept a closely guarded secret I had an unexpectedly enthusiastic welcome from the crowd, particularly service men, with shouts of 'Good Old Louis!'

The Ceylonese team astounded me by playing in bare feet, which, however, did not prevent them from kicking the ball very far and accurately. I should have hated to play barefoot against the RAF who were playing in heavy studded boots. The match ended level with one goal all. An extra ten minutes was therefore played each way. At the end of the first 10 minutes it was still a draw but in the last two minutes of the last period the RAF scored 2 quick goals. The Ceylonese team lost their head and fouled after the last goal had been scored and on their being penalized by a free kick the Ceylonese spectators stormed the ground. Upon this the British Service spectators joined in and a glorious free fight occurred between literally hundreds of people on the football field. It was a perfect introduction to Ceylon life!

In India I am sure that the natives would never have dreamt of supporting that type of fight with the British but here the Ceylonese are quite uncowed and most friendly; even this scrimmage was conducted in a thoroughly friendly atmosphere!

On return I had another meeting with Admiral Somerville in order to go through the final plans for the big Fleet operation against Sabang, and after that he left to hoist his flag in the Fleet Flagship to take the Fleet to sea.

Pownall and I are staying the night with Geoffrey Layton. Our host was my Captain in K.6, in the 12th Submarine Flotilla, when I was doing my Midshipman's Submarine time during the winter of 1917–

Mountbatten, holding a Naga spear, stands on the famous tennis court at Kohima where wave after wave of Japanese attacks were repulsed. The ruin of the District Commissioner's bungalow is in the background.

The docks at Bombay photographed by Mountbatten after the explosion of an ammunition ship in April 1944. The wreck of a merchant vessel can be seen mounted on the sea wall.

The Viceroy, Lord Wavell, with Mountbatten at the Investiture on the battle field at Imphal. Lord Euston, now Duke of Grafton, leads the procession. 15 December 1944.

Generals Sultan, Wedemeyer and, on Mountbatten's left, 'Wild Bill' Donovan at Myitkyina on 16 January 1945.

1918. He seems quite unchanged, the typical, bluff, decided sailor. I hear that he keeps all the Ministers properly in order, with very strong language.

The set-up here is curious: the Governor[1] is definitely under the Commander-in-Chief's orders in all matters pertaining to the defence of the Island and operations generally. The Commander-in-Chief is directly under my orders as Ceylon is part of the South-East Asia Command, so presumably the Governor is indirectly under my orders also.

SUNDAY, 16 APRIL   I drove up to my new Headquarters in the morning. It took two and a quarter hours from Colombo.

The new South-East Asia Command Headquarters consist of the SAC Headquarters in Peradeniya Botanical Gardens, the Army Group Headquarters and the Air Command Headquarters, all three of which are on different roads leading from Kandy, and each about four miles from the centre of the town. The Eastern Fleet Headquarters (SEAC Section) are in Kandy itself and are much smaller than in Delhi, since we have the main Eastern Fleet Headquarters only a short distance away in Colombo.

I am living with my personal staff at the King's Pavilion in Kandy. The most senior officers are living at the Suisse Hotel. Officers of Colonel's and Brigadier's ranks are also living at the Suisse Hotel. Officers of Brigadier General's and Major General's ranks and officers of the Wrens, Wacs, Cwacs, and women civil officers are living at the Queen's.

We were all puzzled why Admiral Jerram had arranged the billeting in this manner, until a bright American officer pointed out that it was the presence of the female officers at the Queen's that had made it undesirable to allow the young Colonels or the very old officers now entering their second youth to be billeted in the same hotel. The Major Generals were considered to be belonging to the most staid level.

The Wrennery, in which all the British and American female ratings and enlisted women live, has been built on the 8th and 9th holes of the golf course. Admiral Layton decided that, since he had had to requisition the Botanical Gardens for us, thus interfering with the pleasure of the natives, he should also requisition a part of the golf course, in order to interfere equally with the pleasure of the Europeans!

[1] Sir Andrew Caldecott.

Micky Hodges has had to put up wireless stations and an elaborate signal system. We are erecting British and American Hospitals, cinemas, officers' clubs, NAAFI, etc. Our Communications flight, however, has to be some distance from Kandy, as we cannot put an airfield among the mountains.

It will be realized that SEAC has become the principal, one might say the only, industry of Kandy, and a lot of buildings have had to be put up. The only brick buildings, however, are the War Room and my own office block. All the remainder are either built out of wood or plaited bamboo, known as bashas or cadjan huts.

All the various organizations (of which there are a surprising number) which work under my orders have established liaison missions in my Headquarters and one way and another we have a very large and motley collection of people in Kandy, though I am glad to think we have kept the numbers down to less than a quarter of what Ike Eisenhower, and later Jumbo Wilson, had to move from Algiers to Naples. In addition to that, I and my three Commanders-in-Chief have to keep a Rear Headquarters running in Delhi, so it will be seen what a complicated set-up it all is.

On the other hand, I am convinced that if we had not carried out this preliminary move now we should never have become sufficiently mobile to move on into reconquered territory when the time comes.

My own office block at Peradeniya has rooms for my personal staff, secretaries, typists etc., on one side and the Chief of Staff and Assistant Chief of Staff with their personal assistants and secretaries sit on the other side of the main entrance. Round this are grouped a series of huts housing Wedemeyer and his staff, Wheeler and his staff, Jerram and his staff, Micky and his signal organization.

All the various roads have been given suitable names. The Press live in Fleet Street with the Public Relations Departments and the censors. Irving Asher[1] and his photographic laboratories are in Hollywood Boulevard. The Medical Advisory Division live in Harley Street. The dentist has set up his shop in Welbeck Street, etc.

After dealing with urgent telegrams, etc. in the office I drove on up to the King's Pavilion, which is four miles away, but as the road is crowded and the Ceylonese entirely without any traffic sense it takes nearly a quarter of an hour from door to door.

The King's Pavilion was built in 1829 on the site of the house of the

---

[1] An American officer with a background in the film industry, who also acted as Mountbatten's ADC on visits to American units.

Prime Ministers of the old Kings of Kandy. It stands in extremely beautiful gardens, which although small are so surrounded by beautiful trees that the town is completely hidden. The Governor has his official residence in Colombo and another one in the hill station of Nuwara Eliya, and I gather he very rarely uses Kandy. By the King's direction the King's Pavilion was kindly put at my disposal and it certainly makes the whole difference having such a lovely house to live in.

Although the house looks quite imposing it has far less accommodation than Faridkot House, having only four big bedrooms and three smaller rooms for ADCs.[1] Luckily this meant that I could not take the whole of the senior officers from Faridkot with me and I decided to make it into a personal residence rather than a Senior Officers' Mess.

My newly married Flag Lieutenant has moved into the secretary's bungalow. I visited Arthur and Margaret Leveson there and found them very comfortably installed. They are, however, driven even more mad than I am by the small temple which adjoins the grounds next door to their bungalow. Beginning at 0600 an indefatigable native band produce very monotonous music. There is an extremely tiresome wind instrument suitably known as a Horronawa, which is accompanied by maddening tom-toms. I can hear these from my bedroom, but Arthur and Margaret have to shout at each other over their meals to drown the band.

A curious feature of this house is that one enters through the dining room, there being no sort of front hall. The rooms, and particularly the central hall, which is between the dining room and the garden, are luckily very high and cool. Everybody has remarked on the fact that the atmosphere of the King's Pavilion is friendly and not pompous. British people liken it to the atmosphere of an English country house, the Americans to the atmosphere of one of their old Colonial houses. Although old-fashioned, thank God it has got modern bathrooms, recently installed, and in general is incomparably nicer than Faridkot House, and that is saying a lot.

MONDAY, 17 APRIL to FRIDAY, 21 APRIL I spent these days in meetings with the Deputy Commanders-in-Chief and in going round the Headquarters and Camps.

---

[1] When Mountbatten visited the house with the Prince of Wales in 1922 he commented: 'It is rather a hopeless house, for although it contains many large and airy reception rooms, there is an entirely inadequate supply of sleeping apartments.'

My arrival in Ceylon has coincided with the christening of a new orchid which rejoices in the astounding name of 'Vanda Pride O'Lanka Lord Louis Mountbatten's Var'. The newspapers announce that this plant is the sister of the original 'Pride O'Lanka'. I never realized plants had sisters before but it is nice to feel that it is a god-daughter rather than a god-son.

SATURDAY, 22 APRIL to MONDAY, 24 APRIL   Pownall and Lushington tackled me this week, saying that they thought it was really necessary I took week-end leave and had a rest. I smelt a rat and said: 'I suppose I am getting irritable and difficult?' To which they replied: 'Not exactly, but it is obvious that your ten-day tour of the Front has tired you out.' On condition that Henry Pownall himself took a week's leave when I came back I finally agreed to go away for the week-end.

The Government had offered to provide me with a little rest bunga-low. This is the custom in Ceylon, where the Governor, Commander-in-Chief, and the Naval Commander-in-Chief all have these little rest bungalows. I therefore decided to visit the bungalow which had been placed at my disposal at Ellatota. I took Douglas Wilson and Peter and Janey Lindsay.[1] Their section has moved from Meerut to Kandy and they have themselves got quite a nice little bungalow about eight miles from Kandy, on the Yahalatenne Estate.

We drove up in the afternoon, stopping for tea at the Hill Club in Nuwara Eliya. This is 6000 feet up and it was quite cold. The golf course looks lovely. Ellatota village is about three miles beyond Bandarawela and a couple of miles short of the naval rest camp at Diyatalawa. Although the distance is only eighty miles it took us just over three and a half hours so twisting and winding is the road. I do not know when I have seen more beautiful country, with waterfalls, tea gardens, jungle, moorland and every possible variety of scenery.

The bungalow itself is very dashing and modern, having only been completed three years ago for a rich Ceylonese planter. It rejoices in the curious name of Sidupiyanilla. We spent Sunday sun-bathing and going for a walk and generally lazing about. On Monday morning we left at 0800 and got back to the office at 1200.

---

[1] The Lindsays were two of Mountbatten's closest friends, and Janey Lindsay was a particularly valued confidante.

TUESDAY, 25 APRIL   I have been invaded by the Dutch Minister for Colonies and Acting Governor General of the Netherlands East Indies, Dr Van Mook, the Dutch Commander-in-Chief, Admiral Helfrich, the Dutch Ambassador to China, Dr Lovink, who are all staying in the King's Pavilion for three or four days.

Irving Asher arrived back from the US this week having crashed in the Persian Gulf in a large C.54 aircraft. He was the only member of the party uninjured and had quite a task getting wounded men to the shore in their rubber dinghy at night. He lost some extremely valuable combat cameras and Leicas, which is a tragedy as they are irreplaceable. He himself seems none the worse.

These air crashes are getting beyond a joke; the same day General Giffard, the Army Group Commander-in-Chief, with most of his staff, crashed in a Hudson on his way back from Comilla. One of the engines apparently blew up and they had to do a belly landing in a field, but mercifully killed nobody.

Captain Betty Lutze, Personal Assistant to General Wedemeyer, said to me on her return: 'I saw your two cunning little daughters at Chester Street and we all fell in love with them.' I was flattered and said: 'I hope they behaved themselves', to which she replied: 'They were both darlings, though one of them did try to bite Colonel Lincoln.' I echoed, with great astonishment: '*Bite* Colonel Lincoln?' She replied: 'Oh! but it was Colonel Lincoln's fault, he was teasing them.' I didn't know the answer to that one and so gave up the struggle. I couldn't make up my mind which of the two was more likely to bite old Abe Lincoln, Patricia or Pamela.

In the mornings here I have been riding with Johnny Papps.[1] There is a jungle reservation immediately adjoining the King's Pavilion garden which is quite lovely. The jungle abounds with every type of curious creature and in the first few rides I have seen a snake, gaily coloured butterflies with a six-inch wing spread, a thing like a flying bluebottle but at least two inches in diameter, a host of friendly monkeys and a colony of several hundred flying foxes. The only snag is that if one rides off the paths into the undergrowth the ponies come back with their legs bleeding profusely from leeches, although apparently this does them no harm.

I dined with Peter and Janey at their lovely bungalow at Yaha-latenne one night and brought over the album of *Oklahoma* records

---

[1] One time banqueting manager of the Dorchester Hotel and now Controller and Military ADC.

which a friend had sent me from America. I became very unpopular with everyone afterwards as I dropped the album and broke every record.

I have now discovered that Betty Lutze was referring to our two cunning little 'dawgs' and so it was presumably Mizzen and not Patricia who took a cutlet out of Abe Lincoln.

SATURDAY, 29 APRIL   I drove down to Colombo and visited the USS *Saratoga* accompanied by Clem Moody, the Rear Admiral Commanding Aircraft Carriers. She is one of the largest American aircraft carriers and took part in the raid on Sabang. It will be remembered that in my communiqué I said an American carrier-borne Task Force took part. I addressed the 2900 officers and men and then went round the ship. In different compartments I was given iced pineapple juice, vanilla ice cream and Coca-Cola. She was very clean. I then went on board the American destroyers who had escorted her.

After that Admiral Somerville gave a luncheon party for me at which most of the Flag Officers of the Fleet were present and I had a long talk with him.

I came back in the SEAC Special which leaves Colombo each night at 1830 and gets to Kandy at 2145. It has a conference room and private car attached in which I gave high tea to eight of our officers who were coming up in the train.

This train runs down at 0805 every morning getting in at 1115. It takes the many people who are going on by air or rail or sea from Colombo. It also takes the people in to meetings and we allow a certain number of officers and men to go down on leave. It saves the wear and tear on tyres on these terrible twisting roads and a lot of petrol.

THURSDAY, 4 MAY to THURSDAY, 11 MAY 1944   Admiral Somerville came to my meeting with the Commanders-in-Chief on Thursday, 4th, and I had a small luncheon party for him which included Frank Owen (who was down on a visit from Calcutta) and John Davies, the State Department representative, whom my spies tell me is reputed to have been responsible for the notorious article in *Time* saying that Stilwell and I had had a disagreement.[1]

---

[1] Davies was energetically opposed to imperialism and fuelled Stilwell's suspicions that the main object of British policy was to restore the British Empire.

I had a meeting of all the War Correspondents to try and find out what all their complaints about censorship are. I think it went well and am glad I had it.

Sergeant Watson, late of Hawes and Curtis,[1] has opened a tailor's shop next door to the officers' shop. He has been so swamped by orders from officers that he has engaged a number of native tailors, to work under him. The first officer who came to try on his trousers found that they would not meet round the waist and came above his ankles. Watson got the Ceylonese tailor to check over the measurements in his presence and was amazed to find that they were exactly as written down. On checking over the tape measure, however, he discovered that the tailor had torn it, folded the ends over, and sewn them together, so that there was about three inches missing out of the tape!

On Saturday I visited the Army Group Camp at Kondesalle. General Playfair[2] received me at the Army Group Commander-in-Chief's beautiful bungalow. It has a magnificent view with the mountain ranges in the distance and cocoa and rubber plantations all round it.

The Guard of the Ceylon Light Infantry turned out and when I was inspecting it I asked the sergeant: 'How many years service have you?', and received the answer: 'Six and a half years, Sar.' I remarked: 'Quite a veteran, eh!', to which the sergeant indignantly replied: 'No Sar, I am the second son of my father and my mother.'

The Army Group Commander-in-Chief and the Air Commander-in-Chief came down on Monday for a series of meetings. I am putting Peirse and Sultan up at the King's Pavilion but Giffard is at his own bungalow. The work is going on very hard while they are here, meetings succeeding each other at a rate comparable to the Quebec Conference.

The other day a Ceylonese looked in at Frank Owen's basha and asked him if he would like him to take away any of his clothes. Frank Owen, who had only recently been asking Irving Asher about having his clothes washed, assumed that this was the Dhobi man come to collect the clothes for washing. Not only did he give him all the clothes he had with him but he stripped off the shirt and underclothes he had on and gave these to him as well.

He has never seen his clothes again and probably never will as the man was not the Dhobi man and was presumably asking for cast-off clothing!

[1] The Savile Row tailors.
[2] The Deputy Commander-in-Chief.

FRIDAY, 12 MAY to TUESDAY, 16 MAY   The Commanders-in-Chief left one by one during this period but work continued feverishly on the plans. On Saturday I had the most difficult of many difficult days in this command, as I had to tell my Army Group Commander-in-Chief, General Sir George Giffard, that I had lost confidence in him, and was asking for his replacement.

General Giffard is the senior General in the Army List; he was given the GCB in the New Year's Honours; he was specially selected by the CIGS to be my Commander-in-Chief, and it required a great deal of courage to sack him.

He insisted that I should write out categorically that I had lost confidence in him. He took it like the great gentleman that he is, and once the matter had been put in writing he behaved admirably and undertook to remain on until an adequate successor could be found. I naturally only told the secret to the Commanders-in-Chief. I was quite surprised at the strength of their agreement, and in the case of the Americans they were extremely outspoken.[1]

I suppose it really is that he is orthodox and extremely cautious, whereas I really feel that we must push on and take all the risks with the troops this monsoon. I am sending Henry Pownall home with my letter to the CIGS.

WEDNESDAY, 17 MAY   I started a two-day tour of Royal Air Force stations in Ceylon today, arranged by my Air ADC Squadron Leader Douglas Wilson. He wanted me to leave by car at 0700 but I was certain he had allowed too much time and refused to leave until quarter past. Even then we arrived at Sigiriya half an hour too soon at 0900 and so we went off sightseeing and had a look at the famous Sigiriya Rock. This is an amazing natural feature consisting of a single colossal rock rising 400 feet above the level of the surrounding plain with vertical sides. It is oval in cross section with an average diameter of two to three hundred feet. It was converted into a great rock fortress by Kasyapa after he had killed his father and had to take refuge from the vengeance of his elder brother. Kasyapa lived about 400 BC and the fortress which he built on this rock must have been one of the most wonderful efforts of building that the world has ever seen.

At China Bay[2] I met the officers and men of the Royal Netherlands

---

[1] Stilwell had refused to serve under Giffard, Peirse considered him negative and uncooperative, while Somerville agreed he lacked 'speed of thought and action'.

[2] Airfield for the great naval base at Trincomalee.

Navy Flying Boat Squadron 321. I found that every single officer and man could speak English, most of them extremely fluently. I therefore addressed them in their hangar and instead of cracking my usual jokes and being light-hearted I talked to them very seriously because I felt that men whose families were left in Sumatra and Java and Holland would not feel much like hearing jokes. Apparently the talk went extremely well and afterwards they gave me lunch at their mess.

The Dutch Navy has a curious custom, grace is not said aloud but a bell is rung for a few seconds' silence during which people are supposed to say grace to themselves. It is then rung a second time to mark the end of the silence. When the Dutch padre is present the silence period is four or five times as long, as the mess president does not dare ring the bell until the padre has opened his eyes again. What the poor padre does not realize is that all the young Dutch officers have a sweepstake on the number of seconds that he will keep his eyes shut and everything is done to encourage him to be as long as possible.

The monsoon appeared to have set in, or at all events there was such bad weather that we were unable to fly straight across the island and had to go north about all the way round to reach Koggala, in the extreme SW corner of the island. It was raining hard and there were thunder storms and altogether our passage was rather rough. Although we took off at exactly the right time we were half an hour late landing at Koggala airstrip at 1730.

This is a newly built Flying Boat Station making use of a large lake whose height is now artificially controlled by a sill[1] leading to the sea. I counted some 20 Flying Boats at anchor on the lake. The remainder of course were all out on patrol.

THURSDAY, 18 MAY It was raining so hard in the morning that we could not see more than twenty to thirty yards through the rain. The meteorological forecast was so bad that the Station Commander strongly advised me to go by car to Colombo. This was extremely annoying as it meant cutting out Ratmalana Air Station, but I finally decided to do so and drove to Colombo, leaving at 0840 and arriving at 1110.

At 1450 I drove to the Queen's House, where I was met by the Governor, Sir Andrew Caldecott, and Geoffrey Layton. I then had the unusual experience of taking the chair at a meeting with the Governor

[1] A word for the timber controlling the entrance to a lock or dry dock.

and the Commander-in-Chief in their own Government House. I went into the effect of certain constitutional proposals on my future operations and was glad to find I was in complete agreement with HE and the C.-in-C.[1]

MONDAY, 22 MAY to SATURDAY, 27 MAY Meetings with Stratemeyer who left on Tuesday. I heard the most lovely story from one of Stratemeyer's staff. The first time that General Stilwell flew over the Hump into China he blew up his lilo mattress fairly tight and lay down on it to sleep. When the aircraft got to 18,000 feet the pressure inside the cabin had fallen so much that the lilo burst and old Vinegar Joe was brought down to the deck with a bump. He woke up with a start, drew both his revolvers and looked round to see whom he could shoot. Fortunately at that moment he passed out from lack of oxygen. It must have been a wonderful scene.

SUNDAY, 28 MAY to TUESDAY, 30 MAY Work continued at the usual high pressure. Ronnie and Micky inform me that the number of signals and papers generally have increased enormously in the last few weeks but I suppose this is inevitable.

Noel Coward arrived in a destroyer from South Africa. I had originally arranged for him and his staff (accompanist and manager/dresser) to be flown to Calcutta via Cairo and a closely worked out programme of visits to the Front was due to start two days after they got to Calcutta. For some reason best known to himself Noel instructed his two assistants to stay in Cairo until they got a telegram from him to say that he had arrived in Colombo, the result was of course that Noel, who already had arrived late through coming in a destroyer, had to wait another week while his staff were located in Cairo and put on an aeroplane. Actually his manager/dresser has developed typhoid and so cannot come but as I am sending Mike Umfreville[2] round as conducting officer, Noel really does not need a manager. Noel is making up for this by delaying his return to England.

---

[1] Mountbatten later added in manuscript: 'In fact I had been asked by the PM whether I considered it essential for the stability of Ceylon as one of my bases to have a Commission to come out to make proposals for Ceylon Independence after the war. We all 3 agree. The Soulbury Commission was appointed in consequence of my recommendation.'

[2] Major Umfreville had formerly been Mountbatten's military ADC.

Noel was in cracking good form full of amusing stories. He was highly amused by my efforts to compete with the extremely polite telephone operators at King's Pavilion who are all American and who have the greatest difficulty in understanding what I am saying. For instance the other day I asked the operator to put me through to General Pow'l, the operator claimed never to have heard of this General. When I patiently explained that he was the Chief of Staff and he really ought to have heard of him by now the mystery was cleared up by the operator saying: 'Oh, you mean General p'*nall*.'

WEDNESDAY, 31 MAY I caught the SEAC Special from Kandy Station at 0805 with Captain Michael Goodenough (the senior British Naval member of my War Staff) and Flags. We arrived punctually at Colombo Fort Station at 1115 where I was met by Rear Admiral Nicholson, the Flag Officer Ceylon and now Deputy Commander-in-Chief, Eastern Fleet. I drove to the harbour where I embarked in Admiral Somerville's barge and proceeded out to where the French battleship *Richelieu* was lying. She is the most lovely looking ship imaginable and quite colossal, being of some 46,000 tons displacement. Although she had only come in from sea that morning she was looking very smart and clean and the whole of her ship's company were dressed in their best white uniforms and fallen in by Divisions. After inspecting the Guard of Honour I went down each Division and at each one stopped and spoke to one or two men. I was most interested and encouraged to find a far better spirit prevailing on board than one would have thought under the conditions. All the men I spoke to were cheerful; most of them had had their last leave at home as late as 1941 or '42.

After the inspection I addressed the ship's company which must have consisted of some 1600 to 1800 men.

During the last half-hour he spent with me before going off to catch his aeroplane Peter Murphy had helped me produce a brief talk. Somerville had kindly given me the tip that the men had been very upset by not having their usual ration of wine but that Algerian wines had been shipped out and were due to arrive on the 9th June. When I referred to this it was received with much laughter and glee.

The visit lasted just over an hour and I then went to see the Commander-in-Chief, Eastern Fleet, in his office. I should explain that the night before he had announced his intention of accompanying me on board the *Richelieu* but I got his Chief of Staff to see him and point out how very awkward it was for me to be followed round by somebody who had 20 years more service than myself in the Navy. I went principally to thank him for having agreed not to come!

I lunched at Government House with Sir Andrew Caldecott. I find him very charming and am very sorry for him as he has a crippled leg and a weak heart and his wife recently committed suicide by throwing herself out of their residence (Queen's Cottage) in Nuwara Eliya.

THURSDAY, 1 JUNE to TUESDAY, 6 JUNE 1944 Thursday was a busy day holding meetings with James Somerville. I must say to have Somerville together with Noel Coward was most amusing. They both have the gift of quick repartee and are used to being the centre of interest. They crossed tongues the whole evening, Somerville's opening thrust being quite unexpected. Noel had just announced that he had been out to Guy Garrod's[1] bungalow to say goodbye when Somerville staggered him with: 'That must have been a relief to Guy anyway.' Noel was not quite certain he had heard correctly until a second and ruder crack came from James, whereupon Noel replied: 'Take care; you are dicing with death! I shall write a song about you.' From then on we never had a dull moment for the rest of the evening.

THURSDAY, 8 JUNE Thursday being the official birthday of the King the senior American, Chinese and Dutch officers of each service came to me in a body to request that my message I sent to HM from the Command should include all the Allied Forces in the command. I thought this a very nice gesture and they were delighted with the King's reply when it came. Both telegrams are being published in *SEAC* as this is the best way of passing this sort of news out to the Command. Usually such telegrams are only published in Orders which means very few people ever get a chance of reading them.

FRIDAY, 9 JUNE I left the King's Pavilion at 0900 and drove to Sigiriya. Here we boarded my flying wireless station, the Mercury. The Hapgift was away with Speck Wheeler who is visiting Stilwell and Sister

---

[1] Air Marshal Sir Guy Garrod was Deputy Commander-in-Chief.

Anne is still in England with Henry Pownall, while the York is having a major overhaul in England so I had the interesting experience of flying in the Mercury amidst all the wireless sets and gadgets.

We arrived at China Bay at 1015 and drove down to the jetty where Clem Moody's barge met me. I got on board the *Illustrious* at 1030 where Moody met me. I addressed the ship's company (some 2000 strong) through a loud speaker and then spoke to selected Petty Officers and ratings.

At 1115 I went to one of the escort carriers, the *Atheling*, I addressed the ship's company, thence I went to *Phoebe*. Next I went to the Dutch destroyer *Van Galen* which is a sister ship of the K Class and which once more made me feel homesick.

I went back to the *Illustrious* for lunch. It was the first occasion on which I had had lunch in the dining cabin which I myself had redesigned in Norfolk Navy Yard, Virginia, and again I felt quite homesick.[1] Charles Lambe who is coming out to take over the command has not yet arrived.

Until quite recently James Somerville has done his very best to prevent my visiting any of the ships but he suddenly turned round and became very friendly and asked me to go round as many as possible.[2] I found Moody and the various Commanding Officers not only very friendly but they kept repeating how glad they were that I had at last come to see the Fleet.

SATURDAY, 10 JUNE to THURSDAY, 15 JUNE   The Governor of Burma has attached Sir John Wise to my staff to help in bringing civil and military legislation for Burma into line. Now that Joe Stilwell and Joe Lentaigne have got right into the Myitkyina/Mogaung area we have reconquered quite a large strip of Burma which is bringing in its trail all the attendant problems of Military Government.[3]

On Wednesday I received the nicest telegram of my life. It was addressed personally to me and was signed: Arnold, Brooke, Churchill, King, Marshall, Smuts. It told how they had visited the British and American Armies on the soil of France and how they had sailed through

---

[1] Mountbatten had been designated as Captain of *Illustrious* before Churchill put him in charge of Combined Operations.

[2] In March 1944 Somerville received a telegram from the First Sea Lord, Andrew Cunningham, urging this change of policy.

[3] 'Whoops! Will this burn up those Limies!' was Stilwell's comment when he captured the airstrip at Myitkyina. Mountbatten does not seem to have been discomposed.

vast fleets of ships with landing craft of many types pouring more and more guns, vehicles and stores ashore. They paid tribute to seeing clearly the manoeuvre in process of rapid development for which I and my Staff at Combined Operations had been to such a large extent responsible. I wonder if anyone has ever had the fantastic luck to receive so nice a telegram signed by the six greatest war leaders from the field of battle?

FRIDAY, 16 JUNE to MONDAY, 26 JUNE   Lushington and Al Wedemeyer have both been pressing me to take a week's leave; they evidently must think I am getting ratty from overwork! Anyway, I agreed to go away for five days to my bungalow at Dimbula, as this is only one and a half hours' journey by jeep and is on the scrambler telephone. Despatch Riders brought up a certain amount of work and on the Monday in particular I worked the entire day on a crisis which has arisen with James Somerville.[1] I found that being away quietly in the mountains enabled me to find a clear solution to this crisis much more easily than I would in the hurly-burly of Kandy.

TUESDAY, 27 JUNE   A party of seventeen left Kandy at 0630 for Sigiriya airfield, and took off at 0830. We arrived at Palam airfield, Delhi, at 1530 after a very pleasant flight. I was delighted to see that Pownall was on the field, as he had just arrived back from London in the Sister Anne that morning.

I drove straight to the Viceroy's House, where the Viceroy had kindly asked me to stay.

The temperature at Delhi, which has been 120°, has dropped to about 110° as there has been some rain recently, but compared with Kandy the atmosphere is terrible. Luckily I have an air conditioner in my sitting room and in my bedroom, but there is the usual trouble when one goes out into the corridor, as one breaks out in a sweat again.

WEDNESDAY, 28 JUNE   Practically the entire day was spent in meetings. It was funny going to my own Intelligence Meeting in my old

---

[1] Somerville had written formally to the Admiralty, protesting about Mountbatten's use of his planning staff; the Supreme Commander was seeking, wrote Somerville, 'a form of absolute control usually exercised by dictators'.

War Room which has been kept running by my Rear Headquarters and the Army Group and Air Staffs. I afterwards had a meeting with the Commanders-in-Chief in my old office. Altogether it was very queer suddenly dropping back, after two and a half months, into the routine which I had followed for so many months at Delhi. After this I had a staff meeting, followed by a conference with Giffard, then lunched with Auchinleck, followed by a conference attended by two Generals, three Lieutenant Generals and a Major General or two. I am getting quite used to being the only sailor in the party. The advantage of wearing a khaki bush shirt at these meetings is that one has to look very closely to see who is a soldier and who a sailor or airman. Even the Americans in this theatre wear bush shirts.

THURSDAY, 29 JUNE   At 0730 Peter Murphy, who has come back with Henry Pownall, came to breakfast with me. I have had to try and fit him in early in the mornings and late at nights as of course I wanted to get all the news from home. At 0830 I had a conference of my own staff at the Viceroy's House.

After the usual Intelligence Meeting I had a meeting with the Commanders-in-Chief and was able to leave punctually at 1200 for Willingdon airfield. At 1750 we arrived at Comilla airfield. We went to the Army Commander's room and at 1800 I held a conference there.

FRIDAY, 30 JUNE   The Sister Anne had to go back to Delhi to do her overhaul so I changed over to the Hapgift. At 1100 we arrived at Tinghawk Sakan airstrip which is just to the north of Shaduzup in the Hukawng Valley.

The American pilot of the Hapgift did a really fine piece of navigation through the monsoon and plunged through the dense rain clouds heading correctly for the centre of the Hukawng Valley. The ceiling was not much over a hundred feet and we hopped along over the tops of trees in the jungle, looking for a landmark. Eventually we came to a very straight and rather narrow river which had sandbanks sticking out of it here and there. This seemed quite new to me and it was only considerably later that I discovered that it was part of the newly constructed Ledo Road completely under water.

Two of our fighter escort succeeded in following us into Tinghawk

Sakan which, observing that they were flying without instruments, was a really good performance.

We transferred at once into six two-seater light aircraft and were flown to Shaduzup, the airstrip of which is too small for Dakotas of the Hapgift type. Here I was met on the airfield by General Stilwell and his staff and he drove me in his jeep to his Headquarters. He invited me to address the American Officers and enlisted men of his Combat Head-quarters and they gave me a very friendly reception. After this we lunched in his tent with the rain beating down on us and the tempera-ture inside so great that we were as wet from sweat as if we had been sitting in the monsoon rain outside.

After lunch I had a long conference with Joe Stilwell and Joe Lentaigne. It will be remembered that the latter succeeded Wingate in command of the Chindits, who have now been placed under Stilwell's orders. Although Stilwell has always shown himself as quite remark-ably friendly to me the meeting was not easy as there were several points of difference to be cleared up. However, he met me very handsomely, more than half way.[1] If only I could see him every day there would never be any difficulties in this Command between the Americans and ourselves. Not that we do have many difficulties, as our relations on the whole are now very good.

Stilwell's Headquarters are at present virtually on an island as the recently constructed bridges on the Ledo Road have both been swept away by the river they crossed, which rose twelve feet in a single night. Since the beginning of this month they have already had over 28 inches of rain here.

I informed Stilwell that I intended to visit Myitkyina and received the most violent protest from him and Lentaigne, as they had the nerve to suggest it was too dangerous although they had both been there themselves! However, as will shortly be seen, they had the laugh on me later on.

Stilwell drove me back to the airstrip and we had no sooner got into our aircraft than we had to get out again as the Japanese sent over a fighter sweep. This is only the fourth time that any Japanese aircraft have flown over Burma during the month of June, and that they should have chosen today was particularly maddening for me. The usual idiotic rumours soon got round that there had been a leakage about my movements and that the Japs were after me. As soon as the sweep had

---

[1] The point of dispute was Stilwell's handling of Lentaigne's Special Forces. The problem was exacerbated over the next two months.

gone by, chased by our fighters, we took off and flew back to Tinghawk Sakan, arriving there at 1515. We then transferred to the Hapgift and got all ready to go to Myitkyina when a further enemy sweep of Zeros was reported and we heard that a sister ship to the Hapgift had just been shot down between Tinghawk Sakan and Myitkyina on the very route we were to fly.

It was evident that we would need to take drastic measures to get to Myitkyina and so I collected the fighter pilots of our escort and asked if they were game to take me in, to which they replied that if there were no more than four Japanese fighters they would gladly do so, but as there were only four Mustangs they could not undertake it if there were more enemy fighters. I cursed the day on which I limited my fighter escort to four, as the last time I came into the Hukawng Valley I had sixteen fighters which I had considered ridiculous.

We now all put on parachutes and carried out parachute drill so that if we were shot down we could bail out. We started up the motors and taxied out, only to be stopped by a very frightened Dakota which landed on the strip and said that it had just been shot at by Japanese fighters. At this moment a sweep of eight fighters was reported over Myitkyina and four over Mogaung and so we were once more grounded.

My pilot reported that if we did not leave within the next twenty minutes he could not get us into Mohanbari that night.

As the air raid warning had not been cleared after the given time I had most reluctantly and furiously to give in and we flew back to Mohanbari. We passed over the Brahmaputra, which I had last seen at the end of the dry weather, a mere trickle in a great bed. Now it was the greatest river I have ever seen in my life. I am told that it is far greater than the Mississippi when in flood. At places it is so wide that one might think that one was flying over the sea. Much of the surrounding country is badly flooded.

We got in during quite light rain at Mohanbari but within five minutes of touching down the heavy monsoon clouds had set in again and there was an absolute downpour through which we could not possibly have found our way, so my pilot was proved to be right and only got us in with five minutes to spare.

I was particularly annoyed at not being able to go to Myitkyina, as the fighting there is very desperate. We have 3 columns of Chindits on the east bank of the Irrawaddy at Myitkyina.

Colonel Ravdin had kindly sent Captain Scheie down from the 20th General Hospital at Ledo to examine my left eye. Scheie expressed himself as very satisfied and said that I was now out of danger, but that the slightly enlarged left-hand iris was never likely to be quite the same size as the right-hand iris. He also shattered me by saying that he thought I ought to start to wear glasses for reading and wishes to test my eyes next time I am at Ledo.

SATURDAY, 1 JULY 1944   We left the bungalow at 0740 and took off in the Hapgift at 0820. We arrived at Dimapur at 0930.

We started off without delay in a convoy of jeeps down the famous Manipur road for Kohima. We followed the advance of the 2nd Division as far as Milestone 37, where the first Japanese encounter occurred. We stopped to have a look at the surrounding country here and then drove to a high point from which we could get an excellent view of Kohima itself.

From 1120 to 1420, a total of three hours, with the exception of a few minutes eating sandwiches, was spent in going all over the Kohima battlefields and a very interesting and instructive three hours it was.

We went first over the famous Naga village which had been completely destroyed by our own gunfire before the Japanese were driven out and then over to Church Knoll from which the Japanese were not driven out until we got two 5.5″ guns up one night that fired 300 rounds (100 lb projectiles) at 1000 yards range. This destroyed all the Japanese bunker defences. At the same time another force started encircling them and the two factors together caused them to withdraw from that side of Kohima.

Everyone seems to have behaved splendidly in Kohima. Pawsey,[1] although a Civil Servant and under orders from the Government of Assam to withdraw, insisted on remaining in Kohima throughout the siege.

The Naga tribesmen did everything in their power to help us and volunteered to carry our wounded back under fire, proudly refusing any pay for their services. I am writing to the Viceroy to ensure that their village shall be speedily rebuilt and that they should be provided with food until they can provide for themselves, and, above all, to ensure that this should be given to them free, as I hear ugly rumours that the Government expect them to repay any rebuilding services by giving their services free.

These Nagas, primitive headhunters though they be, have shown

[1] The District Commissioner, Mr C. Pawsey.

themselves true friends of the British and we must do everything we can for them.

We then moved up to the famous tennis court above the DC's bungalow. This is a very ordinary concrete tennis court, but it will go down in history, because the bank around it was held by the Japanese and many a gallant British charge was wiped out, at the last moment, as they tried to get across the tennis court. No more than 25 feet from this bank was a little hillock, which was held by the British. This was about another forty yards from Garrison Hill, which was held by us to the last. To relieve the men in the hillock men had to dash across in the open for forty yards, under Japanese machine gun fire.

We next went over the whole of Garrison Hill. This is a comparatively small hillock covered with trees in which no less than 2000 men of Kohima Garrison, most of them consisting of odd reinforcements for various British units, held out for 13 days. They had no prepared defences, nor any wire to put out. The Japanese attacked them night and day continuously and it was very rarely possible for them to get any sleep. They were supplied by parachute. All round the hill are dotted little groups of graves, unit by unit, Royal West Kents, Royal Welsh Fusiliers, etc. One could not visit this pathetic little hillock without being deeply moved at the gallantry of this scratch lot of defenders who were never intended to fight as a military formation.

On the other side of Garrison Hill was the FDS Hill which was held by the Japanese. At this point the Japanese and British front lines were separated by not more than thirty or forty yards. When men of the 2nd Division attacked up the side of the FDS Hill many of them were shot by machine guns from Garrison Hill. It was only then that our men discovered that the Japanese had dug themselves in from an overhanging part of the hill from which they were able to bring fire to bear on our men climbing up the other hill.

I have been down the Ledo Road, the Tamu Road, the Tiddim Road and some of the roads we have built in the Arakan but the Dimapur–Imphal (or Manipur) road beats them all for beauty. In many places the sides are so steep and the hills so high that it is incredible that we ever succeeded in driving the Japanese out. It was really partly due to one of Wingate's columns, the 23rd Brigade, who did a left hook and cut off their lines of supply, that they eventually had to withdraw, through lack of food and ammunition. At the end they were very weak and thoroughly disorganized. I was told that our soldiers formed themselves into shooting parties of ten or twelve men, carrying their rifles like shot guns and walking up the sides of the hills making noises like beaters. Every now and then a Jap would leap up and run, to be shot down like a rabbit or a hare.

No quarter is asked or given in this war. British soldiers have given up the idea of being taken prisoner, but the Japanese, curiously enough, are more ready to be taken now and we have some 250, although the British tommy is not too keen to take them alive, as may well be imagined.

SUNDAY, 2 JULY I reached the Headquarters of the 17th Indian Light Infantry Division near Bishenpur at 0800. Here I was met by Punch Cowan, the gallant Divisional Commander. This Division has been fighting in the line for 32 months which I believe is a record for the British Army. It carried out the long retreat from Tiddim followed by the offensive at Bishenpur over the last nine weeks, and is very tired. I was shocked to see how drawn and haggard poor old Punch Cowan looked and must arrange for him to go on leave and his Division to be pulled out of the line as soon as the battle will permit this.

He first showed me his Situation Map and after that I talked to some of his officers and then addressed representatives from the Division. As this is the third occasion on which I have talked to representatives of the 17th Division I was rather at my wits' end to know how to vary my speech, but fortunately ten minutes before I got to the Headquarters Geoffrey Scoones, the Corps Commander, showed me copies of Orders of the Day issued by two of the Japanese Commanders, which I decided to make use of. I thus had the unusual experience of reading out these Orders of the Day from the Commanders on the other side to my own troops as an encouragement. They were very well received and caused howls of laughter.

One of these Orders of the Day is given below:

Special Order by Major General Tanaka Nobuo dated 2 June 1944 commanding 33rd Divisional Infantry.

Now is the time to capture Imphal.

Our death-defying Infantry Group expects certain victory when it penetrates the main fortress of the enemy. The coming battle is a turning point. It will decide the success or failure of the Greater East Asia War. You men have got to be fully in the picture as to what the present position is; regarding death as something lighter than a feather, you must tackle the job of definitely capturing Imphal.

For that reason you must expect that the Division will be almost annihilated. I have confidence in your courage and devotion and believe that you will do your duty. But should any shirking occur, you have got to understand that I shall take the necessary action.

In the front line rewards and punishments must be given on the spot, without delay. A man, for instance, who puts up a good show should have his name sent in at once. On the other hand a man guilty of any misconduct should be punished at once in accordance with the Military Code. Further, in order to keep the honour of his unit bright a Commander may have to use his sword as a weapon of punishment; exceedingly shameful though it is to have to shed the blood of one's own soldiers on the battlefield, and even though the delinquent may be no more than a mere horse's backside.

At 1250 I flew off in the Hapgift taking Guy Garrod with me. After an hour's flight we landed at Sylhet where I was met by the 14th Army Commander, Bill Slim, and Colonel Farr, commanding the US Air Squadrons on this station. The latter lent Slim and me his bungalow for a conference attended by Guy Garrod, and Jack Baldwin, at which we went over the points I had covered at the Imphal conference, since the doctors had not allowed Bill Slim to fly to Imphal and he had had to come from the hospital to Sylhet by car. I was shocked to see how ill he looked and have urged him to take some sick leave as soon as possible. What with his bad bout of malaria and the terrible strain he must have been fighting under it is no wonder he looked ill.

At 1650 we flew on in the Hapgift to Alipore Air Station at Calcutta. Dick Casey had sent his Military Secretary, who drove us to Government House which we reached at 1900.

TUESDAY, 4 JULY [Godavari] At 0800 I started my tour of the military part of the Combined Training Centre, visiting the various camps and establishments, many of which are still in the process of completion, and talked to the various instructional staffs, an Indian Beach Group and the DUKW[1] school. This went on until 1100 when I

[1] The DUKW – pronounced Duck – was an amphibious transport vehicle originating in the United States.

visited the RAF Flying Boat Station and then we all drove back in convoy to Godavari.

I must mention a very curious feature of this visit to Cocanada. To begin with, the most elaborate police arrangements were made. Traffic was entirely suspended along all the road our party were passing over, with police stationed at close intervals in the town and villages. Crowds had collected in the villages we had to pass through and in Cocanada itself they were quite dense. They were kept back by the police but were most friendly and waved and stooped low to look into our car (which was a closed station wagon) and smiled. Remembering what a disappointing reception many of these Indian towns had given the Prince of Wales in 1921 it was quite astounding to think that there should be such a spontaneous and presumably unorganized demonstration for an infinitely less important man in 1944 in view of the reported deterioration in Anglo-Indian relations.

We took off from Godavari in the York at 1310 and landed at Sigiriya in Ceylon at 1625.

WEDNESDAY, 5 JULY to TUESDAY, 18 JULY On return two disasters occurred.

Peter Murphy had bought a new lot of clothes with the special issue coupons he had been allowed to replace the ones he had burnt after they had been eaten by termites in Delhi. These clothes were unpacked by one of the servants and hung in a cupboard in the King's Pavilion which had a powerful electric globe in the bottom to keep the clothes dry. Apparently the rod supporting the coat hangers broke and all Peter's new clothes fell on to the hot globe and got burnt once more! Peter is now reduced to a pair of very brief blue shorts.

The Flag Lieutenant has a new assistant, Third Officer Irene Wigham Richardson, who has been transferred from my Secretary's office. Being an extremely efficient and enthusiastic person she set about getting Flags's files in order. She collected a list of all the people who had been to lunch and dinner and all the social letters that had been written and all the photographs that were waiting despatch home and put them in a new filing cabinet in the bottom of which she placed a powerful electric bulb so as to keep the photographs and files dry.

On the night of July 4th there were great Independence Day celebrations going on in the American camp when an American military policeman rang up the Officers' Mess and said there was a fire in my office! Irving Asher took the message and collected a party to go down. They arrived to find my office on fire as the bulb had been left on in the filing cabinet.

The local fire engine had been sent for but was held up by the sentry at the gate while every member of the Fire Brigade had to show his identity card!

Although most of the papers were burnt, curiously enough the photographs were mostly only singed. Miss Richardson, who is known to her friends as 'the amiable horse', was heart-broken at this poor reward that Fate had bestowed upon her zeal.

A new story has come to us from China. There is a persistent rumour that the Generalissimo is about to become a father but nobody has yet been able to make out who the mother is. In the western world the reverse is often enough true but it takes China to turn the facts of nature inside out!

WEDNESDAY, 19 JULY to TUESDAY, 1 AUGUST 1944   The three Commanders-in-Chief have arrived in Kandy for important discussions.[1] I had Somerville, Peirse and Giffard to lunch alone, and to dinner with a large party of Senior Officers on the 19th.

Carton de Wiart has arrived down from Chungking and is staying with me. There have been various cocktail parties for the Commanders-in-Chief, including Stilwell's representative Sultan.[2] One was held in the Eastern Fleet Bungalow and another by Wedemeyer at the Suisse.

My Deputy, General Stilwell, arrived on 1 August to take over while I am away, and he and Somerville attended my Cs-in-C.'s meeting on 1 August.

WEDNESDAY, 2 AUGUST to FRIDAY, 4 AUGUST   I left the King's Pavilion at 1025 on Wednesday and arrived Sigiriya at 1215. At 1230 we took off for London. We were due at Karachi at 2030, but 200 miles south of there we were told not to land in the Karachi District on account of the monsoon. Thinking that so heavy a shower would be

---

[1] About Mountbatten's two plans: the abortive DRACULA for an amphibious assault on Rangoon, and CAPITAL for the advance by the 14th Army on Mandalay. Mountbatten was about to return to London to discuss these possibilities.

[2] Lieutenant General D. I. Sultan, who was to take over from Stilwell the command of the Chinese–American forces in North Burma.

bound to stop soon, we landed at Chela airfield, in Kathiawar, hoping for news of the Karachi airfields soon being open to us. We only discovered the following day that they were under water and could never have been serviceable that night. Having landed, we discovered that Chela had been completely abandoned by the RAF and it was impossible to get petrol there.

I looked at the map and found that Jamnagar was only a few miles away, so we rang up the Jam Sahib of Navanagar, who sent a fleet of cars to pick up our party, and took us to his Palace. Here we found a large house-party of his friends, and in due course he produced a sumptuous European banquet for us. He then opened another palace, Pratap Villas Palace, in which all our party were put up for the night.

The new Air Vice Marshal, Stevens,[1] very kindly authorized us to fly by day to England, in view of the urgency of getting to London Friday, and the improved War situation in France. I believe we were the first transport aircraft to be allowed to do this passage by day, on the 12th Meridian. We crossed the English coastline at Land's End at 1930, exactly 36 hours after crossing the coastline of India, and at 2030 landed at Northolt, where we were met by Edwina, and various other people. We drove straight to Chester Street.

SATURDAY, 5 AUGUST   The whole of our party have been given very good offices at Norfolk House. We were not allowed to go to COHQ, as the only block available for us was Montague House, which was considered unsafe on account of flying bombs. I saw Pug Ismay and then Al, and I attended a meeting of the Chiefs of Staff Committee, at which we discussed our future plans. After lunch, I met the Directors of Plans and we had a very friendly discussion. Edwina and I drove down to Broadlands in time for a late supper, where we found Mama, Patricia and Pamela,[2] it was lovely being home with the family again.

SUNDAY, 6 AUGUST   We left Broadlands at 1050, and drove to Chequers, which we reached in time for lunch. The Prime Minister was in great form. The rest of the party consisted of Clemmie Churchill, the Prof. (Lord Cherwell), Melchett and his Naval son,[3] and Major Sidney,[4] the new VC.

[1] In Gibraltar.
[2] The Dowager Marchioness of Milford Haven and Mountbatten's two daughters.
[3] The 2nd Baron Melchett and his son Derek Mond, who was killed in 1945.
[4] Later Viscount De L'Isle and Dudley.

Bob and Angie Laycock came over for tea and dinner. I had long and profitable discussions with the Prime Minister.

MONDAY, 7 AUGUST   Edwina returned early to spend Bank Holiday with the children at Broadlands, but I had to go to London. The PM mounted a large guard of the Coldstreams for me. Al and I attended the meetings of the Chiefs of Staffs in the morning and the afternoon.

TUESDAY, 8 AUGUST   We had meetings with the Prime Minister, Deputy Prime Minister, Foreign Secretary, Minister of Production and Chiefs of Staff at 1130, 1800 and 2230.

WEDNESDAY, 9 AUGUST   Saw Pug and then bearded the PM in his bed, and finally attended another full dress meeting at 1230, followed by another at 2230.

Bruce Fraser, the new C.-in-C. Eastern Fleet, came to see me at 1500. Managed to take the children to an amusing play, *While the Sun Shines.*[1] Edwina and I dined with the King and Queen.

THURSDAY, 10 AUGUST   Saw the King and Queen again in the morning and then went down to Supreme Headquarters of the Allied Expeditionary Force (SHAEF). In the afternoon saw Bruce Fraser, CIGS, the PM and Pug. Edwina and I took the girls and Angie to dine at the Savoy.

FRIDAY, 11 AUGUST   Visited Ike Eisenhower and Tedder at SHAEF. We all drove down to Broadlands for a late supper.

SATURDAY, 12 AUGUST to SUNDAY, 13 AUGUST   Delightful weekend lying in the sun and riding with the children.

MONDAY, 14 AUGUST   Drove back to London and attended a meeting of the Chiefs of Staffs Committee, with Al, who left for Washington today.

[1] By Terence Rattigan.

TUESDAY, 15 AUGUST   Meeting at Norfolk House. Saw Secretary of
State for War,[1] lunched with Leigh Mallory (the Allied Air C.-in-C.
AEF) at Claridges, and had an important discussion with him.[2] Saw
various people at Norfolk House, and then went to the M. of I. and saw
Brendan Bracken.

THURSDAY, 17 AUGUST   I had the Planners and Ronnie to breakfast
at Chester Street at 0815, to go through the paper I was putting up to the
Chiefs of Staffs Committee, before leaving for France. Unfortunately,
fog delayed our take-off and we did not leave Northolt until 1100,
arriving at A.9 airstrip at Le Molay. During the outward trip contact
was lost, while climbing through the clouds, with our fighter escort,
consisting of four Spitfires, manned by the French. It was fascinating
flying over the beaches and seeing the vast array of big ships, coasters,
landing craft and DUKWs. The craters from the bombing and the
Naval bombardment were very prominently visible from the air. My
greatest thrill was to see the artificial harbour at Arromanches, which I
and my Staff at COHQ had been responsible for originating and Harold
Wernher had been responsible for putting over. This vast port, the
components of which were towed over soon after the assault, and
erected on the open beaches, is like a great commercial harbour, with
breakwaters, piers, quays, etc., at which ships were busily unloading. I
imagine real estate will boom in Arromanches after the war. On
landing, I drove straight out to Cerise Le Forêt, where I found Ike
Eisenhower's Advanced Headquarters in a beautiful apple orchard.

While sitting in his tent I was amused to hear the telephone ring and
find it was Ronnie, informing me that the Chiefs of Staff wished me to
give a Press Conference and desired that the script should be submitted
to them that same night.

Only Ike's personal staff lunched with us, but they included two
very beautiful WACs. After lunch, I had a good talk with Ike, and then
drove on to Le Beny Bocage, where the Advanced Headquarters of
General Montgomery had been put.

Monty was in great form. He had a map which he himself had
produced, showing the tracks of all the military formations in June, July
and August. I imagined that it had only been drawn up a day or two

[1] Sir James Grigg.
[2] Arranging for him to replace Peirse as Air Commander-in-Chief.

before, since it showed the present disposition with great accuracy. Monty assured me he had drawn it in May to demonstrate to the King and the PM what movements he intended the armies to carry out after landing. But for that disastrous storm of a fortnight after we landed, which held up all supplies, the movements on Monty's map might have been set afoot much earlier. Monty assured me that the German Army in France was 'finished – absolutely finished!' I flew back at 1845 and then had to work till 0300 preparing my script for the Press Conference, but managed to find time to slip away with Edwina to the Hungaria for half an hour.

TUESDAY, 22 AUGUST to THURSDAY, 24 AUGUST   There were more flying bombs than usual last night. I had a rushed morning: 1000 Pug Ismay; 1030 Mr Amery (Secretary of State for India); 1050 vital talk with Anthony Eden on the scrambler.[1] 1100, went through final paper with the Planners, then drove to Northolt with Edwina. Took off 1200. We should have flown direct to Cairo, but Bowhill would not let us fly across the Continent yet, nor use our new overload tanks.

We arrived at Cairo at 1030, where I was met by the Ambassador, Lord Killearn, Pavlo[2] of Greece, and Philip,[3] whose destroyer, *Whelp*, is at Alex. Had long discussions at the British Embassy, first with Philip, then with Pavlo, and then with Georgie, the King, in the garden at the Embassy, and afterwards we all lunched with the Ambassador. Had very satisfactory discussions.[4] The whole party, except Georgie, came to see me off at 1445. We landed at Ratmalana at 1530.[5] I went to say goodbye to James Somerville, who has just given up command of the Eastern Fleet, and then had tea with the Governor.

SATURDAY, 2 SEPTEMBER to TUESDAY, 5 SEPTEMBER 1944   I visited poor Henry Pownall in Katugastota Hospital each day. He had a very unpleasant operation just before I came back and looks very ill and

---

[1] Eden had been almost Mountbatten's only ally in his battle to persuade the Chiefs of Staff to support a forward maritime strategy in South-East Asia. He achieved some success but it was all cancelled a few months later.
[2] Crown Prince Paul, later King Paul I.
[3] Mountbatten's nephew Prince Philip of Greece, later HRH the Duke of Edinburgh.
[4] The main subject was the possible marriage between Prince Philip and Princess Elizabeth.
[5] The following day, the 24th.

worn. I am afraid the doctors will not let him stay out here, though Henry very loyally and self-sacrificingly offered to stay on, even though it might break down his health entirely, but, as he pointed out that he might have to have another operation at any moment and it might come at a very awkward time, he invited me to consider replacing him and this I have reluctantly decided to do. He will be a real loss; he has been such a true and loyal friend to me.

On Monday evening the new Commander-in-Chief, Eastern Fleet, Admiral Sir Bruce Fraser, came to stay. I had two hours talk with him before dinner and a long and satisfactory meeting with him and Max Langley after dinner.

On Tuesday we had meetings again all day with Bruce Fraser and his staff. I gave a naval luncheon party for him which the senior officers of the American, British, Dutch and Chinese Navies on my staff attended. We are still short of a French Naval Staff Officer! In the evening Bruce Fraser gave a cocktail party for the naval officers in Kandy and I never realized before what a very large number of sailors we seem to have here between us. I like him so much – what an improvement on his predecessor.[1]

WEDNESDAY, 6 SEPTEMBER   At 1710 landed Palam airfield, New Delhi, and was met by Claude Auchinleck and Charles Lane, as well as the usual host of other officers. Claude came and saw me off at Delhi Junction where I caught the Calcutta Mail at 2300 for Kalka en route for Simla.

Claude pointed out that in peacetime there would have been a red carpet, palms, soldiers and a special train for me but I was quite satisfied with the arrangements they had made! The Viceroy had sent down his coach which had a large sitting room, three large bedrooms and a bathroom, with a long bath rather bigger than the one at Chester Street! I found it a trifle embarrassing that the Viceroy's gorgeous khitmagars in their scarlet and gold livery insisted on standing in the sitting room while one was trying to read and I eventually persuaded them to move into the pantry. Large tubs of ice were put in every room, which proved a doubtful blessing as most of them leaked all over the carpet.

One forgets what an appreciable difference the broad gauge makes in the size of the railway carriages here, since they must be at least a foot

[1] Admiral Somerville.

wider, but of course it seems even bigger when one is inside the compartment.

We reached Kalka station at 0650. I should mention that the Viceroy had expressed surprise that I was only going to spend six hours in Simla and had urged me to spend a night or two with him. When I refused he then said he would send a motor car which takes an hour less than the rail car so as to have longer in Simla. I again refused this as I said I wanted to work in the rail car.

I now know how Wavell won all his victories in North Africa. It must be through persistence because notwithstanding my refusal he had a motor car and station wagon waiting at Kalka station which I naturally refused to take. In any case the rail car was much more amusing. It is a mixture between a motor car and a railway compartment having a bonnet, headlamps, horn and a comfortable seat next to the driver with a seat for 2 behind in which Johnny and Moore sat.

The railway to Simla must be one of the most remarkable in the world. The track is only 2ft 10 inches wide and one passes through no less than 100 'numbered' tunnels on the journey. I cannot help thinking that they must either have made one or two extra tunnels or cut out one or two to make the number come to exactly 100!

On the way up we had to stop three times on account of a choked petrol pipe but eventually we got it right and the timing of this trip is so slow since the rail car is only supposed to average 15 miles an hour that we were easily able to catch up.

Viceregal Lodge, which was built some 40 years ago, is an enlarged edition of Balmoral but rather more 'Hollywood', but it certainly stands on the most magnificent site, 7000 feet up in the Himalayas, overlooking the most gorgeous view. Every square inch of the gardens and grounds have had to be levelled off and indeed the whole of Simla presents the most unusual appearance.

This town has been built on a knife edge ridge and several small pinnacles in the Himalayas. It was started about 100 years ago by a Viceroy who found the heat of the plains intolerable in the hot weather and gradually the entire Government of India have drifted there for the hot weather. Everything in Delhi is duplicated here, even GHQ, India and the C.-in-C.'s residence. Only three motor cars are allowed in Simla – the Viceroy's, the Governor of the Punjab's (in which province it is situated) and the Commander-in-Chief's. Bicycles are only allowed in certain parts and horse-drawn vehicles are not allowed at all. It follows that apart from rickshaws the only way of getting about is on one's feet or on horseback and here one still finds men and women riding as a means of getting about. The only other form of conveyance is the rickshaw, but on account of the steep hills instead of there being one coolie there are four.

At my earnest request the Viceroy drove me round after lunch to show me the sights, but as it transpired that he himself had been rarely in Simla he proved a very indifferent guide and was unable to tell me what most of the buildings were. I asked to be shown the famous polo ground at Allandale, which is on the only level spot half way down a valley with very steep hills rising up at one end of the polo ground and dropping in a precipice on the other side. It must be an exciting and dangerous ground to play on.

The ADC who accompanied us, a very nice Marine called Billy Henderson, took us in one direction to see the polo ground but the Viceroy and he had a heated argument as to whether one could not get a better view from the other direction, so much of the afternoon was spent in trying different directions to get a better view of the polo ground!

We had a look at Snowdon, the Commander-in-Chief's residence, which is built on two levels connected by a ballroom. Both Snowdon and a large part of Viceregal Lodge have been turned into a leave camp for officers and other ranks of the 14th Army when they come out of Burma. I was taken round and talked to many of the men. Luckily I now know all the divisional signs out here, and so was able to go up to a man according to the sign he wore on his shoulder and talk about the particular part of the Front I knew he must have come from.

Peter Coats,[1] the Comptroller, had turned over a lovely lawn and verandah with little tables for an open air beergarden, but, with the true British dislike of sitting in the open air, the other ranks had asked permission to make themselves a 'pub' in the stables and here we found them, piled into a couple of loose-boxes as tight as sardines, in a terribly frowsy, smoky atmosphere, drinking their beer and feeling thoroughly at home.

Bill Slim is on sick leave in Simla after a bad go of malaria. I had particularly asked to be allowed to have a good talk with him, but the programme was arranged for me to see him after lunch and when we withdrew to another room every ten minutes an ADC came in to ask whether we had finished. I could not think why, until I came out and

[1] Now distinguished as author and gardener.

found that the entire luncheon party was sitting round waiting for the General to come out.

I gave Mrs Slim strict instructions that he was not to go back to the Front until he was really fit.

The Governor of Burma was away on leave, but I received a deputation from the Government to discuss every sort of problem, such as the control of opium traffic, the enlistment of the Burma police force and the new laws which the Government of Burma would like me to make in conformity with their post-war policy.

At 1715 I left Viceregal Lodge for Summer Hill station and at 1725 we left in our rail car. The Viceroy never ceased to express his pain and surprise that I would not stay for a day or two and I gather there is no record of anyone going to Simla for six hours. Seeing that one has to spend nearly thirty hours travelling to spend six hours at Simla I suppose it is not really surprising, but I think the real explanation is the leisurely attitude which the atmosphere of India induces.

FRIDAY, 8 SEPTEMBER   We arrived at 0655 at Delhi station where Claude Auchinleck met me. He took me to Aram Garh, where he has built a rest house and canteen for Indian other ranks and after this we went to see the new Wavell Canteen, also built by Claude, for British other ranks who are travelling through Delhi. These are really necessary institutions, and should have been built when the war started, but have in fact only been built since Claude took over. Previously the soldiers had to lie about without food on the platform for hours.

SATURDAY, 9 SEPTEMBER   At 0930 we landed at Cox's Bazaar. I was met by the new Air Commodore Commanding 224 Group, the Earl of Bandon. Paddy Bandon is a delightful chap whom I knew in Delhi and I am sure he will make a success of it, but in an excess of enthusiasm he mounted a guard of the RAF Regiment for me, which I do not approve of.

At 10 o'clock we left Cox's Bazaar in jeeps to drive to Ramu. We had flown through thick monsoon rain but during our half-hour at the airstrip there had luckily been a fine period. It came on to rain heavily again as we drove off. Indeed, it seems to rain most of the time in the Arakan when the monsoon is on. They had over 50 inches of rain in July and on more than one occasion they had over six inches of rain in a single day.

At Ramu Christison, commanding the 15th Corps, and his senior staff officers, were there to meet me and I held a meeting to discuss the situation in Arakan. We had a sandwich lunch and after inspecting the men of this Headquarters we left, and drove back to Cox's Bazaar, which we reached at 1400.

I went in the Sister Anne to Imphal. We landed at 1620 and were met by Monty Stopford, the Commander of the 33rd Corps. At 1730 I held a conference in their war room and at 2030 we had dinner.

It made me feel rather sad to realize that this Headquarters was the one which had been built for Wingate and was the last place in which I had seen him and from which he left when he was killed.

Just before dinner a large frog jumped on to the table in one of the most amazing bounds I have ever seen and all round was the 33rd Corps farmyard; geese, chicken, pigs, goats, all making suitable farmyard noises. At dinner we had a roast sucking pig which had been running about as a pet the day before and which everybody ate with mixed emotions.

MONDAY, 11 SEPTEMBER [Ledo]   We arrived at 0700 at Ledo airstrip and took off in the Sister Anne at 0715. We should have taken off at least 15 minutes earlier, but two of the fighters had gone out of action and they insisted on waiting for two more to be flown in.

At 0845 we arrived over Myitkyina airstrip, only to find that as our fighter escort, who had lost us in the clouds, was landing we were put into the circuit with some 15 or 20 other Dakotas of the Air Supply Squadron. As we circled through the monsoon clouds we missed a right-angle collision with another Dakota by about six or eight feet. The result of the fighter escort mix-up was that we landed half an hour late.

It was fascinating seeing the Irrawaddy for the first time. It must be at least half a mile wide at this point and is a most majestic-looking river.

We landed in a typical monsoon downpour and then drove into the town, or what there is left of it. Every house except three has been destroyed and the railway station is a complete shambles. I was shown with pride the one locomotive they had succeeded in repairing and they think they can get two others right in due course.

I was taken into one of the three houses which are still standing, where I met my old friend, Lieutenant-Colonel Seagrave, the American missionary doctor who has spent all his life in Burma and who had been the first one to attend to my eye in his hospital at Taipha Ga.

He has a tremendous lot of Chinese in his hospital and has taken on twenty Burmese girls from Myitkyina to join his original twenty Burmese nurses. He took me with pride into a very tumbledown room which he was using as an operating theatre. Here three surgeons, one British, one American and one Burmese, were carrying out operations. Why doctors always insist on taking me to see the most sick-making operations I shall never understand. I really can't bear to see someone's stomach being cut open and all their guts being pulled out, but it is difficult to refuse what is evidently regarded as a great privilege.

At 0950 we went to see the new rail head established just outside Myitkyina and embarked in a jeep train. I sat beside the driver of the jeep, an American officer of the railway engineers, and behind sat Lieutenant General Sun, who has now been promoted to command the 1st Chinese Army. The rest of the party got into a goods waggon of the '*8 chevaux – 40 hommes*' type. Fortunately the railways in Burma are metre-gauged (3' 4"), which appear to be the normal width of a jeep's wheels, so by putting on flanged wheels instead of tyres they can be used to run on the railway. The way in which a jeep will draw a train has to be seen to be believed. They are running four trains a day between Myitkyina and Mogaung, taking about 1000 passengers and 200 tons already.

There is no road between Myitkyina and Mogaung, except the railroad, and consequently all troop movements for which there is not room in the train take place along this road. The mule companies of the 38th Chinese Division were moving from Mogaung to Myitkyina and as there is very little room on either side of the track we had the terrifying experience of passing through lines of very frightened mules, who invariably turned their heads away from the train, laid back their ears, and appeared to be on the point of kicking us as we passed. Very frightening! The Chinese insisted on walking down the middle of the line and only got to the edge when we blew our hooter. The Chinese guards on the back of the train spent their time in kicking those of their comrades who had remained near enough to be within reach of their boots!

We reached the Mogaung river at 1140, where we were met by Major General Frankie Festing, commanding the British 36th Division, which I had sent up to help Stilwell out after Lentaigne's forces had been withdrawn.

The bridge over the Mogaung river had been destroyed by our own Air Forces and American engineers were busy repairing it and expected to have the first train over within 24 hours. At the other bank we got into another jeep train and as we drove through Mogaung the worst monsoon downpour of all occurred, the water coming down in solid sheets and soaking us all to the skin. Another bridge was destroyed, and we had to cross by a ferry made up of Japanese pontoons which they had obligingly left for us.

We arrived at the Headquarters of the 36th Division at Sahmaw at 1300 and had lunch in Divisional Headquarters, after which I held a conference. I was supposed to inspect the British Casualty Clearing Station but time did not permit so I promised Frankie Festing that I would send Edwina to visit the Casualty Clearing Station instead.

The Americans are very thrilled about the prospect of her visit here and are already working out plans to take her to all their hospitals right up to the Front so she will be in for a pretty tough time.

At 1515 we went off in jeeps and drove at high speed to Pahok along a terrible road, past Hill 60, which had been the scene of some very fierce battles with the Japanese.

The Japanese are completely demoralized and beaten in this area. Frankie Festing told me that he had had a friend of his, a teacher at the Quetta Staff College, on a visit and they had gone out with a couple of carbines one morning and each got a Jap before breakfast and on the way back the Staff College teacher had bagged another Jap! Actually they were watching a counterattack when these Japs appeared!

Festing is the greatest possible success with the Americans and Chinese and they all think that he is wonderful. I entirely agree with them; he is a grand leader. (On return I found a War Office telegram appointing him to the War Office – which I am challenging.)[1]

We landed back at Ledo at 1800 and at 1900 General Pick had asked a large party of British and American officers to meet me. At 2000 he gave a big dinner party at which I was, as usual, expected to make an after-dinner speech. However, this time the party was enlivened by four American coloured GIs, who sang negro songs.

TUESDAY, 12 SEPTEMBER   It was announced on the radio this morning and published in the papers that General Stilwell, who is

---

[1] Successfully, Festing remained with the 36th Division until the end of the war.

supposed to be in command of this Front, had left for Quebec.[1] I can hardly believe he would have done this without informing me! (Later on I discovered he had gone to Chungking.)

We landed at 0810 at Chabua in a dense monsoon downpour and transferred to the York. The Sister Anne got bogged in turning for the runway, which caused a considerable delay in the transfer and we were not airborne until 0850. The Station Commander said that on the previous day three Dakotas (the same class as the Sister Anne) had been shot down by Japanese fighters which had come over for the first time in many weeks. I am afraid that my visits to the front will become unpopular among the transport pilots if the Japanese persist in these habits.

We flew direct across the Bay of Bengal to Ceylon and landed at Ratmalana at 1700.

I arrived at Kandy station at 2145 and drove to the King's Pavilion. Here I found two important telegrams from the Prime Minister from Quebec, which necessitated some very quick thinking, and hard work.[2] At midnight I came to the conclusion that I should have to send a representative to Quebec and pulled poor Brigadier Kimmins out of a bridge party and told him to go. He left Kandy at 0300 after various discussions and is being taken in the York to Karachi, where he will catch an American air liner which goes to New York, from whence he will fly on to Quebec, taking some 61 hours from Ceylon to Quebec!

WEDNESDAY, 13 SEPTEMBER to SATURDAY, 16 SEPTEMBER   I found a vast pile of work waiting for me which kept me very busy.

Al Wedemeyer and Irving Asher got back on Friday. Al had brought me some champagne from Paris, where he had stopped on the way.

He was held up three times by engine trouble and at Naples had a terrifying experience, when the B.29 bomber he had transferred to somehow got one of its landing wheels jammed up and another one down. After spending two and a half hours circling over the airfield wondering whether to make a parachute drop, which with inexperienced and elderly men usually means at least a broken leg, or whether to remain in the air and try a crash landing, they eventually landed, completely wrecking the machine but luckily killing nobody. Al said that during this two and a half hours in the air he spent his time thinking of

---

[1] Where the Second Quebec Conference was in progress.
[2] About the additional forces needed for the projected maritime assault on Rangoon.

all his shortcomings as a Deputy Chief of Staff, and made plenty of good resolutions to do better if he were spared!

SUNDAY, 17 SEPTEMBER to MONDAY, 2 OCTOBER 1944
During this time we have all been working extremely hard in connection with the Quebec Conference.[1] During the meetings with the Commanders-in-Chief, which were held during this period, I gave a dinner party confined to Generals, Admirals and Air Marshals, and excluding Brigadiers, Air Commodores, Commodores (2nd Class) and civilians ranking as Major Generals, and found the total number was thirty; but C.-in-C., Eastern Fleet, Admiral Sir Bruce Fraser, was indisposed, and my Chief of Staff, Sir Henry Pownall, was still on the sick list, which reduced the number to 28.

TUESDAY, 3 OCTOBER   Left Kandy at 0805 by the SEAC Special. We had breakfast in the train. On arrival at Colombo at 1115 I went to see C.-in-C. Ceylon to have a discussion with him, then drove out to Ratmalana airport, which we reached at 1215. We embarked in the York and flew to Madras, landing at St Thomas' Mount airfield at 1445. The Governor, Arthur Hope, was away at Ootacamund, but Lady Hope was there; a rather quaint creature who described herself as being most unsuited to be a Governor's wife. I am afraid she is right, although she turned out to be a very pleasant hostess.

WEDNESDAY, 4 OCTOBER   At 1130 we took off from the St Thomas' Mount airfield for Bombay, which we reached at 1450. We drove straight from Santa Cruz airfield to Princes' Dock, Bombay, where the usual crowd met us. It was the first time I had seen the immense damage caused by the explosion last April. Wrecked ships still lay everywhere, new dock walls were gradually rising from the ruins of the old, and the scene appeared to be one of continued devastation. When one went into the matter more closely, one realized that an immense amount of work had already been done, and that the reconstruction was now well under way, so that within another month

---

[1] All the resources required for DRACULA seemed to have been made available. Mountbatten was 'in the seventh Heaven of delight', wrote General Pownall, going on: 'He is so very simple-minded. For my own part . . . I wouldn't get over excited . . . until I was plum certain of the resources.' Pownall's pessimism was soon proved justified.

all this vast dock area should be ready for use again. The improvement which will result from the reconstruction has to be seen to be believed.

Vested interests had got solid buildings and warehouses in sites from which they could not be dislodged. Slum dwellings crowded round the docks and any attempt at modernization or improvement had proved impossible. Then, fortunately, an Indian coolie dropped a lighted cigarette on a bale of wool, which caught fire, and in due course caused the ammunition in the ship to blow up, with these remarkably beneficial results. The fact that 200 lives were lost and that damage ran into many millions of pounds sterling may well prove to have been a light price to pay for the vital modernization at Bombay, as without this railway lines could not have been extended and the areas could not have been cleared for the vehicle waterproofing pools or for troop assembly points. In fact, this explosion will immeasurably have improved Bombay as a military mounting port.

No doubt the Chief Magistrate at Bombay had this in mind when last week, instead of giving five years hard labour to two coolies who were again caught smoking on board an ammunition ship, he gave them a five rupee fine.

The actual effect of the explosion must have been quite astounding, as a 5000-ton ship was lifted bodily out of the water and deposited at right angles across the dock wall. I obtained a photograph of this amazing phenomenon.[1]

At 1645 we drove to Colaba Transit Camp, which, as it only holds 3000 soldiers, is being replaced by a magnificent new transit camp at Kalyan, to hold about 30,000, to compete with all the resources I hope will one day come to us from the European theatre.

One of our problems, of course, is to prevent the outgoing soldier from 'infecting' the incoming soldier, since men who have spent five or six years under the appalling conditions out here take a fiendish delight in frightening newcomers, partly on the well-known schoolboy principle of the Sixth Form boys trying to frighten the new boys, and partly because these men have been through conditions far worse than they are likely to be in the future.

An unfortunate incident occurred at Colaba, where the local General, in an excess of enthusiasm, had collected 2000 men for me to speak to, but as these men were in General Auchinleck's command, I felt I

[1] Reproduced opposite page 128

could not do this, and they had to be fallen out again, as I do not wish at any price to appear to be interfering in his command.

THURSDAY, 5 OCTOBER   Just after midnight we arrived at Deolali and were shunted into a pleasant siding. At 0850 the usual crowd of senior officers met us, including Major General Rees, commanding 19th Indian Division.[1] We drove out to Mashrul Camp, where I inspected the 62nd Indian Infantry Brigade, carrying out my usual routine.

By now the news that I hate having men kept hanging about for my inspections has got round and become exaggerated to such a degree that I found the parades of Indian troops so organized that in each battalion only one company would be on parade as I arrived on the parade ground, and when I got about ten files from the end of the first company the second company would be marched on, halted and turned into line with the remainder. As I got past the first ten files of the second company the first company would be marched off again, so that in fact no man spent more than three minutes on the parade ground.

I thought this was a bit much, and for the remaining brigades decreed that battalions should be fallen in complete before I arrived and should not be marched off until I had finished! However, it certainly shows the right spirit, as I am informed that for an inspection by the Viceroy it is customary for the men to be fallen in at least three hours before he comes, partly, I believe, on the principle that the longer they have to wait the bigger the respect shown to the great Sahib who is coming. By this standard they must think I rank somewhere below a Second Lieutenant. As a matter of fact, General Rees, who is one of the most experienced soldiers in the Indian Army, told me that the Indian troops were wildly excited at the prospect of seeing me, not because I was their Supreme Commander, or that in fact they had heard anything favourable about me, but because I was a second cousin to the King Emperor, who, in their simple way, they still rank with but after Buddha, Siva, or whatever particular deity they fancy.

SATURDAY, 7 OCTOBER   Our train arrived at Byculla station over two hours late and refused to move on to Victoria terminus until they

[1] Mountbatten was to see more of General Rees in 1947 when Rees commanded the Punjab Boundary Force, charged with checking the massacres that accompanied partition.

had cleared all packages. As in India every package has to be signed for, it may take anything up to half an hour before a goods train can leave a station, so we disembarked at Byculla. While waiting I was interested to note the various suburban electric trains going by. They have big double doorways in the centre of each coach, rather like the London Underground, but the doorways were wide open and crowds of natives were clinging to the doorways and standing on the footboards. I at first assumed this to be due to overcrowding inside the carriages, but a closer inspection showed that there were many empty seats inside the carriages and it is evidently the schoolboy mentality that makes them think it smart to travel on the step. I remarked to the General: 'I suppose there must be many accidents as a result of their travelling like this', and before he could answer a stretcher was carried by with the inert form of an Indian, dripping with blood, providing the most unexpectedly vivid answer to my question.

We dashed across Bombay to Santa Cruz, and were able to leave punctually at 0900 in the York. We landed at 1115 at Hakimpet airport and drove to Begumpet airport, which was the civil airport for Hyderabad City, with a very dashing modern airport building, but unfortunately built so close to the city that it is incapable of extending runways to take modern aircraft. It is extraordinary how many cities have planned their airport on the assumption that nothing bigger than a Moth would ever want to use it.

I spent the rest of the morning meeting various Indian pupils at this school. [No. 1 Elementary Flying Training School] and at the schools of technical training and non-technical training. It was very interesting to note that the Indian other ranks appeared if anything as brighter and more willing than the officers. They have abolished the caste system and food restrictions in the Indian Air Force, as they have done in the Indian Navy. Unlike the Indian Army, where Urdu has to be taught to many a wretched Indian soldier to whom this language is strange, in order that he may try and haltingly converse with a British officer who is also learning Urdu, I am glad to say the Indian Air Force and Navy have had the sense to make English the common language for all the various Indian nationalities. Why they do not do this in the Indian Army passes my comprehension, unless it is that Clive taught Urdu to his soldiers and they do not wish to change such a venerable institution. This is where the Air Force has the great advantage in that there was no Air Force in the days of Clive.

It has, however, one unfortunate result, and that is that the higher caste members of the warrior tribes will not enter the Indian Air Force, and the type of Indian who goes in for a commission, although well educated, is apparently quite unsuitable. I was told by Douglas, and this was confirmed by his Group Captain, that of an average class of 25 Indian officers who go through the Elementary Flying Training School, rarely more than 11 pass out and at the Secondary Flying School we are lucky if 7 or 8 pass out. Thus only 30 per cent of all the Indians who start ever get wings. In many cases the right to wear wings is the final ambition of Indian Air Force officers, and having got their wings, three or four out of the seven or eight apply to be transferred to the Administrative Branch, where they can walk about wearing their wings without having to fly any more. In fact the present system seems to me to be a great waste of time and I shall certainly take this up with the Air C.-in-C. next time I see him.

After finishing with the various Air Force establishments, I started my inspection of the various big hospitals that have recently been put up in the Secunderabad area.

No wonder Claude Auchinleck was keen for me to visit these hospitals, as they certainly are the showpiece of India. They have taken over the magnificent buildings which the Nizam of Hyderabad erected many years ago for the British cavalry and Infantry brigades stationed at Secunderabad and money was no object. The buildings really are magnificent and could hardly be improved on if they had been specially designed for hospitals – lovely flower gardens and grounds have been laid out round them and all that was wanted was to build an operating theatre, X-ray rooms, dispensaries, etc., and to convert the large dormitories into wards.

The cheerfulness of the wounded is quite remarkable. Men who had lost an arm, or a leg, or sometimes both legs, appeared to look forward to the future with undaunted courage. All of them were high in their praise of the way they were being looked after in these hospitals. They particularly appreciated the steps I had taken to ensure that the evacuation from the Front should be by air from the first possible landing ground and thence mostly by hospital ship to Madras, and hospital train to Bangalore, but all of them said the worse part was being carried on stretchers or mules or jeeps from the battlefield to the airstrip.

In 127 Hospital I was particularly interested with the occupational therapy centre, where war neurosis cases are being taught leather work, carpentry, radio repair, toy manufacture, etc., etc. I asked five men what part of the Front they had been on and in every case they replied that they had never been to the Front. On enquiring from the chief psychiatrist, I found that 70 per cent of the war neurosis cases in India are from men who are too frightened to go to the Front and who collapse with neurasthenia at the mere prospect of going to battle. This was quite a revelation to me, as I could not imagine anybody getting shell shock until they had been shelled. I cannot imagine why the War Office send out men in such a neurotic condition that they cannot even face the prospect of action.

At 1800 I went to 128 IBGH. The part I found most interesting in this hospital was the penicillin research surgical ward, where particularly serious wounded are receiving the new penicillin treatment. I suppose I have a weak stomach, but I must say that going through the wards where men have had legs or arms smashed by gunshot wounds makes me very nearly sick. The new idea of leaving the plaster cast on indefinitely over suppurating wounds produces a stench only one degree less horrible than that of the battlefield. The men themselves gradually get used to the appalling smell which their wounds exude and presumably no longer notice it. I feel it is terribly important to go round with a natural expression when visiting badly wounded men. This is difficult enough to achieve, but when one opens one's mouth to talk and takes a breath it requires the utmost mental resolution not to retch.

The sprue wards I also found very difficult to take. To see really bad sufferers from sprue,[1] looking like living skeletons, with the skin falling in under their cheekbones, with their arms so thin that they are scarcely capable of raising them, I found peculiarly horrible, and yet the men remain astoundingly cheerful. There really is nothing to beat the spirit of the British Tommy in hospital, particularly when they feel that every possible attention is being lavished on them.

Actually, they are now establishing further hospitals on this scale at Bangalore, so that our battle casualties and front-line sickness cases can be decently looked after. Secunderabad and Bangalore both have very lovely climates and surroundings and both have the buildings readily convertible into hospitals, but the quickest trip a wounded man is likely to do from the Front to the hospital is a week and the distance is comparable to sending the wounded from the Russian Front to recuperate in Hampshire. The other hospitals in India I gather are not so good

---

[1] An unpleasant tropical disease characterized by flatulence, diarrhoea, emaciation and other unmentionable symptoms.

and I shall try one day to go to one of the worst hospitals, without warning.

I addressed the up patients before leaving this hospital and I began by saying: 'Will any of you to whom I have spoken before at the Front put up your hands' and was gratified to find that 90 per cent of their hands went up.

SUNDAY, 8 OCTOBER   Had breakfast 0845. Sir Arthur Lothian[1] told me he had been the Resident in Jammu when I was out there with the Prince of Wales in 1922. I asked him if he remembered the Prince and I going off on pad elephants with our partners, after the State ball. He replied that he remembered the incident, and indeed, he would never forget it, since the Sub-Inspector of the Kashmir Police had been in a frenzy lest His Royal Highness should be electrocuted against the overhead high tension wires, and in endeavouring to stop the elephant procession from starting had danced up and down in front of the leading elephant, waving his arms and shrieking. The Prince had not been able to understand what the Sub-Inspector was saying for, although he had been trained at Scotland Yard, in his excitement I suppose he had relapsed into his native accent. At this moment the Resident arrived and asked what was the matter, whereupon the Prince said in a loud voice: 'What the hell does the bloody fool want?' Lothian eventually found out and explained, upon which the elephant procession took a different route.

The next day the Resident was astounded to receive a call from the Sub-Inspector, who asked him to bear witness that His Royal Highness had indeed referred personally to him in his remarks and requested that they should be recorded in the form of a written testimonial. Lothian said: 'But do you realize what he was saying?' 'Yes,' replied the Sub-Inspector, evidently deeply moved, 'but any remarks concerning me by His Royal Highness are the greatest honour which I wish to keep recorded among my family archives.'

Sir Arthur Lothian then wrote him out a chit as follows: 'This is to certify that Sub-Inspector ——, on the night of —— 1922, endeavoured to stop the Prince of Wales's elephant from advancing in the direction of high tension cables. His Royal Highness deigned to pass the following comments on the Sub-Inspector: "What the hell does the bloody fool

---

[1]   British Resident in Hyderabad.

want?" It is at the Sub-Inspector's special wish that I gladly record His Royal Highness' comments.'

MONDAY, 9 OCTOBER to SATURDAY, 14 OCTOBER [Kandy] Hardly had the papers announced the arrival of the Prime Minister, Foreign Secretary, Chief of the Imperial General Staff and General Ismay in Moscow, then I received a telegram from the Prime Minister warning me to meet him in Cairo in about ten days' time to discuss new plans. I therefore called a meeting of my Commanders-in-Chief and invited the Commander-in-Chief (India) to attend the meeting. All the Commanders-in-Chief arrived on the Thursday evening, and we had meetings on the Friday and Saturday with them.

SUNDAY, 15 OCTOBER   We landed at 1315 local time at Cairo West, thus going from Ceylon to Cairo in 19 hours, including refuelling. Paget[1] drove me to the Villa of the Resident Minister, Lord Moyne, where I am staying.

Telegrams came saying the Prime Minister's party were delayed in Moscow, which is very annoying as our planners had to work through three days and nights in Kandy getting our papers ready for this trip.

I sent a telegram offering to fly up to Moscow to meet them there, not only to save my hanging about, but because I had a great desire to make the acquaintance of Marshal Stalin. This suggestion was very poorly received. I was told on no account to come, as it might cause severe political repercussions, as Russia is not at war with Japan! In fact, 'Most Immediate' telegrams flashed all over the Middle East saying that if I had already left my aeroplane was to be turned round and sent back to Cairo!

THURSDAY, 19 OCTOBER   After lunch I was taken to call on the King of Egypt. I had been officially invited by the Embassy to do this, to help Anglo-Egyptian relations. We set off in a 20-year-old Rolls. The Palace has all the least desirable qualities of a palace, and lives up to Hollywood's worst ideas on the subject. We were met by rows of Court officials, in frock coats and red fezzes, and bowed about from room to

---

[1] General Sir Bernard Paget, Commander-in-Chief, Middle East.

room. Meanwhile, the King's private muezzin started to call the faithful to prayer from the front door.

King Farouk was very pleasant, and seemed to me to be very shrewd and well informed. He looks at least 34 but is actually only 24. He reminded me that the last time we had met was at the Regal Cinema, Marble Arch, in May 1937, at a Ginger Rogers film, and that we had brought him back to Brook House for a drink. He informed me that he had met her in person since then, and had been very thrilled. I was able to counter that I had also met her in person since then, and had not been very thrilled!

He said that he had noted that I had been three times through Cairo without coming to see him, and that he had been interested to see whether I would go away again this time without coming.

I asked him about the political situation and he told me that if he had not been allowed to get rid of Nahas this time, that in six months' time there would have been real trouble, as the country would not any longer stand for the corrupt administration.[1]

I gather from all the British officials with whom I discussed the matter in Cairo, that it is generally considered an excellent thing that the King has been allowed to change his Government, since the new Prime Minister appears to be very friendly. If Miles Killearn had not been away in South Africa on holiday, I understand that it is unlikely that the change of Government would have been able to take place, as he has been backing Nahas and Wafd to the full up to now.

Pavlo and Freddie of Greece came in again for a good long gossip. They are of course not happy at not being allowed to go into Greece at once to help. Pavlo volunteered as long ago as June 1943 to go in with our agents and fight with the regulars, but although at first he was granted permission, this was later withdrawn and so he has not been able to get back. I must say he was very honourable and did not ask me to mix myself up in any way in Greek politics. He did however ask my advice, and I advised him to write a line to the Prime Minister and ask for an interview with him or, if he did not have time, an interview with the Foreign Secretary, and this I know he did.

FRIDAY, 20 OCTOBER   At 0640 I drove with Walter Moyne to Cairo West airfield, where for once I found myself among the large crowd of

---

[1] Farouk had dismissed the Wafd ministry of Nahas Pasha ten days earlier.

notables awaiting the arrival of an aeroplane, and realized to the full what a damned bore it is going to meet important people, especially as aeroplanes never arrive at the time they say they will.

The PM's party, consisting of two Yorks and a Liberator, arrived at 0750. The entire party consisted of over fifty, in two Yorks and three Liberators, but two of the Liberators and their passengers flew home direct to England without stopping at Cairo. He had with him Anthony Eden, Field Marshal Sir Alan Brooke, General Sir Hastings Ismay, and quite a large staff. I drove Pug Ismay out to the Villa in my ancient Rolls. I had forgotten how uncomfortable the 1924 model is to sit in behind, and felt quite sick.

The whole party had breakfast with the PM, who, considering he has been recently indisposed, was in remarkably good form.

After breakfast I went through the usual business of being told that I opened my mouth too wide, asked for too many resources, and that my Army had too big a tail. However, I know the procedure well, having heard other commanders go through it at the hands of the PM in the past.

At 1030 a Conference was held at Mena House, with the CIGS in the chair, attended by my staff, Pug Ismay, Ian Jacob, etc. It is too funny having a meeting again at the same place and under similar conditions to last November. I found myself in almost the same position, asking for some help and assistance to our theatre, in almost the same terms as last year.

At 1330 had lunch at the Villa, with the PM, Anthony and Walter, and at 1500 a full-dress conference was held, with the same people as at the morning conference, but this time including the Prime Minister, Foreign Secretary and Minister of State. It lasted 2½ hours, and I must say that considering the gloomy circumstances in which it started, it ended very happily.[1]

There was a large dinner party at the Villa, attended by all who were at the Conference. The PM on arrival had announced he would stay until 2300 on Saturday, but when he went into dinner at 2100 he suddenly announced that he would like to leave at 1100 the following morning, and appeared to be very surprised when most of us had to leave the table, some immediately and others as soon as dinner was

---

[1] Mountbatten, as always, was resolutely looking on the bright side. In fact this Cairo Conference ensured that the main thrust of the offensive against the Japanese must be by the 14th Army through the jungle and that only the most meagre resources were available for amphibious operations.

over, to try and get minutes written up, telegrams drafted and arrangements made to meet this unexpected advance of 12 hours in the time of departure. The PM was feeling tired after his trip, and so the party got up from the dinner table at midnight, and most had left the Villa at 0100. A very early night for the PM!

I was able to get quite a lot of business done between midnight and 0100, and got a number of vital telegrams approved by the PM, the Foreign Secretary and the CIGS. In fact the feeling everyone had, that we must get matters settled up quickly, for which we would otherwise have had the whole of the next day, undoubtedly helped me to get the answers quickly which I wanted, and which might have taken much more argument on the following day, so I was all for the changed programme.

The PM showed me the most mournful and historic document, which he had only just received; a letter written by Count Ciano on the night before his execution. As far as I remember, it began something like this –

> I have but a few hours to live, and have been granted permission to write one or two letters. One I feel must be to you, on whom the whole future well-being of the civilized world depends. It is true that you have said some hard things about me in the past, but my chief crime has been that I was powerless to stop Mussolini from selling all of us, his countrymen, into Nazi bondage.

The letter was not very long, and continued in this strain, but I was very struck that even in enemy countries, the one man that people who are not of a Fascist outlook pin their hopes on is Winston Churchill.

SATURDAY, 21 OCTOBER   I spent the morning dictating letters for the CIGS and Pug to take home, and also wrote rapidly to Edwina, Patricia and Pamela, as the PM had offered to take some letters home himself for them.

I then dashed out in the rickety old Rolls and saw the whole party off. On returning, I had a bathe in Walter's beautiful swimming bath, and then drove to the Embassy for lunch with Anthony and Walter.

I had two hours at the Embassy, and over an hour's excellent gossip with Anthony, about the future, both military and political. I was much encouraged to find that his views remained progressive and bold.

He told me one most encouraging thing, and that is that the PM, on his drive to the airfield that morning, had said to him: 'I give Dickie full marks; we gave him a lousy job, and we have given him absolutely no help or assistance ever since he has been there, in fact the reverse; but nevertheless he has kept the show running and always turns up smiling whatever we do to him. We really must try and help him all we can in the future.'

I record the above since it is so rare that one ever hears anything directly encouraging in this way, and it is nice to know that one's masters appreciate one's difficulties.

At 1615 the whole of our party once more embarked in the York and took off. We had tea at 1630, and then set our watches on 3½ hours, to 2000; and soon after this had dinner!

TUESDAY, 24 OCTOBER [New Delhi] I attended a special parade held in front of the Red Fort in Old Delhi, at which the Viceroy presented four Victoria Crosses and one George Cross. All the army commanders (Slim, and Auchinleck's four Indian Army commanders) were present. It was a well-staged and quite dramatic ceremony. The first to receive the VC was a 19-year-old Punjabi, who gained it in Italy. I could not help feeling from the citations that the standard of the 14th Army VCs was higher than the 8th Army, and when I discussed this with Slim afterwards he absolutely confirmed this. On the other hand, the George Cross which was given to the widow of one of the Madras Sappers and Miners in Italy showed the highest form of courage, in that he threw himself on to an anti-personnel mine, the fuse of which had started to work, in order to save the lives of the rest of his party, at the expense of his own.

Of the three VCs in the 14th Army, one was given to a widow. I had a talk to the other two. Naik Nand Singh, of the 11th Sikh Regiment, gained his VC on the 11th March, with the 7th Indian Division on the Maungdaw/Buthidaung road. He led his section up the very steep knife-edged ridge under heavy machine gun and rifle fire, and, although wounded in the thigh, rushed ahead of the section and took the first trench with the bayonet by himself. He then crawled forward alone under fire and though wounded again in the face and shoulder by a grenade which burst one yard in front of him, he took the second trench at the point of the bayonet. A short time later when all his section had been either killed or wounded, Naik Nand Singh dragged himself out of the trench and captured a third enemy trench killing all the occupants with the bayonet.

He was a magnificent-looking man, who had completely recovered from his wounds.

Bill Slim was bursting with pride when he introduced me to Rifleman Ganju Lama, of the 7th Gurkha Rifles, the regiment of which he is Colonel. Ganju Lama was with the 17th Indian Division north of Ningthoukhong. After an intense artillery barrage our position was overrun by a strong enemy attack, supported by five medium tanks. After fierce hand-to-hand fighting, the perimeter was driven in in one place, and a company of the 7th Gurkha Rifles was ordered to counter-attack. They came under heavy enemy machine gun fire at point blank range, which covered all lines of approach.

Ganju Lama, a typically unimaginative and simple-minded Gurkha, was the No.1 of the Piat gun. During his course of instruction he had been taught that his object was to destroy tanks. To do so he must make sure of hitting them. To hit them he must get within 30 yards of them. The counterattack was halted more than 100 yards away from the tanks. 'This will never do,' thought Ganju Lama, 'I cannot hit them from here,' and so he went forward, on his own initiative, by himself, and engaged the tanks single-handed. He was hit on the left wrist, pretty well smashing up his hand. I examined what was left of his left hand, and enquired how he managed to get on without it. He replied: 'Sahib, I only require the right hand to fire the Piat gun.' Finally, when some 30 yards from the tanks, he was hit in the left leg, which was smashed. Although this happened on the 12th June, he was still in a wheel chair on the 24th October.

'Sahib,' he said, 'it did not matter about my being hit in the left leg, as I was then near enough, so I lay down and fired the gun.' He knocked out the first tank, and he then knocked out the second tank. Meanwhile one of our anti-tank guns interfered (!) and knocked out the third tank, the other two being out of reach. The tank crews started to come out, as their tanks were on fire, and so Ganju Lama proceeded to produce three grenades which he had had concealed about his person; when he was hit in the right hand. 'But, Sahib,' he said, 'that was all right; I could pull out the pins with my teeth.' He then jumped on his one good leg and hopped after the retreating Japanese, throwing grenades at them with what was left of his right hand.

He succeeded in killing the lot! Meanwhile, the remnants of his company joined him, and when his Company Commander ordered him back to the Regimental Aid Post, he was terribly upset, 'Who will look after the Piat gun?' he protested. 'No one else knows how to work it.'

On the conclusion of the parade, the troops marched past the Viceroy and the VCs. I sat next to the four VCs we already have out here at the parade, and later managed to see Group Captain G. L. Cheshire, who not only has the VC, but three DSOs and the DFC. He was full of good ideas of what should be done out here, and did not have too high an opinion of the dash and leadership of the pilots in our Strategical Air Force. I pointed out that we were not expecting to get all the 'first eleven' out here until the war with Germany was practically over, and that he was the first of the new team to arrive out here. I have written to Leigh Mallory about this.

WEDNESDAY, 25 OCTOBER We throttled down so as to make a more comfortable trip, and took 8 hours instead of 7, landing at Ratmalana at 0700. I drove up with Henry to the office, which we reached at 1115, and started work at once. The Governor of Burma, Sir Reginald Dorman-Smith, arrived out with General Giffard, and he and his Military Secretary are staying with me, and arrived in time for lunch. H.E. (as he refers to himself when quoting other people talking to him) has first-class ideas on the future of Burma and we see eye to eye on all Burma questions.[1] He writes excellent letters but is an extremely poor debater in person.

THURSDAY, 26 OCTOBER to MONDAY, 30 OCTOBER This period was taken up with feverish planning activities and meetings with the Commanders-in-Chief, who attended all the meetings in person, including General Stratemeyer, but excepting Bruce Fraser who is in London.

I received the information that the American China–Burma–India Theatre has had China separated from the Burma–India element, which seems a logical improvement on the previously complicated set-up.[2] It was a great surprise, however, to hear that General Stilwell was leaving. There had been trouble a year before when I was in Chungking between

---

[1] This happy unanimity was not to last for long.
[2] Stilwell's job was broken up into three parts: Wedemeyer moved to Chungking, Sultan took over the campaign in North Burma, while Wheeler replaced Wedemeyer in Kandy.

him and the Generalissimo, which I was able to smooth over personally, which is one reason why I think old Vinegar Joe always appeared to like me.

It was however the greatest possible shock to me to be informed that my beloved Al Wedemeyer was being appointed as the US Commanding General of the China Theatre, in place of Stilwell. As I am about to lose Henry Pownall, whom I am afraid is being invalided home, and as Al Wedemeyer's British Deputy, Max Langley, is about to be relieved next month, and I am in the process of getting three new Commanders-in-Chief, I really feel that the strain is going to be very great. I shall be the only senior officer left in any of the services or on my staff who has any knowledge of the theatre and of the current and impending operations.

I had hoped that I would have been able to stabilize my staff in such a way as to take a good deal more of the strain off me, but it now appears that the entire strain is going to be thrown 100 per cent on me. However, I have learned a lot about my job in the last year, and feel I can take it.

On the Saturday afternoon I gave a farewell luncheon for Al Wedemeyer, at which all the Commanders-in-Chief and the senior officers of the headquarters were present. (Some 34 in all.) Al and I made brief speeches, and afterwards I mounted a guard of honour of the Ceylon Light Infantry for the official departure of the new Commanding General of the China Theatre. In my speech I said that I could not believe that Eisenhower or MacArthur had an Englishman who meant so much, or had been of such loyal help as Al Wedemeyer had been to me, and I believe this is quite true.

Another excitement this week has been the arrival of the French Mission to my Staff, under General Blaizot, consisting of Naval, Military and Air Officers, most of whom speak very little English. I gave them a large dinner, at which I proposed the health of *La France* in a little speech in French.

The news has at last come through of the decorations which the King has approved for my American Generals. Although I was delighted when Bill Slim got the KCB and his three Corps Commanders the KBE, as it seemed unique that the Army Commander and all three Corps Commanders should be knighted for the same successful campaign, I was worried that I had not been able to get any decorations through for the Americans, but it took rather longer than the British ones. But I am glad to say that the King has approved the KCB for

Stilwell, KBE for Speck Wheeler and CBs for Al Wedemeyer, Sultan and Stratemeyer. This news comes at an opportune moment at the change round between Stilwell and Wedemeyer.

Speck Wheeler was really touchingly delighted. I wrote him the news in a letter and he dashed round to see the Chief of Staff and said he was quite overcome at being made an Honorary Knight Commander and that this was far beyond his fondest hopes, would it be in order for him to sit down and write to His Majesty and express his great sense of honour? Henry Pownall told him it would be enough if he wrote and expressed his sentiments to me.

I have agreed to let Richard Peirse give Stratemeyer his CB when he says goodbye to him at Eastern Air Command Headquarters in Calcutta. Stilwell I suppose will get his from Halifax[1] but I propose to give the insignia to the other three here in Kandy later on.

SATURDAY, 4 NOVEMBER 1944   Took off in a Fairchild Argus at 0815 and flew to Vavuniya airfield, in the north of Ceylon, which I reached at 0900. Here Johnny Papps met me and we went off in a jeep to visit the 28th East African Brigade.

Two of the battalions talked Swahili, so I was able to get off my pet phrases to them, but I was defeated by one Battalion being a Somali Battalion, since nobody had prepared any Somali phrases for me! They are a magnificent lot of men, but quite unstable and apt to refuse duty at odd moments, unless in the face of the enemy, when they are reputed to fight very well. Seven men were in the guardroom for refusing to carry the heavy pack with which they were practising for the first time the day before.

When I was inspecting a platoon of the Uganda Regiment which had been fallen in separately under an African sergeant, a delightful incident occurred. The sergeant called the platoon to attention and then, with his eyes almost popping out of his head, suddenly spotted a man in the rear rank whose thumbs were not down in line with the seams of his trousers. Leaping forward like a man in a Bateman cartoon, he seized the offending Negro's thumbs and pressed them back against the seams of his trousers, whilst volubly reproving him in Swahili. He then came back and reported the platoon to me as though nothing had happened.

On returning to Vavuniya, I was told that there were such monsoon

---

[1] Lord Halifax was then British Ambassador in Washington.

storms about that it was inadvisable for me to fly back. However, the young Flying Officer who was piloting me was quite prepared to take the risk and so we left at 1730 and flew round the edge of all the thunderstorms and landed without any difficulty at Dambulla, which is a temporary airstrip a few miles south of Sigiriya.

I found that there are all sorts of Air Force regulations for the Viceroy and myself, and that it is necessary for a fire engine, an ambulance and a doctor to be present when we landed anywhere! This makes the use of temporary airstrips rather difficult.

I got back at 2000 and a few minutes later Sir Ronald Cross arrived from his visit to the Front. He is our High Commissioner in Australia and a pleasant man, although he had been the cause of demonstrations in Trafalgar Square demanding his removal after he had said that he hoped that the Germans would kill as many Russians as possible. I had a small dinner party for Cross.

SUNDAY, 5 NOVEMBER to TUESDAY, 14 NOVEMBER   It was a terrible shock to hear of Walter Moyne's death in Cairo, as I was so recently staying with him in the very house on the doorstep of which he was assassinated. He lived in a simple way and did not like police protection; he was entirely sympathetic to my refusing to have police protection for myself.[1]

Sir John Dill's death is a really serious blow to me.[2] Not only has he been an extremely kind friend to me, ever since I did the higher commanders' course at Aldershot under him in 1939, but he proved an invaluable link between me and the US Chiefs of Staff. In particular he was a great personal friend of General Marshall's, and I simply cannot think who can replace him.

On Friday Lieutenant-General Sir Oliver Leese arrived to take over from General Sir George Giffard the command of the 11th Army Group. In addition I am appointing him as Commander-in-Chief of the Allied Land Forces in South-East Asia, for British, American and Chinese, which will take a great load off my shoulders, as up to this moment I have been acting as Allied Land Forces Commander myself.

It has taken many weeks to get everyone's agreement to this decision, and finally I announced that I would make the appointment at

---

[1] Lord Moyne was murdered by terrorists from the Stern Gang on 6 November 1944.
[2] Field Marshal Dill, who had been British representative on the Combined Chiefs of Staff, died on 4 November 1944.

midnight on Saturday. General Marshall's agreement reached me at 2030 that night!

On Sunday 12th, Bruce Fraser came up to stay in the King's Pavilion on a farewell visit before taking part of the Battle Fleet with him to the Pacific to form the new British Pacific Fleet.

We had had an awful setback about the decorations for the Americans for, though Joe Stilwell and Al Wedemeyer are to be allowed to keep theirs, there is going to be great difficulty about Speck Wheeler, D. I. Sultan and Stratemeyer, since all three of these are concerned in Lend-Lease agreements, the rules of which apparently preclude them from being given decorations. It seems particularly hard that this should apply in the case of Stratemeyer, who has been nearly a year in active command of the British and American Air Forces fighting in Burma, and who had the CB hung round his neck in the presence of a large gathering in Calcutta, before we heard that the Americans were not going to agree to the decorations. As far as we were concerned, the matter had been cleared in London and it was therefore a tremendous shock to hear that it had not been cleared in Washington.

WEDNESDAY, 15 NOVEMBER There were only four of us at dinner – Geoffrey Layton, Bruce Fraser, Lushington and myself, and we let our hair down and had a thorough gossip, mostly about the Admiralty. We all four found ourselves in very complete agreement.

I shall miss Bruce Fraser so much; he has been such a wonderful change after James Somerville, and has produced an entirely new atmosphere throughout the whole of the Eastern Fleet Staff. A new era of friendship and close co-operation now exists between my Naval Staff and the Fleet's and I am therefore particularly sad to lose him. He will be succeeded here by Vice Admiral Sir Arthur Power, who is luckily an old friend of mine, who will take over the East Indies Fleet on the 22nd.

THURSDAY, 16 NOVEMBER We left the house at 0630, and drove to Ratmalana. After a long argument with Air Command, my staff had eventually got them to agree to let me fly to the great Naval and Air base at Addu Atoll, in an American B.25 Mitchell bomber. This bomber has only two engines, and is a tricky aircraft, but it is very fast and we expected to do the trip at about 270 miles an hour. By this means it would be possible to do the entire trip there and back, including the time needed for the visit, during daylight. However, I found at the last moment that Air Command had been so nervous about my safety that they had got the Eastern Fleet to send a destroyer out halfway to pick us up if we fell into the ditch and were sending a Sunderland to escort us. 'Escort' is perhaps hardly the right word, as the Sunderland only flies at a little more than half the speed of the Mitchell. Furthermore, they insisted that we should do dinghy drill before embarking, as everyone seemed quite convinced we should end up in the sea.

Landfall was made with some of the Maldive Islands, ninety miles north of Addu Atoll. We then turned south, flying over the various atolls. Addu Atoll lies 40 miles south of the Equator. It is the first time I have crossed the line by air.

I had never seen an atoll in my life, and had only heard them described. No description can give one an adequate idea of the amazing beauty of these atolls, particularly when one sees them from the air. The various shades of blue and green, according to the depth of the coral, are indescribably lovely. In the places where there is any land, it sticks out above the coral, beginning as a bright fringe of glistening white sand, which merges into glamorous palm groves.

We landed safely at Addu Atoll, on Gan Island, at 1030. After inspecting the guard of honour, I drove all round the island and visited in turn all the various naval and military units, of which there were about a dozen. In the hospital I met my No.1 Typhus Research Team, which I had been instrumental in getting started. The entomologist showed me the scrub typhus mite which they had succeeded in isolating. They were barely visible to the naked eye and looked like minute little red pin-points; but under the microscope they revealed themselves as revolting looking crabs that were scrabbling about in a solution. It is incredible to think that the bite of one of these mites could bring on scrub typhus, which has proved fatal in the past in about 15 per cent of all cases. Indians are far more prone to die from this typhus than white folk. I was particularly interested to see some Maldivians in the hospital.

The Prime Minister of the Maldives, Amin Didi, had flown down to meet me and he introduced me to five local Maldivian officials. Amin Didi proved to be a young and very presentable man, who talked English as well as Peter does. He told me that the population of the Maldives was 98,000. Luckily Colonel Johnson, whom C.-in-C. Ceylon had the foresight to send with me, was able to deal with the problems of food, etc., that the Prime Minister wished to bring up. I left Colonel Johnson behind to hold a council meeting with him.

We returned to the coral airstrip on Gan Island and took off in the B.25 at 1440.

Shortly after we left the runway the rudder jammed hard-a-starboard, and as we spun round over the barrier reef I thought we were definitely going into the sea at 200 miles an hour; and so, incidentally, did the pilot but by heroic measures he managed to pull her out of the spin, giving the starboard engine full boost. We then had a most uncomfortable crabwise progress whilst he was fighting to gain control. Luckily our enforced right-hand circuit brought us back over the airstrip, on which he succeeded in putting us down safely.

I then had the Sunderland recalled, and went off to have a bathe. I had been bemoaning the fact that my programme did not allow time for a bathe and quite welcomed this change in programme. The atoll is roughly circular in shape, having a diameter of some 5 or 6 miles, and is large enough to contain the whole of the Eastern Fleet. The islands themselves only fill up about two thirds of the circle, the remainder being closed by a coral reef, which is clearly visible from the air, but which at sea level at high tide (as it then was) cannot be seen. All one can see is a dark blue wall, which is formed by the swell outside rising above the reef. It is continuously changing to white as the surf breaks.

We were recalled after we had swum out about a quarter of a mile, as it appears that once you get beyond the inner reef, there are sharks in the harbour.

The Sunderland eventually got back at 1630. She was piloted by Group Captain Geoffrey Francis. I had pulled his leg about how much quicker the B.25 was than an old Sunderland and that I had thought he was flying backwards as we passed him. He told me after that, that his crew were laughing so much when they saw me come out to the much-despised Sunderland that he had to give them orders to stop laughing! Geoffrey Francis himself was rather worried at the prospect of taking me back because one of his engines had been giving trouble and he had not got a weather forecast for the night at Kogalla, since he had expected to land in daylight. However, he gallantly undertook to fly me back and after refuelling we took off at 1745 and got to Kogalla at 2230. I went up to the control position to watch the landing. I must say it was a very eerie experience doing a landfall through clouds by Radar.

The flarepath at Kogalla is curved, because the lake does not give a sufficiently long straight run. I noticed that he did about three circuits before making up his mind to go in, and then I must say did a beautiful landing. When he had finished he wiped the sweat off his face and said:

'I haven't done a night landing for over two years, and my co-pilot has never done a night landing.' I was glad I had not known this when I asked him to take me back by night!

On arrival I was met by the shocking news that Trafford Leigh Mallory[1] and his wife were missing in his new York aircraft in which he was coming out to take over the air command. This is an absolute body blow, for, having at last succeeded in collecting a team of really young and dashing Commanders-in-Chief whom I know and like and can work well with, it is disheartening to lose one of the team before he has even taken over.

FRIDAY, 17 NOVEMBER   We took off from the landstrip at Kogalla at 0815. At 0905 we landed at the large new RAF station at Kankesan-turai, in the extreme north of the island. Here Colonel Tollemache, Royal Marines, met me and we drove in a jeep to Hammenheil Camp on Karaitivu Island. This is the base which I have had started for the Small Operations Group I have formed out there.

It was nice meeting again Lieutenant-Colonel 'Blondy' Hasler, the hero of the Bordeaux raid, who took eleven other Marines in six canoes 70 miles up the River Gironde and succeeded in sinking three blockade runners due to start for Japan. He and one Marine got back alive to tell the tale. I also met Lieutenant-Commander Wright of the Canadian RNVR, whom I originally met at Broadlands in May of last year, where he succeeded in persuading me over tea of the need to form a Special Swimming Unit. Afterwards I saw demonstrations by the various parties, including the Special Boat Section of the Commandos, who have been putting up such a grand show in Burma, only recently capturing an enemy motor boat on the River Chindwin having killed the Commanding Officer and crew.

FRIDAY, 24 NOVEMBER to FRIDAY, 1 DECEMBER 1944 [Kandy]   The Commanders-in-Chief, Oliver Leese and A. J. Power, arrived for meetings in Kandy on Monday evening (Guy Garrod is permanently here[2]). On Tuesday night Speck Wheeler, who as DSAC

---

[1]   Leigh Mallory was on his way to succeed Air Chief Marshal Peirse as Air Commander-in-Chief. His plane crashed in the mountains 16 miles west of Grenoble.
[2]   Air Marshal Garrod was temporarily acting as Commander-in-Chief after the death of Leigh Mallory.

now draws an entertainment allowance of some 10,000 dollars, threw a large dinner party for the Commanders-in-Chief at the Suisse Hotel.

On Wednesday I gave luncheon to the Ministry of Information and Political Warfare Mission, which has arrived out here for meetings.

They are an odd-looking collection and I believe have a couple of female secretaries with them. Anyway, there was nearly an incident in the SEAC Special when they came up, as they were unable to get into my conference coach, which was occupied by the Combined Ops Mission, and so sat in one of the open first-class coaches. One high-spirited young officer, after carefully examining the M. of I. party, remarked in a loud whisper: 'If this is the best ENSA can send us, they had much better not send us anyone!'

On Friday 1 December my new Deputy Chief of Staff, Major General Fuller, joined us. There is a curious inversion of ages between the Chief of Staff and his Deputy. Henry Pownall is 56, Al Wedemeyer is 48; Boy Browning is 47, and Horace Fuller 58![1]

Fuller was Military Attaché in Paris when the Germans marched in. He has married an English wife. He commanded the American 46th Division during three of the landings in the Pacific, and was Task Force Commander for one. He seems a very charming man.

THURSDAY, 14 DECEMBER   I left Kandy at 0805 in the SEAC Special. By 1130 our party was airborne in the Sister Anne. We landed at Barrackpore airfield at 1930. Here I was met by Oliver Leese. I am staying in his Mess at Flagstaff House, Barrackpore.

FRIDAY, 15 DECEMBER   I took Oliver with me in the Sister Anne at 0715. I had put on my jungle green bush shirt and trousers, but Oliver Leese appeared in a collar and tie and a very smart tunic, and persuaded me that on such an occasion up on the cold heights of Imphal I ought to wear a monkey jacket, so I changed in the aeroplane. It is the first time I have ever worn anything but khaki or green on the Front; but Imphal is hardly the Front now. At one time the Japs were within three miles of the airfield, now the nearest Jap is 130 miles away.

I was delighted to see my new Chief of Staff, Boy Browning (who is relieving Henry Pownall), and who had arrived direct at Imphal from

---

[1] Mountbatten was 44.

London. He has practically been pulled straight out of the battlefields of Holland to the battlefields of Burma, and had with him Captain Jim Collins, his American ADC, who had himself been in the thick of the battle of the Airborne Army of Arnhem a few days ago.

It is grand value having a young man like Boy as my new Chief of Staff; he is only three years older than me. The Governor of Assam and his wife, the Clows, arrived by air. Clow was very worried that we would not get in a line to receive the Viceroy in time; so I finally left him in charge of the high-ups, and told him that if he could form them into a line, he was welcome to do so, whilst I went off with the AOC to receive the Viceroy and Lady Wavell, who landed at 1100. At 1100 we all got into cars and drove across to the parade ground, which was in a hollow surrounded by hills on the edge of the Imphal Plain, which we reached at 1120. We deposited the Wavells in a refreshment tent whilst I took my two Cs-in-C., Oliver and Guy, with me and we went across to the parade and were received by a general salute. After this we collected the Viceroy, who was given a Royal salute. The whole party then inspected the Army and Air Force Guards of Honour.

I should perhaps explain that this being an inter-Service SEAC show, the invitations to the Investiture and the official luncheon were issued in my name, although they were run by the staff at Imphal. After the inspection of the guards, the Investiture followed, and I heard for the first time in my life the remarkable order: 'Lieutenant Generals – Quick March!', as Bill Slim and his three Corps Commanders stepped off smartly. Bill Slim and Geoffrey Scoones were in the Gurkha Rifles; Monty Stopford was in the Rifle Brigade, and poor Christison was the only heavy infantryman present, and had the greatest difficulty in keeping up with their fast Rifle step. The opportunity was missed of saying: 'Lieutenant Generals – form fours!', which might have made the occasion even more unique.

The Viceroy's Military Secretary had brought with him a lovely gold and plush stool, which replaced the petrol can and sandbag which the 14th Army had produced for the dubbing ceremony. I felt it did not look nearly so well.

The King had given special permission to the Viceroy to knight these Generals on the field of battle and so each of them in turn received the accolade. Monty Stopford was so nervous I thought he was going to pass out. He was chugging up and down as though he had swallowed a small auxiliary engine. The Viceroy's sword clattered on his shoulder badges, and at one time I thought the only solution would be to send for a hundred Japs to steady his nerves! After the four Lieutenant Generals had been knighted, the Viceroy presented medal ribbons to twelve selected officers and men.

When the ceremony was over, I was introduced to the new Ladies – Slim, Scoones and Christison, and their daughters, and much wished I could have had Edwina, Patricia and Pamela with me for the ceremony. The only one without relations present was Monty Stopford, whose wife is at home. He had telegraphed to her: 'Have been trying to make a lady of you for 22 years. Have today succeeded!'

SATURDAY, 16 DECEMBER [Kalewa. 11th East African Division]   At 0830 I was introduced to some 60 officers of the Headquarters staff, including some old friends from the Special Boat Section of the Commandos, who have been doing a grand job on the Chindwin.

At 0900 I inspected the African other ranks, and then addressed the British officers and other ranks.

At 0915 I left by jeep and crossed the main river Chindwin, over the newly constructed Bailey Pontoon bridge, which is, I believe, the longest Bailey bridge in the world, being 1152 feet long. The pontoons took about 200 lorry-loads, along impossibly difficult tracks, over miles of rough country. It had only been completed three days previously and no sooner had it been finished than the Japs came and attacked it with six aircraft. Three of them were shot down by the anti-aircraft guns; a very fine effort, for which I was later able to congratulate some of the crews.

On the east bank of the Chindwin I addressed some of the British units attached to the 11th East African Division, and a battalion of the Royal Berkshires belonging to the 2nd Division, who were about to embark in DUKWs. I then watched the unusual sight of some 16 great DUKWs, each crammed full of British soldiers, waddling down the sloping banks of the Chindwin, then plunging into the swift flowing stream and setting off in single line ahead down the river. At 1000 I walked down to 'Grub Bridge' (as the Chindwin Bridge is called) and watched them ferrying tanks down the river on large rafts made of pontoons; a remarkable feat.

At 1100 we arrived at Kyawzin airstrip, where I met and talked to pilots of the American light aircraft liaison squadron attached to one of the US Air Commandos. These pilots do a grand job ferrying our wounded out, and I saw them loading wounded into their aircraft. I saw a notice inside the cockpit of one of these aircraft saying: 'This aircraft will not be spun when there is a stretcher case on board.'!

At 1120 we left in our L.5s and flew low down over the Chindwin and the road to Shewygin. Beneath us was a most inspiring sight – an army in hot pursuit of a beaten enemy. The 2nd British Division were in process of passing through the 11th East Africans. Down the river Chindwin an endless stream of DUKWs and other craft were carrying soldiers; along the track on the river bank lorries and motor vehicles of all types were ploughing on in an endless stream like the traffic leading to Epsom on Derby Day. Alongside them marched the Infantry in single file, interspersed with mule trains.

It is just one vast forward surge, and one of the most exhilarating sights I have ever seen. We flew back down Myittha Gorge as far as Kalemyo, and then by the Kabaw Valley to Yazagyo, which we reached at 1215. Monty Stopford and his staff met us and drove us to his Headquarters, where we had a conference and a discussion on the tactical situation. He then gave us lunch.

George Crosbie, the DDMS of 33rd Corps (who was at Christ's with me), told me of the great success of our DDT spraying. We had made the most malarial district in Burma, the notorious Kabaw Valley, into a reasonably healthy and safe place for our troops to operate in. The Japs had died like flies in this valley. The medical advisory division which I set up in September 1943 are paying me rich dividends.

We left Yazagyo at 1415 in the Sister Anne, landing at 1500 at Imphal, where I held a conference on the airstrip with the Army Commander, Slim. We went carefully through the tactical situation, which was most encouraging. At 1600 we re-embarked in the Sister Anne and flew up the Manipur Road to Dimapur, which we reached at 1700. We set off right away in jeeps, but it took some two hours to reach Kohima, as half the drive was in the dark. I dined with the senior officers of the 7th Divisional Headquarters, where we are staying.

SUNDAY, 17 DECEMBER   At 1230 we arrived at General Warren's mess,[1] where I met his staff. During lunch the pipe band of the 4th Battalion of the Jammu and Kashmir infantry (loaned to SEAC by Hari Singh[2]) played some excellent selections. When I went out to thank and congratulate the Pipe Major in Urdu, he staggered me by saluting and

---

[1] Major General Warren was commanding the 5th Indian Division.
[2] The Maharaja of Kashmir.

saying to me, in very curious English: 'Jolly good fellow!' I thought this a bit patronizing, until I discovered that the band were breaking into the tune 'For he's a jolly good fellow', which sounds extremely weird on the pipes.

At 1400 we left by jeep and drove back to Kohima. At 1530 we visited all the memorials which had been put up on the battlefields. I must say they are very nice and simple, and very moving. The whole of the District Commissioner's bungalow grounds have been turned into a vast cemetery, where row upon row of graves stand. Boy had promised to send Willie Goschen's sister a photograph of his grave. It was of course uniform with all those of his men, surmounted by a plain white cross with 'Brig. W. Goschen, Grenadier Guards' stencilled across it.

One of the nicest memorials was a joint memorial shared by the Queen's Regiment and a Gurkha regiment, who charged together, and fell in almost equal numbers, side by side. Their names are on one large slab. But the most impressive is that of the 2nd British Division, the inscription on which runs as follows:

> When you go home, tell them of us, and say for their tomorrow we gave our today.'[1]

At 1030 I attended a demonstration by Lieutenant Colonel Grant Taylor. He is a most extraordinary man, who looks like a rather prosperous country parson, but in fact is probably the greatest British gunman. For 8 years he was the British representative with the FBI and spent most of his time in tracking gunmen in Chicago. He took part in the killing of Dillinger, and is bringing a new technique and enthusiasm to our troops for killing men at ranges from 15 yards and less, with revolver, automatic and sub-machine gun.

At this demonstration he was passing out a class of officers and men after a five-day intensive course in which they learn to become instructors for their own units. The most impressive item was where the candidate comes into a room, or large dugout, in which there are six of the enemy. Until he enters, he does not know the shape of the room, the number of the enemy or where they will be. In this case one was put high up, representing a man coming down stairs, another one was lying down horizontally, and four others were gathered in different positions

[1] There has been much debate over the origins of this epitaph. Once thought to be derived from a Spartan text, it was finally decided to be the work of J. M. Edmonds in about 1916. The word 'their' should have read 'your', and an amended plaque was erected in 1963.

around the room. The soldier has to enter, select a position from which to do his killing, and then kill each man with a slug through vital parts, represented by a target 12 inches by 16 inches in the centre of the human figure. The bull's-eye is an oblong about two inches by three inches long. After opening the door, the soldier has to advance some 8 paces to reach the most convenient position from which to fire.

A young Gurkha soldier killed all six men, four of them through the bull's-eye, in 6½ seconds from entering the room. The day before a man had done it in 5½ seconds.

MONDAY, 18 DECEMBER   At 0815, Boy Browning and I had a half an hour's lesson in 'close quarter battle' from Grant Taylor, which was really very thrilling. He taught us how to shoot from the hip, and it is surprising how accurately you can hit the bull's-eye after a little practice, if the range is not too great.

At 0845 we drove to the little airstrip where a parade of the representatives of all units of the 7th Indian Division was drawn up. As I was presenting the ribbon of the Burma Gallantry Medal to one of the Burma Rifles, I turned to the CO and said: 'This man received the same ribbon from the Viceroy two days ago; why have you brought him up again today?' The CO blushed crimson, and appeared covered with confusion, as he replied: 'None of this man's regiment was at Imphal and we were so keen that he should be decorated in front of his comrades that I put him in again. I'm afraid we never thought there was a chance of you noticing!'

By 1500 we were airborne in the Sister Anne and at 1640 landed at Chiringa airfield where Air Commodore the Earl of Bandon, AOC 224 Group, met me. I like Paddy Bandon a lot, and he is a great fighter and a grand pilot, but typically light-hearted. He had not read the instructions on how I like my visits to be carried out, with the result that he had some 1200 RAF officers and men on parade, fallen in by squadrons, which completely wrecked my usual method of dealing with the situation.

At 1730 we left again and landed at Cox's Bazaar, where Sir Philip Christison, Commander of the 15th Corps, met me. This Corps has been taken out of the 14th Army, and is now directly under Oliver Leese.

The whole morale problem of how to build up the prestige of the various units has now got to be faced up to. Only about a month ago every British, Indian or African (other than 36 Division) fighting in

Burma belonged to the 14th Army. Now less than half of those in Burma still belong to the 14th Army. The only communal name for all our troops fighting in Burma now is 'SEAC' and we shall have to try to build up this name instead of the 14th Army in future. It only took 15 minutes to drive to the main Headquarters of the 15th Corps at Cox's Bazaar, and I immediately had an hour's conference with Christy in his Operations Room.

WEDNESDAY, 20 DECEMBER   At 0730 I inspected the entire 3rd Special Service Brigade on parade. When they marched off the band played such a slow cadence that it was almost impossible for the men to keep time, which rather spoilt the effect.

At 0845 I left by jeep and suddenly came across a detachment of about 40 American paratroopers dressed for battle and fallen in in the jungle. I stopped to find out what they were doing and discovered they were some of Bill Donovan's crowd, so I inspected them and gave them an address.[1]

I finally reached the Teknaaf jetty at 0900 and embarked in a motor launch commanded by a South African. I proceeded across the Naaf river to Maungdaw, which we reached at 0930. The change in this place between the wreckage I last saw and the flourishing little port with ships, lighters, etc., all working hard, was quite remarkable.

At 1010 I reached the Headquarters of the 25th Indian Division where the new Divisional Commander, Sam Wood, met me. He introduced me to the senior officers of his staff and then took me to his Ops Room to explain the very encouraging situation in which the division found themselves. He promised to reach Donbaik at the tip of the Mayu Peninsula by the end of the week (and kept his promise). His Headquarters are in Razabil and he took me over to address representatives of his division in the same place as I had seen their representatives before some months ago and which had in consequence been christened 'Mountbatten Copse'.

At 1050 we left by jeep to visit the Headquarters of the 51st Indian Infantry Brigade where I was met by the officiating Brigade Commander, Lieutenant Colonel Thimaya.[2] This Brigade is making history for the Indian Army. It is the first time there has been a Brigade

---

[1] William 'Wild Bill' Donovan was founder of the OSS, the American intelligence service.
[2] Colonel Thimaya went on to become Chief of Staff of the Indian Army.

consisting entirely of Indian Battalions, each commanded by Indian COs, and the whole Brigade commanded by an officiating Indian Brigade Commander. He has been doing remarkably well in the current operations. He and his COs all gathered around Boy Browning, who had been one of their instructors at Sandhurst.

After light refreshments, I said goodbye to Sam Wood and at 1145 reached the Headquarters of the 82nd West African Division, where I met Major General Bruce, a tall and fiery Canadian from the Lincolnshire Regiment.

At 1230 we came to the first big chaung but this had been crossed by a Bailey Bridge which had been built during the night and which was being completed as we drove up. Ten minutes later we came to an unbridged chaung which had some planks across it. I have since heard that the Japanese have been laying planks across chaungs and putting land mines under the planks so that the first jeep that goes over them blows up. However, they evidently had not had time to put land mines under these planks as we got over in safety. A few hundred yards further along we came to another chaung where there were no planks, but our bodyguard of some 20 West African soldiers pushed the jeeps through the mud and water with much splashing, noise and laughter.

At 1245 we got to a third muddy chaung, which was much more difficult to cross, and in fact our own jeep stuck in it, and it was only with the greatest difficulty that it was pushed and carried through. We therefore decided that none of the rest of the jeeps should follow. This meant dispensing with the African bodyguard but Boy Browning took the loaded rifle of one African, the 15th Corps Staff Officer had a tommy gun, Bruce an ivory-handled pistol, and I had an automatic, so off we set to try to and find the Front.

As we drove along Bruce said to me: 'They have probably left some booby-traps and mines on this road, as we have not had time to clear it yet. Please keep a good look out on the road.' Five minutes later he said: 'Do you see those foothills on the left? Yesterday they were full of Japanese snipers; I don't know whether we have managed to clear the hills yet, so keep an eye open for snipers.' At this, I suggested we should take off our hats and remove the flags from the car so that we should look less conspicuous. To this he readily agreed.

He was without exception the most dangerous and fiery driver I have ever driven with. There was no proper track; we constantly had to cross small chaungs and banks. His method of negotiating these was to go into four-wheel drive, double reduction gear, and then go as hard as possible at the obstacle. Having practically thrown us out of the jeep at the first obstacle we refused to sit in the jeep when he was negotiating subsequent ones. One of us used to guide him if it meant going off the narrow track but after he had nearly run down Boy we refused to guide him any more and left him to his own devices. When we got back into the jeep he frequently started off before we had sat down so that we all fell over backwards. He had not been able to find out where the Front was that morning and I began to wonder whether we should find the Japanese lines before our own, since warfare here is very open and fluid, and the Front is moving rapidly.

Finally we came to two British doctors, both very blood-stained and one heavily bandaged, standing in the road, so we stopped and Bruce asked what had happened. They said they were under mortar fire and had had their Advanced Dressing Station hit, to which Bruce replied: 'More fool you for putting your Advanced Dressing Station in a silly place. However, let's go and see what has happened.' So we all scrambled out.

Three of their very precious British personnel had been killed and a number of Africans.

I climbed up to the Command Post of the front-line Battalion, and saw a Japanese machine gun they had captured a night before. Below us to the left we could see the Japanese positions from which they were withdrawing, and to the right there were fires, presumably from the dumps they were burning as they retreated from Kinduang.

FRIDAY, 22 DECEMBER to THURSDAY, 28 DECEMBER [Kandy]. On Sunday [Prince] Philip [Mountbatten] arrived, as he had 48 hours' leave over Christmas. I took him and Boy Browning to a small Christmas Eve party given by Janey at her bungalow at Yahalatenne. It seems strange to think that it is a year ago since Bunnie and I attended her Christmas Eve party at Meerut.

The cook had gone mad, and started roasting the turkey a couple of hours too late; so we had an inverted dinner, with the sweet, savoury, fruit, coffee and cigars before the turkey!

I spent Christmas Day going round from one mess to another, making speeches and drinking toasts, and lunched again, as on last Christmas Day, in the Wrennery.

Christmas festivities out here are greatly enlivened by a liberal use of elephants. Every mess I went to appeared to have at least one large elephant outside and one small elephant inside. At the Wrennery, in fact, I went for a ride on one of the elephants, surrounded by Wrens.

Philip Joubert arranged the Christmas festivities for the Men's Hospital in Katugastota, which included a procession, with the inevitable elephants and buffaloes. An elephant misbehaved itself at the front door in a notable manner; one of the buffaloes kicked a nurse in the stomach, so that she retired to bed as a patient.

On Christmas night, the British Officers' Mess in A.1 Camp threw a most colossal party, to which they invited the messes from all the other camps, Navy, Army, Air Force, civilians; male, female, British, American, French, Dutch, Chinese, including the various Secret Services. I have never seen such a gathering nor heard so many different languages spoken at one party.

I went meaning to stay half an hour for two or three official dances, but was finally swept out at midnight. It really went extremely well, and was very gay and light-hearted, without any of the usual signs of Christmas inebriation. There is a grand *esprit de corps* throughout the SEAC Headquarters in Kandy; in spite of the high pressure at which we have to work (or perhaps because of it).

MONDAY, 1 JANUARY to TUESDAY, 9 JANUARY 1945   On 2nd January the departing Commander-in-Chief, Ceylon, H.E. Admiral Sir Geoffrey Layton, and his successor, Lieutenant General Wetherall, came to lunch with me at the King's Pavilion. The Guards of Honour were a difficult thing to arrange because I wanted Weatherall to receive a guard on arrival as the new C.-in-C., and Layton one on departure as the outgoing C.-in-C.

I shall miss Geoffrey Layton, who has been a most loyal friend and supporter. I wish sometimes he would not give 'bridge' decisions without weighing up all matters first, but this is a failing that many fighting Admirals have.

Curiously enough, the decision which is causing me the worst headache is the one by which he ordered that all WAAF personnel should be allowed to wear plain clothes when off duty, in the same way as the WRNS. This has caused a storm of protest from Air Command, who do not like unilateral orders given in one area of their command by the local Commander-in-Chief. It has gone to my Chiefs of Staff's Committee, which did not prove to be a sufficiently high level. It was also no good taking it at a meeting with the Commanders-in-Chief's representatives and I finally had to put it on the agenda for our next operational meeting with all three Commanders-in-Chief in person, and after discussing plans for Akyab and Ramree the third item was women's clothes!

The 9th was a very busy day. Oliver Leese flew down from Calcutta. Power came up from Colombo, Garrod and Wheeler were of course here, and we spent most of the day having meetings with the Commanders-in-Chief, at the end of which I decided to send Boy Browning home to London to represent a certain matter to the Chiefs of Staff.[1]

WEDNESDAY, 10 JANUARY I left in the special train at 0805 for Colombo, accompanied by Flags. We changed in the train into white tunics and on arrival I went straight to the Queen's House, where I met Harry and Alice Gloucester.[2]

I had known for many months that they were coming and had invited them while in London last August to come and stay in Kandy. I had been informed by Harry that they were arriving during the first week of January and had made all my plans accordingly. Then came a telegram to say that they would arrive on the 9th January and stay with me until the 11th. This was very awkward, as I had arranged to leave on the 10th to open up Advanced Headquarters in Calcutta to direct the combined operation against Akyab from there. However, the crumbling of Jap resistance meant that a full-scale assault did not have to be mounted, and it became unnecessary and even undesirable for me to move the Advanced Headquarters to Calcutta. Thus the Gloucester situation was eased once more.

Then came a telegram to say that the Admiralty had made a mistake in calculating the speed of their liner and they would not arrive until the 10th, and would have to go on the same day. (This reminds me of the mistake the Admiralty made in laying out the Prince of Wales's tour in 1920 to Australia, when they forgot that one loses 24 hours on crossing the 180th Meridian from east to west.)

I cancelled the arrangements I had made for the Gloucesters in Kandy and was thus able to arrange the urgent meeting with the

---

[1] Probably Wedemeyer's recommendation that the Chinese Army in India and Burma should return to its homeland. This complicated matters for the 14th Army in its advance on Mandalay.

[2] The Duke of Gloucester was on his way to Australia to take over as Governor General.

Commanders-in-Chief which has already been described, for January 9th. Then came a telegram to say they were arriving at 7 o'clock on the 9th and not leaving until the 11th. This was assumed to be 7 a.m. and caused the most terrible excitement, as I could not put off my Commanders-in-Chief's meeting. However, it finally turned out to be 7 p.m. and so it was agreed that I should go down and spend the day with them in Colombo.

On arrival at Queen's House I was shown the children. William, the eldest son, has grown tremendously since I saw him last at Barnwell, and I was introduced to the latest member of the family, who I must say looks very sweet.[1]

At 1200 there was an official sherry party for Ceylonese dignitaries, whom I met for the first time. Several of them said, rather sourly: 'We had begun to think you were a myth, as none of us ever met you', to which I replied: 'Socially you can continue to regard me as a myth, as I am only out here on a war job.'

After lunch we had arranged to take the Gloucesters down for a picnic and bathe at Bentota, which is about 40 miles south of Colombo on the road to Galle. I drove them in my Cadillac, and we three sat in front, with William on Alice's knee. Just as the door of the car was slammed, Alice shouted out: 'Look out, his fingers are in the door.' There was a terrible moment when we all thought his fingers had been cut off and he started to howl; but it transpired that they had fortunately been missed by a fraction of an inch.

THURSDAY, 11 JANUARY   At 0700 the Gloucesters' ship, the SS *Rimutaka*, sailed for Australia. Flags and I drove out to Ratmalana and took off in the York at 0750. We flew over the mountains to Kandy and then went down to inspect the new site for the proposed SEAC airstrip, finally landing at China Bay at 0900. By my decision, the RAF Station at China Bay has now been turned over to the Navy under the title of Royal Navy Air Station, Trincomalee (HMS *Bambara*).

I should explain that I had been invited to visit the British Pacific Fleet on the eve of their departure to the Pacific. They were due to carry out one more operation in my theatre and then go on.

The curious thing is that when I first came out in October 1943 and the whole of the Fleet was in the South-East Asia Command, with no

---

[1] Prince Richard, now himself Duke of Gloucester, had been born the previous year.

proposal that it should leave, all attempts on my part to visit the Fleet were sabotaged by James Somerville.

It was only through Admiral King inviting me by telegram to visit the US aircraft carrier *Saratoga* while she was with the Eastern Fleet that I first gate-crashed into the Fleet and this was followed by an invitation to visit the battleship *Richelieu* from the French. In fact, it was only at the very end of James Somerville's time that it was made possible for me to go on board any British ships at all.

Of course, with the advent of Bruce Fraser and Arthur Power, all this was changed and from the beginning they extended the most warm and friendly invitations for me to visit the Fleet, and it was my intention to do so once it was clear which ships were going to the Pacific and which ships were going to remain in the East Indies Fleet. Judge then of my astonishment when I received an invitation from Power to visit the Pacific Fleet before they left, since these were precisely the ships which were passing out of my command. I tactfully declined and thereupon Philip Vian, who was at that time in command of the Fleet, wrote and pressed me. Even then I felt chary, until Admiral Rawlings, the actual commander, who was visiting Kandy, added his pressure. I finally accepted and must say I have never had a better or more thrilling day.

From 0915 to 1900 I went round solidly from ship to ship – battleships, aircraft carriers, cruisers and destroyers. The party included no less that four fleet carriers, the greatest number I have ever seen together in one harbour. I was given lunch in one of the battleships by Philip Vian who had been human enough to transfer his dinner in the evening to the *Illustrious*, although his flag was flying in another carrier.[1] Here all the Flag Officers and Captains of the British Pacific Fleet were invited to dinner and it was a very cheery party. Boy Browning,[2] who had come up from Kandy to meet me in the evening, also came to dinner in the *Illustrious* as well as Philip.

I was very thrilled to go on board the *Indefatigable*, which Mama launched what seemed to me to be such a short while ago on the Clyde. The Captain showed me the lovely silver bowl she had given the ship and promised to send photographs of my visit for her.

I had made a special point of going on board Philip's ship, the *Whelp*, and meeting all his officers and having a look at his cabin,

---

[1] Presumably in view of the fact that Mountbatten had once been set to command *Illustrious*.

[2] General Browning in 1948 became Comptroller to Princess Elizabeth and the Duke of Edinburgh.

wardroom and bridge, etc. They have had a very exciting time towing back a damaged submarine, which had been constantly attacked by the Japanese.

I must have talked to over 12,000 sailors in the course of the day and shaken hands with hundreds of officers and selected men, but it was a great thrill being back with the Fleet and I felt very homesick, particularly, of course, on board the old *Illustrious*.

FRIDAY, 12 JANUARY   We landed at 0700 at Palam, New Delhi. I was driven straight to the Viceroy's House, where I found Edwina, who had arrived the night before from England, via Karachi, where she had spent a couple of days visiting hospitals, etc.

It was really lovely seeing her again and finding her in such good form. I had hoped to have two days' rest in Delhi with her, followed by two days' holiday with her in Jaipur. It will be seen that Fate decreed otherwise.

At 1630 I picked up Edwina and drove her in a jeep to the old Viceregal Lodge (which is now a university) in Old Delhi, where we went, hand in hand, to visit the room in which we got engaged 23 years ago, next month. We then went and looked at the little pavilion which had been built for David[1] and looked in at his sitting room, to which he had given us a special key. We got back about 1830, when Edwina had to go round various welfare centres and clubs and I went to the cocktail party given by Air Marshal Hollinghurst.

SATURDAY, 13 JANUARY   This morning the bearer, whom Major Brian Hunter had engaged with so much care for Edwina, gave notice. He had looked after the Viceroy's daughter and had been engaged by me for two months and had been supplied with two complete sets of khaki uniform. However, having taken one look at Edwina, he threw in his hand and so all Delhi had to be combed today to find another one. When ordered to return the cheque he had received the night before for an advance of wages, he protested violently that he was a poor man.

I went to the Old Fort, Delhi, to see CSDIC (Combined Services Detention Interrogation Centre). I must say it was most interesting to see how we handle the various Japanese prisoners of war that are being detained for interrogation.

[1] The Prince of Wales, later King Edward VIII and Duke of Windsor.

To begin with, it is astounding the way in which they readily, and indeed willingly, and almost enthusiastically, give away information on any point about which they are asked. Only the naval prisoners show any sign of reticence.

It appears that they can in no circumstances bear solitary confinement. 24 hours is enough to reduce the strongest Japanese to tears. Indeed, when a Jap has given away some particularly important information and it is desired to protect him from possible retribution at the hands of his fellow prisoners (to whom he is almost certain to confess), it is the custom to separate him from the remaining prisoners, in his own interests. There is no known case of their being able to stand more than a fortnight of this without going almost off their heads, so this presents quite a problem.

I came into one interrogation cell to find the interrogator, a very worthy Oxford don disguised as an Army Captain, red with excitement and emotion. He could hardly wait to say to me: 'Sir, this man has just voluntarily confessed that his platoon was in charge of some 300 British prisoners of war engaged on the building of the railway line from Bangkok to Thanbyuzayat. He states that on an average 120 prisoners of war were flogged a day, many of them so badly that they had to be taken away on stretchers and were useless for further work. He gleefully admits that they were even beaten for no reason at all, other than that their guards did not like their faces!'

When I went into this case further, I found that a Japanese officer had gone so far as to make a gramophone record of a confession, in the first person singular, of inflicting brutalities on British prisoners of war. What their object can be in making these voluntary confessions which, had the cases been reversed, would have involved their probably being flogged to death, I cannot imagine.

I came across one class of Japanese learning basic English with great enthusiasm. It is interesting to note that most of the prisoners assume that they could never go back to Japan and in many cases their ambition is to become Honourable Members of Honourable British Empire.

Many of the more senior officers try to pretend that they are private soldiers. They are dealt with in a very simple way, by being made the batmen of the junior Japanese officers. Altogether, a most interesting morning.

I asked for a return of prisoners, month by month, from December, 1941, to the time when I took over command. The monthly figures were put down with unfailing regularity as 'o', 'o', 'o', ending up with the words 'Total: o'. We have now about a thousand, although even this figure is not much when you compare it with 55,000 killed and over 80,000 wounded, which is our score for 1944.

Although I was clear by 1700, Edwina did not get out of her meeting with Lady Wavell until 1730. This gave us just time for a quick run round in the jeep and we visited some of our old haunts like Humayun's Tomb, which we last saw by moonlight in 1922. We attended a cocktail party given for us by the senior members of Rear Headquarters and later on Edwina and I went quietly to dine at Maidens Hotel, almost the first time we had had a quiet chance of seeing each other, owing to the amount of appointments we have both had to keep.

SUNDAY, 14 JANUARY   At 1500 Edwina and I took off in the Hapgift. At 1600 we landed at Jaipur airfield, where the Maharaja and Maharani met us. We drove to the Palace outside the town. This is very lovely and on the whole in good taste. Of course Jai[1] is very Europeanized, having spent so much of his time in England playing polo. He has been for some years a Captain in the Life Guards and served with the Regiment in London in peacetime and in the Middle East during the war.

He has invited me on several occasions to come and stay and promised that we would have a complete rest and holiday; he would make no arrangements for our entertainment, or engagements of any type. Edwina and I thus looked forward to a quiet time together.

Although Jai undoubtedly refrained from giving the impression that he had made any arrangements, it transpired that in fact he must have had a pretty closely worked out programme in the back of his mind. After tea we visited the city and the city Palace. This was most interesting, as Jaipur City is probably the most beautiful in the whole of India. A Maharaja some 200 years ago had ideas so modern and dashing as to be far ahead of anything which had been done in India in subsequent years. The city is really beautifully laid out, with wide rectangular streets and properly designed façades linking up all the houses and shops.

Of particular interest was the original Jantar Mantar, the smaller copy of which I had shown Edwina in Delhi the day before.[2] This one

---

[1] The Maharaja of Jaipur.
[2] Largest of the five great astronomical observatories built by Jay Singh.

was enormous and beautifully laid out and looked as though it had been designed in 1950 instead of in 1710.

I found that Jai knew absolutely nothing about the astronomical uses of the various erections, and I was able to guess how they operated better than their present owner.

The pictures and early Persian manuscripts in the Palace Library are quite fascinating. It is clear that Jaipur is really a richer state than Rampur, but Jai has been sufficiently Europeanized not to wish to display all his riches and wares, and even the ones he showed us were faintly under protest.

MONDAY, 15 JANUARY   Edwina and I tried vainly to sunbathe, but what with telephone calls from Delhi, telegrams from the Mercury and Jai hovering about, obviously wanting to get us started, we finally resigned ourselves to getting dressed and joining him and Ayesha in their lovely Rolls-Bentley. We went off into the town to the Maharaja's stables, to see his polo ponies. A shamiana[1] had been erected at the head of the riding school and 72 beautiful ponies were led past. We also saw the polo grounds, which must be two of the best anywhere in the world. Polo had been played up to the day before, but with the move of the Cavalry to their training camp it had been stopped. Jai's three sons were playing bicycle polo with friends. As the eldest must be at least 12 years old and Ayesha can hardly be more than 20, we were very puzzled as to the relationship. I later discovered from the Prime Minister that the two eldest sons are by a first wife, now dead, and the third son from a second wife who is living in the same palace as we are, but in purdah; and that Ayesha herself has not yet had any children.

We next drove some 20 miles from the town to a big lake, or tank, as they are called out here, on the edge of which a very modern dashing country house had been built quite recently by Jai.

After lunch we went out in a motor boat on the tank to shoot crocodiles. I politely refused and asked to be allowed to steer the boat while Jai took a shot at about seven of them, all of them slipping back into the water, some of them possibly dead. I must say a crocodile shoot is very fascinating, as one can often get quite close to these great ungainly creatures before they slip into the water. We ran aground once, but Jai's ADC with great gallantry got out and shoved us off again.

[1] A large, richly decorated marquee used for ceremonial purposes.

While we were out after crocodile, another boat came out, with much shouting and gesticulation and Jai said, 'Come on, I have a tiger for you.' It then transpired that they had a tiger shoot arranged and that a tiger had just been located at the kill. I was very firm and refused categorically to shoot a tiger, as I feared that there might be a leakage to the Press and it would indeed be bad if it were thought that I was busy shooting tigers while my troops were busy shooting Japs at the Front. However, I agreed to accompany the party and off we went to the other side of the tank. All the ladies, except Edwina and Ayesha, went the last part of the trip on howdah elephants.

Jai, Ayesha, Edwina and I climbed into a machan[1] half-way up the side of the hill. Here a further dispute took place, as they wanted Edwina to shoot the tiger, which she also very wisely refused to do. Finally it was left to Ayesha, backed up by Jai. I found the beating of the jungle as fascinating as ever, as one gets that eerie feeling when the whole jungle starts to move towards you. A great sambhur broke out just above us and other game broke out below us. Finally the tiger himself appeared at the edge of the clearing, but refused to come out and wandered backwards and forwards in front of us until finally he appeared almost immediately under our machan. He was unfortunately not killed by the first or the second shot, and I must say it is unpleasant to see even a beast of prey like a tiger in its death agonies, and I cannot understand these tiger record hunters like the old Maharaja of Bikaner, who shot over 200 without having a single tiger in his state. I am even told that one minor native Prince shot over 2000 in his lifetime – one a day for nearly six years!

We did not get back until after 1800 and during tea I discovered that I was expected to go and visit the Barracks of the Jaipur State Forces, whilst Edwina was expected to go and visit a hospital; so much for our holiday!

TUESDAY, 16 JANUARY   I took off in the Hapgift. We landed at 1745 at Myitkyina South airfield. General Cannon met me, and drove me to General Sultan's house. I must say I was immensely impressed by the terrific development which the Americans have done at Myitkyina since I last saw it. There are now two enormous airfields with pipe lines delivering petrol direct from India down the Ledo Road. The air traffic is busier than La Guardia airfield ever was in peacetime. Many of the

---

[1] A raised platform.

houses have been rebuilt and vast supply dumps have been erected everywhere.

I arrived at D.I.'s house almost simultaneously with himself and Al Wedemeyer, who had been visiting forward areas at Namkhan. Al and I fell on each other's neck, after which I ticked him off for daring to come into my theatre without previously informing me.

We talked from 6 o'clock to practically midnight and cleared up a great many misunderstandings and difficulties.[1]

WEDNESDAY, 17 JANUARY   After breakfast with D.I. and Al, the former drove me down to the airfield. We flew off at 0800, landing at Akyab at 1215, where Sir Philip Christison and various staff officers met me. I had not seen Akyab since I had last flown over it in a Mosquito in December 1943.

I was intensely interested to see the beaches and their defences across which we would have had to do an opposed assault if the Japanese garrison had not pulled out a day or two before we came in. They would certainly have been quite tough propositions. I was thrilled to see that the Beach Group was handling more supplies from the landing craft across the beaches that day than the civil port of Akyab used to handle a day in peacetime.

I went to the Tactical Headquarters of 15th Corps for lunch and after lunch I had a meeting with the Force Commanders, when we discussed future operations, including the assault on Ramree. At 1500 we went back to the airfield, where I congratulated three pilots who between them had shot down five out of six enemy fighters which came over Akyab the day after the Spitfire squadron had been installed.

We then took off in a Sea Otter, which is merely the old Naval Walrus Amphibian converted to air-sea rescue work by the RAF. We took off on wheels and then flew over Baronga Island, and landed as a flying boat in Hunter's Bay after half an hour's flight. We were then taken ashore in an LCP and landed at the 'follow-up' beach on the Myebon Peninsula.

We visited the beach on which the actual assault was carried out, which was further to the east. It was strongly defended and it is almost a miracle that the Commandos had only four killed in the assault, particularly as they themselves buried 95 Japs. I feel it was largely due to

[1] Many more remained; notably about the division of responsibilities in Siam and French Indochina.

the heavy naval and air bombardment which caused the Japanese to get to their shelters, as three 37mm guns were captured intact. We then drove on in a jeep towards the Front. We got to within about 3000 yards of the enemy, against whom the Gurkhas were at that time in action, when we had unfortunately to go back because there are no night flying facilities on Akyab and it was getting late.

THURSDAY, 18 JANUARY   We took off from Akyab airfield at 0900 and flew to Htizwe airstrip well to the north of Akyab. Here I was met by Major General Hugh Stockwell who had just taken over the 82nd West African Division from General Bruce.

It will be recalled that during my last visit General Bruce had taken Boy Browning and me for a most dangerous jeep ride in search of the fast-moving Front, in which he kept saying, 'I hope we run into our own forces and not the Japanese.' Luckily for us, we ran into our own forces. I was now to learn that my new Deputy Chief of Staff, Major General Horace Fuller, had not been so lucky. He had spent Christmas Day with General Bruce and so far as I can make out much the same occurred as with me. They started off with a large convoy of jeeps, containing a strong bodyguard. They ended up with the two Generals and three staff officers in one jeep. This time they ran straight into the Japanese front line and the first thing they knew about it was when a machine gun opened up on them. They all jumped out of the jeep in record time. The problem was then what to do. They were cut off without any hope of getting help. However, General Bruce, who is the stuff of which VCs are made, leaped back into the jeep in order to turn it round. Needless to say it would not start. Bullets whistled all round him but luckily at the third attempt the jeep started and he was able to turn it round.

Meanwhile General Fuller was directing operations in the field. He disposed his British staff officer on the left flank, his American staff officer on his right flank and the 15th Corps Liaison Officer in the centre, to avoid the jeep being surrounded. They then had to crawl on their hands and knees through a paddy field back to where the jeep had been driven. They leaped in and drove off to safety and it was only then that they turned round and discovered that they had left General Fuller behind. A counterattack had to be staged. Firing their ivory-handled revolvers and tommy guns, the party charged back at the Japanese and retrieved General Fuller, who, at the age of 58, had not been able to crawl quite as quickly as the staff officers.

When they ran into their first party of African troops on their way back, General Bruce, greatly excited, stood up and made them a speech in Hausa, to the following effect: 'On this festive day, you will be pleased to hear that I, your General, have been engaged in hand-to-hand combat with the Japanese. We have come off victoriously.'

Wild and enthusiastic cheers followed from the Africans, who clustered round and started trying to pull General Fuller out of the jeep. It was only then discovered that the Africans understood that poor old Horace Fuller was a Japanese General whom their General, Bruce, had gallantly captured for them as a Christmas present, and they were about to take delivery of him with glee.

There was considerable difficulty in persuading the Africans to realize that, far from being an enemy, General Fuller was a highly placed and highly valued ally. Finally, the two Generals had to shake hands in public in the jeep to try and convince the Africans that they were on the same side.

General Bruce has now succumbed to an in-growing toenail which has put him on the sick list and so Hugh Stockwell has taken over and it is possible to visit his Front in greater safety! I can hardly imagine a better Divisional Commander than the latter.

SATURDAY, 20 JANUARY [Hladaw. 2nd Division Headquarters] Cam Nicholson took me at 0800 in his command car to visit the forward areas. At 0900 we got to the Headquarters of the 4th Infantry Brigade, which was at Sadaung. Most Headquarters are in pongyi chaungs, as the compounds are called in which all the pagodas and shrines are erected, since the local priests or pongyis live all round them. They usually have plenty of trees planted there to give good shade, and these provide the ideal cover for a Headquarters.

I went into one of the shrines, which was really rather beautiful, and had a photograph taken of the Buddha idol inside, as I thought it was so lovely.

After talking to the Headquarters of this Brigade, we drove on to some high ground some miles northwest of Mandalay. The town itself of course is hidden by a range of foothills about 1000 to 1400 feet high, but the outskirts of Sagaing can just be made out.

Any idea that the Japanese are not putting up quite a tough rearguard action should be dismissed. It is only that as we have got tanks forward we are usually able to force them to withdraw far sooner than was possible in the days when we were fighting in the mountains and could not get tanks up.

The 2nd Division, for example, has only had 24 killed, but have buried 235 Japs in their recent advance.

On the way back I addressed the 1st Battalion Royal Scots, then went on to meet representatives of the 6th Brigade. All three Brigade Commanders are of course new, since I originally visited this Division, as their predecessors were killed or wounded at Kohima.

We landed at Barrackpore airfield, Calcutta, at 1800, where Oliver Leese met me, and drove me to his Mess at Flagstaff House. Here a conference had already been assembled, on my instructions.

At 2020 I had a meeting with Captain Ian Coster, Royal Marines, and Captain Maynard, US Army, the new co-editors of the *Phoenix*.

I must explain that there has been a minor tragedy about the *Phoenix*. I had originally intended to have one daily paper, *SEAC*, particularly for the British troops to give them accurate news and thus build up their morale. It has been a great success. Its circulation is already 35,000 (price being rather more than one penny a copy) and some 2000 copies are bought by the Americans.

However, I wanted to have a joint Anglo-American publication so as to bring the American and British forces closer together in this theatre. I thought a weekly picture magazine, on the *Life–Picture Post* model, would be the best. Everyone, even General Stilwell, agreed. Needless to say, the Americans produced their staff several months before the British were able to produce anybody, and the Americans got fed up with waiting and drafted their staff away, so that when the British staff became available they had no American colleagues.

As one has to prepare a magazine of this type at least three weeks ahead, they produced no less than three numbers which were all-British. There was alarm and despondency when I ordered 75,000 copies to be pulped and told them to start again. However, this Command could not run at all if people were at liberty to change my policy and subsequently blackmail me into agreeing to a *fait accompli*.

I ticked off Coster severely for having resigned and told him to get on with it with his new American colleague. I must say he took it very well and I am sure together they will produce a grand magazine.

TUESDAY, 30 JANUARY [Kandy]   I went down to Colombo in the special train, having breakfast on the way as usual.

At 1745 we landed at Poona where Edwina was waiting with the Governor of Bombay and Lady Colville and their daughter. The Colvilles had taken her up in their special train to carry out her programme in Poona.

We drove straight to Government House, where we had been given the rooms which were originally used by David when he and I were out there in 1921. After dinner I had a discussion with Edwina and Sir Cameron Badenoch, the Chief Commissioner of St John's in India, about the Red Cross and St John's Organization in Burma.

Edwina has had an extremely strenuous tour and seems to have killed off her staff. Miss Lees is in bed with a high temperature and will not be fit to go on to the Front with her, which will be a blow to them both. Brian Hunter has also collapsed (he said he had been stung by a Portuguese Man of War) and had only just recovered.

Major General Rankin, the Director of Medical Services for the Southern Army, who accompanied her for a fortnight round his hospitals, wrote her a letter of such eulogy that I can only suspect him of having fallen in love with her. It is wonderful having her here and she is going to have two complete rest days when we shall be able to spend a good bit of the time together.

WEDNESDAY, 31 JANUARY   I had arranged the morning's programme leaving at 0900, and was astounded to find that Edwina insisted on coming and doing part of the programme with me, and this on her rest day too! Eric Dunstan, the Officer in Charge of ENSA in the India and South-East Asia Commands, fetched us and drove us all round ENSA activities, including their workshops, office, and the hotel and theatre they wished to requisition. At 1000 Major General Beard, who now commands this area, met us and took us round the Bombay Docks, which have now been completely repaired after the explosion.

Edwina and I then went shopping, and she bought all the things she has not been able to get in England for several years, such as silk stockings, gloves, bags, scent, lipstick, shoes etc. etc.

After an early dinner we went with the Governor to see the opening night of George Formby's[1] shows for the troops. It was held in the open so that some 5000 troops were able to see the performance. Needless to say, it was a very great success. What a difference it makes getting these big stars out here to entertain the troops.

[1] Star of music hall and screen who sang to a ukulele.

After the show we went to the Taj Mahal Hotel to supper, but as it was not a late night we found the dining room in semi-darkness and had to content ourselves with eggs and bacon. Edwina was very content as she had three eggs, which is about a month's ration in England, at least she says so. The management refused to let me settle the bill.

THURSDAY, 1 FEBRUARY 1945 At 0900 I drove out to the Combined Operations Experimental Establishment at Marve, which is about three-quarters of an hour's run from Bombay. Here I carried out my usual type of visit, but also saw a number of interesting demonstrations.

They are woefully behind-hand with their experiments, and I shall have to take up the question of speeding everything up when I get back.

We finished at 1215 and met Edwina on the way back at Juhu Beach. The ADCs left us and we spent a delightful afternoon entirely alone. We bathed twice, ate a picnic lunch, and lay about on the sand; one of the most restful afternoons I have spent for a long while.

Edwina and I dined alone at the Ritz Hotel, in plain clothes. We sat next to a Sapper Major from the 5th Indian Division, who kept leaning across and joining in our conversation. He told us he was a Norwegian and this was his first leave for three years. All he wanted to do was to play golf, and he had been unable to get even one ball, although he had advertised in the papers and asked all his friends. I offered to send him a ball, and he told me that as he thought I had a nice honest face he would believe me; so I am arranging to send him two old balls when I get back.

FRIDAY, 2 FEBRUARY I had planned to leave punctually at 0900, but what with Edwina writing letters up to the last moment for me to take to send in my bag, and the Governor wishing to take a snapshot of us both and she being still in her dressing gown, it was not until 0920 that I got away. We drove at a very high speed to the airfield and had the level-crossing gates opened for us, and managed to get to the airfield only two minutes late at 0947.

We arrived at Cochin at 1315. I was really thrilled to see the developments, all of which had taken place since I arrived out here. It has been made into a great landing craft base and is nearing completion.

I spent an hour going round all the buildings and repair facilities, including a run round the harbour in a launch, but I did not address any of the men as it is my intention to come back here another time.

I was shown the theatre which had just been built by the Indian Army. As it was nearing completion they started to build a wall right across the stage in a position indicated on their plans, but which clearly would have prevented any performers from getting on to the stage (Basil Dean[1] tells me that this was an out-of-date plan drawn up for cinemas before they realized that they would also require live entertainment on the stage).

The Captain in command requested the Engineer Major not to continue building this wall as it would prevent the stage from being used by actors. The Sapper agreed, but said that he was powerless to order the work to be stopped and that the wall must be completely built. Once it was built he did not mind if it was taken down again.

The Navy then watched the soldiers build up this wall brick by brick, and when the last brick was put in place the same men proceeded to dismantle the same wall brick by brick, to the intense amusement of the sailors.

If the story had not been vouched for by a Captain RN and corroborated by the Officers standing round, and had I not seen the marks in the wall where the bricks had been taken away, I would not have believed that lunacy could reach such a pitch in the Indian Army.

We took off again at 1430 and landed at 1600 at Ratmalana. We came back at 1830 in the special train where I had my usual dinner party for the Senior Officers on board.

SATURDAY, 3 FEBRUARY to FRIDAY, 9 FEBRUARY I went to our Naval dentist in the Headquarters. There is no doubt that he is better equipped and, I believe, a better dentist than the American dentist or the Army dentist. He tells me that he does not think three dentists are enough for our Headquarters. It seems a grave reflection on our teeth, because our numbers are still very small when compared with Eisenhower's or Alexander's Headquarters.

While sitting in the dentist's chair in front of a window in his 'Basha' hut with most of the dentist's hands and tools inside my mouth, I noted a Ceylonese gardener come and stare very rudely at the window. I was even more mortified when he went and collected 6 American GIs who all came and stared and appeared to be showing the greatest possible interest at the free performance the dentist was putting up on me. I was

[1] Founder and Director General of the Entertainments National Service Association (ENSA).

about to rise in my wrath and protest when one of the GIs picked up a log of wood and threw it. It landed a few feet from the window, and a large snake some 7 to 8 feet long slid off into a tree. I leapt out of the window with my bib round my neck. The dentist followed me with a hand full of tools and we joined in the chase for the snake. I regret to say however, the snake escaped.

SATURDAY, 10 FEBRUARY to WEDNESDAY, 14 FEBRUARY
Although I managed to rest last week-end, this week-end work proved unusually heavy.

On Monday I had Frances Day[1] to lunch on her way through to entertain the Fleet, and in the evening an all Royal Marine dinner party including three Major Generals.

THURSDAY, 15 FEBRUARY   I worked all day at high pressure until 1840, when I drove to Colombo. At 2200 I went to Radio SEAC studios to make a recording for a broadcast to the troops on the occasion of the fall of Mandalay, in case by any chance it fell unexpectedly in my absence! I also sent a telegram to the Chiefs of Staff saying what I proposed to broadcast.

At 2315 I took off in the York from Ratmalana and turned in right away.

FRIDAY, 16 FEBRUARY   Had breakfast on board the York and landed at 0800 at Monywa No.1 strip where I was met by Bill Slim. We drove out to the new 14th Army Headquarters which we reached at 0815 for a discussion. At 0900 I attended the Intelligence Meeting in their War Room, which is in one of the few houses where enough was left standing to make it worth while patching it up for use. After the War Room meeting Lieutenant-Colonel MacDonald of the War Office Film Unit, who was the producer of *Desert Victory* and is now starting on a second Burma film, inveigled me into having a sound shot made talking to the Army and RAF Group Commanders.

Before starting he cautioned us against using bad language because it appears that, on the last occasion he 'took' a discussion between senior officers, Bill Slim, in saying goodbye to Monty Stopford said:

[1] An actress and singer, who originally made her name in cabaret.

'Well, goodbye Monty, good luck to your attack and don't make a xxxx of it!' Needless to say, this bit will not get past the censor.

At 1045 we took off in the Hapgift which had come to meet us here, and flew with an escort of six Spitfires to Sinthe. There I was met by Frank Messervy, who took over the 4th Corps from Geoffrey Scoones two months ago, and after a discussion on the air supply situation we flew on at 1140 in four L.5 light aircraft and landed at 1200 at Myitche airstrip on the banks of the Irrawaddy. Here Major General Geoff Evans, the new Commander of the 7th Indian Division, who took over from Frank Messervy, met us. He showed us the situation of the division on his map and after a quarter of an hour we drove off in a jeep and at 1315 we arrived at the beach head at Kukyun further upstream on the Irrawaddy. At this point the Irrawaddy is about a mile wide. The rivers in Burma are on a different scale of magnitude to the rivers in England, for although it must be some 400 miles from the mouth, the river must be more than six times the width of the Thames at Waterloo Bridge.

I was fascinated to see what a beach head looks like in a river crossing and found that it bore a fairly close resemblance to a beach head in an amphibious assault, except that the soldiers run all the craft themselves.

At 1340 we embarked in a DUKW and crossed to the further bank of the Irrawaddy, and went forward to see the troops of the 7th Indian Division who were fighting at the bridgehead.

The Irrawaddy is now in the process of being crossed at four widely separated points, though some of the crossings have not started yet. The casualties in the crossing have, up to date, been surprisingly light when you think that the successful crossing of the Irrawaddy with sufficient British troops will mean the end of the Japanese Army in Burma. Altogether I felt it was quite an historic occasion to set foot on the opposite bank of the Irrawaddy so soon after the first crossing.

I was glad to see a number of Sherman tanks had already crossed. They will form the armoured spearhead of the 17th Indian Division's thrust to Meiktila and I hope that before this diary can be despatched we shall have been able to announce its capture.

We returned across the Irrawaddy at 1415 and drove to Myitche, where I met Major General 'Punch' Cowan, who commands the 17th Indian Division and whom I had not seen since he fought that extremely gallant action with his division between Tiddim and the south of the Imphal Plain. He was in great heart and full of dash and confidence.

I was much amused by the following story. In the 28th East African Brigade a murder had recently been committed. In due course three Africans arrived at 4th Corps Headquarters. The biggest and smartest of the three, and the only one who could speak English, reported to an officer of 'A' Branch and said, 'Please, we are murder cases.' The other two were immediately thrown into clink with the first one as guard. He guarded them faithfully for three days, when the documents arrived, and it transpired that he was the murderer and the other two were the escort!

We landed at Bhamo at 1730, where Lieutenant General Sultan, the US Commanding General, who commands the allied forces in the Northern Combat Area Command, India Burma Theatre, met me and drove me to his Headquarters in a school, one of the few houses in Bhamo which had not been utterly destroyed in the war. We immediately went into conference, which was only interrupted long enough for dinner, and then continued again until late, except for a quarter of an hour's interval while Major Scheie checked over my eyes for spectacles.

SATURDAY, 17 FEBRUARY   At 0830 I held a two-hour conference with General Sultan, Admiral Cooke[1] and their staffs. We then drove round to see the sights of Bhamo. I must say I like old Savvy Cooke, and have arranged for him to be entertained by Wheeler and Browning in the King's Pavilion when they go down to my Headquarters. I sent Flags a telegram telling him to have the photograph which Savvy gave me at Quebec put in a conspicuous position, though Heaven knows he is no oil painting.

At 1130 we took off in the Hapgift. We landed at 1210 at Myitkyina East airfield. It was an amazing sight to see no less than four full-sized, all-weather airfields in the Myitkyina area. This is now the principal terminal for the route across the Hump into China. Petrol for the aircraft is delivered by pipe-line from Ledo and the most recently announced totals of stores lifted into China have reached the staggering figure of 40,000 tons a month, and it is still increasing at a very rapid rate.

At 1410 we took off from Myitkyina North in the Hapgift and at 1440 we landed at Warazup. I inspected a C.47 which had just been loaded, and talked to the 'kickers', that is the three men whose duty it is to push the supplies out as they fly over the dropping zone.

[1] Admiral Charles Cooke had just been appointed Deputy Chief of Naval Operations.

All these C.47s have had their doors taken off permanently, so as to make it easy to throw the supplies out. General Sultan told me an almost incredible story, which he swears is true. During the recent move of the 22nd Chinese Division back into China, they were flown in supply-dropping aircraft which had the doors off. As they were flying over the Hump, the Chinese soldier nearest the door stood up and with his hands on his knees, bent forward to look out of the door.

The soldier sitting opposite the open door leant forward, with his hands stretched forward and palms vertical, behind the soldier who was looking out. He then looked up expectantly at the two rows of Chinese soldiers, who all laughed and nodded vigorously. On receipt of this encouragement, he pushed the first soldier out of the door, amid the paroxysms of laughter of the remaining Chinese, who were quite overcome by this ultimate high spot in slapstick humour.

We got back at Bhamo at 1715, and I worked with ACOS until 1900, when a cocktail party was given by General Sultan. At 1930 we were invited to dinner by General Davidson,[1] who had succeeded in improvising a wonderful house round a fireplace which was all that was left of the original. His dining room was a marquee worthy of the Mayfair Catering Company at its best. At dinner I sat between General Davidson and Miss Lili Pons,[2] and opposite her husband, Mr André Kostelanetz. Throughout dinner, a Chinese 'candid cameraman' took pictures and altogether we might have been in the Stork Club, New York, from which, incidentally, General Sultan's chef comes.

After dinner I was asked whether I would like to hear Miss Lili Pons do a broadcast and, greatly wondering how this could be arranged in ruined and desolated Bhamo, accepted. We were driven to a large bell tent, hung with blankets, in which there was a 'one rat-power' little local broadcasting set. Miss Pons became somewhat temperamental and said: 'Where is my orchestra? I never broadcast without an orchestra!' I thought she must be barking mad, to expect an orchestra in the jungle, but it transpired that in fact they had collected from the 200,000 American soldiers in this theatre some 50 or 60 really high-class musicians who had been rehearsed by Kostelanetz and had then gone round with them giving high-class concerts to the troops. A really excellent idea.

Even so, it would have been quite impossible to get any part of the

---

[1] Major General Davidson commanded the 10th US Air Force.
[2] An American opera singer and film star, eponymous heroine of the Maryland town of Lillypons.

orchestra into the tent, apart from one small man who was there with a flute and who kept on struggling for possession of the microphone with Miss Pons. Altogether a most unexpected evening in Bhamo.

SUNDAY, 18 FEBRUARY   The same party as yesterday took off at 0840 in Hapgift and landed at 0910 at Muse. The Chinese 11th Army Group had only withdrawn from Muse a day or two before. This was part of the Chinese Yunnan Force who had met SEAC forces at Wanting when opening the Burma Road. During the time they were in Burma they came under my orders.

I wonder whether any soldier, or, for that matter anybody at all, has ever had simultaneous command of two Army Groups both bearing the same number, since the British Army Group out here, which includes the 14th Army, 15th Corps, etc., is also the 11th Army Group.

We transferred to about a dozen L.5s and flew down the old Burma Road as far as Kutkai, where we landed, on a rather rough and undulating piece of ground, at 1000. Here I was met by Lieutenant-General Li Jen Sun, commanding the First Chinese Army. We drove off in a convoy of jeeps and at 1030 arrived at the Command Post of the 90th Chinese Regiment. We walked up to the top of the hill, and then crept on hands and knees to the edge, from which we watched a battle which was in progress on the road to Hsenwi.

It was extremely difficult to believe it was a real battle, as it so much resembled the Aldershot Tattoo or the Royal Tournament. 1500 yards in front of us there was a conical hill, which was held by the Japanese. On one side of it there was another hill which had just been captured by the Chinese, and at the other side there was a long line of high ground which had been in our hands since the day before.

Tanks had recently been in action, and artillery on both sides was firing, and there was a constant rattle of rifle fire. General Sun was a great showman. He would say: 'Do you hear that machine gun? That is a Jap.' After a short pause he would say: 'Do you hear that machine gun? That is a Chinese.' Once, when some mortar shells burst on the road in front of us, he remarked, somewhat superfluously: 'Those are Japanese mortars.'

At 1345 we arrived at the Headquarters of the Mars Brigade which consists of the 475th US Infantry Regiment, and the 124th US Cavalry Regiment (dismounted). Each regiment, which consists, of course, of three battalions, has an artillery battalion with it. The Mars Brigade are the direct successors of the old Merrill's Marauders, whom I originally got sent out by General Marshall.

The 124th Cavalry are immensely proud of two brothers called Knight, one of whom commanded a company and lost his life after great acts of heroism in the taking of a strongly held hill. His brother, a sergeant in the same company, who refused a commission in order to remain with his brother, was very badly wounded in the same engagement. Sultan is putting Captain Knight in for the Congressional Medal of Honour. The 124th Cavalry called this hill 'Knight's Hill' among themselves, and when I addressed them I informed them that I was going to have this name printed on the maps of Burma of the future; which went down very well.

At 1545 we took off from Hosi airstrip, which is in a valley and is consequently a very tricky take-off. The airstrip is covered with wrecked aircraft, since it would be difficult enough to land with all the cross-currents in peacetime, but this strip was until recently under heavy fire, and the casualty evacuation planes had to land with shells bursting all around them.

At 1600 we landed back at Muse. We left in the Hapgift, and at 1700 landed back at Bhamo, where we spent the night.

MONDAY, 19 FEBRUARY At 0840 we took off in 'Sultan's Magic Carpet', as General Sultan's Dakota is called. It is very nicely fitted up, with a private cabin for the General, with a bed and a little dining table for two, as well as a larger passenger compartment.

At 0910 we landed at Bahe airstrip, where Major General Frankie Festing, commanding the 36th Division, met us. At 0930 we en-jeeped and were driven by Frankie to his Headquarters at Mahlarnggon, where he explained the tactical situation to me on his maps.

At 1050 we arrived at the Main Headquarters of the 72nd Brigade. After a ten-minute talk we continued, and at 1100 arrived at the 28th Indian Mountain Battery, whom I addressed in Urdu. We then drove on in jeeps, and walked the last stretch down to the banks of the Shweli River. Only the four Generals were allowed to come with me, and we crawled on our hands and knees up to the river bank. The river at this point is 270 yards wide. Well over to our right, we could see some troops moving on the opposite bank. Frankie told me that these were on the left flank of our bridgehead across the river. I replied, 'You must mean the right flank.' He said, 'No, the left flank.' Then I asked, 'In that case, who is holding the bank immediately in front of us?' Frankie had evidently been waiting for this (he is a grand showman), for he replied dramatically, 'The Japanese.'

This Division has had 600 casualties in the last five days' fighting, and over 2000 rounds of artillery fire had fallen on the area in which we then were.

General Sun put up a good show yesterday, but it was nothing compared to what Frankie Festing put up today. As we lay there, the Air Force went to attack an island three or four hundred yards upstream, which was held by the Japanese. Wave after wave of Mitchell bombers came over and in fact had been coming over up to our arrival, dropping 500-pound bombs from a very low level. They were followed by Thunderbolt fighters, dropping napon oil fire-bombs, and carrying out ground strafing with their machine guns.

We were lying so close that some of the hot cartridge cases fell all round us and we had to duck. Altogether, it was a thoroughly inspiring performance, having been so often at the receiving end of air attacks myself at the beginning of the war when we had no air cover.

We drove back to Bahe airstrip, and took off at 1230 in the Hapgift, which had come to fetch us, and landed an hour later at Monywa, where General Slim had come to show me the latest situation, which is indeed encouraging. We transferred to the York and left at 1350, landing at Comilla at 1520.

At 1710 we left in the York, arriving an hour later at Alipore. We got to Government House at 1850, and found that Edwina, who had arrived a couple of days before, was still out on her visits. She arrived back looking as fresh as a daisy, with poor Brian Hunter wilting in her trail.

Before dinner I had the most interesting conversation with Major General Patrick Hurley, the US Ambassador to Chungking, who is on his way through to Washington with Wedemeyer. It is unfortunate that I had already arranged to go to China at the very time they have now been called away, but Pat Hurley confirmed that the Generalissimo would take great umbrage if I postponed my visit because Wedemeyer was not there; so I shall have to go on with it.

After dinner, I left at 2130 for General Stratemeyer's house and had a two-hour conversation with Al Wedemeyer and gave him his CB.

TUESDAY, 20 FEBRUARY   We took off at 1050 and landed at 1110 at Chakulia airfield, where I met and addressed the 40th B.29 Group.

After this was over, I emplaned in a B.29 of the 25th Squadron. I was put in the bombardier's seat in the very nose of this colossal aircraft, completely surrounded by plexiglass, and only some seven or eight feet above the ground. This aircraft is so huge that the B.29 transport version takes a hundred passengers, and the bomber version takes forty 500-pound bombs.

The 20th Bomber Command has actually carried out raids against the Southern Island of Japan, by staging from India through China, and then four airfields had to have their runways practically doubled to take them.

The actual take-off was a great thrill. I could hear the co-pilot chanting the speeds: 70, 80, 90, 100, 105, 110, 115, and just before we got to 120 miles an hour, she took off, having run for over a mile on the runway at this terrific speed.

Normally, the B.29s fly at about 20,000 feet, at which altitude they reach a speed of 300 miles an hour, but on this occasion we went hedge-hopping over to Kharagpur, where we landed at 1235. I must say the landing is a terrific thrill. The aircraft comes in at about 145 miles an hour, and touches down at about 120, the ground fairly leaping up at one as one goes roaring over the concrete strip, running on for about a mile and a half before finally pulling up.

We transferred to the Beechcraft and landed at Barrackpore at 1320, reaching Flagstaff House, Oliver Leese's Headquarters, at 1330. I had lunch alone with him and a long and profitable discussion on the present tactical situation and future strategy. I left at 1450 and at 1530 arrived at the Headquarters of Group 'A', Force 136.[1] I visited all sections of the Headquarters, and addressed the Heads of Sections on future strategy in the War Room. I was also introduced to all the French officers, and found it rather a strain making separate conversations in French with each of them.

At 1720 we arrived at Force 136 War Signal Station, which I found extremely interesting. We left at 1735, and at 1750 arrived at the Calcutta Headquarters of my Psychological Warfare Division. I was very interested to find in one room three Japanese prisoners of war hard at work helping us to convince their colleagues how wrong they were to continue the struggle. I finished my visit at 1830, and got back to Government House at 1845.

---

[1] The paramilitary force working with the Burmese National Army.

WEDNESDAY, 21 FEBRUARY   At 0820 I went all over the RN and RIN establishments in Calcutta. I addressed the English-speaking ratings in English and the remainder in Urdu, and I then visited the Landing Craft Base to congratulate the maintenance crews on the magnificent job they have done in keeping our pathetic old landing craft running in the Arakan.

I went back to Government House to change from whites into khaki, and then drove out to Flagstaff House, and at 1120 started being introduced to some 200 officers of Oliver Leese's staff. It took 1¾ hours to have a few words with each, and at 1310 I met Edwina and had a long talk with her and Oliver Leese about her recent tour of the Arakan Front, and it was not until nearly 1400 that we went into lunch.

At 1515 I left with Edwina for my Tactical Headquarters in Fort William. I showed Edwina round and then she went on, but I stayed and worked until 1800. On return we both had various people to see. This was Edwina's rest day, but she seemed to have spent most of it working. However, we took Peter Murphy, who had come up from Kandy, to dine at the '300', which proved to be quite a nice little restaurant.

THURSDAY, 22 FEBRUARY   This was supposed to be a clear day, which Edwina and I had asked should be kept free, so that we could see something of each other.

At 0800 I worked with my Secretary and Conference Secretary. At 1215 I made a new record at the All-India Radio studio of my Mandalay broadcast, as the Chiefs of Staff wanted some of the wording altered.

At 1315 Major Scheie came to bring my new reading glasses.

At 1330 there was a lunch party to meet four Ministers of the Bengal Government.

During the afternoon there were more interviews, but Edwina and I managed to get one hour away in a car. We could not think where to go, so we went to the Victoria Memorial, which was closed, but which we nevertheless walked round.

At 1830, I attended the beginning of a cocktail party of the Welfare organizations given for Edwina.

At 1900, I left for my Tactical HQ for an hour's meeting with my staff, who had all flown up that day from Kandy. I then drove out to Oliver Leese's house for dinner at 2100, and at 2200 we had our usual 'off the record' meeting with the Commanders-in-Chief, which included Air Marshal Sir Keith Park, who has just arrived here to take over from Air Marshal Sir Guy Garrod.[1]

I got back about 0100.

FRIDAY, 23 FEBRUARY   At 1000 I held a preliminary conference of Commanders-in-Chief, including General Sultan, and we had photos taken.

At 1030, the full conference of fifty senior officers. All the Commanders-in-Chief were present in person, including General Stratemeyer. I took some of them back to lunch at Government House at 1330, as we had to go on again at 1440 with meetings. I finally left the Headquarters at 1800, and had a meeting with the Governor, Dick Casey.

That night a colossal dinner was given for all the Commanders-in-Chief. I had to come late for dinner, as although I was dressed in plenty of time, I had to redictate one of the draft telegrams, and at 2200 after dinner I had a meeting in my room with the Commanders-in-Chief, which lasted till after midnight. I was about to go along and swank to Edwina how hard I had to work, when I found that she had not yet got back to her room.

By 0100 I was worried that she had not turned up, and then discovered that she was still hard at work clearing correspondence. So she was able to have the laugh on me for hard work.

SUNDAY, 25 FEBRUARY to SATURDAY, 3 MARCH 1945   This was an astoundingly busy week because the strategic decisions taken in Calcutta released a spate of papers, which have been held up pending decisions. Added to this I have had a host of visitors and functions. On Sunday I gave a farewell luncheon for Guy Garrod, who has been Acting Allied Air C.-in-C. for the three months since Richard Peirse left. He had been such a grand and loyal supporter that I shall miss him very much. Although we do not usually make speeches and I only spoke for two minutes, he stood up and said that he wanted an opportunity to say that he had seen the South-East Asia Command grow up under the most difficult circumstances imaginable, to a point where the higher command had reached the top level of happy and loyal brotherhood, and that he thought that a new example had been set in how an Allied inter-service campaign could be conducted.

[1] Park had been sent out instead of Leigh Mallory who had been killed three months before.

This week we have had Air Chief Marshal Sir Christopher Courtney, (Air Member for Supply and Organization), Lieutenant General Sir Archibald Nye (Vice Chief of the Imperial General Staff), Lieutenant General Godwin-Austen (QMG in India), Major General McMullen (Director of Transportation, War Office). Each of them come with appropriate staffs of Air Marshals and Generals, with the result that we spent the entire week in conferences and in looking after all these high-level visitors.

However much trouble it is having to look after all these people in addition to dealing with ordinary work, the feeling that at last Whitehall is beginning to take an interest in South-East Asia is so grand that everybody is delighted to see them.

I went out one day to see the SEAC airstrip. In the 7 days they have been at work they have cleared 7000 coconut trees, and have got a real move on.

TUESDAY, 6 MARCH   On Tuesday I left Kandy at 1730 by car, and drove to Admiral Power's Headquarters. Here we changed, and went with the C.-in-C. to the 'Silver Faun' for dinner. We left after a hurried dinner at 2130 for Ratmalana, and were airborne in the York at 2200.

WEDNESDAY, 7 MARCH   We coasted the whole way, as permission had not yet been given to cross the Bay of Bengal, and landed at Monywa airfield at 0630. Here we were met by Bill Slim, and had a good hour's discussion on the present situation and future plans of the 14th Army. The attack on Mandalay is developing very satisfactorily.

At 0730 we flew on with Spitfire escort, and landed at Myitkyina South at 0900. Here D. I. Sultan met us, and we went to 'Sultan's Magic Carpet' and held a conference on the operational situation. During the conference Edwina arrived in the Sister Anne from Sukrating. She had just finished her very strenuous tour of the forward areas.

At 1020 our two parties joined up and all left together in the York. We landed at Kunming at 1250 Chungking time. We left by car at once for Claire Chennault's house, where he gave us lunch. His 14th Air Force are certainly doing wonders.

The landing at Chungking is so tricky that there was no question of being able to go on in the York, and so the party split up into two Dakotas.

We took off at 1415 and landed punctually at 1630, at Chiu Lung Pu airfield, Chungking. An enormous mixed gathering awaited us here of from 80 to 100 notables headed by Dr Soong, the Foreign Minister and Vice President, and all the senior British, American and Chinese officers and Embassy staff. There was the usual Guard of Honour of 300 with a large band which insisted on playing (not only very badly, but also most improperly) two or three verses of 'God Save the King'. We drove in a large procession of motor-cars to Dr Soong's own house at Hung Ai Hain Tsun, which he had placed at our disposal.

We were all astonished to see the Generalissimo himself awaiting us on the lowest step of the front porch. This was a surprise he had sprung on everyone, including Dr Soong, and I believe it is without precedent for him to meet visitors on the doorstep of the house allotted to them. He was quite exceptionally friendly, smiling the whole time in his very charming way, and overwhelming us with compliments.

THURSDAY, 8 MARCH   At 0845 I had a brief conference with Adrian Carton de Wiart, and at 0945 we all, including Edwina, left to pay our official call on Dr Soong. Our Ambassador, Sir Horace Seymour, and John Keswick were awaiting us at the entrance to Soong's house to take us in.

At 1030 Dr Soong took us on to call on the Generalissimo at his town house. There was a large gathering here, both political and military, British, American and Chinese. The first quarter of an hour was spent in exchanging courtesies with Edwina, after which the Ambassador took her off to meet the heads of the various Chinese Women's Services.

We then got down to military business, and I gave a long ex-planation of the whole of the campaign in Burma, from the time that I had last seen the Generalissimo at Ranchi in December 1943.

Lieutenant Colonel MacDonald, who is producing the new Burma Campaign film, had come over to take a picture of our meeting, but as there was insufficient lighting in the house, the Generalissimo very graciously consented to a special sitting in the garden where a sound film could be taken.

After this the whole party lunched with the Generalissimo, while Edwina was given lunch by the Chinese Red Cross. After lunch, Edwina attended a mass open-air meeting of 7000 Chinese women, which she addressed.

I spent the afternoon paying official calls. We got back to Soong's house with only just time to spare to change and drive out to the official country residence of the President of China at Shan Tung. This had only been taken over by the Generalissimo when he succeeded the late President Lin Sen in 1943.

The Generalissimo met us in the front hall, and conducted us in to the drawing room where those who had the 'entrée' were assembled. It appears the Generalissimo made advances to Edwina at this moment, and asked her to consider his home her home.

After having been introduced to all those in the drawing room, we set off in a procession up a hill to a large official banqueting hall, where some 80 to 100 guests were assembled. Edwina and I sat on either side of the Generalissimo and were warned just before dinner that he was going to make a speech to which we would be expected to reply.

I remember so well that in October 1943 at Huang Shan, which is on the other side of the Yangtse, there had been a soft background of Chinese music on a radiogramophone. At the moment the General-issimo stood up, the volume control was switched full on, so one could hardly hear what he said. I could not help wondering what would happen this time.

The lights had been at half brilliancy throughout the banquet, but the moment the Generalissimo stood up to speak, they went almost completely out. Needless to say, I got a fit of the giggles, and when the lights suddenly went up to full brilliancy I had the greatest difficulty in controlling my features.

I must add the Generalissimo was not the least put out, and had started to try to read his speech by the poor light, which, as it was written in Chinese, must in any case have been very difficult to read!

The Generalissimo said some very charming things about the campaign in South-East Asia, and how much China owed to us. He also said some very flowery things about Edwina, and was evidently well informed as to her activities.

Edwina and I replied to him in turn. I had never heard her speak in public before, and was astounded at how good she was, though I must say that she began by forgetting there was an interpreter and I had to catch her eye to stop her from going on too long before she gave him a chance to interpret.

The Generalissimo had invited us to stay with him in his official residence that night, as it is three-quarters of an hour's drive from Chungking.

FRIDAY, 9 MARCH We had been bidden to breakfast by the Generalissimo at 0845, and at 0930 Edwina left by car to see the hospital, etc.

Adrian arrived by car and we all walked around the garden with the Generalissimo and T. V. Soong after which I dictated some telegrams, and at 1000 all the high-ups were collected in the drawing room, whereupon the Generalissimo, after making me a little speech, handed me the insignia of the 'Special Grand Cordon of the Order of the Cloud and Banner', which, he announced, was the highest class of the highest order that he could bestow.

At 1010 we retired to the dining room, where the conference of the previous day was continued, at which the Generalissimo, Dr Soong and General Shang Cheng, the new Minister for War, set out the future programme that they wished to carry out in China.

General MacClure attended, at my special invitation, on behalf of Al Wedemeyer. It was most unfortunate that he and Pat Hurley had been recalled to Washington just at the time that I had arranged to come to Chungking, for it was really at Al's suggestion that I had come; but there is no doubt the Generalissimo would have taken umbrage if we had tried to postpone the visit on account of the absence of his American Chief of Staff!

When the conference broke up, the Generalissimo announced his intention of coming to see me off at the airfield at 0800 the following morning. I begged him not to but he insisted that he wished to indicate his high esteem in this manner, and although he was subsequently put to bed by doctors, having caught a slight chill, and was unable to come, I gather that in China it is sufficient to announce an intention of this type for the honour to be done. I gather he has hardly ever seen anyone else off from the airfield, and this gesture was therefore very good for British 'face'.

Incidentally, when Edwina left three days later, he sent Dr Soong to represent him, and showered her with gifts, ranging from 13th century Ming and a 1000-year-old musical instrument to bales of white silk.

That evening Dr Soong entertained us in the house of his brother-in-law, Dr Kung. I arrived early and had a separate interview with Dr Soong and then Mr Wellington Koo, the Chinese Ambassador in London, who happened to be at Chungking on a visit.

T.V.'s very romantic sister, the widow of China's national hero, Dr Sun Yat Sen, acted as hostess. She is not of course so lovely as her younger sister, Madame Chiang Kai-shek, but is if anything more charming. She proved to be a chain smoker and a most fascinating talker. She is the only member of the Soong family I have met with any progressive ideas.

There were three round tables in the dining room and most of the evening was spent in going round all the other tables and drinking various people's healths, in accordance with the usual Chinese custom.

SATURDAY, 10 MARCH   We left the house at 0700, Edwina coming too in case the Generalissimo's cold should have been better and he should have been able to come to the airfield. The Guard and band were drawn up at Chiu Lung Pu airfield, but this time had been told not to play 'God Save the King' and played an entirely unrecognizable tune.

Edwina stayed behind for a further three days' visit.

We landed at 1100 at Kunming, where we were met by General Chennault and General Ho Ying Ching, who announced to me that a few hours previously the Japanese had attacked French garrisons in Indochina, which I can foresee is going to involve me in quite a lot of headaches. The two Generals showed me the latest position on the map in Chennault's war room.

At 1140 Chungking time we took off in the York and had lunch on board. There was a headwind of between 70 and 80 miles an hour over the Hump, which made us half an hour late landing at Jorhat.

I met on landing Major General Mansergh, who has just taken over the 5th Indian Division from poor Warren, who has been recently killed in an aeroplane accident.

At 1500 General Mansergh drove me out to a parade ground on which representatives of the 5th Indian Division were drawn up and I pinned medal ribbons on 85 officers and men of the division. They are in great heart and longing to get back into the battle. One Brigade has already moved off; the remainder will be in action before I shall have time to get this diary typed out.

We were airborne again in the York at 1715 from Jorhat, and arrived at Barrackpore at 1920.

SUNDAY, 11 MARCH   We should have taken off at 0800, but as there was fog we were delayed and did not take off until 0940.

I took Oliver Leese with me and we landed at Palam airfield, New Delhi, at 1340. Here we were met by the usual crowd. I did not get to

Edwina Mountbatten starts on a tour of hospitals on Ramree Island in February 1945.

With General Festing, watching the bombardment of a Japanese-held island in the Shweli River. 19 February 1945.

With General MacArthur in Manila. As the photographer appeared, MacArthur 'pulled his cap on, his whole manner changed, his jaw stuck out, he looked aggressive and tough'. 17 July 1945.

Claude Auchinleck's lunch party until 1415, where the guests had been waiting for over an hour; most unfortunate!

After lunch Donald broke the news to me that the Hapgift with Boy Browning etc. was missing. I had a very unhappy afternoon wondering who I could possibly find to replace these key men. I spent most of the afternoon in conference with Claude Auchinleck and later with my joint planners, who were up in Delhi. In the evening we heard the good news that it was a false alarm about the Hapgift and she was not missing.

At 2000 I had a conference with the Viceroy, who in his extra-statutory capacity as a member of the War Cabinet is really Minister of State for South-East Asia.

At 2030 I attended a dinner party given by the Viceroy, at which Sir Ronald Storrs, whom I had last seen when he was Governor of Cyprus, was present.

After dinner, instead of leaving pompously in my Packard, we found the starter out of action, and so all the ADCs, headed by myself, pushed the Packard round the courtyard three times, after which we gave up the effort and went home in a jeep.

MONDAY, 12 MARCH   Had a busy morning addressing a meeting of some of my own inter-Service commanders from 0800 to 0900, supported by Oliver Leese. From 0900 to 0945 I addressed all the heads of services in GHQ (India), numbering in all some 80 officers of Brigadier's rank and above. I gave them a review of our past operations and a general forecast of the future, and took an opportunity of expressing my great appreciation for all that India Command had done for us.

I then drove off to Palam airfield and spent half an hour working on board the York, dictating and having urgent letters typed. We landed at Ratmalana at 1715, where Admiral Power met me and drove me to his flat for a discussion. I caught the SEAC Special at 1830.

TUESDAY, 13 MARCH to SUNDAY, 18 MARCH   Lord and Lady Keyes arrived to stay with me for a few days on their way back home from Australia. They are both in grand form, although the Admiral of the Fleet had been very ill and is looking much older.[1]

---

[1] Lord Keyes had been on a protracted lecture tour of the Commonwealth countries and the United States. He died nine months later.

THURSDAY, 22 MARCH   We landed punctually at 0730 at Monywa, where Oliver Leese, Vincent, etc. met us. I drove straight off to Oliver's Tactical Headquarters, which he has established alongside Bill Slim's.

I had a preliminary talk with him and at 0930 a conference collected, which I had summoned by telegram the night before, which included of course the two Cs-in-C., Oliver Leese and Keith Park, the American Generals Sultan, Stratemeyer and Fuller, General Slim, Air Vice Marshal Vincent, etc.

The conference broke up after two hours, and I then flew in a Beechcraft with Keith Park and the ADCs to Mandalay North airstrip.

Mandalay had only been captured two days before and I was very anxious to see it. I was met on landing by Major General Pete Rees, who commands the 19th Indian Division. We started off in a jeep procession and were met halfway into Mandalay by Monty Stopford, the Corps Commander, who joined the party.

We drove round Mandalay Hill and walked about a third of the way up the covered stairway of the Buddhist colony and had a picnic lunch.

After this we drove into Fort Dufferin, and I inspected the damage done by medium artillery firing over open sights at point-blank range in an endeavour to breach the walls. So thick were these wonderful old walls that the guns really failed. The only reasonable breach was one made by a 2000 lb RAF bomb.

The Japanese had set fire to the historic old wooden palace, merely as an act of spite and vandalism.

I had not been here since 1922. It was sad to see the ground where David and I played polo burned black as a result of the battle.

I well remember that in the match we played here I committed a foul by pulling up on the ball. The player behind me rode into me, shot over his horse's head and landed astride my horse with his arms round my neck. We rode off to the side of the ground, where he dismounted with great dignity.

I addressed representatives from every unit in the 19th Division, both in English and later in Urdu, round the flagstaff at which the Union Jack fluttered again for the first time in three years. Pete Rees gave me the flag afterwards as a souvenir.

We then had a look at various captured Japanese tanks and guns, etc., and then I had tea in the bungalow which the Press correspondents had taken over.

We got back to Monywa at 1820, and after further talks with Oliver Leese we had dinner, after which I held a further meeting. The conference ended at 2320 and we took off in the York at 2350 to fly straight across the Bay of Bengal this time.

FRIDAY, 23 MARCH   When I woke in the morning I noticed that the York was quieter than usual and on enquiring found that one of our engines had given out halfway across the Bay of Bengal and that we were flying on three engines. It is nice to know that she can keep height on three engines!

It is amazing the distances one flies here. On my way back from Delhi last time I completed 100,000 miles flying since I was given this job, and in order to attend this one conference I had flown 3000 miles.

THURSDAY, 29 MARCH   I went down in the SEAC Special and on arrival at Colombo was met by Rear Admiral Nicholson, Flag Officer Ceylon, who accompanied me during the day. I went by barge direct across the harbour to the Headquarters of the Ceylon RNVR. I inspected representatives from the Ships' Companies etc., and addressed them. On the way back I went on board the old *Renown* who was in Colombo harbour. The Captain, Basil Brooke, was a watchkeeper in the *Queen Elizabeth* with me in the last war. The last big ship I had served in in Colombo harbour curiously enough was the *Renown* in 1922.

At 1330 I went to Queen's House where I got involved in a colossal lunch party which the Governor and Lady Moore were giving for all the Red Cross and St John lady workers in Colombo. However, I was able to slip away before the end of lunch as I had to go and make a record at the Colombo Broadcasting Station, after which Nick collected me again and we went to visit HMS *Mayina*, the Naval Transit Camp. It is commanded by Captain Briscoe who has succeeded in introducing a thoroughly naval atmosphere into the camp which is clean and smart and 'tiddly' just like any other naval barracks, in complete contrast to the sloppy appearance that military camps of an exactly similar nature seem to have out here. I watched a football match and on conclusion addressed the whole ship's company on the football ground.

We left at 1700 and went to see the RN Barracks (HMS *Lanka*). The ship's company were all drawn up on the football ground for me to address but just as I approached them a tropical rainstorm of great severity descended upon us and we all scuttled to the canteen for my talk. The remarkable feature of this very pleasant day with the Navy was that I saw no less than five old 'Kelly's', three in *Mayina,* one in *Lanka,* one in *Renown.* As less than half the ship's company survived the Battle of Crete and many survivors were killed in action with other ships in the Mediterranean, I was indeed in luck to come across so many in one day. What shook me most was that all five were now Petty Officers whereas most of them had been ordinary seamen when they were with me in the *Kelly.*[1]

I got back to Queen's House at 2000 expecting to have to apologize for being so late and found that Edwina had not yet returned from visiting hospitals, whilst two people were waiting to be seen by her when she did arrive! She finally turned up after 2100 and by the time she had her two interviews and got dressed it was 2145.

FRIDAY, 30 MARCH   I left at 0900 to go round the whole of the Colombo Headquarters of Force 136. At the conclusion, I drove to Ratmalana and at 1130 took off in the Hapgift arriving after 20 minutes at Kogala. I drove to the lovely old town of Galle where I met Edwina at the conclusion of her St John inspection.

We drove all round the fascinating old Dutch town and went shopping, finally ending up at Klosenberg Bay where we bathed and had a picnic lunch. We picked up no less than four hermit crabs to give to Peter Murphy and have christened them James, Jeremiah, Victor and FitzWilliam.[2]

MONDAY, 2 APRIL 1945   I held a small meeting in the morning with Commanders-in-Chief. Edwina and I lunched at Oodewella Bungalow with Peter Wildman-Lushington. This was really Peter's farewell party as he is leaving this afternoon to take up command of a Special Service Group. He came to me originally in December 1941 and early in 1942 was promoted to Major General and became my Chief of Staff in COHQ. He followed me on out here as Assistant Chief of Staff. He has been longer with me than any member of my staff and nobody could have been more loyal, straightforward and helpful during the last three

---

[1] Since Mountbatten had gone from Captain to acting full Admiral in the same period, his surprise seems misplaced.

[2] Though he was always known as 'Peter', these were in fact Murphy's Christian names.

and a half years, and I don't know what I should have done without him.

After lunch I had a full dress meeting with the Commanders-in-Chief to go through the final plans and to discuss our future strategy and discuss the question of the combined operations for the capture of Rangoon.

THURSDAY, 5 APRIL   I gave a luncheon party for all the Flag, General and Air Officers in Kandy, British, American, Chinese, Dutch and French, to meet Edwina. I also included the senior women officers of the appropriate services, making 30 in all. I had to leave out American Brigadier Generals as there was nothing like room for them!!

In the evening Edwina and I attended a cocktail party given by General Blaizot of the French Mission in her honour, after which we attended a dinner party given for her by General Wheeler at which American Officers of full Colonel or Captain USN rank and upwards were present, but no other nationality; this produced about two dozen officers.

FRIDAY, 6 APRIL   Edwina left at dawn for Nuwara Eliya to do her tour of the welfare centres and hospitals in that district and spent the night at Queen's Cottage with the Moores. She was expected to dine at 2000 but when I rang up at 2200 she had not yet got back from her tour! The poor Moores have a lot to put up with when they have Edwina!

I heard only recently that after I left Fort Dufferin for Mandalay they killed and captured a few Japanese who were still in the Fort. I am sorry to have missed the fun.

TUESDAY, 10 APRIL   Drove at 0800 to Sigiriya and took off in the York at 0950. We landed at Barrackpore airfield at 1520 where Oliver Leese met me and drove me to Flagstaff House. Here I had a long discussion with him on the combined operation to capture Rangoon. I insisted on putting back the parachutists who had been cut out of the plan and on the 14th Army speeding up their advance so as to get airfields nearer Rangoon.[1] After a private talk with Oliver we had a meeting with his senior staff officers.

[1] This was the first of what was to be a series of violent disagreements between Leese and Mountbatten.

The conference ended at 1800 and by 1830 we were airborne in the York and had dinner on board. We landed at Palam airfield at 2230. We drove to the Viceroy's House. While Lord Wavell is in London, Sir John Colville is the Viceroy and Acting Governor General and is living in the Viceroy's House. I had half an hour's interview with him and then joined Edwina. We are living in the Wavells' own suite.

THURSDAY, 12 APRIL   This morning we transferred from the Viceroy's House to the C.-in-C.'s house. Lady Auchinleck is at home and his sister, Mrs Jackson, is acting as his hostess. Most of his Army Commanders are up and I was glad to meet Geoffrey Scoones again. He has recently taken over Central Command.

In the afternoon I had a discussion with Claude after which Edwina and I drove out to the Qutb. Whilst we were admiring the Minar we were inveigled by an amusing old rascal to come and see the Jumping Well. He showed us men who jumped (at 4 rupees a jump) from heights up to 60 feet and the old grandfather offered to jump from the top, which must have been nearly 100 feet, for 8 rupees. It quickly became a most expensive afternoon's amusement and we had great difficulty in restraining the whole population from jumping. On the way back we stopped to take a quick look at the deserted city of Tughlaghabad.

In the evening Edwina and I attended a reception given by the members of the Overseas League. It was practically the first social function I had attended in India but as I am the President, Edwina inveigled me into going.

FRIDAY, 13 APRIL   At 0930 I helped Edwina interview the Head of the War Transport Department and the Chief Commissioner of the Railway Board. She shook them by telling them she had done an 18-hour railway journey in a 3rd Class compartment full of BORs!! I hope something comes of this interview.

Claude drove us out to Palam airfield, and at 1720 we took off in the York and landed at 1830 at Nal airfield, Bikaner. We were met by the Maharaja of Bikaner and his staff. Hiru is probably my oldest friend among the Indian Princes since I knew him at Wolfsgarten in 1907, in London in 1911, and we were on David's staff in 1921/22. I had stayed with his father in 1921.

A special shamiana had been erected on the airfield in which we were given tea. After this he drove us in an open car to visit the shooting palace at Gujner. It is a delightful oasis in the middle of the great Bikaner Desert and is built on the edge of a lake (or tank as it is known out here). After visiting the palace we drove through the game reserve. We then drove into the capital city of Bikaner and reached Lallgarh at 2100. Here we changed for dinner and at 2130 Hiru drove us out to the Vallah Gardens where dinner was served in the open. These are charming gardens which he himself has laid out since I was last in Bikaner. He is well on in the course of constructing a very delightful modern villa. We got back to Lallgarh about midnight.

SATURDAY, 14 APRIL Edwina left shortly after 0800 to do her hospitals, and I to visit the Japanese POW Camp. Actually Edwina and I joined up for the visit to the Japanese Hospital, but the rest of the time I was going into the question of this camp very carefully.

Although there are nearly 1000 prisoners here, only 200 are sufficiently disciplined to fall in when ordered to do so. These fell in for me to see. The remainder are extremely surly and ill-disciplined; and I must say I was most dissatisfied with what I saw and am taking it up with Claude Auchinleck. When I think of the way the Japanese overwork their prisoners of war and flog them at the slightest excuse I am horrified to think that when the Japanese are the prisoners of war and we are the jailors they seem to get the better of us. However, I am sure that Claude will change all that.

Edwina and I also joined up at the Old Fort which Hiru showed us around. A large lunch party was given in the new dining room which Hiru has built and which has all his own heads hung on it – no more than 2 of any kind of animal. I should think there must have been 70 different types; there were lions, tigers, giraffes, rhinos, all types of antelope etc. The Maharaja's band played for lunch. After lunch, at Hiru's urgent request, I had a long interview with him and found his views on the future of India as reasonable as any ruling prince could be expected to express.

We took off at 1600. At 1830 we landed at Mauripur air station, Karachi. We drove to Government House where we are staying with the Governor of Sind and Lady Dow, with whom we dined.

SUNDAY, 15 APRIL At 0520 the whole party drove to Mauripur airfield to see Edwina off to England. It was very sad seeing her go. She has certainly done a wonderful job and will have completed 34,000 miles in three months by the time she gets home. Brian Hunter tells me she has talked to over 15,000 men in hospitals, apart from numerous public addresses and conferences. There is no doubt that she has done a grand job and everyone is singing her praises.

At 0930 we took off in the York and landed at 1540 at Alipore airfield where I was met by General Browning. We drove together to my temporary Advanced HQ at Fort William, Calcutta, where I held a meeting with the senior members of my staff and the planners. I drove out to Flagstaff House at 1945 to stay with Oliver Leese.

MONDAY, 16 APRIL   At 0945 I attended the investiture of General Sultan by General Wheeler of the second oak leaf cluster to his DSM. There was a remarkable gathering of senior officers to witness this ceremony as they were all taking part in the conference. General Sultan told me that one of his staff worked out that there were 63 stars present. I asked him what he meant and he explained that according to the American system of stars, i.e., four stars for myself as an Admiral, 3 for Keith Park as an Air Marshal, 3 for Wheeler, Sultan, Leese and Browning as Lt Generals, 2 for the Major Generals, Rear Admirals and Air Vice Marshals, and one for the Brigadier Generals and Commodores, the total in the conference room amounted to 63!

At 1000 I held a full meeting in my HQ which was attended by the various Commanders who were to command the amphibious assault on Rangoon. After they had submitted their plan, the Base Commanders for Rangoon, a Brigadier, a Captain RN, and a Group Captain, gave their plan for opening up the port. The meeting considered various other items and I consider we did very well in getting through in three hours. We started the conference again at 1445 with a reduced attendance. We had some very knotty problems to settle about the move of Chinese and American forces. We dined with Oliver Leese again.

TUESDAY, 17 APRIL   I took off at 0800 for a Civil Affairs tour of Burma in the York and landed at 1050 at Myitkyina. I visited all the Civil Affairs activities in Myitkyina including the Civil Affairs offices, the Welfare Shop, the store go-downs, and the hospital. Edwina had given me all the notes she had made during her visit to the Civil Affairs Centres and so I was able to check up and see whether her suggestions had been complied with. On the whole I found that they had, but I think it shook Civil Affairs people considerably to find that I knew exactly what deficiencies to look for as a result of her visit. I also inspected the temporary gaol and went personally into the cases of five prisoners awaiting confirmation of the death sentence. I found in one barbed wire enclosure a dozen ordinary and rather pathetic lunatics and arranged to have them removed to some suitable asylum.

At 1300 we took off in a Beechcraft and flew to Katha where we were met by the local Civil Affairs officers and police. We drove straight to the District Commissioner's bungalow which is one of the few houses which has not been destroyed.

A large crowd had collected to attend the auction of the local river Fishery Rights. I saw my first Pwe since 1922 in progress. Three attractive young Burmese girls were striking attitudes in the form of a dance to the music of a Burmese band. These girls occasionally moved their feet, but I am told that the classical way of doing a Pwe is to keep the feet stationary.

After lunch I did a tour of the Civil Affairs activities as usual including the local power station, which I believe can be repaired, and of course the gaol. We then went down to the railway station where I saw Frankie Festing's private coach which he used as his Headquarters while the 36th Division were advancing down the railway corridor. The Army were busy salvaging as many of the sunken rivercraft as possible because our greatest problem in Burma is communications and it is difficult to lift rice from a surplus area to a deficiency area. In places the natives are reduced to living on boiled roots which they collect in the jungle and which did not appear to me to be very appetizing.

WEDNESDAY, 18 APRIL We took off in the York at 0800 and landed at Monywa at 0915. On arrival at 14th Army Headquarters I first of all had an operational conference in which I urged Bill Slim to push on hard with the 4th Corps and try and get to Toungoo by the 25th April. He said he did not think he could possibly get there before the first week in May but agreed that I should try and put pressure on the Corps Commander myself.

Bill Slim told me that he personally launched the first two of the Chindwin River Gun Boats and that he had christened them after his young daughter and my young daughter; so now we have HMS *Pamela* flying the White Ensign on the rivers Chindwin and Irrawaddy.

We took off in the Beechcraft at 1300 and had a picnic lunch on board. At 1340 we landed at Meiktila West and were met by Lieutenant General Frank Messervy, the Commander of the 4th Corps. I had a long operational meeting with Frank in which I explained to him the vital necessity of getting the Toungoo airfields by the 25th April so as to be able to give close air support to the airborne and sea assault on Rangoon on the 1st May. He thought it would be impossible to get there before the first week in May, but I told him that I would personally take responsibility for his getting anything up to 3000 men killed in an attempt to speed up the advance, and he promised to go down that afternoon to the forward elements of the 5th Division and stick a sharp spur into them.[1]

I don't think I have ever seen such activity on any strip as at Meiktila West. As I went glider after glider came in with the Air Commandos Aviation Construction Battalion ready to fly on to make up the forward airfields. They had everything on board including bulldozers.

We took off in the Beechcraft at 1450 and flew direct to Kyaukpyu, the small port in the north of Ramree Island. Here I was met by the senior officers of the three Services and had a look at the new all-weather airfield. This was to have been finished by the 15th May, but I gave orders at Calcutta that they were to finish it by the 26th April in order that it could be used for the support of the amphibious assault on Rangoon. It was clear that they were going to be able to finish up to time.

I transferred to an L.5 and flew on down to Minbyin where we landed after ¼ hour's flight. This is an airstrip halfway down the west coast of the island. Here I was met by the Assault Force Commanders for the Rangoon assault. I had only said I wished to hold a consultation with the Assault Force Commanders Staff, but in an excess of zeal General Chambers (who had only recently taken over the Division from General Lomax) had most of the Division[2] formed up on the beach and I had to go down and address them in English and in Urdu.

It was now getting very late for the discussion and to my horror when I arrived at the large marquee tent I found at least 100 staff officers of the three Services sitting in rows with a big map in front evidently expecting me to address them. I had not thought of anything to say as I had meant to have a high-level discussion with the senior officers sitting round a table. However, there was no alternative and I gave them a ¼ hour's address on the operation giving them the strategical background.

---

[1] Toungoo was captured on 22 April, with only a few hundred casualties.
[2] The 26th Indian Division.

It was now getting really late as the sun sets so much earlier in Burma by Indian Summer Time. We took off at 1815 in the L.5 and at Kyaukpyu transferred to the Beechcraft. As we left Joubert said, 'I am afraid this is rather a dangerous adventure; our pilot has never landed in the dark and there are only very primitive night flying arrangements at Akyab.' When we reached Akyab it was completely dark; we circled around the field once or twice and then landed with a heavy bump at 1910 at Mawmubyin East. We drove to 15th Corps Headquarters for dinner, and after dinner had a large Civil Affairs meeting to deal with the Arakan. Wing Commander Bradley, who is the Civil Affairs Officer at Akyab, was stationed there in the Burma Civil Service before the war and was welcomed back with great enthusiasm by the local populace.

We took off at midnight in the York from Mawmubyin.

SATURDAY, 28 APRIL to MONDAY, 30 APRIL [Kandy]   On Saturday I had symptoms which appeared to me to indicate that I either had bacillic or amoebic dysentery. I reported to the doctors at once and they diagnosed it as amoebic dysentery. As luck would have it Brigadier Hamilton Fairley, one of the world's greatest authorities on tropical diseases, both in Bombay and in London, and who is now in the Australian Army, came to have lunch with me on his way back to Australia. He immediately volunteered to stay and look after me which turned out to be very lucky for him later on as he himself had to retire to bed!

I accordingly called all the senior members of my staff together and informed them that I was retiring to bed to be treated for amoebic dysentery but that I would retain the Command and continue to hold the more important meetings in my bedroom, and would be available on the scrambler telephone at any time.

The injections on Sunday and Monday were not too bad.

TUESDAY, 1 MAY to MONDAY, 7 MAY 1945   On Tuesday morning I had a very important and not too easy interview with Oliver Leese, who has arrived down from Calcutta for a Commanders-in-Chief's meeting.[1] Wheeler, Power, Park, Leese and Browning met in my bedroom to discuss future operations. The Commanders-in-Chief had

[1] It was as a result of this meeting that Leese considered himself empowered to relieve Slim from command of the 14th Army.

collected in Kandy for the control of the amphibious assault on Rangoon, the airborne element of which starts on Tuesday with the naval element on Wednesday.

On each day I saw an average of about 3 to 4 senior officers.

Major General Thompson, who is coming as my PMO, has been responsible for instituting a sort of blitzkrieg against amoebic dysentery, whereby they do three drastic treatments simultaneously, which make most people feel frightfully ill. Anyhow one of the forms of treatment is particularly revolting and uncomfortable but I must say it has not got me down.

TUESDAY, 8 MAY to TUESDAY, 15 MAY I continue to have regular meetings and to see important people each day.

VE Day celebrations passed off quietly in Kandy, Boy Browning taking the salute at a big inter-allied parade.

Peter and Brice are being driven mad by the amount of work I am giving them both, since they, unfortunately, are the only members of the office staff who are now working whole time in the King's Pavilion. I am having a particularly trying time over General Aung San and his Burma National Army. I am completely on their side but keep on being advised to arrest him and declare his Army (who have been fighting on our side) illegal![1]

On the 15th May the Bishop of Newcastle[2] came to see me after having visited the Front. He was a young Battalion Commander in the last war with the DSO and MC and seems a thoroughly good sort.

It was sad saying goodbye to Air Vice Marshal Whitworth Jones, my Assistant Deputy Chief of Staff (Air). He is the last of the original Chiefs of Staff to change and it is curious to think that within a few months I have lost my COS, DCOS, ADCOS (N) and now ADCOS (A). I do not include Air Marshal Joubert, for though he is a DCOS he is not on the operational side and, in any case, his time is up this summer also.

On the 15th also, Brigadier Hamilton Fairley carried out a most astounding inspection with a telescope 18″ long with a light in the end and pronounced me cured.

---

[1] The matter was not quite so clear-cut as Mountbatten suggests. There were strong grounds on which Aung San could have been tried for the murder of Burmese civilians hostile to the Japanese.

[2] The Rt Rev. Noel Hudson. He was a former Bishop of Labuan and Sarawak, hence presumably his presence in the area.

It appears to be almost a record cure which is largely due to my virtue in reporting the disease within 48 hours. Many people wait until they have abcesses and ulcers and are really ill.

He insists, however, that I shall carry on the treatment to the full limit which is up to the 21st. He then wants me to go on 15 days' sick leave. This I cannot afford so I have compromised on 5 days in Kashmir.

MONDAY, 21 MAY and TUESDAY, 22 MAY   Oliver Leese had flown down specially to report to me over a certain matter and I gave him dinner. He then went to his bungalow to think over what I had told him and on Tuesday morning came back to see me. This particular problem, a knotty and difficult one, has now been settled.[1]

I am still only supposed to do half a day up and I am going fairly steady.

THURSDAY, 24 MAY   At 0830 we landed at Willingdon airfield. We drove to Bikaner House, where I had an hour's business talk with Adrian Carton de Wiart about China and Wedemeyer's difficulties, and at 1015 we took off again in the Sister Anne landing at 1300 at Srinagar.

It was a lovely flight over the Himalaya Mountains into the valley of the Jhelum, which lies some 5000 feet up in the mountains. The mountains, which rise to heights of 26,000 feet, are snow-capped and quite lovely.

On landing we were surrounded by bees which were swarming underneath Mercury's starboard wing, and deeply resented being dislodged by the slipstream of Sister Anne as she taxied in.

We drove to No.2 Guest House, which the Maharaja had placed at our disposal. There are several of these guest houses, and it is an admirable idea. Each house is self-contained. Every house has four separate 'flats', each containing two bedrooms, bathrooms, sitting room and dining room. In addition, there is a main dining room and sitting room when the house is occupied by a single party.

The food of course was incredibly good, and it was a joy to find English fruit and vegetables in season, such as strawberries, cherries and green peas.

We sunbathed in the garden after lunch and then I drove out to Drappahama, one of His Highness's shooting and fishing lodges.

[1] Leese had been told that Slim must be reinstated in command of the 14th Army.

It was only in the early part of this century that trout were introduced to Kashmir. It appears that about 1900 the Duke of Bedford wrote to the then Maharaja and asked for some Bara Singh (giant deer) to be sent to his estate in England for cross-breeding. The Maharaja refused to accept any money for this, and so the Duke, wondering how he could repay them, sent out 50,000 ova, with which to stock the streams in Kashmir with trout. They have proved a great success, although the streams run very fast, and except in the Maharaja's own river there are few pools. It is very cold here after the sweltering heat of Delhi, but unbelievably lovely.

FRIDAY, 25 MAY to MONDAY, 28 MAY   I stayed in bed till noon and then went and called on the Resident. The Residency garden is really lovely, just like the best of England only much more so. We went round picking the most glorious ripe strawberries and other English fruit and admiring the lawns and flowers and the trees in the park. We then drove out to the new Palace of the Maharaja of Jammu and Kashmir.

I had not seen Hari Singh since Deauville and I could not help telling him that the whole of Srinagar and its layout with polo grounds, flower gardens, and the lovely lake reminded me more of Deauville than anywhere else! The glorious snow-capped mountains behind of course did not fit into the Deauville picture, nor of course did the surrounding country.

In the afternoon we went out to Drappahama to fish. We saw a large black bear on the hillside. Indeed the Maharaja wanted me to shoot bear but I refused on principle.

Hardly had I started to fish when I was violently sick and felt ghastly and so we drove back and I went to bed. The doctor came and told me I had a bad chill and after an examination he told me I still had amoebic dysentery so I was put back to bed feeling rather depressed.

However, on Sunday 27th, when the rest of the party came back from visiting the Kashmir Ski Club at Gulmarg, a small town some 9000 feet up in the mountains, I felt well enough to go out for a drive. We drove round the lovely Nagim Bargh lake with all the houseboats on it and then drove further up the valley to the Dal Lake and on the way looked in at the two Moghul gardens built by Shah Jahan when he used to come up for the hot weather.

TUESDAY, 29 MAY   I stayed in bed till lunchtime and then, after a most excellent lunch, drove to the airfield where I flew off in the Sister Anne to Delhi.

We landed at Willingdon airport at 1730 and then drove to my Rear Headquarters where I had a meeting with the Chief of Staff and Directors of Plans. I am staying at the Viceroy's House which is full to overflowing with all the Generals I have summoned for my meeting on the following day.

WEDNESDAY, 30 MAY   I spent a very busy day at Delhi. In the afternoon I had a political meeting on the future of Burma to which I invited the Governor of Burma and some of his staff as well as Leese, Slim, Stopford, Rance and all my Civil Affairs people. Some very important decisions were arrived at at this Conference.[1]

THURSDAY, 31 MAY   I attended my War Room meeting and then I addressed some 250 planners who had assembled in my Rear Head-quarters. I spent the rest of the day seeing various officers, including General Gale, who commands the Airborne Corps.

After dinner I took off in the Sister Anne from Willingdon airport.

FRIDAY, 1 JUNE to THURSDAY, 7 JUNE 1945   We landed at 0845 on Friday morning at the new SEAC airstrip. We were the first aeroplane to land officially and thus opened the airstrip. Hundreds of workmen lined the side of the strip as we landed and cheered.

The SEAC airstrip is 2000 yards of Bithess all-weather strip, with a 200-yard over-run each end, which is 2400 yards right in the heart of the mountains only 19 miles from Kandy. It will make a great differ-ence, though like so many of the airfields in Ceylon its use is uncertain during the monsoon.[2]

This week I have started my new treatment which consists of taking pills morning and evening and spending the mornings in bed; the afternoons I spend mostly at meetings.

---

[1] Relations between Mountbatten and the Governor of Burma, Sir Reginald Dorman-Smith, were already deteriorating – 'Damn it all, I'm governing Burma – not he, whatever his title,' wrote Mountbatten indignantly shortly before this meeting. The main decisions related to Aung San and the Burmese National Army. Dorman-Smith was overruled.

[2] Its use was, on the contrary, far from uncertain. It was almost certainly going to be unusable.

WEDNESDAY, 13 JUNE   Edwina's little tree rat Boogie Woogie had grown so extremely tame and cheeky that he used to run about loose and leap on to one at the slightest provocation. Alas! his tameness has led to his untimely end. He was running loose in the bathroom one night when someone – not me – having left the Lulu cover open, he fell into it and was drowned.

After a very rushed day's work I left Headquarters at 1630 with Micky Hodges, whose ship is here for a week and drove to Colombo.

We arrived on board the *Duke of York* at 1900, of which Micky is the Commander. His Captain, Nicoll, met me and took me down to the Action Information Centre where I saw the new automatic Radar plot. The scientific gadgets in a modern battleship have developed at such a startling rate that I find myself completely lost and had to start having everything explained to me like a young Sub. I went to have a drink in the Ward Room afterwards where one of the Marines who had been at the King's Pavilion with me came up and said how much he would like to come back to the King's Pavilion. He then said to me: 'You may remember I was one of your bodyguard.' As I have naturally never had such a thing, since the 4 sentries on the front door can hardly be described as a 'bodyguard', I was dumbfounded. I now realize how it is that ridiculous stories get about, for people seem to delight in inventing them.

Teddy Lonsdale told me the other day that a Commander recently out from the Admiralty asked why it was that I always went about dressed in full whites and Teddy replied that so far as he knew I had only worn this twice, once to go on board the *Saratoga* and once on board the *Richelieu*, in both of which ships the officers were wearing a corresponding uniform, and he presumed I would wear it at the Rangoon Parade for the third time!

I got to Government House at 2015 to spend the night and arrived 5 minutes late for dinner at 2035. When I apologized to Lady Moore, she said: 'Please don't worry. When any of the Mountbattens come here we always have cold meals!' (This comes from Edwina being 2 hours late for every meal.)

THURSDAY, 14 JUNE   I left Government House at 0520 for Ratmalana where I met the two Commanders-in-Chief, Park and Power, and at 0550 we took off in the Sister Anne for Rangoon.

The monsoon rain had soaked everything but it luckily stopped

Reading the announcement of the Japanese surrender from the steps of the Municipal Buildings in Singapore on 12 September 1945. From left to right, Admiral Power, General Slim, Mountbatten, General Wheeler and Air Chief Marshal Park.

General Itagaki signs the Instrument of Surrender.

Signing autographs for Australian ex-prisoners of war at Changi in October 1945.

In Singapore with Field Marshal Alanbrooke on 5 December 1945.

raining 10 minutes before we arrived and the sun was out. We drove first to the Parade Ground where the ceremonies on the following day were to take place and then we drove on to Government House which we reached at 1800 where I inspected the Guard.

Government House is perfectly hideous and might well have been intended for St Pancras Station. The furniture of course has all been removed but we had brought camp beds and managed to get hold of some chairs. In my sitting room there are still some Japanese paintings and a host of small booklets entitled: 'How to learn Japanese'.

Brian Kimmins,[1] had only arrived the day before but had managed to get hold of most of the old Burmese servants. They were in rags and had to have Army clothing issued to them. I am putting up about 50 guests, practically all of whom are General, Air or Flag officers. We are so crowded that we have as many as six Major Generals per bedroom.

We sat down 50 to dinner and having borrowed some port from the Fleet we were able to drink the King's health as it was his official birthday. After dinner I had a meeting of the Commanders-in-Chief to discuss again the situation that has been brought about by the Secretary of State for War's announcement in the House that he would reduce the period for Army repatriation from 3 years 8 months to 3 years 4 months.[2]

FRIDAY, 15 JUNE It was a fine morning which was lucky as the troops had begun to assemble for the parade from dawn.[3] At 1058 exactly, I stepped into an open car with Major General Kimmins in front and Lieutenant General Wheeler beside me. I had an escort of armoured cars, motor cycle outriders, etc, and we drove off to the Parade Ground which was only two minutes away, under the shade of the great Shwe Dagon Pagoda. This famous Pagoda is covered with gold leaf and rises to a height greater than the spire of St Paul's.

The streets were lined and the Burmese population gave me quite a friendly reception, nothing startling, but many of them waved and smiled. On arrival at 1100 at the Parade Ground, a battery of the Royal Field Artillery fired a 17-gun salute. It was the first time I had ever been received by a gun salute and it must be rare for a serving officer to go

[1] Major General Kimmins was Chief of Staff to the Air Commander-in-Chief.
[2] P. J. Grigg's announcement to this effect, on 8 June, with no previous consultation with Mountbatten, had the effect of removing many of the skilled personnel needed for the forthcoming maritime operations against Malaya.
[3] A Victory Parade to celebrate the liberation of Burma.

straight to the 17-gun salute of a full Admiral missing out the lesser salutes through which one works in peacetime.

After inspecting the Guard I mounted the rough and ready dais on which were standing the Commanders-in-Chief, Army, Corps and Divisional Commanders and the General, Air and Flag officers of all the Allies. On the distinguished visitors' dais next to us Major General Aung San of the Burma National Army was present in a full Japanese General's uniform; also about 50 of the most prominent citizens of Rangoon. All around the Parade Ground the raised banks were covered with crowds of people. A microphone and pulpit had been arranged on the dais from which I read out my formal address followed by a message which the King had graciously sent for the occasion. This same address and message was read out simultaneously throughout the whole of the South-East Asia Command and to all troops in India who had fought in South-East Asia.

At the same time I had a million leaflets dropped all over Burma proclaiming the 15th of June the Liberation Day of Burma to be a public holiday and declaring the friendly and liberal policy which my Military Administration intends to follow. I also had a special edition of *Lay Nat Tha*, my Burmese vernacular paper, printed and had 300,000 copies distributed by air.

Halfway through my address the monsoon settled in again. Fortunately the loud speakers carried my voice above the noise of the rain. The rain spoilt the fly-past of the Royal Air Force for, although they could be seen flying at 50 ft within sight of the middle of the Parade Ground, they could not fly immediately overhead since the top of the Shwe Dagon Pagoda was in the monsoon clouds so they had the grave risk of running into the Pagoda.

The ceremony finished by my handing to the representative of the Rangoon Port Commissioners the Red Ensign captured from the Port Commissioners' building by the Japanese and recaptured subsequently by the Americans at Attu. General Marshall had sent it through Field Marshal Brooke to me and I returned it to a representative of the Port Commissioners. After which it was ceremoniously re-hoisted on the flagstaff at the centre of the Parade Ground, whilst the band played the National Anthem. After this all the National Anthems of the Allies were played and at 1130 I left the Parade.

At Government House hot rum punch was served and we all tried to keep ourselves warm before the March Past. Meanwhile the rain came down in absolute buckets, but as luck would have it by the time I got to the saluting base in China Street at 1240, the rain had slowed up to a mere drizzle. So far from spoiling the March Past it made it somehow more impressive, as one of the soldiers afterwards said to Frank Owen:

'We fought through the fucking rain and it's bloody well right that the bull shit should take place in the rain.'[1]

The March Past took over half an hour in columns of sixes. First came the Royal Navy and then the Royal Indian Navy, then the Burma RNVR followed by the French Navy (the ship from which the Dutch Naval contingent was to come had received sailing orders at the last moment). Next came the Army; every Division was represented by a composite unit of 600 men and every battalion in every Division had sent a platoon. Thus, apart from the fact that all the men in a particular group wore the same formation sign, every 4 or 5 ranks the type of soldier changed; Sikh, Pathan, Punjabi-Mussulmen, Ghurka, Madrassi, etc. Not to mention the most magnificent-looking British troops I have ever seen on parade.

They swung by drenched to the skin in their jungle green battle dress, their bronzed heads erect and a proud look on their faces, which affected all the spectators profoundly. I did not meet anybody in discussion afterwards who was not moved almost to the verge of tears by the feeling that these men had had to fight their way yard by yard over the worst country and in the worst conditions in the world, for 18 months, in order to get to Rangoon.

After the 14th Army had gone by we had detachments from the American Army, the Chinese and the various Burma Guerillas – Chins, Kachins, Karens and finally the Burma National Army itself dressed in Japanese uniforms with a large red armlet to distinguish them from the Japanese and doing the Japanese goose step! They, of course, got a tremendous ovation from the Burmese crowds and I am sure that having Aung San and his Army take part in this Review will have done more to prevent strife and civil war and to establish friendship than anything I could have done.

Next came the Allied Air Force, preceded by the Royal Air Force Regiment and followed by British, Australian, Canadian, South African and American air crews. The procession was wound up by mechanized artillery of all types rumbling through the streets. Luckily the tanks which were to have taken part had to go up to take part in a battle just north of Rangoon with the Japanese – I say luckily, because I am sure

---

[1] The expletives were omitted in the original typed version of this diary but later added by Mountbatten in manuscript.

they would have torn up the streets of Rangoon. I had a particularly friendly reception from the crowd on driving back and the rain stopped as I got into the car.

I drove back to Government House where I was giving a cocktail party for 30 members of the Press including 17 US editors who are making a tour of the Eastern War Fronts. It was an informal, off the record, talk but they kept on expressing constant surprise (rather rudely I thought) at my assurance that we had not come in to start political persecution, curfews, banning of meetings, political censorship and generally to screw down the Burmese. It is horrifying to think that the American and Indian press evidently still regard us as merely Imperial monsters, little better than Fascists or Nazis.

SATURDAY, 16 JUNE It was a lovely day today (which is most unusual during the monsoon) and there were only very few rain squalls and none that interfered with any of the ceremonies.

At 1100 I left in the open car with General Wheeler at the head of a procession of some 20 staff cars and jeeps carrying all the rest of the party. At 1120 I embarked in a green Admiral's barge with a full Admiral's flag in the bows and my SACSEA flag at the mast head. Actually this was contrary to the instructions I had given as I do not think that one should fly more than one flag at one time and therefore thought it was improper that they should also have put up an Admiral's flag.

In the barge with me was Vice Admiral Moody, commanding the Units of the Fleet that were present, and General Wheeler. We were escorted by 4 LCPs and followed by a flotilla of motor gunboats carrying the Commanders-in-Chief and senior officers and one of the Burma gunboats carried the Burmese guests.

At the head of the line lay two 10,000-ton cruisers, the *Cumberland* and *Ceylon*, really beautifully painted up and very tidy. They looked as good as any ships did in the Spithead Coronation Review. As my flag was broken in the barge the *Cumberland* fired a 17-gun salute and all ships manned and cheered ship as we went by. Among the smaller ships were some manned by the Royal Indian Navy and some by the Burma RNVR. There were some 15 merchant ships in the harbour all of whom voluntarily manned and cheered ship and gave us a great ovation.

However, I must say I got a particular thrill from the two smallest units in the whole review: His Majesty's motor gunboats *Pamela* and

Una flying the white ensign, commanded by Naval officers but manned entirely by soldiers in jungle green.

We got back to the jetty an hour and a half later and arrived back at Government House at 1300. After lunch I had a meeting with General Blaizot and at 1500 I saw all officers of the Burma Civil Affairs Service of the rank of Lieutenant Colonel and above, about 50 in all. I handed them out my printed policy directive and generally told them I would have no more of these proposals to declare the BNA illegal, or to arrest Aung San or in fact to impose any form of political discrimination on the Burmese.

When I invited criticism the Chief of Police, Brigadier Chettle and Colonel Sir Alexander Campbell[1] informed me that it was a great mistake handling the Burmese too softly and that I would make the British Administration of Burma difficult for years to come by starting off in this way. I reminded them that there would be no British Administration in Burma in the years to come, since Burma was being given Dominion Status and the right to secede just as soon as they could hold elections after the country had been rehabilitated a bit. I pointed out that my policy would make them wish to remain a member of the British Commonwealth once they had Dominion Status, but that their policy would ensure that they voted themselves out of the British Empire the moment they were given the chance.

After light refreshments a formal entertainment was given by the foremost troupe of Burmese dancers, led by an old man of 60 whom I had last seen dance as a comparatively young man in front of the Prince of Wales in Rangoon, 23 years ago.

The Burmese included the Buddhist High Priest, aged 92, who is too holy to be touched by anybody and had fallen asleep by the time I came into the room. The only way to wake him up was to rock the bath chair in which he was sitting. All the ex-Prime Ministers and political leaders (except those who had accompanied the Japanese to Moulmein!) were there.

The party included Than Tun and the leaders of the Anti-Fascist organization as well as Major General Aung San and his staff officer Colonel Ne Win.[2] I took care not to take too much notice of them during the ceremonies as I do not wish to build them up too much.

At the end of the dances I addressed the Burman leaders and told

[1] Sir Alexander had been with the Burmese government in exile during the war with the title of 'Reconstruction Officer'.
[2] Still the effective ruler of Burma.

them of our liberal and conciliatory policy. I told them that I had placed a flying boat at the disposal of H.E. Sir Reginald Dorman-Smith, to enable him to land in the Rangoon River and then transfer to HMS *Cumberland*. I said that I had arranged for him to invite twenty Burmese leaders representing all parties to a conference at which he would explain the Government White Paper on the future of Burma. This announcement was very well received.

As the representatives of the Burma National Army and the Anti-Fascist Organization had asked to see me separately I let them stay back discreetly after the others had left and had a meeting with Major General Aung San, Colonel Ne Win, and Than Tun[1] in the presence of Generals Stopford and Rance and the Governor of Burma's representative, Mr Hughes. It was an extremely interesting meeting and I thought it went very well. I directed General Stopford to discuss one or two outstanding points with General Aung San and the Governor on the 20th. Aung San then said: 'I regret very much but I have to go on an important tour of inspection starting on the 19th June.' I replied: 'What nonsense, a Conference is far more important than a tour of inspection. You must stay.' Aung San replied: 'Very well, if you insist.' I cheered him up with: 'Surely your tour of inspection could not really have been important', to which he replied: 'No, indeed it was only an attempt to get out of attending the conference.'

SUNDAY, 17 JUNE   Left Government House at 0800 and at 0830 we took off in the Sister Anne. We were due to get to Delhi by 1800 in a direct flight but when we were some 540 miles out at sea we developed engine trouble in one engine and started to lose height; not much fun in the monsoon! We all had to put on life-saving jackets and do 'ditching drill'. When we jettisoned all our spare petrol, we luckily managed to maintain level flight and got in safely to Akyab in a monsoon downpour.

I asked to see Anthony Eden's son, who is a Sergeant here but he was away on a flight and I left an invitation for him to spend his next leave at the King's Pavilion.

We took off again at 1345 but were forced down at Agra at 2200 as there was a heavy dust storm over Delhi. We had supper in the transit camp and afterwards we drove out to see the Taj Mahal by moonlight as

---

[1] Than Tun broke with Aung San in October 1946 and headed the Communist revolution two years later.

I had not seen it since the ghastly scaffolding had been removed from the dome. There is no doubt it is twice as lovely now the scaffolding has been taken away.

MONDAY, 18 JUNE   We landed at Palam airfield at 0200.

I was horrified to find a couple of Air Vice Marshals and a Brigadier to meet me for I had sent a special message asking that no one should meet me owing to the lateness of the hour. Got to bed at the Viceroy's House at 0250.

At 1500 I went to pay a farewell call on Lieutenant General D.I. Sultan at the US Headquarters of the India-Burma Theatre. He is leaving the Command and I feel in him I have lost a good friend. Nevertheless I cannot conceal my great satisfaction that my Deputy, Speck Wheeler, is going to be the new Commanding General as well as remaining DSAC and PAO, SEA. This unifying of all American Forces in my theatre under my own Deputy Supreme Commander I am sure will prove to be the perfect arrangement.

At 1630 I had a long interview with Lord Wavell who told me all about his vicissitudes in London, which I found extremely interesting.[1] There was a large dinner party, but I got away early and worked until 0100.

TUESDAY, 19 JUNE   At 0900 we took off in the Sister Anne from Willingdon. At 1150 we landed at Srinagar airfield. We went off to the Government Silk Factory where I bought some extremely expensive silk. The only reason I bought it is that I presume it is unobtainable anywhere else in the world today.

I lunched with the Maharaja [of Kashmir] and the Maharani in their Palace and at 1540 I drove out to Trikka Lodge. Immediately after tea we went out on to No. 3 Beat of the Trikka river and in spite of the strong north wind and a heavy rainstorm, I killed six trout and put six back, my biggest being 2½ lbs.

WEDNESDAY, 20 JUNE to FRIDAY, 22 JUNE   This little lodge is quite delightful: it has only four bedrooms, a sitting room and a little dining room and it is very restful, there being only four of us.

---

[1] With the end of the war in sight, all Churchill's doubts about a rapid transfer of power to an Indian government were re-emerging.

Charles[1] disgraced himself by killing a 8¾ lb trout which was 28½ inches long and was only 3 inches less round the waist than the Empress of Austria. As there are probably only 2 such trout in the whole of Kashmir this caused a sensation. The Maharaja arrived out the next day and hardly had he stepped out of the car, when he said: 'Is he still on your staff or have you sacked him?'

SATURDAY, 23 JUNE   Just after midnight we had an earthquake which shook the house fairly intensely for about 30 seconds so that all the water in my bottle nearly splashed out. Everyone felt it except the two Air ADCs who apparently took it in their stride.

We left Trikka Lodge at 0750 very regretfully as it has been a perfectly lovely holiday. The doctors had tried to make me take 15 days' sick leave but as I spent three of the five I agreed to take in bed I had come back to make up the three days. In all I had killed 20 trout and 8 country fish and put back 32 trout, having landed a total of 60 fish in 3½ days. Even the trout put back averaged about one pound. Kashmir certainly is a fisherman's paradise and I could not have enjoyed myself more.

The meeting between the Governor and the leading Burmese on board the *Cumberland* on the 20th June had apparently gone off extremely successfully and, in fact, I was staggered to find that Boy Browning, who was my representative at this meeting, had himself pressed and got the Governor to agree that Aung San's forces should have their title changed to 'Patriot Burmese Forces' and that Aung San should be made Deputy Inspector General of the regular Burma Army with the rank of Brigadier; a very far cry indeed from arresting him and declaring his Army illegal![2]

MONDAY, 25 JUNE to SATURDAY, 30 JUNE   Monday being my 45th birthday, the Americans rallied round and gave a colossal party in the evening; a sort of dinner dance, at the Kandy Officers' Club. I had no idea that I had so many Americans in Kandy, as there must have been

---

[1] Squadron Leader Charles Harris St John was Mountbatten's Air ADC. A Spitfire pilot, he had been awarded the DSO with bar and the DFC with two bars.
[2] Mountbatten's conviction that Aung San would have made a responsible constitutional leader was never properly tested, since the Burmese was murdered with most of his Cabinet in July 1947.

between two and three hundred Americans, officers and civilians, of both sexes. They had asked the senior British, French, Dutch and Chinese officers as well.

During the dinner our host, Speck Wheeler, asked who a pretty platinum blonde was, and on being told it was daughter of Big Bill Tilden, the American tennis star, he took an early opportunity of going over towards her when he saw her alone, to be friendly. 'I do hope you are enjoying this party,' he said, to which she replied, 'Do you want me to tell you the truth?' Speck said, 'Of course.' 'Well then, candidly the answer is no,' she replied, and Speck came back rather crestfallen to our table. However, I think she was the only one who did not enjoy it, since I have never seen such gaiety and good feeling. All sorts of people had come long distances to attend this party, Admiral Power having undertaken a five-hour round motor trip from Colombo to come to the party, and General Stratemeyer had flown down from Calcutta.

He told me that he had applied to General Arnold, on behalf of the American Air Force in SEAC, for permission to give me American Command Pilot's wings. Apparently, the US regulations do not permit these to be given to an officer unless he already holds the wings of his own country; so if I ever qualify for the RAF, Stratemeyer says I shall automatically get the American wings as well!

The situation reminds me precisely of Topaze, where he says: '*Figure-toi que M. l'Inspecteur d'Académie a déclaré à M. Muche, qu'il me décernait les palmes académiques moralement,*' to which his friend Tamise replies, '*Moralement? Qu'est-ce que ça veut dire?*', and on Topaze saying, '*Ça veut dire qu'il m'en juge digne et il a chargé le patron de m'annoncer, en propres termes, que je les ai moralement.*' Tamise sums up the situation with, '*Oui, ça doit te faire tout de même plaisir, mais enfin tu ne les as pas.*'[1]

This is the case with the wings; *Enfin, je ne les ai pas!*

On Tuesday I had Rear Admiral Cecil Harcourt to lunch. He is out here in command of the Light Fleet Carrier Squadron. As he was recently Naval Secretary, I asked him what my present Naval position was, since on the 30th I have eight years seniority on the Captains' List. He informed me that I should reach the top of the Captains' List in one

[1] 'Just imagine, the secondary school inspector has told M. Muche that, morally speaking, he was awarding me academic honours.'
'Morally speaking – what does that mean?'
'It means that he considers me worthy and has told the head to announce in so many words that, morally speaking, I've got them.'
'Well, that must please you, but, all the same, you haven't got them.'

year's time, and that he does not then see how I can possibly avoid promotion to the substantive rank of Rear Admiral, since they would not retire me in my present job. He strongly advised me against asking for an exception to be made to keep me on the Captains' List.

On Thursday I went to Colombo for the day and went to inspect the new caravan I am having reconstructed in the Colombo Workshops. The object of this is to prevent the Army Commander from always giving up his own caravan to myself or very important visitors, since in future we will be able to use my caravan at Army Headquarters. I had hoped there would only be a Major and a Sergeant draughtsman to see me; but a hundred yards from the entrance a Brigadier was waiting to pilot us in. I jokingly said to Dusty Dunsterville: 'Most unusual, only having a Brigadier when I asked to see a Major; I had expected that they would have produced at least a Major General!' Never was a truer word spoken in jest, for the General Officer Commanding Ceylon Army Command was there all right in the caravan waiting to receive me, with eight staff officers and a guard of the Sappers turned out.

I told them that if they did this to me again, I should not feel free to come and look at the caravan.

We then drove to the Naval airfield on Colombo racecourse, as I had said that if the weather was suitable I might like to fly back in a light aircraft instead of going by train. I had asked that no special steps should be taken. They had therefore confined the arrangements to turning out a guard of honour of the Royal Marines, commanded by an Officer, to having some two dozen blue-jackets lining the route, and a dozen men fallen in at the aircraft, with the Captain, Commander, and a large staff to see me off. The weather turned out to be unsuitable, and so we went by train.

I explained to the Captain that unless he could really allow me to slip in quietly and use his airfield unobtrusively, it would mean I should always have to go by train, as I could not face completely dislocating the life of the station every time I wanted to come to Colombo.

On Saturday I had to write a very important letter to Oliver Leese and send an officer to take it to him personally in Kashmir.[1]

THURSDAY, 5 JULY to TUESDAY, 10 JULY 1945 This period was fairly fully occupied with meetings. Oliver Leese left from Calcutta on Saturday and sent me a friendly message before leaving.

[1] This letter informed General Leese that he was to be replaced as Commander-in-Chief by General Slim.

The whole of Sunday, from 0930 to 1730, with only a short break for lunch, was spent at a very big and important meeting.[1] I just had time to change and rush to St Paul's Church, Kandy, for the Naval Thanksgiving Service, the collection of which was for King George's Fund for Sailors, of which I am President.

WEDNESDAY, 11 JULY   Major General Penney, the new Director of Intelligence, picked me up and we drove out to the SEAC airfield together and at 1045 took off in the York. We landed at 1600 at Barrackpore, where senior British and American air officers met me. We had tea at 228 Group Headquarters. We took off at 1815 and flew direct from Calcutta to the Philippine Islands, via Lashio over the Hump and over China and the China Sea. As we were having dinner, the navigator came in and said: 'We are just passing over Kennedy Peak.' I looked at the altimeter and saw it was reading 9700 feet, which is the exact height of Kennedy Peak, so I replied, 'Only just!'

THURSDAY, 12 JULY   We landed punctually at 0730 at Nichols Field, Manila. We were met on this airfield by the greatest gathering of generals I can remember out of a series of great gatherings of generals on airfields.

The party was headed by General of the Army Douglas MacArthur, Commander-in-Chief of the Army Forces in the Pacific, and he was supported by numerous four, three, two and one-star generals, to whom I was introduced. MacArthur drove me in his car to the house he had lent me. We had to drive through the entire town of Manila, and I was horrified to see the degree of destruction which had been wrought everywhere. Unlike Rangoon, where at least 40 per cent of the town is intact, I doubt if 5 per cent of Manila is habitable. The siege lasted some three weeks, during which those houses that had not been destroyed by American artillery or aircraft were blown up by the Japanese before they left. The large ferro-concrete buildings had walls and pillars bulging outwards in all directions, but their iron skeletons held them from falling down completely, though they could not of course save them.

The General had found an undamaged house in the Santa Mesa

[1] About Operation ZIPPER, the projected maritime assault on Malaya, and arrangements during Mountbatten's forthcoming visits to General MacArthur and to Europe.

district, which had been occupied by the Japanese Ambassador up to the last moment. The house immediately opposite, which was also undamaged, was placed at my disposal.

After bath and breakfast I went through the admirably prepared programme and drove to General MacArthur's Headquarters at 1100. His Headquarters occupies about the only large building in Manila of which the majority has been saved, the new City Hall.

I had a long and interesting conversation with MacArthur, or, to be more precise, I listened to a fascinating monologue, and found the same difficulty in trying to chip in as I have no doubt most people find in trying to chip into my conversation (a very useful object lesson for young Supreme Commanders!).

At 1130 an ADC reported that our combined staffs were present for the meeting, but General MacArthur waved him lightly aside, and it was not until 1150 that he took me up to the meeting. At this meeting General MacArthur's staff presented the plans for his next operation in full detail, and answered all our questions. My staff then presented the plans for my next operation, in equally great detail. There was the most complete and frank exchange of information. The meeting did not break up until 1320, when the Commander-in-Chief drove me to his house for luncheon.

Mrs MacArthur and Ronnie [Brockman] were the only other two present, but young Arthur MacArthur, to whom I was introduced, kept passing through the room with a bundle of music under his arm. 'Don't take any notice of him,' said Mrs MacArthur. 'He's only trying to attract your attention.' Sure enough, when we didn't pay any attention to him, he sat down at the piano and played. Incidentally, he played extremely well. He is quite a prodigy.

Douglas MacArthur is the younger son of the great general Arthur MacArthur, who first conquered the Philippines for America at the end of the last century. Young Douglas took part as a Second Lieutenant. The elder son Arthur went into the Navy and had two sons. When he died 'Uncle Douglas' wrote his two nephews, who had recently married, urging them to produce a son who could carry on the traditional name of Arthur MacArthur. They tried hard, but could produce nothing but a series of daughters. Finally, in disgust, when he was 57 years old, Douglas MacArthur married for the second time and wrote to his two nephews; 'Since you have failed in your duty, it now behoves the elder generation to produce an Arthur MacArthur', which he successfully proceeded to do.

Mrs MacArthur described to me her life on Corregidor Island from Christmas 1941 until they left in March 1942. We had flown low over the Bataan Peninsula and Corregidor Island coming in, and the buildings and even the trees on the island had been knocked flat by bombardment.

At 1730 I called on the President of the Philippine Islands at Malacañan Palace. This was fortunately undamaged, except for the usual bullet holes and splinters, as the Japanese General had lived there. I found President Osmeña a most charming and distinguished grey-haired gentleman. I discussed his problems of Civil versus Military Administration as compared with my problems in Burma.

He quite honestly admitted: 'My landing with the General was only a gesture. I am powerless to achieve anything here, as I have not the means at my disposal. General MacArthur is and must remain the virtual Governor of the Philippines until the period of military operations is well over.' In other words, the position in the Philippines is no different from that in Burma. Indeed, the President hadn't even any clothes and was dressed in an ordinary American GI's issue uniform without any badges.[1]

He showed me round the house afterwards. What a funny thing memory is! I had not been to Manila for more than 23 years, and yet when he showed me that State Dining Room, I was certain that this was where we had danced; and he then admitted that many years ago the ballroom had been turned into a dining room.

FRIDAY, 13 JULY I ended the morning with another long and interesting talk with the Commander-in-Chief, to whom I am taking the most tremendous liking. I then drove out to Admiral Kinkaid's house. This is a house in the Cavite direction, which has also miraculously escaped damage. Kinkaid commands the 7th US Fleet.

In the afternoon, Admiral Kinkaid and Commodore Sullivan took me round the harbour. They had estimated that there were some 400 ships and craft sunk in the harbour and Manila Bay, from 12,000-ton ships to small 50-ton craft; but Commodore Sullivan (the great salvage expert of Naples and Cherbourg fame) assured me that he had already raised 400 and estimated that he still had another 200 to raise. We steamed round the wreck of a Japanese cruiser and two destroyers and

[1] The Philippines became independent in 1946, by which time Sergio Osmeña had retired.

then went and visited all the berths where ships were being discharged alongside. In addition to some 20 ships alongside, another 100 must have been lying in the harbour and bay, and an endless stream of landing craft, lighters and DUKWs was pouring backwards and forwards; so much so that it was quite a job to thread one's way through the traffic lanes.

Incidentally, the traffic ashore is greater than Manila ever knew in the piping times of peace, for the Americans have landed 300,000 trucks, which jam all the roads worse than London in mid-season. If they didn't send one everywhere with motorcycle police escorts and sirens, one would never get through in time.

I got back to our house just in time to receive President Osmeña's return call, and had an interesting half hour with him.

At 1815 General Kenney, who commands the Far Eastern Air Forces, called for me and drove me to his house, which stands outside the town and is also undamaged. We began the party by bathing in his swimming pool, and had a most valuable air gossip during dinner. It is interesting to note that this group of Air Generals has a different view as to how the war will end from the Ground Generals I met the previous night, and from the Admirals I met at lunch. General Kenney drove me back after dinner and remained talking to me until nearly 0100.

SATURDAY, 14 JULY   I called a conference of the whole of my staff at 0900, when we went through all the items which each member had been directed to discuss with his opposite number, and I was most happy to know the results which had been achieved by all.

At 1000 I drove to the City Hall to see General MacArthur and to comply with requests from the Press for photographs of both of us together.

Contrary to popular conception, he gives the impression of being a rather shy and sensitive man who regards compliance with the needs of publicity as a duty. He has not got a grey hair on his head at the age of 65, though the hair is beginning to thin out and recede. He does not look at all fierce or commanding until he puts his famous embroidered cap on. As we went out together to face the photographers, and he pulled his cap on, his whole manner changed. His jaw stuck out, he looked aggressive and tough; but as soon as the photographers had finished he relaxed completely, took off his hat, and was his old charming self.

At 1430 we drove on to Clark Field, where General Whitehead[1] met me and showed me round his Headquarters at Fort Stotsenberg.

General Whitehead then drove me round Clark Field, which has been enormously developed. Dozens and dozens of all types of Japanese aircraft abound all round; some utterly wrecked, others not too badly damaged, and one I even saw being got ready to fly under American colours.

At 1620 we took off in General MacArthur's own C.54, the Bataan. We flew out over the district where fighting is still going on and landed at Nichols Field at 1710.

I drove out to the 'Admiral Apartments', which is the only apartment house left standing, where most of my staff are accommodated. In a room there they had arranged for me to meet the Press informally. I explained I was not allowed to give a conference and they agreed to treat all my remarks as 'off the record'.

From there I drove to GHQ for a final conference with the Commander-in-Chief, at which I presented a memorandum embodying all our agreements, which we signed and exchanged copies.

On my return I found the Chief of the Australian Air Staff, Air Vice Marshal Jones, waiting to see me. I had a hurried conference with Jones, which I hope will be fruitful and then went over to dine with the MacArthurs. We had an extremely interesting dinner, at which the Commander-in-Chief waxed really eloquent. Finally at 2200 we left for Nichols Field, Mrs MacArthur promising to bring the General to visit me at the next favourable opportunity. He has invited me to attend the Victory March in Tokyo.

During the half-hour's drive to Nichols Field I had the most satisfactory of all my many talks with MacArthur. I fully admit I am completely under his spell; he is one of the most charming and remarkable characters I have ever met, and so sympathetic and friendly towards the South-East Asia Command.

SUNDAY, 15 JULY   We got over Akyab at 0640 after a ten-hour flight from Manila. As we were ahead of schedule, we flew round and landed at 0700. I was met by Air Commodore Hardman who delivered up to me some of the most intimate and private belongings of Sergeant Simon Eden, son of Anthony and Beatrice, who is still missing after an

---

[1] Commanding the 5th Air Force.

operational flight, some two or three weeks ago. It is now pretty certain that there is no longer any hope for him.

At 0720 we took off in a Dakota since Mingaladon airfield has not yet been lengthened to take a York. We landed at 0930 and were met by Lieutenant General Stopford. I drove with Monty Stopford to Government House, where I had an immediate meeting with him and Major General Rance[1] on Civil Affairs.

At 1530 Major General Symes, who commands the South Burma Area, arrived to take me round the various Army units connected with port activities. We started with the Sule Pagoda Wharf, where I walked round and shook hands with the officers of all the ships which were unloading and the officers of all the Dock Companies who unload them. A big parade of Indian Units in the dock area was spoilt by a heavy monsoon downpour starting shortly after my inspection, but we had been very lucky, as the rest of the day had been fine. I addressed the British troops of the Transport Columns in a recently repaired dock shed, having to shout to make myself heard above the rain. I got back at 1700 to Government House for a meeting with Stopford, Rance and Hughes (the Government's representative).

At 1800 Major General Aung San, Commander of the Patriot Burmese Forces, arrived for a meeting. This meeting went just as well as the last one, and I must say I found Aung San a very reasonable man to deal with. After three quarters of an hour this meeting broke up and I then took the chair at a big meeting of 45 Civil Affairs Officers from all districts in Burma, which lasted about 1¼ hours. We got very good value out of it; last time I had had to read the Riot Act among the Old Blimps, who were often oppressive and dictatorial. This time they all reported a much better attitude of the Burmese population, which I am sure is largely due to the fact that they have adopted a better attitude themselves. What a fight it has been to get a progressive and liberal and conciliatory policy going in Burma. Philip Joubert fought me so hard on this. He wanted to arrest Aung San and declare the Patriot Burmese Forces illegal and I find he has been sabotaging my policy in a most disloyal way behind my back. As he has now left my staff, matters are considerably easier in my relations with Burma Civil Affairs.

Those who opposed my policy when I first laid it down are now beginning to come round and see that I was right. Rance (who replaced

[1] Rance was Chief Civil Affairs Officer, 'a progressive and high-minded officer' in Mountbatten's words, who was eventually to replace Dorman-Smith as Governor of Burma.

Major General Pearce, who was one of Joubert's companions in disloyalty), told me that Than Tun, the Secretary of the Anti-Fascist organization, had told him, after a dinner one night, that for the first month the progressive Burmese could not believe that all the things we were saying and doing really could represent the policy we would carry out. They felt that they must be misunderstanding us and that they would soon be disillusioned. Finally, after they had had a talk with me and realized that this policy emanated from the top, and when they found that the Governor, a few days later, was proclaiming his intention of continuing with a co-operative and lenient policy, they realized that a new era had been born for Burma. As Than Tun sadly remarked: 'If the British Government had at any time during the last 100 years behaved to Burma as you have been behaving during the last few weeks, none of the troubles between us would ever have arisen, and no Burmans would have dreamed of supporting the Japanese.'

MONDAY, 16 JULY   Rance came to see me at 0820, to report further conversations with Aung San's staff last night, and drove out with me to Mingaladon. Here I had a ten-minute talk with Monty Stopford, and at 0900 we took off in the Dakota, landing at 1115 at Akyab. We transferred to the York and took off again at 1130.

I sat in the co-pilot's seat and we followed the blind landing procedure, flying in on our two radio beacons for the SEAC airfield.

TUESDAY, 17 JULY to SATURDAY, 21 JULY   Reggie Dorman-Smith stayed until 19th July and we had a series of excellent meetings with him and his staff, trying to solve the knotty problems of preparing a programme of how and when I could hand over various parts of Burma to him. He has agreed to support my proposal strongly that Aung San should be offered a commission as an acting Brigadier and as one of the two Deputy Inspectors General of the Burma Army, under a British Major General. If this comes off, it will indeed be a triumph, for Joubert spent most of his time trying to persuade me to shoot him as a traitor. I wonder what would have happened if we had tried and shot Botha and Smuts after the South African war?

MONDAY, 23 JULY [New Delhi]   At 0900 I attended an inter-command meeting in Claude's office. The meeting ended at 1100 and I then went to my own office, for some work.

At 1145 I went to Viceroy's House for an interview with H.E. He and I lunched alone at 1230, and I left him just after 1300.

We took off from Palam airfield at 1330, seen off by the usual crowd of senior officers.

At 1700 we ran into a violent monsoon rain-squall. The York dropped so violently that all of us left our seats by several feet. As we landed, we ploughed our way through inches of water. It is curious to think that almost exactly a year ago we were held up by a similar cloudburst at Karachi, and bearing this in mind I refused to be kept back and insisted on taking off before the heavy rain came on again. (This turned out to be lucky, as several other officers in our party were held up for two days on account of the rain at Karachi.) We were airborne at 1800 and had dinner on board.

TUESDAY, 24 JULY   We landed at 0145, Cairo Local Time. I was handed a most immediate telegram from Pug Ismay, telling me not to go to Paris, where I had arranged to spend the night with the Duff Coopers but to go straight to Berlin to join the Potsdam Conference. We hurriedly worked out a new route and at 0230 took off. We flew across the southwest corner of Greece. As I woke up, I recognized the harbour of Argostoli, where I have so often been with the Mediterranean Fleet. We flew on across the Adriatic to Brindisi, and then straight up to Venice and from thence over the Italian Alps into Germany.

Fortunately it was a lovely day. Whereas Jack Matthews usually flies the York at over 10,000 feet, when I went forward to the cockpit for the passage of the Alps we were only flying at 9200. As the Alps at this point are 11,000 feet high, I expected to see him climb; but in fact he went down to about 8400 feet, and flew through a valley, with mountains towering up on either side of us!

We were routed over Frankfurt, presumably in order to fly over the American and British zones rather than the Russian zone. We had no large-scale maps of this part of the world, but luckily I knew my way around pretty well and we circled the Heiligenberg[1] once, which was undamaged but had been painted a dark khaki colour. We flew twice over Darmstadt, which was unrecognizable, it had been so severely bombed. The whole damage was done in a 25-minute raid, and Merck's big chemical works had not even been touched, so a second raid was

[1] Heiligenberg Castle was the family home of Mountbatten's father. It had been sold in 1920.

necessary to destroy them. The New Palace was flat, but part of the Schloss still seemed to be standing. We then flew on to Wolfsgarten and circled it twice.[1] It appeared to be undamaged.

No one, not even Gloucester W/T Station, would tell us what the local time in Berlin was, and we were led to believe that it was one hour ahead of GMT, which is the normal pre-war European time. Actually they were keeping double summertime in Germany, which was three hours ahead of GMT, and so whereas we thought we had arrived at 1110, in point of fact we were told on landing at Gatow airfield that the time was 1310.

We drove with a smart British motorcycle escort along roads lined in many places by well-turned-out Russian troops. Presumably they belong to a Guards Division. The sentries stand in pairs and although they are dressed in khaki they have blue breeches, high black boots, brass buttons and blue or green piping and facings to their tunics. The officers wear gold shoulder straps. The line regiments apparently wear khaki breeches.

The women of the Guards Divisions wear smart blue skirts, with high black boots; the women of the Line Divisions wear khaki skirts. They carry out traffic control duties with semaphore flags.

We arrived at 1340 at House No. 1A, which had just been vacated by Field Marshal Alexander and Major General Laycock and which had been turned over to our party. We had lunch in No. 44 Mess, where I met Pug Ismay, Bob Laycock, Anthony Head, and Alex.

At 1445 I called at the PM's house, and was told he had bidden me to dinner that night.

At 1500 I had a discussion with the CCO[2] and at 1615 I had tea with the British Chiefs of Staff. At 1730 I went with them to attend the 200th meeting of the Combined Chiefs of Staff, which had been called for the purpose of meeting me. I addressed the meeting for half an hour on past and future operations in SEAC, and after that for another half an hour answered a series of questions by the US Chiefs of Staff.

I can never describe the friendliness of the reception I had from the American Chiefs of Staff. Hard-boiled old Fleet Admiral King took my hand in both his hands and shook it a dozen times with great warmth. Bill Somervell appeared even more pleased to see me.

General Marshall and General Arnold invited me to come back and

---

[1] Last remaining palace lived in by the former royal family of Hesse-Darmstadt.
[2] Chief of Combined Operations, Major General Laycock.

have a drink with them. Then Marshall swore me to secrecy and said he would reveal to me the greatest secret of the war. It appeared that the team of British and American scientists who had been working on the release of atomic energy had at last succeeded in utilizing the release of energy from the fission of element 235, an isotope of uranium, and that when this had been applied in a bomb the results had been quite shattering. An experimental bomb exploded in New Mexico and had had unbelievable results. A steel girder structure half a mile away had either melted or been vaporized; there was nothing left of it. It was estimated that all human beings within a radius of two or three miles would be killed, and those beyond this radius for a mile or two, would be so burned as to be unlikely to recover.

Marshall told me they now had an atomic bomb on the way over to Okinawa, ready for release round about the 5th August.

I said: 'This will surely mean the end of the war within the next few days, or anyway within the next few weeks?'

Marshall and Arnold both agreed that this was so, and that they couldn't possibly visualize the war going on beyond the end of 1945 in any case.

I then asked why the meeting of the Combined Chiefs of Staff that afternoon had given the official date of the end of the war as the 15th November 1946; and they pointed out that on account of secrecy the planners had had to work without knowledge of the bomb's existence, and that this was a fair estimate of how long it might have taken if there had been no bomb.

Finally General Marshall reminded me of my promise not to tell a living soul – not even the Prime Minister, with whom General Marshall knew I was dining that night.

I left them at 1930 and had a brief talk with Pug Ismay. I then returned to the house and wrote a letter to Generalissimo Stalin, asking if I might come and pay my respects the following day. I was going to send Johnny Papps round to his house with it, when I thought a mere Major might not cut sufficient ice with the Russians, and therefore decided to send Major General Kimmins with him. Even so, they had no luck; after being kept 1½ hours outside his house while being interviewed by Russian officers of ever-increasing seniority, they failed to get an answer to the letter. Indeed, the first two officers refused even to take hold of the letter! The Russians are certainly extremely suspicious and security-minded.

At 2030 I dined alone with the Prime Minister in his house, having been excused for this purpose by the Combined Chiefs of Staff, who had also invited me to their dinner.

After dinner we moved into the study, and the Prime Minister closed the doors. After looking round in a conspiratorial manner, he said: 'I have a great secret to tell you' – and proceeded to tell me the story of the atomic bomb. He said it would be dropped on the 5th and that the Japanese would surrender on the 15th. He advised me to take all necessary steps to compete with the capitulation as soon after this date as possible. I therefore sent a telegram to Boy Browning to take all the necessary steps, without of course being able to give him the reason.

I had come back convinced that Labour would get in by a handsome majority and was astounded to find that the Prime Minister and indeed everyone I met at Potsdam was quite confident that the Conservative Party would get in.[1] The most pessimistic majority I heard was 30, and the Prime Minister himself told me he thought he would have 100.

The Prime Minister has never been so friendly to me in his life. He kept on telling me what a good job I had done, and how I had vindicated his judgement when he selected me for the job. He said: 'When the war is over I am going to arrange a great ovation for you and for your battle-green jungle warriors. When we get back to London come and see me and we will talk about your future, as I have great plans in store.' It was a mournful and eerie feeling to sit there talking plans with a man who seemed so confident that they would come off, and I felt equally confident that he would be out of office within 24 hours. However, I was particularly glad to have a three-hour heart-to-heart talk with him, when he was in such a good mood. It would indeed have been terrible if I had not been able to see him until after his defeat at the elections. For once he did not keep me up late, and I was home before midnight.

WEDNESDAY, 25 JULY I called on Anthony Eden at 0900 and brought him the intimate personal possessions of his son, Sergeant Simon Eden, who was lost in a Dakota Squadron from Akyab recently. We had a half-hour's very interesting talk on future operations, and Anthony promised to support my point of view to the full; but again I had a curious feeling of talking to someone who did not realize he would no longer be Foreign Secretary on the following day.

At 0930 I called on President Truman at his house, and had an

---

[1] Mountbatten's views were largely based on some remarkably accurate predictions made by Peter Murphy.

hour's interview with him. The President told me, as a great secret, the story of the atomic bomb. He also agreed that it would bring the war to an abrupt conclusion. I suggested he should tell MacArthur of this, as when I was with him he gave no indication of knowing. I then pointed out to the President how extremely difficult it was for theatre commanders, especially in far distant theatres, if they were not kept fully informed of all developments that were likely to have such a profound effect on their theatres. I also suggested that the timing of successive bombs should be so arranged that everyone would have time to get ready for this surrender and not be caught unprepared. The President agreed that this should be given consideration, but his view of course was that the war should not continue for one unnecessary day. Since the atomic bomb had cost $2,000,000,000 (about nine days' cost of the war), he felt that the sooner the war could be brought to an end, both from the point of view of human life and economy, the better; although it is clearly going to present the wretched commanders with extremely difficult problems.

The President could not possibly have been more forthcoming or friendly and thanked me on behalf of the United States for the way I had looked after American interests in SEAC. He said: 'Just as the British feel that Eisenhower was very fair in looking after the British interests in SHAEF, so all of us Americans feel you have been very fair in looking after American interests in SEAC.'

After this I had a brief interview with Pug Ismay, when we discussed my relationship with the Chiefs of Staff, which on the whole, he told me, had never been better.

At 1100 I left by car for Berlin, with my staff. On arrival at the Adlon Hotel (or what was left of it) we transferred to the car which Hitler had given to Admiral Doenitz; this was a supercharged, armoured Mercedes, the windows of which were two inches thick. It was driven by an RCNVR Lieutenant, since it had been taken over by the British Navy in Berlin. We had a sightseeing tour, ending up at the Chancellery.

When one looks at the streets superficially, the majority of the houses appear to be standing; but when one drives down the streets one realizes that extremely few of the houses are habitable, since most of them are gutted.

The Chancellery was very interesting, particularly Hitler's own study, which was of gigantic proportions. We also went and had a look at the dugout in which he and his girlfriend, Eva Braun, committed suicide; and saw the place where his body was burned, and the five petrol cans which were used in burning it, which were still on the scene. The Russians, however, claim that his death was faked, and that he is still alive somewhere. As I believe he was out of his mind from time to time at the end of the war, this seems unlikely, as one cannot easily conceal a man during his periods of insanity, when he is not in a position to cooperate.

We arrived at the Cecilienhof punctually at 1230, as arranged by the Prime Minister, only to find that the conference of the Big Three had broken up a few minutes earlier. However, Generalissimo Stalin was still there, and it was arranged I should go and see him at his house.

To save both his time and mine (since my aircraft was due to depart at 1330), I suggested that I might drive with him in his car, or if this was not possible that my car should follow his, so that we would not get lost or turned back by the guards. Both these suggestions were considered to be quite out of the question. The arrangements for his safety are infinitely greater than those made for poor Uncle Nicky.[1]

After having lost our way, we eventually arrived at Stalin's house, where we had a very friendly reception. The Generalissimo himself came out of his study and advanced across the hall to meet me.

At the meeting he spoke through his interpreter, Pavlov, and I through the British interpreter, Major Lunghi. He has a curious way of using an interpreter, whereby he speaks half a dozen words, pauses long enough for the interpreter to put them into English, and then goes on again; so that one gets a barely intermittent running commentary.

Stalin was very friendly, and asked about the Burma campaign. In reply to my questions, he agreed that the war against Japan was going to end in the very near future, and said that Russia would come in before the war ended.

We had a great rush to get out to the airfield, because so many VIPs were taking off that day that, if we had missed our take-off time between 1330 and 1345, we could not have again got into the queue until 1530. The PM had already upset their plans by leaving long before his expected time, and had taken off just before us.

We landed at Northolt just after him. Edwina and Patricia were there. Owing to the difference in time of two hours, we arrived at 1500. We drove straight to Chester Street, and after a talk with the family I went on to the offices which had been arranged for the SEAC Mission at 1, Richmond Terrace, next door to COHQ. I shall have some 20 officers with me, because we expected to have a lot of hard work ahead of us.

[1] The last Tsar of Russia.

Mama, Alice and Louise came to dinner. By great good luck, both the sisters were here.[1] It is the first time we have all been together for six years, and I was glad to find them very unchanged in appearance.

Edwina gave me the Gestapo dossier on me, with a minute by Hitler saying I should be tried by a People's Court if captured!

THURSDAY, 26 JULY At 1700 Edwina and I went to Buck House to have tea with the King and Queen. The news of the sweeping Labour victory came out today; it appeared to surprise everybody I met. The King was seeing the old and new Prime Ministers (Winston Churchill and Attlee) as soon as we left.

We took the girls to the theatre and dined with them at Claridges afterwards. Later I had an interview with General Bill Donovan in his room at Claridges.

FRIDAY, 27 JULY A very busy day, with interviews all day, including Admiral Helfrich, the Dutch C.-in-C., who was in London from SEAC.

I attended a meeting of the Chiefs of Staff at 1130, and after lunch at Chester Street Duff Cooper (our Ambassador in Paris) came to see me to discuss plans for stopping in Paris and calling on General de Gaulle on my way back to make up for my having been diverted from Paris on the way home.

After lunch we left in the Admiralty car and drove to Kensington Palace, where I picked up Mama, Alice and Louise, and the whole lot of us drove down to Broadlands where I am to have 10 days' leave – the first since 1941.

SATURDAY, 4 AUGUST to MONDAY, 6 AUGUST 1945 On Sunday Sir William and Lady Slim came for a short weekend. He is on leave from the 14th Army prior to relieving Oliver Leese as C.-in-C. ALFSEA.

The four Planners came down for lunch and we spent the entire afternoon in conference. As I had been told to keep the existence of the atomic bomb such a close secret, I could not do more than repeat to the Planners what I had been telling them since I got back – that the war would end about the 15th August, and I was not allowed to give them

[1] Mountbatten's sisters, married to Prince Andrew of Greece and the Crown Prince (later King Gustav VI) of Sweden respectively.

the reasons. It followed that most of the detailed work which we did, which was for our contribution to the final assault on Japan, seemed very unreal to me, as I knew it was going to prove abortive. However, we got through a lot of work.

After tea Patricia, Edwina and I drove to Windsor. We are staying in the rooms in which my sister Alice was born. We saw the King and Queen and Lilibet and Margaret soon after arrival, and I had a long, separate and very profitable interview with H.M.

Everybody was in good form over dinner, as the atomic bomb had just fallen and we were busy discussing the prospects of an early peace.

TUESDAY, 7 AUGUST   We left Windsor after an early breakfast, and I had a meeting with my staff right away, followed by a meeting with the Chiefs of Staff at 1130. I saw Mr Bevin, the new Foreign Secretary, in his office, and drove with him to lunch at Chester Street, where Mrs Bevin met us. The new First Lord, A. V. Alexander was there.[1]

Edwina, in a fit of absent-mindedness, had asked two more people than the dining room table would hold. She only succeeded in borrowing a big enough table at the last moment and it appeared in a horse-drawn van ten minutes before the guests.

I continued seeing people all day, including Lieutenant General Bimbo Dempsey, who is to succeed Bill Slim in command of the 14th Army, and Field Marshal Montgomery.

WEDNESDAY, 8 AUGUST   I called on the new Secretary of State for Air, Lord Stansgate, and the new First Lord. After this I had an hour with the First Sea Lord (Admiral Cunningham).[2]

I attended a luncheon given by the Kinema Renters Society for me at Claridges, at which there were many speeches.

At 1530 I attended the first Defence Committee meeting of the new Government at No. 10 Downing Street, at which we discussed my future plans and those of General MacArthur. I am afraid I blotted my copy book with the First Sea Lord by trying to get the Light Fleet Carriers back into South-East Asia.[3]

---

[1] He had been First Lord in the wartime coalition government.
[2] Admiral Sir Andrew Cunningham had been First Sea Lord since October 1943. He was succeeded by his namesake John in 1946.
[3] Cunningham was indignant that Mountbatten raised this issue in the Defence Committee rather than proceeding through 'the usual channels'.

THURSDAY, 9 AUGUST   I began the morning at 0900 with meetings with Mr Isaacs, the new Minister of Labour, followed by Lord Pethwick Lawrence, Secretary of State for India and Burma.

At 1110 we drove to the Ministry of Information, where I had an interview with the new Minister, Mr Williams.

At 1145 I met about 150 of the principal editors, broadcasters, etc., for an off-the-record discussion which lasted till 1300, and seemed to go very well. I was able to enlarge on our policy in Burma, which was very well received.

At 1300 Edwina picked me up, and we drove to the Mansion House for luncheon with the Lord Mayor. I had been warned I had to make a speech, but had not thought out what I was going to say, as I intended to do so in the car going down. However, Edwina was very gay and chattered, and I hadn't the heart to stop her, with the result that I arrived at the Mansion House with no idea of what I was going to say.

There were about 30 people at lunch, including all the important city people, and I was the only speaker. I tried hard to marshal my thoughts during lunch, but both my neighbours occupied my attention fully, so that when I got up on my feet I really had not strung two words together. The consequence was that I made what Edwina informed me was one of the best speeches of my life. Anyway, the various city magnates all rallied round and were very polite about it.

At 1500 I was back at the Ministry of Information for a large open Press Conference of four or five hundred reporters.

From here I went to have meetings with Sir Stafford Cripps, President of the Board of Trade, and Mr Lawson, the new Secretary of State for War.

FRIDAY, 10 AUGUST   I spent the morning making recordings at Broadcasting House for the broadcast which was to be put on immediately after the 9 o'clock news that night.

At 1115 I attended a meeting of the Chiefs of Staff, and at 1230 I went to pay my respects to the Prime Minister. I was alone with him in the Cabinet room at No. 10 Downing Street when his Secretary burst in with the news that the Domei Agency had broadcast the Japanese offer to accept the Potsdam terms.

Edwina and I lunched at the Chinese Embassy with the Wellington Koos. During lunch the butler came in and said: 'Mr Churchill to speak to you on the telephone.' I went down and found Winston on the telephone saying: 'Well, Dickie, it's happened – and on the 15th, too, just as I said.[1] I hope you have made all plans and that you are ready to send your first aeroplane into Singapore tomorrow. Mind you, I no longer have the right to talk to you like this, but speak as a friend who hopes we will press on quickly.'

I had a very hectic afternoon with the various ambassadors, etc. Edwina and I had tea with Queen Mary at Marlborough House, after which I went to see the new Secretary of State for the Colonies, Mr George Hall.

SATURDAY, 11 AUGUST   At 1100 I went up to do a fresh series of recordings to broadcast, since the offer of capitulation had completely put my previous recordings out of date, and they had not been used.

SUNDAY, 12 AUGUST   At 0330 Pug Ismay rang me up from the country to say that the Prime Minister wished me to return at once. As I had only just previously sought instructions, and been told to go back on Monday, this was very disconcerting, and meant cancelling my visit to Paris a second time. I spent a busy day squaring off everything, and after dinner we went to Stoney Cross airfield nearby and were airborne in the York at 2115.

MONDAY, 13 AUGUST to TUESDAY, 14 AUGUST   We stopped at Cairo for refuelling, and at Karachi for refuelling, but apart from that flew on straight through, reaching the SEAC airstrip at 0930 on Tuesday the 14th, having been exactly 30 hrs 45 minutes from Stoney Cross – a record flight, in spite of having to make a wide diversion to miss a monsoon storm.

Keith Park, Speck Wheeler, Boy Browning, etc., were there to meet me. I drove back with Boy, who had only that day got up from a bed of sickness and looked very ill. He told me everything was well in hand as a result of the signal I had sent from the Potsdam Conference telling him that the Japanese were going to capitulate on the 15th August.

---

[1] Since this conversation took place on 10 August the reason for Churchill's self-congratulation is obscure. Possibly Mountbatten meant to write '5th', the day on which the bomb was dropped.

WEDNESDAY, 22 AUGUST to TUESDAY, 28 AUGUST   Edwina and Brian Kimmins arrived out on Thursday. She very gallantly flew out at a moment's notice to help me with the repatriation of the prisoners of war, of which she had great experience in Europe.

On Saturday the great Victory Parade was held in Colombo, at which some 3500 representatives of all the services marched past in 35 minutes. At this rate, the 1,380,000 men in SEAC would take nearly 9 days and 9 nights to march past!

Incidentally, few people realize the immense scale of the enlarged South-East Asia Command, which includes a million and a half square miles of territory, has a population of 128 millions, nearly half a million Japs and over 200,000 prisoners of war and internees to be repatriated.[1] From the northwest corner of SEAC, which starts a few hundred miles west of Karachi, down to the new easternmost limits, halfway through New Guinea, is a distance of 6050 statute miles. This is 150 miles more than the distance from the northwest corner of SEAC to St Johns, Newfoundland!

On Tuesday, while I was holding my Cs-in-C.'s meeting, Boy Browning arrived back from Rangoon where he had been holding the preliminary South-East Asia surrender negotiations with Lieutenant-General Numata, Chief of Staff to my Japanese opposite number, Field Marshal Count Terauchi, who is the Supreme Commander of the Army, Navy and Air Forces of Japan in the whole of the Southern Regions.

We had been ready to start re-occupying Penang on the 22nd August, and all other territories shortly after, but on the instructions of General MacArthur, who has been made Supreme Commander for all the Allied powers for the surrender, I have been made to keep back all my forces until he has finished the official surrender negotiations in Tokyo on the 2nd September.

SATURDAY, 1 SEPTEMBER to MONDAY, 3 SEPTEMBER 1945   At 1100 on Saturday, the Lieutenant Governor General of the Netherlands East Indies, Dr Van Mook, arrived at the SEAC airfield. Edwina and I drove out in a jeep to meet them. I am putting H.E. up in KP.

I worked hard all the afternoon, during which the Siamese Military Mission arrived at my headquarters; but I personally refrained from

[1] At Potsdam it had been agreed that South-East Asia Command should be widened to include French Indochina, Java, Borneo and the Celebes.

having any dealings with them until they had had their preliminary meetings with my staff.

We got back[1] early on Monday morning, as Edwina had to leave for her tour of the prisoner of war camps, beginning with the transit area at Rangoon and then to Bangkok for the terrible camps in Siam.

TUESDAY, 4 SEPTEMBER   I had a large Siamese lunch party, to which I invited the entire Siamese Military Mission, and those members of my Headquarters who had been dealing with them. The Siamese Mission consisted of eight, headed by the Deputy Commander in Chief, Lieutenant-General Sena Narong. There were Naval, Military, Air Force and diplomatic representatives on the Mission, as well, and all were very humble and very anxious to please. SEAC had been in the ludicrous position of having an integrated Allied Headquarters, the British half of which was at war with Siam, and the American half of which was at peace with Siam. Some eight months ago the Regent of Siam offered to place the Siamese Army under my command, and asked me to equip it. It is sufficiently unusual to be offered command of the enemy army in war, but to be asked to equip it as well seemed a shade over the odds. I prevented them from coming into the open on our side, as they would have been massacred by the Japanese before I could have got in to help them. But now we were prepared to kiss and make friends.

The Siamese General and Admiral were particularly small. The General had the added disadvantage of having an enormous sword with a heavy silver scabbard. I feared he would never be able to sit down at luncheon, and that his sword would probably keep him propped up out of his chair. I therefore said to the interpreter: 'Ask the General to let my ADC take his sword.' The General turned very white and handed over his sword. He ate little and talked nervously and humbly throughout the meal. After lunch I had a meeting with the Heads of the Siamese Mission, and my Commanders-in-Chief, at which a military agreement was drawn up in two parts; one part which they had authority to sign at once, and the other part for which they said they had insufficient authority. I then ordered the General to remain behind while he sent the rest of the Mission back to obtain the necessary authority. At this he almost collapsed. Just as he was leaving the house, I called to his

---

[1] From a weekend at Dimbula.

interpreter and said: 'Tell the General he has forgotten his sword.' The General's face lit up with relief as he recovered his sword.

I only discovered afterwards that the General thought that I had demanded his sword in token of surrender, and had subsequently ordered his retention as a hostage!

At 1700 I had a colossal meeting with the Netherlands delegation and the senior members of my Dutch staff, at which we settled many questions on the future of those parts of the Netherlands East Indies which I have now taken over. Unfortunately we already have a local Resistance movement in Java, known as the Indonesian Republic, which will require very careful handling.

WEDNESDAY, 5 SEPTEMBER The Dutch Mission left and the Burmese People's Mission arrived. They are led by Major General Aung San, who has with him each of the Area Commanders of the Burmese Patriotic Forces, as well as representatives of some of the other racial, irregular forces. The Anti-Fascist People's Freedom League was represented by their Secretary, Than Tun. Thus I have 11 Burmese, as well as the Governor of Burma's delegation, which includes Tin Tut, who has been most valuable as a preliminary go-between.

Air Vice Marshal Maltby, who has just been released from the senior officers' prison camp at Mukden, came to lunch. I used to know him in the old days in Malta, and was shocked to find how thin he had become. He had terrible tales to tell of the way the Japanese set out to humiliate the senior officials. The Governor of British North Borneo was made to sweep the streets of his own capital. British Generals were invariably made to salute Japanese privates, and bow to them. Lieutenant General Heath, one of the Corps Commanders, had a crippled arm from a last war wound. The Japanese sentries took a delight in calling him to attention, knowing that he couldn't get his arm down, which gave them the necessary excuse for striking him each time.

THURSDAY, 6 SEPTEMBER My York came back from Okinawa, where it had taken the SEAC delegation to the Tokyo surrender. It brought back Lieutenant General Percival, the late General Officer Commanding Malaya, who surrendered Singapore to the Japanese. I had only seen Percival once or twice since the old Malta days, when he commanded the Cheshires. I found him woefully thin and aged. He had been present at the great surrender in Tokyo Bay, and Charles Gairdner[1] had brought him thinking I would like to take him on to Singapore, but I am afraid I took the view that since we had not reconquered Singapore by force of arms, bringing Percival in a second time rather savoured of hawking him round from surrender to surrender. Percival quite understood my point of view.

He too had sad tales to tell of having his face slapped in public by Japanese privates and was most interesting on the Malayan campaign.

The house is now full to overflowing with high-ups in every possible room, and I seem to be dealing with French, Dutch, Siamese, Burmese, and MacArthur's party almost simultaneously.

At 1100 I had a full-dress meeting with all the Burmese of both delegations, except the Governor himself, who was meeting the Burmese politicians off the record. I had been warned by General Stopford (who was present at the meeting) that he thought a rebellion was about to break out in Burma, unless I was able to obtain satisfactory agreements at this meeting.[2] At their request a verbatim record was taken of all our meetings, and I began by putting Aung San in his place by pointing out the comparatively small share that his forces had had in the liberation of Burma, compared with the Karens, Chins, Kachins and Nagas. After two hours we reached a provisional agreement on which staff meetings could continue for the rest of the day.

Monty Stopford asked Bill Slim after the meeting: 'Do meetings always last as long as this here?' I was therefore intensely amused to find the staff meetings with the Burmese, at which I had instructed him to take the chair, lasted from 1430 to 2100, without a break!

In the evening I had a dinner party to meet all my house guests, and we showed the American film *Stilwell Road*. This was the film which I had originally suggested should be an Anglo-American venture, but when it was found impossible to reach agreement on the script in Washington, I agreed with General Marshall that they should make an American version, *Stilwell Road*, and we should make a British version, *Jungle Victory*. We both pledged each other that we would be fair about the share of the other nation, and I must say Marshall has kept his word, for this film is excellent.

---

[1] Lieutenant General Gairdner was Mountbatten's representative at General MacArthur's Headquarters.
[2] Aung San was disturbed at the bad terms which he thought his followers were getting over integration with the regular army.

FRIDAY, 7 SEPTEMBER   I was to have had a final meeting with all the Burmese at 1100, only to find that they were still holding staff discussions; and so the meeting could not start till 1200. I felt it was going to be a two-hour meeting, and so it turned out.

Meetings went on in different parts of the house all the evening; and as midnight struck I had General Sena Narong waiting to sign the final agreement with the Siamese in the dining room, with the Chief Political Adviser and those concerned with Siam. In one corner of the lounge, the Governor of Burma and his staff were having final discussions with Aung San, Tin Tut and U Ba Pe, over the final agreement which I was about to sign with them. In another corner Brian Kimmins had laid out an enormous plan of the Municipal Buildings at Singapore, and with little marked Halma men was busy going through the ceremonial for the Singapore surrender. In yet another corner of the lounge, the Director of Intelligence and one of the Saigon Control Commission were drafting a reply to an unsatisfactory signal from Field Marshal Terauchi, for my approval. Luckily the French and Dutch Cs-in-C. had by this time returned to their respective houses, and the party from Tokyo were drinking quietly in the only free corner.

If Hollywood had attempted to stage such a scene at the residence of a Supreme Allied Commander, I am afraid it would have been regarded as burlesque.

SATURDAY, 8 SEPTEMBER   It is lucky I am off tomorrow, because I really cannot compete with the rate at which high-ups are arriving in Kandy. Today the High Commissioner for French Indochina, my old friend Vice Admiral d'Argenlieu arrived. It was reported he was bringing a staff of 61, but this turned out to be a false alarm. He merely had a Rear Admiral and a Colonel, and a small staff.

SUNDAY, 9 SEPTEMBER   I left the King's Pavilion at 0615 and at 0700 took off. I took Sir William Slim with me. I also took Mr Tom Driberg, an old acquaintance who is out here in the dual capacity of MP and War Correspondent.[1] At 1720 we landed at Mingaladon airfield, Rangoon. As a result of an official reprimand which I had to pass out for lack of proper reception arrangements when Boy Browning went as my

---

[1] 'Bevin is behaving like the *worst conservative diehard*,' Edwina wrote indignantly a little later. But Tom Driberg was coming to dinner, 'so I'll get the leftist views on Java, etc'.

representative for the surrender negotiations in Rangoon I found a transformation scene. 200 men of the Royal Air Force Regiment were paraded under arms along the length of the strip and a special guard of RAF police lined it as Sister Anne landed.

Stopford drove me to his bungalow after which he took me to meet a deputation of all the men overdue for repatriation in the transit camps in Rangoon. After hearing their complaints I was luckily able to satisfy their requirements and all passed off well.

Rangoon is one of the staging points for the great air traffic moving to Singapore for the surrender and at dinner in the Army Commanders' Mess was General Carton de Wiart on his way through. After dinner I had a meeting with Generals Slim, Stopford and Gracey, who is going to be my representative in Field Marshal Count Terauchi's Headquarters in Saigon. Air Marshal Park also attended this meeting.

At this meeting we decided, amongst other things, to visit between us all the British prisoners of war that had arrived in Rangoon by air from Bangkok.

MONDAY, 10 SEPTEMBER At 0800 I started off going to various hospitals and transit camps where our repatriated prisoners of war were being taken care of prior to their onward passage by sea. In all I addressed some 4500 prisoners and had the most tumultuous reception I have ever experienced. It was almost impossible to start speaking when one first stood up on account of the excited condition of the men who went on cheering and clapping the moment one stood up. I was much touched by the constant references, from the various prisoners I spoke to individually, to Edwina's visit to their camps in Thailand; her visit evidently went down extremely well with everybody.

At 1030 our Dakota flight took off and at 1730 landed at Penang. At 2000 we went to the Residency which had been prepared for our visit. I must say the Japanese had left it in very good order. I had not been to Penang for 23 years and had forgotten what a lovely island it is. The people gave the British a tumultuous welcome on their return which is all the more remarkable considering the shameful way in which we left them in the lurch. It only came to my knowledge now that in 1942 the British community apparently arranged to leave in secret. No natives, nor Eurasians and not even Eurasian wives of British officials were allowed to be in the secret and all were left behind. The British community went to their offices as usual in the morning and during the luncheon hour secretly embarked in a ship and went down to Singapore. I think that it was only right that they were subsequently interned by the Japanese. The Japanese must have treated the population very badly for them to be so pleased to see us back after such a shaming evacuation.

TUESDAY, 11 SEPTEMBER   We left the Residency at 0800 and our flight of Dakotas took off at 0845. At 1000 we arrived over the Port Swettenham area and flew over the great invasion fleet for Operation ZIPPER. September 9th had been the D-Day for this great invasion and although the Japanese had capitulated I had kept the assault phase of this operation in being in case there was any treachery since I had no atomic bomb to take its place!

The original invasion force was to have been 7 Infantry Divisions, one armoured Brigade, one Parachute Brigade, one Commando Brigade – a total of over a quarter of a million men. Actually we only landed 100,000 and of course without opposition but I feel sure that it must have had its effect on the Japanese to find that three days before their official surrender in Singapore we came in overwhelming forces from the north in addition to the 5th Indian Division which had been landed by arrangement with the Japanese in the south.

At 1030 we landed at Kelanang near Port Swettenham airfield where we were met by Lieutenant General Ouvry Roberts, commanding 34th Indian Corps, as well as the usual crowd of other senior officers. I was immediately attacked by the Commanders-in-Chief, who complained that the Naval Force Commander, Rear Admiral Martin, had taken the bigger and better of the two Headquarters ships, *Bulolo*, to Singapore for the surrender, turning out his air and military colleagues into the smaller HQ ship *Largs* at a moment's notice.[1]

I began by addressing the airmen of 902 wing at the airfield and was delighted to discover that they already had 200 Jap prisoners of war working on the airfield. We then drove along the road to Klang.

All along the road the local inhabitants were putting up triumphal arches, of which the biggest and best was still in the course of erection in the town of Klang. We had a very friendly reception from the population. After this I saw a party of Chinese guerillas raised by two of my

---

[1] The partial breakdown in communications that resulted from this action, coupled with faulty intelligence on the state of the beaches, turned ZIPPER into something less than a total success.

Force 136 officers. They were very smart and enthusiastic and I addressed them through a Chinese interpreter. These men would have done great work if we had had to invade the country and we had raised an irregular army to assist them all over Malaya.

After this we had lunch at the Klang Club which had been taken over as 25th Divisional Headquarters. We drove back in a monsoon downpour and arrived to find the Kelanang airfield almost under water. We were in a terrible quandary since the great Surrender Ceremony was to take place the following morning. But fortunately the rain stopped in time for our flight to take off and we reached Kellang at 1730. The three Dakotas landed in swift succession at Kellang airfield which is really one of the greatest airports in the world, comparable to La Guardia in New York for it has excellent concrete runways as well as flying boat quays within the same airport.

We drove straight from the airport to the Municipal Buildings in order to inspect the parade ground and Council Chamber where the Surrender Ceremony was to be held on the morrow. A colossal crowd was collected round the parade ground to watch the most pleasant sight which the population that had been suffering under the Japanese yoke for 3½ years could possibly wish to see – 100 Japanese soldiers were busy filling in the slit trenches on the Padang by hand.

Outside the Council Chambers I saw Edwina with some of her Red Cross workers and arranged that she should see the parade from the first-storey balcony where she would be able to see not only the parade but the entry of the Japanese delegates and of the high officers taking part in the Surrender.

Speck Wheeler tried hard to persuade me to find a place for Edwina and his daughter, Peggy, within the Council Chamber but to do so would have meant displacing some of the prisoners of war whom we have invited to witness the Ceremony and would undoubtedly have given any hostile pressmen a chance of a dig at us. Edwina nobly supported me in this decision for after all she had come here to work for the prisoners of war and not just to attend the Surrender Ceremony.

WEDNESDAY, 12 SEPTEMBER   To receive the unconditional surrender of half a million enemy soldiers, sailors and airmen must be an event which happens to few people in this world.[1] I was very conscious that

---

[1]   Mountbatten later added in manuscript '⅔ million actually'.

this was the greatest day of my life and curiously enough everyone else also appeared to have an electric feeling throughout the day. The entire route which I imagine must have been close on two miles was lined at 4-yard intervals by sailors and marines from the Allied Fleet and a friendly crowd was already collecting along the entire route.

We arrived at the Municipal Buildings precisely at 1030 and were received by the three Commanders-in-Chief, and all the high Allied officers in Singapore. On the Padang were drawn up 4 Guards of Honour, Royal Navy and Indian Army to the left, Royal Air Force and Australian paratroopers to the right. The edges of the Parade Ground were lined by massed formations of Allied soldiers, sailors and airmen. The massed bands of the Fleet played 'Rule Britannia' and the Royal Artillery fired a 17-gun salute. I then inspected the Guards and the troops on parade.

Then my entire party walked up the great steps of the Municipal Building to thunderous cheers from the huge crowds which had collected all round. Our party was shown into a small waiting room whilst arrangements were made for the audience to assemble.

Major General Brian Kimmins was the 'producer' and had staged a marvellous show. He had found a picture of the King and the Royal Arms hidden away in the museum and had put them in the Council Chamber. The flags of all the Allies including the Australians were hung in the hall. In the vestibule local Chinese guerillas were drawn up under their British officers. At each of the eight pillars there stood an armed guard; a British soldier, an Australian soldier, an Indian soldier, an American soldier, a Chinese soldier, and at the door stood a British airman.

In the very centre of the room two long tables were arranged 6ft apart, and in the centre of our table there was a raised desk and dais for myself. It was arranged that on my right should sit General Wheeler (United States), Admiral Power (Allied Fleet), General LeClerc (France), Brigadier Thimayya (India), Major General Penney (D. of I.), on my left General Slim (Allied Land Forces), Air Chief Marshal Park (Allied Air Forces), Air Vice Marshal Cole (Australia), Major General Feng Yee (China), Colonel Burman van Vreedon (Netherlands, representing their C.-in-C. Admiral Helfrich who was taken ill at the last moment). Behind us sat the Flag Officers of the Fleet, the Army and Corps Commanders, the Air Commanders, the representatives I share with the Prime Minister at the Generalissimo's and General MacArthur's Headquarters (Lieutenant Generals Carton de Wiart and

Gairdner respectively), and senior officers of my own staff. The Sultan of Johore came as an old acquaintance and as a private guest.

The opposite table was reserved for the Japanese delegation, consisting of the three Area Army Commanders, the Air Commander and the two Fleet Commanders. Behind each there was an armed officer of the appropriate service as their escort. Behind them there must have been 300 or 400 distinguished spectators including representatives of the released prisoners of war and internees, prominent among whom was the Bishop of Singapore. Officers in command of HM ships, troops and Air Forces below Flag rank also sat here. The two galleries were filled with about 140 press representatives and beneath the galleries on each side selected photographic and film teams had been installed. In front of my desk were microphones erected by the BBC, AIR (All India Radio) and news reels.

This was the arrangement of the audience but the method by which they came in had also been carefully organized. First came the photographers, then the Press, then the spectators, then the high-ranking officers, then the Allied delegates followed by DSAC, and the three Commanders-in-Chief. When all were seated General Penney said: 'The Japanese Delegation will now arrive, please do not rise.' When the Japanese Delegation came in there was a stony silence as they took their seats. Then all were bidden to rise and I have been informed by half a dozen different people that the minute during which they stood in silence was the most impressive moment imaginable.

I must now admit that I had seen none of this for I was being held back in a waiting room until sent for. The moment came and as the double doors were flung wide and I advanced, followed by my 4 ADCs, I felt like some actor taking a cue at the climax of a great opera. In complete silence I walked over to the dais and invited everyone to be seated. I then addressed the following remarks to the Assembly:

> I have come here today to receive the formal surrender of all the Japanese forces within the South-East Asia Command. I have received the following telegram from the Supreme Commander of the Japanese forces concerned, Field Marshal Count Terauchi:
>
>> The most important occasion of the formal surrender signing at Singapore draws near, the significance of which is no less great to me than to your Excellency. It is extremely regretful that my ill health prevents me from

attending and signing it personally, and that I am unable to pay homage to your Excellency. I hereby notify your Excellency that I have fully empowered General Itagaki, the highest senior general in Japanese armies, and send him on my behalf.

On hearing of Field Marshal Terauchi's illness, I sent my own doctor, Surgeon Captain Birt, Royal Navy, to examine him, and he certifies that the Field Marshal is suffering from the effects of a stroke. In the circumstances I have decided to accept the surrender from General Itagaki today, but I have warned the Field Marshal that I shall expect him to make his personal surrender to me as soon as he is fit enough to do so.

In addition to our Naval, Military and Air Forces which we have present in Singapore today, a large fleet is anchored off Port Swettenham and Port Dickson, and a large force started disembarking from them at daylight on the 9th September. When I visited the beaches yesterday, men were landing in an endless stream. As I speak there are 100,000 men ashore. This invasion would have taken place on 9th September whether the Japanese had resisted or not. I wish to make this plain; the surrender today is no negotiated surrender. The Japanese are submitting to superior force, now massed here.

I now call upon General Itagaki to produce his credentials.

Terauchi's credentials were produced, which I read aloud and after this I read (very hurriedly I am told) the Instrument of Surrender. These were signed first by Itagaki and then by me. 11 copies of the Instrument of Surrender were signed for the following Governments: British, American, Chinese, French, Dutch, Australian, Indian and Japanese. The other three copies were for the SEAC Official Records, for the King and for myself.

The Instruments were passed back and forth by Ronnie Penney and Ronnie Brockman. The latter very skilfully so arranged it that I was able to use separate pens, the 11th pen being used by the Japanese. Of these pens, I retained the Japanese pen and one of mine for myself. Five others I handed to DSAC and the 3 Commanders-in-Chief and Ronnie Brockman, the other 4 I intend for the Royal Naval, Military and Air Force Colleges, and the British Museum, as I presume they will one day be of historic significance. In doing this I was following the precedent set by Eisenhower and MacArthur.

The signatures completed, I invited the Japanese Delegation to withdraw. With the exception of Numata,[1] who looked almost human, I have never seen six more villainous depraved or brutal faces in my life. I shudder to think what it would have been like to be in their power. When they got off their chairs and shambled out, they looked like a bunch of gorillas with great baggy breeches and knuckles almost trailing on the ground. The two Admirals were dressed in khaki like the five Generals, and the only way you could tell the difference was that the Generals wore spurs.

The audience then withdrew in the reverse order that they had come in and this is the moment when I must recount an unbelievable incident.

The representative of the great Republic of China, Major General Feng Yee, produced in the middle of the Ceremony a Leica camera which he actually proceeded to focus on the Japanese in turn. The Japanese delegates looked absolutely furious, for to be photographed from the opposite table, and by a Chinese, must have been particularly galling to their pride. Not even Hollywood, had they been called upon to stage such a ceremony, could have thought up the idea of the Chinese delegate taking pictures from the table.

As everyone went out they took up positions on the terrace and on the steps, and finally I went out with the Commanders-in-Chief to the top of the steps of the Municipal Building where a microphone stand had been erected and here I read my Order of the Day which was being simultaneously read at that moment throughout the South-East Asia Command. After this I advanced to the saluting base and the Union Jack which had been preserved secretly in Changi jail, was rehoisted to the strains of the National Anthem, whilst the large Fleet in the bay thundered a Royal salute of 21 guns.

There followed the National Anthems of the Allies which must have been moving indeed to the various prisoners of war watching the ceremony.

Anti-climax – I turned to go and found no cars. For a moment I was lost and asked the assembled Cs-in-C. and ADCs: 'What do we do next?' No answer. I then said: 'Very well, bring up the cars.' As I stepped into my car three ringing cheers broke out from the crowd. This struck a chord of memory and I suddenly realized that I had not completed the official ceremony. I jumped out of the car and called, as had been

---

[1] Lieutenant General Numata, Chief of Staff to Field Marshal Terauchi.

pre-arranged, for three cheers for the King. They were the heartiest cheers I have heard for a good long while.

I then drove off with a small motor cycle and jeep escort. By this time the crowds that had collected all along the road were so dense and cheering so wildly that I felt (foolish as it may seem) it would be better to stand up. My doing so was a signal for renewed outbursts of cheering and I had the amazing experience of driving through 2 miles of densely packed crowds to one never-ending thunderous roar of cheers. When one remembers how silent the Chinese and Malays are by nature and how unusual such a demonstration is I think it is a remarkable demonstration of the delight of the people of Singapore to find the British back once more.[1]

Poor Driver Miller, who had for 3½ years been under the Japanese, was so overcome by emotion that his eyes filled with tears and he said afterwards that he was in constant terror of driving into the crowd through not being able to see properly.

Speck, Arthur Power and I found that we had all three of us been deeply affected. I can never hope to describe the whole feelings of this memorable day.

THURSDAY, 13 SEPTEMBER   At 0820 Edwina and I left for a tour of the Indian prisoner-of-war camps. At each place I gave a short address in Urdu to them and met and talked to each officer. Considering that they had been the worst treated of all they were in wonderful spirits. Our security police had captured a set of the most revolting pictures showing the fate of some of the Indians who refused to join the Japanese 'Indian National Army'. The first photo shows two dozen Indian soldiers kneeling upright in front of the graves that they had dug, with their eyes bandaged. The next photo shows Japanese soldiers lying down at 100yds range with rifles. The next photo shows Japanese NCOs standing among these, evidently instructors in teaching backward marksmen how to shoot. At 100 yards' range even good marksmen could not expect to kill a man at the first shot. These poor devils must have taken many shots for in the last photo one can see the Japanese soldiers finishing off the living with a bayonet.

Christison told me what happened to a personal friend of his. He was Captain Hari Bad Hwar of the 3rd Cavalry who was educated at

---

[1] In a calmer moment Mountbatten would have agreed that it was the departure of the Japanese rather than the return of the British which produced this euphoria.

Cambridge. The Japanese hung him up in a cage in Bangkok for 38 days to try and persuade him to join and lead INA forces. He was exposed to hot sun by day and a spotlight overhead at night. There was no room for him to lie down, and the only food and water he got was from the Siamese when the guard's attention was distracted. The only article in the cage was a bucket which was emptied once a week. He survived all this and was sent to Singapore where he has had a most excellent effect on raising morale. He is now fit and has been evacuated.

After tea at Government House I went to the Sime Road civilian internment camp. Here I stood up on a table and gave a talk to 2000 of the internees, and afterwards signed photographs for them for nearly an hour. I then went round the camp. This was quite a different experience to the prisoner-of-war camps. For here was a large population of civilians of all ages, conditions and nationalities. I went into one of their miserable squalid huts where 80 men where given one metre width apiece in which to lie down. A few had been lucky and had been able to bring in their camp beds, others had lain on the floor for 3½ years. All their clothes were worn out. About half of them had singlets or ragged shirts to put on but the rest were completely naked except for shorts or bathing drawers, all of them very much patched. They had no shoes and had to walk about the stony roads bare foot, and yet they retained that distinguished air which bank managers, civil servants and retired generals always have, and they appeared to be completely unconscious of the ludicrous figure they cut, herded together half naked; a really pitiable sight.

One boy of eight who had been in the camp since the age of 4½, on being told that they were now free and asked what he wanted to do, said: 'Please may I move up to the men's camp?' Their morale was really wonderful and the reception they gave me was overwhelming.

FRIDAY, 14 SEPTEMBER   At 0800 I went with Edwina on a further tour of prisoner-of-war camps. This took us up to 1330 when I had a luncheon party which included the Bishop of Singapore and leading internees.

The Bishop (Leonard Wilson) is the most remarkable man. I persuaded him to give me some account of what he suffered at the hands of the Japanese. At first he was left free, but later, having raised money from the Chinese to buy food to supplement the rations of prisoners who were dying from malnutrition, he fell under suspicion and he was thrown into Changi jail. From there he and 56 others were taken and transferred to Outram Road jail for inquisition by the Kempei Tai (Japanese Gestapo). He was for 7½ months in solitary confinement. Every day from 7 or 8 in the morning, until 9 or 10 at night they had to sit alone in the cell cross-legged on the floor without moving. If their hands so much as touched the floor they were immediately flogged. In the first six weeks they were not allowed out at all, later however, they sometimes had 10 minutes a day in the open. The sanitary bucket was only emptied every 3 or 4 days. Throughout his seven and a half months he cannot recall any prolonged period when the entire jail was not ringing with the cries and screams of the inmates as they were taken up in turn to be tortured.

I will describe only 2 of the many tortures which were inflicted upon him. One consisted of being made to kneel on the ground with a sharp triangular steel rod behind the knee joints whilst Japanese soldiers in hobnail boots jumped on his thighs. He is of course scarred for life. Another time he was strapped face upwards on a table with his head over the edge. A team of seven men then flogged him for seven hours each day for 5 consecutive days with triple-laid wetted ropes. He counted just over 200 lashes before he fainted for the first time, but the Japanese were most ingenious in reviving him before going on with the flogging. At the end he confessed to me: 'I was in rather a mess.' On his birthday they gave him a great feast and the next day started torturing him again. This went on for 7½ months.

I spent the entire afternoon from 1500 to 1845 at Changi jail where there were between six and seven thousand English, Australian and Dutch prisoners of war. This was a peacetime jail intended to house 600 convicts sentenced to rigorous imprisonment. In each of the minute cells 4 white men or three white women were made to live. They showed me samples of their daily meals. Each consisted of a miserable portion of rice, some rancid coconut oil and for lunch a few green weeds from the garden and for dinner some putrefied fish paste. It smelt so terrible that I could hardly imagine being hungry enough to face eating it. Rats and cats fetched a fancy price when they could be got, for the food was definitely below the rate which would support a human being in health and some of the men looked like the pictures of the Belsen Horror Camp. All, however, were in fantastically high spirits. They showed me ingenious wireless sets which they had constructed and operated without the knowledge of the Japanese. In each case detected, those concerned had been flogged to death. Altogether a most disturbing afternoon.

I brought back with me 3 BORs to dinner. They kept on repeating that they could hardly believe it was true that they were sitting in an armchair drinking gin at Government House when a few days before they had been starved, beaten and in terror of their lives. A young Subaltern of the Argyles, who had been acting as my guide, told me that although he had been captured in uniform, wearing officer's pips, he had been accused of being a spy, in disguise. He had 200 days' Japanese solitary confinement, after which he became so ill that they sent him to hospital to revive him, only to continue his sentence – which was 4 years' solitary confinement. On the next occasion he went mad and has only just recently recovered his sanity.

A Corporal told me that he had been taken among a party to the Siam/Burma Railway. They were marched 220 miles through the thick monsoon rain and on arrival they immediately had to turn to work. They had to work 16 hours a day and foul were the conditions. They were constantly struck and flogged by guards with thick green bamboos. They were beaten across the chest, over the head, their noses and teeth were smashed in. Men too ill to get up were made to break sticks where they lay. Men with dysentery were flogged each time they were forced to relieve nature. It was no uncommon thing to wake up in the morning and find the man in the next bed had died in the night. He owes his escape to the fact that having very bad malaria he had a fit of the shivers and could not hold his shovel. He was flogged with a pickaxe handle and finally a guard struck him with the metal end, and paralysed him. For some reason he was carried away and survived whereas most others in similar circumstances were left to die.

SATURDAY, 15 SEPTEMBER   At 0900 I parted from Edwina at Government House as she is off to Sumatra and Java in the Sister Anne. We landed at 1500 at Mingaladon and were met by the usual crowd of high-ups.

At 2000 I was the guest of honour at a dinner given by the Orient Club. There were 160 guests present, mostly Burmese of all shades of opinion. There was a printed list of speakers which included three prominent Burmese, the GOC (Monty Stopford), and myself.

I was mortified to find that Aung San had been left off the list and insisted that he should be invited to speak. All four of the Burmese made extremely friendly speeches and caused a lot of amusement by referring to the fortunate coincidence that my name in Burmese is pronounced

Maung Ba Tin, since this is the name of Burma's most popular film star! Aung San presented me with a Japanese officer's dagger on behalf of the Patriotic Burmese Forces.

Afterwards we attended the Pwe and altogether the evening was a great success. We did not leave until after midnight.

MONDAY, 17 SEPTEMBER to FRIDAY, 21 SEPTEMBER   On Monday Speck Wheeler and I had a farewell tête-à-tête lunch; after lunch he and I had a mutual decoration party. I invested him as an Honorary Knight Commander of the Order of the British Empire. Speck said to me before the ceremony: 'Do I kneel, Admiral?' I replied: 'If you do I shall have to say "Arise Sir Speck" and you will be the first titled American!'

After this he invested me with the US Army Distinguished Service Medal. In this connection I feel I must relate a very flattering thing that happened.

At the Rangoon Victory Parade last June D. I. Sultan announced to me that the President had approved the award of the Order of the Legion of Merit in the degree of Chief Commander to the Viceroy, General Auchinleck and myself. He pointed out that this was the highest order in America and included a broad ribbon and star like an order of Knighthood. I felt immensely honoured and told him so. The King gave his approval in August to these three decorations but as soon as Speck Wheeler heard it he dashed up to me in great despair and said: 'Admiral, D. I. has done a terrible thing, he has put you in for the Legion of Merit!' I replied: 'I am very honoured and you will be glad to hear the King has given his consent.' Speck said: 'But you don't understand, that is a brand new decoration intended only for foreigners. You must get the same as Eisenhower and MacArthur; I insist on having it changed to a DSM.'

So with much trouble the decoration was changed from a Legion of Merit to a DSM.

WEDNESDAY, 26 SEPTEMBER   We left KP at 0700 and took off at 0800 in the York. We flew over Sabang Island at the north tip of Sumatra which interested me very much as it was one of the places that Winston Churchill always wanted me to seize as a preliminary to taking the north tip of Sumatra (Operation CULVERIN).

At 1630 we landed at Kellang airfield, Singapore, where Bimbo

Dempsey, Paddy Bandon, etc. met us with the news that the Secretary of State for War, Mr Lawson, who was due to land from Hong Kong that evening had been delayed 24 hours. We drove to Government House where Edwina had that day got in from Java with a lot of extremely valuable and interesting news.[1]

The other day at one of my SAC meetings an announcement was made that all the prisoners of war had now been cleared out of Sumatra. There was a general murmur of surprise since according to our programme they should not have started moving the first one. I said: 'I bet that's my wife', and on enquiry from Edwina this proved indeed to be right for she had bullied the various Commanders to produce landing craft and aircraft to evacuate all our prisoners long before we could send in our troops. She estimates that most of them would have been dead within three weeks the situation had become so serious.

THURSDAY, 27 SEPTEMBER   At 0800 I went with Boy and Bimbo to visit the notorious jail at Outram Road.

I went through some of the prison blocks and had General Saito brought out of his cell. This was the man under whom all the tortures in the prison camps were inflicted and who himself had recently been humiliated. I asked through an interpreter: 'Any complaints?' To my great astonishment he said: 'None', but he looked pretty shaken.

At 0845 we got to the Sea View Hotel where I talked to about 120 prisoners of war from Sumatra. They were the first lot I had seen who were so cowed and gloomy that I got no reaction from them at all.

Bimbo, Boy and I then collected Major Wild[2] and drove to Pt 348 which is a high hill in the centre of the Island where Wild explained the disposition of our troops during the last days' battle before the fall of Singapore. The Japanese had forced the British prisoners to build a memorial on this hill which our sappers have blown up.

We then drove on to the Ford Motor Works and sat round the table in the Conference Room where General Percival and his 2 Brigadiers and Major Wild (interpreter) surrendered the British Forces in Singapore to General Yamashita. Wild gave us an exact description of everything that occurred and mournful it was to listen to.

After lunch I went with Boy to Seletar Flying Boat Station to meet

---

[1]   As to the extent and enthusiasm of the indigenous independence movement.
[2]   Major Wild had enjoyed the invidious honour of carrying the Union Jack at the surrender of Singapore.

the Secretary of State for War, who landed at 1500 in a Sunderland from Hong Kong.

I drove the Secretary of State to Sembawang Naval Air Station which the Navy had just taken over and after that we drove to the Naval Base. Practically all the living accommodation is intact but the American B.29s have made a horrible mess of the Dockyard itself, though the great dry dock can soon be put into working order.

We arrived at Government House at 1800 and at 1900 the Secretary of State and I attended a Press Conference of some 50 or 60 correspondents. At 1950 Edwina and I drove with the Secretary of State to a cocktail party given by General Christison and at 2030 the Secretary of State and I went to dine with Bimbo Dempsey and the senior members of the 14th Army Staff. During this day we motored no less than 126 miles in Singapore Island.

FRIDAY, 28 SEPTEMBER   At 1130 I had a meeting with Bill Slim and Christison to hear the evidence of Wing Commander Davis from Sumatra and Lieutenant Colonel Maisey from Java whom Edwina had discovered and given me particulars of. They painted rather a different picture of conditions in the NEI to that we had gathered from other reports.

I had sent for Maisey and Van der Plas from Batavia and called the latter in for a later meeting at 1215. At 1330 I gave a luncheon to all the Generals in Malaya. I was astounded to find that at the other table there were between 60 and 70 people all of whom appear to be living in Government House and very few of whom I remember inviting! I really cannot keep track of what goes on in Government House. It is like the Dorchester Hotel and I only hope that the uninvited guests will pay their bills!

After lunch I started a series of meetings on FIC with Gracey and Cedille whom I had sent for from Saigon, following the same routine as with the NEI meeting of having Gracey in first and Cedille joining us later. At 1730 I had a big SAC meeting which was attended by the Secretary of State, at which we settled problems about French Indochina and the Netherlands East Indies and the future Command set up in Singapore.

SATURDAY, 29 SEPTEMBER to SUNDAY, 30 SEPTEMBER   Said *au revoir* to Edwina who is off to Morotai and Borneo today. I left at 1015 in the York with the Secretary of State. We landed at 1800 at the SEAC airstrip and were met by a row of our Generals and Air Vice Marshals. I drove the Secretary of State in my jeep to King's Pavilion where we had a large dinner.

On Sunday morning I took the Secretary of State down to Head-quarters to address selected officers and other ranks and to hold a meeting with my Dutch staff about NEI. I drove him to the SEAC airstrip in the jeep, and was quite sad to see the old boy off. He has done a grand job out here.[1]

TUESDAY, 9 OCTOBER 1945 We took off at 0800 in the York. At 1200 we circled low over Port Blair and watched the 116th Indian Infantry Brigade disembark from a convoy which had just arrived at Port Blair to take the surrender of 8947 Japanese. We then flew up the Andaman Islands and landed at 1430 at Mingaladon.

The object of this visit was to bid farewell to the people of Burma and the Civil Affairs Staff who had served me throughout the time that I was the Military Governor of Burma.

It was on the 1st January, 1944, that I issued my Proclamation No. 1 and took over the administration of that 5 per cent of Burma then in our hands. Five months ago at the fall of Rangoon we had 85 per cent in our hands and one week hence (on the 16th) I shall turn this over to the Civil Government under Sir Reginald Dorman-Smith, leaving only a part of Tennasserim and Karenni under my Military Administration because we still have some Japanese soldiers to disarm in this area.[2]

The Burma Navy provided the Government House Quarter Guard and Guards of Honour were found by the Royal Navy, British and Indian Armies and the Royal Air Force Regiment. Other troops on parade were: on the right flank Detachments of the Burma Regular Army and on the left flank Detachments from the Burmese Patriotic Forces. The latter, thank God, have given up their Japanese uniforms and are now wearing British jungle green battle dress but they are still wearing their own Burmese badges of rank. They are, however, shortly

[1] Lawson had been told by Ernest Bevin not to become engaged in local politics. Mountbatten, however, soon recruited the Minister in support of his liberal policies in Indochina and the Netherlands East Indies.
[2] The handover was contrary to Mountbatten's wishes and subsequently he used to claim that the change of policy which resulted was responsible for driving Burma out of the Commonwealth.

being absorbed into the Burma Regular Army as a result of my meetings in Kandy.

On arrival on the dais after the general salute and an inspection of the troops on parade I read a suitable Order of the Day and then the South-East Asia flag was lowered for the last time at Government House, Rangoon.

The guards then marched off and I shook hands with the senior Naval, Military and Air Forces officers stationed in Burma, all the senior Civil Affairs officers and all the Burmese leaders including the 90-year-old Buddhist Archbishop. It is normally regarded as sacrilege for an unbeliever to touch him but on this occasion the old boy held my hand for five minutes while he blessed me for having liberated Burma and befriended their people. I then made a short speech to the Burmese leaders followed by refreshments indoors.

I was much touched by the warmth of the thanks which I received from all the Burmese leaders at the Parade, Aung San, Than Tun, U Ba Pe and a dozen others. What surprised me most was the way that the Civil Affairs officers expressed their regret at passing from my administration to the Civil Government because I have been extremely rude to many of these in the days when my policy was not being loyally carried out by some of them.

I had summoned General Gracey (in command of the Allied Land Forces in French Indochina and my representative in charge of the Saigon Control Commission) together with General LeClerc to meet me in Rangoon. LeClerc welcomed me very effusively in French (he speaks no English) saying that it was a great privilege to be present on such a historic occasion. I replied: 'It is indeed a happy day when I get rid of the headaches of controlling the Independence Movement in one country and I can assure you that it will be an even happier day when I can go to Saigon and haul down the SEAC flag and leave the French Indochina headaches to you!'

I held a meeting with Gracey and the French after the Burma meeting broke up, in order to formulate future policy to deal with the increasingly difficult situation between the Vietnam Republic and the Allied Forces in French Indochina.[1]

After dinner I attended a Pwe given by an ex-Mayor of Rangoon, at

[1] On 17 September the Viet Minh proclaimed the independence of the Republic of Vietnam. To preserve order Gracey found it necessary to proclaim martial law and back a French *coup d'état* in Saigon. Mountbatten pressed LeClerc to negotiate with the Viet Minh but to no purpose.

his house. It took place in a small garden adjoining the street and a crowd of Burmese collected to see it. Two clowns put on an act representing a Japanese medical officer inoculating a Burmese citizen. The Japanese officer slapped and punched and kicked the Burmese to roars of laughter and applause from the crowd; ending up by doing the inoculation with an enormous knife which brought the house down.

WEDNESDAY, 10 OCTOBER I left with our party at 0915. We landed at 1600 at Kellang airfield three minutes before Edwina landed in the Sister Anne from Hong Kong. As we had not been in touch with each other for several days this was a well-timed coincidence.

I drove straight to Government House where I had a meeting with General Christison whom I had summoned from Batavia. After a preliminary meeting at which I heard with dismay about the seriousness of the situation, we held another meeting at 1815 which was attended by Lieutenant Governor General Dr Van Mook, the Dutch C.-in-C. Admiral Helfrich and Mr Van der Plas whom I had also summoned from Batavia. This meeting went on for two and a half hours.

We had a big dinner party organized by Johnny Papps and Sergeant Charles Smith, at which I had Van Mook and Helfrich next to me and worked on them like mad throughout dinner.[1] Immediately after dinner the meeting reassembled and lasted until after midnight. It went much better.

It must surely be exceptional to have to run three Government Houses simultaneously, so widely separated as Kandy, Rangoon and Singapore, and to give dinner parties on three consecutive nights in the three Government Houses.

THURSDAY, 11 OCTOBER Mike Goodenough had produced a draft telegram in the course of the night and at 0900 we started off again, first with an all-British meeting on the NEI and then at 1000 the Dutch Delegation joined us. We were able to reach complete agreement on the proposals to be put up to our respective Governments. At 1130 they left to fly back and I went to look at our offices in the Cathay Buildings. When we came back after looking at the Wrennery we found that, although Admiral Helfrich had been able to get off in a Catalina, Van

---

[1] Mountbatten was trying to persuade the Dutch to negotiate with Dr Sukarno and the Indonesian nationalists.

Mook, Christison, Mr Van der Plas and Colonel Liddell had been held up because their B.25 could not take off owing to all the petrol at Kellang being condemned that morning. We therefore gave them lunch which was a bit awkward as we had a large Chinese lunch party arranged. They left in the middle of lunch to go off in a Sunderland flying boat from Seletar.

FRIDAY, 12 OCTOBER to THURSDAY, 18 OCTOBER   At 0915 on Friday, Edwina and I took off with the same party and landed at 1660 at the SEAC airfield in the middle of the monsoon. We were met by Bill Slim and had a meeting with him prior to his leaving for Batavia.

THURSDAY, 1 NOVEMBER to SUNDAY, 4 NOVEMBER 1945   At 1045 on Saturday we took off in the York from the SEAC airfield. After a six-hour flight we landed at Bhopal where we were met by Hamidullah (the Nawab of Bhopal). I began by addressing the officers and airmen of the RAF Station. At 1700 we drove off to Chiklod with HH and staff. This is a shooting box about an hour's drive from Bhopal City. Unfortunately we arrived as it was dark which was obviously a great disappointment to Hamidullah as he particularly wanted us to see the view. We had been delayed by bad weather in our flight and so we changed our plans and arranged to stay on until luncheon on Sunday.

Hamidullah has let himself go at Chiklod for, in addition to the two conventional houses built some 20 years ago, he has recently completed an extremely modernistic house based on the lines of an aeroplane with two wings and a fuselage but the tail has not yet been completed! He is an honorary Air Commodore and extremely keen about the air!

We had dinner in a shamiana in front of the nose of the aeroplane and an Indian Regimental Band played for dinner, followed by pipers around the table. After dinner I had a long talk with Hamidullah on the future of India, which was particularly interesting as he is the present Chancellor of the Chamber of Princes.

Edwina and I shared one guest house which has two or three world record 'heads'. We thought we would have breakfast alone on the verandah in the sun. Apart from the fact that there were the usual half dozen khitmagars there was a very distinguished-looking Indian gentleman and a rather less distinguished-looking English gentleman who stood on each side of us and made polite conversation during breakfast.

We could not make out if they were butlers or equerries! By dint of asking questions and making requests we gradually got everybody away on different jobs until finally I was able to lean across to Edwina and say: 'Don't look now, but I think we are alone.'

The Begum and other ladies of the family have only recently come out of Purdah, because the old Begum of Bhopal, although herself a ruler, refused to let anyone else come out of Purdah until just before her death. Some of the girls are very lovely but they wear the oddest sort of clothes, a short dress no longer than a bush shirt over silver, gold or white jodhpurs. Hamidullah took Edwina and me out in his jeep through the jungle, where we saw sambhur deer, langur monkeys and, what fascinated me most, dozens of large colourful spiders in webs stretched between trees a dozen foot apart.

We eventually made our way back to the main road to where the regular cars were waiting and drove on into Bhopal City. Every car and jeep here always has rifle racks in it with half a dozen guns and rifles ready to shoot anything which may come into sight. We all lunched at the Palace of Bhopal with the Nawab and Begum and took off at 1430 in the York. We landed punctually at 1630 at Palam and found the usual crowd of high-ups, headed by Claude Auchinleck and tailed by Third Officer Mountbatten there to meet us.[1] We drove straight off to the Viceroy's house where all our party are being put up. Edwina, Patricia and I have a nice little flat to ourselves.

MONDAY, 5 NOVEMBER   On Monday we three swam in the Viceroy's pool in the morning and then had a quick ride on two of the bodyguard horses and my own horse Viceroy, which is kept with the bodyguard.

I drove with Claude to meet the CIGS at Palam where he arrived at 1630. I had one of the rare chances of seeing what a VIP arrival looks like from the ground. There was a guard and band and much ceremony. Claude had all the India Command high-ups drawn up on one line and I had all the SEAC high-ups in another line which we introduced to Lord Alanbrooke. As there is already a Lord Brooke, the CIGS has been very ingenious in running his Christian name into his surname for his new title.

---

[1] Patricia Mountbatten had declined her father's pressing invitations to join his staff in Kandy but eventually secured a posting to New Delhi.

After dinner I persuaded the Viceroy to hold a meeting with the CIGS, Bill Dening, Boy and myself to discuss the NEI.

THURSDAY, 6 NOVEMBER   We rode in the morning and I had a meeting with the Viceroy and a further discussion with Dening before he left to return to Batavia.

Later in the afternoon, I was presented with my citation and certificate for the American DSM. I was proud to note that my name is inscribed as 'Admiral Mountbatten, British Army'.

Lieutenant-General Gale, the Airborne Corps Commander, came to say goodbye and at 1200 Bimbo Dempsey came to report to me on accepting my offer to become Commander-in-Chief, Allied Land Forces in succession to Bill Slim who is required for an important job at home.[1] I then held a meeting with the Cs-in-C.

SATURDAY, 10 NOVEMBER   Claude and I drove together to see the CIGS off officially from Palam. As soon as his York had left we left in the Sister Anne. We arrived after 2 hours at Jodhpur where we were met by the Maharaja of Jodhpur.

I first addressed the officers and airmen of the RAF Station and then we were driven to the guest house which the Maharaja had placed at our disposal and there we had a private lunch. After lunch we visited the Chittar Palace, the magnificent new residence which the present Maharaja of Jodhpur has just built for himself. It is still only partly furnished on account of the war holding things up. We then drove to No. 2 Polo Ground where an exhibition game was played by Jai's team and Hanut's team.[2] It made me feel very nostalgic to see good polo played after all this time. After polo, Edwina, Patricia and I rode and I knocked about for the first time for years.

After this we drove round sightseeing, including Ratnagar Palace where I stayed during the Prince of Wales's visit exactly 24 years ago, and we had a look at the polo ground where I played the first chukka of polo in my life in November 1921. We ended up with cocktails at Hanut's house and an evening party at the Chittar Palace of 300 guests, followed by dinner, during which the Jodhpur State Band played.

---

[1] The resuscitation of the Imperial Defence College.
[2] Maharaja of Jaipur and uncle of the Maharaja of Jodhpur respectively.

SUNDAY, 11 NOVEMBER   At 0800 Edwina, Patricia and I went to No.2 Polo Ground where we again knocked about. At 1000 we visited the old Jodhpur Fort with the Maharaja's brother and saw the jewels, armoury, etc.

After this we drove out to Sardar Samand, a country residence recently built by the present Maharaja some 30 miles from the City. It stands on the banks of an artificial lake from which we could see crocodiles basking in the sun. We bathed in the swimming pool and had lunch. After lunch we visited the Maharaja's experimental farm and then drove back to Jodhpur City.

Edwina very virtuously went off to the hospitals whilst the rest of us went partridge picking on horseback. This consists in riding across country until one puts up a covey of partridges and then galloping wildly after them until they sit. One then puts them up again and this performance in all is carried out three times after which the Trades Union of partridges prevents them taking the air again and they can then be picked up by hand. We started rather too late in the day and only put up one covey but it certainly carried out the regulation three flights and then refused to get up again. Unfortunately it was in such a thick thorn hedge that we could not get the partridges out.

MONDAY, 12 NOVEMBER to SUNDAY, 18 NOVEMBER   Patricia and I knocked about on the polo ground on Monday morning, and at 0940 we took off in our respective aircraft. Edwina and I went in the York to Ceylon. We tried to land at the SEAC airfield but a terrible storm closed down five minutes before and we finally had to be diverted to Ratmalana. Edwina took off in an Expeditor to Kaggola as she insists on going to Batavia again; the rest of us came up in the SEAC train. Bimbo Dempsey is staying at KP with us.

On Tuesday, I had Admiral Auboyneau, the new Commander-in-Chief Afloat of the French Fleet in the Far East, and some of his staff to lunch, and in the evening I had General Gubbins and Colin Mackenzie to dine with Bimbo Dempsey and me, on the occasion of their organization becoming dissolved.[1]

MONDAY, 19 NOVEMBER to THURSDAY, 22 NOVEMBER   I caught the SEAC Special to go and meet Edwina, who was due from

---

[1] Major General Gubbins was executive head of the Special Operations Executive (SOE). Colin Mackenzie was in charge of the organization's work in Burma.

Singapore. Unfortunately, after I arrived I was told her flying boat had had to turn back on account of an engine failure. I called on the Governor, the Commander-in-Chief East Indies Fleet and the Commander-in-Chief Ceylon to say goodbye to them and their staffs. Admiral Power is not coming on to Singapore and is going to the Admiralty as Second Sea Lord. He has been a most loyal friend to me.[1]

I had a final full-dress meeting with my Commanders-in-Chief on Tuesday morning, followed by a farewell lunch for A. J. Power. In the afternoon I drove out to the airstrip to meet Edwina who had flown up in Sister Anne from Kogalla. She looked frightfully tired and was obviously feeling seedy and run down but refused to cancel her onward passage to England the following day. On Wednesday morning, however, she listened to reason and agreed to postpone her departure until the following Sunday from Delhi.

FRIDAY, 23 NOVEMBER   Edwina and I said goodbye and gave tips to the whole of the King's Pavilion staff and those Goanese stewards whom we were leaving behind. We took off from the SEAC airstrip in the Sister Anne at 0845.

We landed punctually at 1800 at Willingdon airfield and drove at once to the Viceroy's house. Here an officer from Saigon was waiting to see me and the Viceroy also wanted an immediate meeting, on top of which Patricia had to go on night duty at 1900. So it was a very busy evening. I attended a big dinner party given by Claude Auchinleck for the Viceroy, which was attended by all his Army Commanders and the senior Naval and Air Force officers.

SATURDAY, 24 NOVEMBER to TUESDAY, 27 NOVEMBER   On Sunday evening, less than an hour before Edwina was due to take off in the Sister Anne, Elizabeth Ward rang up from Karachi to say that the passenger York Edwina was to go home in had caught fire and returned to Colombo. The only other York that day was a freighter without any seats. However, she decided to go by that. After she arrived, it turned out that this aircraft had also gone unserviceable but she finally got off on Monday morning and will have completed 40,000 miles by air by the time she gets home.

---

[1] He was to be Mountbatten's Commander-in-Chief in the Mediterranean when Mountbatten rejoined the Navy in 1948.

She has done a truly magnificent job out here and I was intrigued to hear from Ronnie Brockman that she had been put in for a 'Mention in Despatches' for her work; not, I might add, by me!

WEDNESDAY, 28 NOVEMBER   Edwina's birthday, I only hope she gets home in time to be with Pamela for it. I took off in the Sister Anne at 0030. At 0915 we landed at Akyab, where Lieutenant General Symes, the Acting Army Commander, met me for a short conference on the military situation in Burma. We had breakfast in the Sub Area Commanders' Mess and took the air again at 1030.

At 1430, we landed at Port Blair, the capital of the Andaman Islands. After inspecting the Naval Guard of Honour, I visited and addressed practically the whole of 116 Brigade in groups, and later went round the magnificent harbour and went on board HMIS *Kistna*.

The population consists of some 12,000 natives and 6000 convicts who have been released and pardoned. Wherever we drove, every single native, without exception, stood up and saluted as we passed, a relic from the Japanese who beat them up if they did not salute. However, I think they were pleased to see us as they were being starved to death by the Japanese. There are about 9000 Japanese on the Islands under a Vice Admiral and Major General.

THURSDAY, 29 NOVEMBER   At 1100 we took off and landed at 1630 at Saigon, where a tremendous crowd of high-ups met us. I drove first to the house of the High Commissioner, Admiral d'Argenlieu, where a very smart French Naval Guard of Honour was mounted. After a valuable interview with him I went on to the Governor of Cochin-China's house, which General Gracey is using as his residence. At 1740 I held a conference with Generals Dempsey, Gracey, Kimmins and others who had come up from Singapore to meet me. After this Gracey gave a large dinner party for all the French officers.

FRIDAY, 30 NOVEMBER   At 1000, the Supreme Commander of the Japanese Expeditionary Forces, Southern Regions, Field Marshal Count Terauchi, surrendered his two ceremonial swords to me in the Government House grounds. The old boy is 67 years old, had a stroke last April, and is practically ga-ga. He is semi-paralysed and walks with a stick and I am recommending to HMG that he should not be tried as a war criminal, since I do not consider that he is any longer in full possession of his faculties. He handed over to me two swords, between 500 and 700 years old, the smarter of which I have asked the King to accept.

These swords were handed to me in boxes, which aroused my suspicions as I thought it was an unusual way to receive a defeated Commander's sword, but it appears it is genuinely a sign of special humility to a high personage to place them in a box.

I spent the afternoon visiting units of the 20th Indian Division with Gracey and saw some 270 of the Kempei Tai in the new French jail. They were extremely servile, all the officers and NCOs simultaneously shouting, saluting and bowing wherever I went. Gracey doubles the role of my representative and Head of the SACSEA Control Commission in Saigon, as well as being Commander of the Allied Forces in Southern French Indochina. He is doing a first-class job and LeClerc said to me, 'Your General Gracey has saved French Indochina!'

SATURDAY, 1 DECEMBER 1945   I left Gracey's house at 0750, to visit the RAF personnel at the air station.

When this was over, at 0845 I granted an interview to Count Terauchi. The old Field Marshal had apparently been very upset that I had refused to allow him to utter a word at his personal surrender ceremony, as he had prepared a beautiful speech. I finally agreed that he could come and make his speech to me at the airfield, provided it did not last longer than one and a half minutes. He read it out to me in Japanese, and it was then translated. It was a fulsome eulogy, and among other things thanked me for granting the Japanese a holiday on their Emperor's birthday. As I had said in reply to his request that, provided all Japanese soldiers working for the Allied Command continued to work the full hours, I did not mind if those engaged on duties not for us had a holiday, his thanks seemed uncalled-for.

We took off in the Sister Anne at 0900 and landed punctually at 1315 at Kellang airfield, Singapore.

We have taken over the biggest building in Singapore, a ten-storey 'sky scraper' constructed on top of a large cinema, known as the Cathay Building. My office is on the top floor overlooking the harbour.

I have reduced my staff from the 600-odd officers we used to have, to 114 British officers and 42 American, French, Dutch and Chinese officers. The inter-service Intelligence staff of another 140 officers nominally belongs to me, but actually serves the three Commanders-in-Chief as well, so we are a very small party compared with what we used to be, and have all been able to fit easily into one building, instead of being scattered over several acres of garden in huts. In addition I have been able to allocate floors to each of the three Commanders-in-Chief's advanced echelons, besides leaving inter-service public relations and broadcasting studios in the building.

Our local Reuter's correspondent launched an attack on the move, which he said had cost two and a half million pounds, and for leaving the camp at Kandy, which he said had cost six million. On going into it, we found that the move had cost £100,000 and the camps in Kandy £600,000 and the latter are all being used by Ceylon Army and Air Commands, RAF Training Schools, and for the Dutch women and children refugees.

Government House is of course a vast edifice. Most of the bedrooms are the size of an average house, and as they have practically no furniture look ridiculous and are very uncozy. I have firmly established myself in a very charming flat over the secretarial wing, for which we have been able to scrape together enough furniture to make it very pleasant. It consists of a sitting room, two bedrooms, a dining room and a kitchenette.

The first evening we caught a colossal moth, with a wing spread of 9 inches and a depth of 4 inches.

SUNDAY, 2 DECEMBER to WEDNESDAY, 5 DECEMBER In the evening I had a full-dress meeting with my Commanders-in-Chief at Government House to discuss proposals about French Indochina and the Netherlands East Indies.

On Monday I had a further big meeting with the Commanders-in-Chief and then sent off some very long telegrams to London.

A friend of Yola's,[1] Count Chambure, turned up on his way to Saigon. He told me that no matter what price he offered a Raffles Hotel for a room, the best they had been able to do for him was to give him one of five beds in a small room, such is the overcrowding in Singapore.

On Wednesday in the afternoon I went to meet the Chief of the Imperial General Staff, Field Marshal Lord Alanbrooke, who had come direct from Sydney in his York.

[1] Yola Letellier was a French lady and one of Mountbatten's oldest and closest friends.

I mounted three Guards of Honour, one from each service, and a Royal Marine band. At Government House I turned out the guard for him, which was found by the very smart Australian Parachute Battalion I have here.

We both had discussions with General LeClerc over tea, and we dined with Bimbo Dempsey to meet Gracey, Christison, and other generals, for informal discussions on French Indochina and Siam and the Netherlands East Indies.

THURSDAY, 6 DECEMBER to FRIDAY, 7 DECEMBER   On Thursday I gave a lunch for all Admirals, Generals and Air Marshals who had come into Singapore for the meeting with CIGS. On the American rating of stars (counting CIGS at 5 stars and myself at 4) the total worked out at 78 stars at the luncheon.

After lunch I went down to meet the Governor General of the Netherlands East Indies, Dr Van Mook, the Dutch C.-in-C., Admiral Helfrich, as well as many other Generals and the Governor of Sumatra who has just distinguished himself by refusing to pass on the Queen of the Netherlands' message to the people of Sumatra as he considers it too 'progressive' and refusing to shake hands with the Indonesian leaders when called to meet them by Christison.

I had a discussion with Van Mook and Bill Dening on policy and in the evening I held two meetings with all my Commanders-in-Chief, CIGS being present. The first meeting was on the subject of French Indochina and went very well, being finished in under an hour. It was followed by a more difficult meeting with all the Dutch representatives and General Christison from the Netherlands East Indies.[1] We also discussed Siam with General Evans.

On Friday I saw CIGS off at 0800, the French party at 0830 and the Dutch party at 1200.

SATURDAY, 8 DECEMBER   I left Government House at 0615. By an error the safe with all my most secret files was left behind so we had to go back for it and did not eventually take off in Sister Anne until 0650. We were originally intending to land at Labuan in North Borneo at 1310 local time and expected to have lunch given us. As we found that

---

[1] At this Conference the British said they would only help the Dutch maintain law and order if some sort of dominion status was offered to the Indonesians.

they were keeping 1½ hours and not 1 hour, as we had thought, fast on Singapore, we did not land until 1340 and therefore had a picnic lunch in the aircraft.

They had taken no notice of the changed hour of our arrival and took us off to lunch at the 2/6 Australian General Hospital at which Edwina had stayed a few weeks ago. I admitted that we had already had lunch but we volunteered to struggle through another one! After lunch I attended the Water Carnival and handed out prizes for the best '1890' bathing beauty contest among the sisters and kissed the winner, which went well with the troops. After that I gave a short address on the beach and then carried out a regular round of visits and addresses to the various units of the 9th Australian Division.

At the last parade I was introduced to two Australian heroes with the good old Australian names of Starcevitch and Stickpevitch. The former had won the VC at the Labuan landing and the latter was one of the only six survivors of the notorious death march into central Borneo of 2600 British and Australian prisoners of war. I brought Stickpevitch back to Headquarters and had a gruesome but fascinating hour's conversation with him about his experiences.

SUNDAY, 9 DECEMBER   We took off at 0730. We landed at 1145 at Makassar at the southwestern tip of the Celebes. We went and had lunch with the Dutch Governor at his Headquarters which are in the Dutch Governor's Palace which was only completed in 1940 and is very modern and dashing. I was quite amazed at Makassar as I had no idea there was such a lovely town in the Celebes. It is beautifully laid out with wide avenues lined by shady old trees. Practically all the houses are of Dutch design, some of them very old, others quite modern. There is no trouble with the Indonesians here and the Dutch are running civil affairs quite peaceably.

MONDAY, 10 DECEMBER   I was called at 0600 with the news that most of our party were suffering violent internal upsets, presumably from something they had eaten. We had to leave behind General Milford's[1] ADC and batman and Marine Thompson. Only the two old men, Milford and I, were immune from tummy trouble. I had a great rush packing my things and could not find half of them until we

---

[1] Major General Milford was temporarily in charge of Australian Land Forces.

searched Thompson's room and found that he had taken them, like most of my clothes, into his own room.

We took off eventually at 0740 and landed at 1000 at Balikpapan on the east coast of Dutch Borneo. We carried out a pretty strenuous programme visiting one unit after another throughout the day, including a Dutch unit and an American Naval Unit. I saw also the beaches on which the Australians carried out their landings in July and the various Japanese defensive positions. Edwina had also been here and everyone spoke in glowing terms of her visit, as they do everywhere.

TUESDAY, 11 DECEMBER We landed at 1200 at Kellang airfield, Singapore. I had an amusing report from Gracey about an action with the Annamites which said that some Ghurkas were engaged by three home-made Annamite guns. After one round had been fired the gunners fled into the jungle. There were no casualties to our own forces as the projectiles carried only 10 yards. The rebel casualties were believed slight as our own troops were too amazed to open fire.

I found a telegram awaiting me containing an offer of a Barony in the New Year's Honours List which put me in an awkward position, as a Peerage is the last thing I want but it is very difficult to explain this at a distance. However I had a brainwave and replied that although I was deeply honoured by his offer I was sure the Prime Minister would allow me not to accept it at this time whilst my men were still losing their lives in French Indochina and the Netherlands East Indies.[1]

FRIDAY, 14 DECEMBER to THURSDAY, 20 DECEMBER The *Duke of York*, flagship of the Pacific Fleet, arrived on Friday morning. I had a large predominantly Naval lunch party of sixty for the Commander-in-Chief, Admiral Sir Bruce Fraser. After lunch Admiral Fraser came to one of my meetings with the Commanders-in-Chief.

On Saturday Arthur [Leveson] left, taking with him Field Marshal Count Terauchi's very beautiful short sword as a gift for the King. In the evening I had a small dinner party in my 'flat' of high-ups for Admiral Fraser.

On Sunday Peter invited Irene Brown and Hazel Terry, who are here

[1] This is slightly disingenuous. Mountbatten was most offended that he had been offered a barony while Alexander and Montgomery became Viscounts. 'I would gladly have the Garter *instead* . . . ,' he told Edwina. 'The Order of Merit would be next best.'

with Gielgud's company, to lunch, and we drove to Johore in the afternoon. In the evening I attended a dinner party on board the *Duke of York*.

On Monday I had John Gielgud and his leading lady, Marion Spencer, to lunch.

In the evening I had a small dinner party and we all went to *Blithe Spirit*.[1] In the interval Patricia, Peter and I went round to see the company, including of course Irene Brown and Hazel Terry.

On Wednesday morning Patricia and I rode round Bukhit Tima Park. As she refused to take any notice of the deep stone drains with which the island is interlaced she finally succeeded in bringing His Majesty down and cutting his knee badly, fortunately without hurting herself too much. Every time we rode past the RIASC camp, the Indian quarter guard used to turn out. I tried to prevent them, but Patricia said it would hurt their feelings.

We lunched alone at the house, and dined and danced together at the Phoenix Club in the Cathay Building. This was the restaurant of the flats, and makes a very charming restaurant and dance club for all the members of the SEAC group of Headquarters; three nights a week for officers, two nights for other ranks, one night for WOs and sergeants, and nothing on Sundays. Patricia remarked that it was far more dashing and pleasant than any night-club she had been to in London or Delhi.

On Thursday I threw a lunch party of forty for all the Americans. In the evening I had a small dinner party and we all went to see Gielgud's *Hamlet* which was quite excellent.

FRIDAY, 21 DECEMBER to THURSDAY, 27 DECEMBER   I went in the Sister Anne to Kuala Lumpur for lunch with Lieutenant General Sir Frank Messervy, the General Officer Commanding Malaya. I had various matters of business to discuss with him, and after lunch we went and looked at my own caravan, which had been specially built for the Malayan campaign, to be attached to the Headquarters of XIV Army. It is really lovely and I feel is a great success. After that we drove up in a jeep to Fraser's Hill, a distance of some sixty miles. It is over 4000 feet high, and has the only view which I believe beats the view from Dimbula. Unfortunately, except for a fleeting moment in the early morning, most of the hills seem to be covered with cloud.

The insects seem even more magnificent than in Ceylon, and the

[1] Noel Coward's comedy of 1941.

local 'tube trains' (millipedes) are far longer and finer. I measured one and it was ten inches long.

We spent the weekend sunbathing and walking between the showers. A direct wireless telephone has been installed, which proved useful, as well as a despatch rider service from Kuala Lumpur, since I cannot yet afford to be out of touch with Headquarters.

We went back by jeep and Sister Anne on Monday, getting back to Government House on Christmas Eve in time for tea. The Hon. Seymour Berry, son of Lord Camrose, has come on a visit representing the *Daily Telegraph* interests. I am putting him up at Government House. He proved to be a reactionary bore.

FRIDAY, 28 DECEMBER to MONDAY, 31 DECEMBER I went to have a look at Flagstaff House, which used to belong to the General Officer Commanding Malaya and which was completely looted between the removal of the Japanese sentries and the arrival of the British sentries. Everything has been torn out – baths, lavatory basins, electric light switches and even doors. If the new Governor General takes up his appointment before I am relieved, I have decided to move into this house, and am going to get it ready in the meanwhile either for myself or my successor.

TUESDAY, 1 JANUARY to TUESDAY, 8 JANUARY 1946 This week I started to sit for Bernard Hailstone, the new official war artist, who is doing an official painting of me in a green bush shirt.

On the 1st, Sir Harold MacMichael[1] and his staff came to stay. He has completed his mission of negotiating treaties with the Sultans of Malaya on behalf of HM Government. It was originally my idea to have a high official appointed to undertake this duty, in place of myself. He seems to have made a great success of the job, and has certainly taken a load off my shoulders.

In the afternoon the Siamese political delegation signed at Government House the final agreement terminating the official state of hostilities between us. Bill Dening acted as the plenipotentiary of HM Government for these negotiations. In the evening I gave an official dinner party for the Siamese delegation, and all the various political and

[1] A former High Commissioner in Palestine, who followed this task with the negotiation of a new constitution for Malta.

financial advisers who had been attached to me from Australia and India, and of course the Foreign Office and Treasury.

On Thursday I visited the *Jamaica* and *Bulolo*. The latter is going home to be reconverted to a liner. She was the first Headquarters ship in history, and was invented by Mickey and me in 1942. I am sure the right solution for the future is to have a special Royal Yacht built which is capable of conversion to a Headquarters ship in wartime. By this means the King can have a really fast and modern yacht, and the Navy can have a well-designed Headquarters ship in wartime, whereas I feel certain they would never go to the expense of keeping one up in peacetime.[1]

On Sunday a large ceremony was laid on for all the guerilla leaders. An inter-service parade was held with the Royal Marines Far Eastern band and the Cameronians pipe band. The presentations took place on the steps of the Municipal Building, and I took the opportunity of delivering an address to the peoples of Malaya and Singapore. A colossal crowd had collected.[2]

I had learned off by heart a few phrases in Mandarin Chinese and Malay, which went very well with the various recipients. We took the whole party up for cocktails at Government House.

On Monday evening I gave a farewell party for Air Marshal Victor Goddard, who is leaving after more than two years as AOA at ACSEA. We ran *Snow White and the Seven Dwarfs* in the ballroom. Nearly a hundred Chinese children from all over the Government House estate, hearing the film was on, crowded round all the windows, so we let them come in, and they swarmed all over the seats and floor. They sat nice and quiet throughout the whole performance. Peter nearly sat on the smallest Chinese baby hidden in a large armchair.

THURSDAY 10 JANUARY to SATURDAY, 12 JANUARY   We took off on Thursday, and landed at 1200 at Palam, Delhi. I went straight to the Commander-in-Chief's house. Patricia was still on watch, but joined us for lunch.

It is sad to think that Claude has had to divorce Jessie Auchinleck. I well remember with what consternation I discovered that she and the then Air C.-in-C., Richard Peirse, were carrying on an affair under

[1] Mountbatten revived this idea on several occasions but never floated it successfully. He was more successful with his project for a combined royal yacht and hospital ship.
[2] Cynics said that the photographs taken on this occasion were most useful some years later to the security forces trying to identify terrorists.

Claude's nose, when I first arrived out in October 1943. Richard was divorced by his wife a few months ago, and now Jessie has been divorced by Claude, which is all very sad and difficult for him.

I met most of the Parliamentary Delegation that was visiting Delhi.[1] Boy Munster told me that the leader of the delegation had said at one of the meetings, to the leader of the Anglo-Indians, 'How do you become an Anglo-Indian?'

SUNDAY, 13 JANUARY to MONDAY, 14 JANUARY I took off with Patricia and Captain Lord Brabourne, Coldstream Guards (my new Military ADC),[2] from Willingdon airfield. We circled Udaipur Lake, and flew over the lovely old city and palace, where I stayed in 1921, and at 1245 we arrived at Deesa airfield, where we were met by the Nawab of Palanpur and his staff. The Nawab and I were together on the Prince of Wales's staff in 1921–22, and although his state is tiny, his personal prestige stands high. He has long been pressing me to visit him, and having seen nothing but enormous Indian states I thought it would be fun to see a very small one. We drove to Palanpur City (though it is hardly big enough to be dignified by such a name), some 18 miles away.

There was a large lunch party, after which we had our photo taken.

His Highness has married a remarkably handsome Australian wife, who has become completely absorbed into the country and wears nothing but saris and fits admirably into the picture. I thought she was a very nice and amusing person.

In the evening we drove out to H.H.'s summer residence at Balaram. There was a large dinner party in the small but ornate palace. On Monday Patricia and I went riding with H.H.'s cousin and ADC, and on return we changed and drove round the 'city' and had a look at the special train of H.H. the Maharaja of Porbandar.

THURSDAY, 17 JANUARY [New Delhi] We left the Viceroy's House in the dark, with the intention of being airborne at 0700, but on arrival we discovered that the ADCs had between them left my green despatch case in my room, and we had to wait while it was fetched. We were not airborne until 0730. Luckily I had intended to fly down the Central

---

[1] An all-party 'good will' mission, with no powers to negotiate.
[2] Lord Brabourne became engaged to Patricia Mountbatten in July 1946; they were married on 26 October and lived happily ever after.

Burma Plain from Mandalay, and by cutting out this diversion we were able to reach Mingaladon airfield punctually at 1600.

I went to Monty Stopford's Headquarters, where I inspected the West African Guard and band, and took the salute at the march past. I then inspected 552 Indian Infantry Troops Workshop, where they, among other things, gave me a wonderful demonstration of assembling a jeep from about a hundred different parts in 3 minutes, 40 seconds, after which it was driven away.

After this I went on to see some of the Indian Army Service Corps Transport Companies. The idiotic CO had spaced most of his men at 10-yard intervals along the road, and as we shot by in a closed car in a cloud of dust, with a police escort, there was no chance of their seeing me or my seeing them. It was with the greatest difficulty that I persuaded him to collect them, since he was far keener to show me his store tents and transport lines than his men!

We then went to Government House, where Reggie Dorman-Smith metaphorically kissed me on both cheeks and gave me an effusive welcome, greatly at variance with the remarks he has been making about me and my Burma policy to some of my senior officers!

Lady Dorman-Smith has certainly done a marvellous job of making Government House much more liveable. It was an interesting experience to find myself a guest in one of the Government Houses in which I have so often been host.

Reggie produced some Burmese of the new party about which he is so enthusiastic, and which he seems to think may stand some chance against Aung San and Than Tun's AFO. They are being organized by Sir Paw Tun, who has been released from a mental home in time to take over the office of Home Member.[1]

Brian Kimmins and a large party have flown up in the Hapgift from Singapore to meet me. They brought the tragic news that Victor Goddard, to whom I had lent Sister Anne to take him as far as Hong Kong, had taken her on to Tokyo in spite of the fact that it would be impossible to get her back in time to take me on my state visit to Siam; since we required a minimum of two Dakotas to carry the whole party. Sister Anne had had to do a forced landing on Sado Island, northwest of Japan, and I am afraid has flown her last flight – a really tragic ending to

---

[1] The following month Dorman-Smith tried to give his protégé a helping hand by arresting Aung San for murder. Whatever the rights or wrongs of the charge, this would probably have produced revolution in Burma.

a grand aircraft on a flight she had no business to be on, but fortunately nobody was hurt.

FRIDAY, 18 JANUARY   At 1000 we took off. Our three Dakotas, with a large Spitfire escort, landed at Don Muang airfield punctually at 1200. I inspected the RAF Guard of Honour and later the Royal Siamese Air Force Guard of Honour.

At 1425 I drove into Bangkok, which was gaily decorated for the peace celebrations which the Government had decided to hold after the dates of my visit became known. At 1500 arrived at the Udorn Palace, which has been placed at my disposal by the King. Here I inspected a Guard of Honour of the Siamese Army. I then changed into white full dress for the State Audience with the King.

The Master of the Protocol arrived to give us instructions on the procedure at the audience, and accompanied me to the Palace. We arrived at the Royal Grand Palace at 1640, in great pomp, with 16 British and Siamese police outriders. In the outer courtyard a Guard of Honour in khaki was drawn up and in the inner courtyard a guard of Honour of the Siamese Guards Regiment, in scarlet uniforms. Fifes and drums played continuously as we mounted the main marble staircase, which was lined by the Guards Regiment in full dress, and by the Siamese Palace Guard in medieval uniform with blue sarongs pulled up between their legs, and ancient spiked blue and gold helmets.

We were met by the Lord Chamberlain and various notables and Court officials, and were marshalled in one of the main waiting rooms.

We were then led to the Great Throne Room, and as we arrived colossal double doors were thrown open, revealing a colossal room with very ornate Victorian decorations. Down the length of the Throne Room were drawn up the Senior Statesman, the Prime Minister, members of the Cabinet, and Commanders-in-Chief of the Siamese forces in white full dress. At the distant end, in front of the high golden throne which was mounted on four tiers, and which stood under a ceremonial umbrella of nine tiers, stood a frightened short-sighted boy, his sloping shoulders and thin chest behung with gorgeous diamond-studded decorations; altogether a rather pathetic and lonesome figure.

We advanced in a series of short rushes, stopping every ten yards to bow simultaneously taking our time from the Master of Ceremonies, who walked beside me. It is only seventy years since all Siamese, however important, had to prostrate themselves before the King.

When I arrived in the presence of His Majesty King Ananda Mahidol, his nervousness increased to such an alarming extent, that I came very close to support him in case he passed out. He whispered a little halting speech of welcome in so low a voice that I had to bend forward to catch what he said.

The programme had said we were to have ten minutes' conversation, but after his first speech His Majesty never volunteered another remark. It was clearly impossible to observe the royal protocol of not speaking unless His Majesty spoke to me, and I therefore carried on a monologue as best I could, obtaining replies from the King only if I put him a direct question, such as: 'Is your Majesty going to remain in Siam?' Reply: 'No.' Question: 'Does your Majesty plan to go back to Switzerland?' Reply: 'Yes.' Question: 'I believe we have the honour of dining with your Majesty tonight?' Reply: 'Yes', etc., etc.

As there was no sign of the King dismissing me, I finally said: 'I feel I should not detain your Majesty any longer.' Reply: 'Thank you.'

We then withdrew backwards for the first ten yards, and bowed. We were then allowed to turn about for the next ten yards, and turn about again and bow; after which we were allowed to go as far as the main doors before all turning round again and again bowing.

Hollywood could not possibly have improved on the King's first State Audience.

I feel I must digress at this moment to describe the situation in which the Boy King finds himself. Some 40 years ago, a small baby was found in a basket and taken to the Queen (the present Queen grandmother), where she was brought up and became an additional maid to Her Majesty. When the time came for her to earn her own living, the Queen kindly offered to pay her expenses to train her for any profession she desired. The foundling girl chose to become a registered nurse, and was accordingly sent to America to be trained.

The Queen's youngest son in the meanwhile was a qualified doctor attached to an American hospital. His Royal Highness met what was probably the only Siamese woman in American medical circles, the foundling probationer nurse. They fell in love, and were married. They produced three children, a daughter (who is unfortunately married to the son of the leading war criminal of Siam) and two sons. They settled at Lausanne, in Switzerland, and then the Doctor Prince died. I gather that to the Prince's medical knowledge and energy much of the extremely up-to-date system of public health in Siam is due.

Some 12 years ago, King Prajadibok, his elder brother, abdicated in favour of his nephew, the 8-year-old Ananda Mahidol, and his found-ling princess became the Princess Mother. They paid a brief visit to Siam but were so horrified by Siamese Court life that they hastily returned to live at Lausanne. Here they led an extremely secluded and simple life, the King and his younger brother taking their studies very seriously. He has at present completed two years out of the four years' course in Swiss Law, and as he told me later, his life's ambition is to take a degree as a Doctor of Law: Swiss Law, incidentally, not Siamese!

Meanwhile the country had been run by a Regency Council, of which the outstanding member was Nai Pridi Pranomyongse, who was given the title (which he has now abandoned) of Luang Pradit.

The 1942 Prime Minister and Government of Siam were violently pro-Axis, and as soon as they heard of the sinking of the *Prince of Wales* and *Repulse*, came to the conclusion that the Allies' number was up, and declared war on the British and Americans. The British accepted the declaration (indeed they could hardly do otherwise, since Siamese soldiers ranged themselves with the Japanese against us on the bound-ary of Burma). The Americans, however, who saw no prospect of a physical encounter, rejected the declaration. Thus I was put in an extraordinary position, in my integrated Anglo-American Headquar-ters, of finding that part of my staff was at war with Siam, whilst the other part was not. This anomalous situation has now been put right by the agreement to terminate hostilities, signed in Singapore on the 1st January. To celebrate this event, four days' peace celebrations, to coincide with my visit, had been proclaimed, and everywhere through-out Bangkok flags were out, booths had been put up, and there were great gaieties and festivities throughout our visit.

The declaration of war took place whilst Luang Pradit was at his home near Ayuthia, and he, who has always been violently pro-British, rushed back and claimed that the declaration was illegal without his signature. It was however too late to undo the harm. Meanwhile, the Regency Council gradually disappeared, but whether they resigned or died I never found out.

Even before Luang Pradit became the sole Regent, he entered into negotiations with the Allies and in August, 1943, the very month in which the formation of the South-East Asia Command was announced, a significant but highly secret meeting took place in Chungking between the Regent's emissary and a Lieutenant Colonel of the British Army who had taken the code name of 'Arun'. In reality this was a Prince of the Royal House of Siam, Mom Chao Subha Svasti. The Regent was allocated the code name of 'Ruth', and when I arrived in South-East Asia he placed the whole Siamese underground resistance movement, which he had been organizing, under my command and promised his fullest support as soon as we could come and drive the Japanese out of Siam. He also sent me a pair of cuff links, which I returned.

After leaving the Royal Grand Palace we drove to the Boromphiman Palace, which was within the walls enclosing these two palaces and the principal temples of Bangkok. Here we were received by the Princess Mother and her younger son. She was dressed in Siamese traditional costume, with a Grand Cross of an Order, and decorations; the younger son in white full dress, also covered with decorations. Unlike her sons, the Princess Mother was extremely talkative. She is extremely attractive and vivacious, and had I not known that she had a 22-year-old daughter I should have put her age at between 30 and 35. Incidentally, Siamese children are rated as one year old at birth; so that, although the King has nominally attained his 21st birthday, he has only been 20 years in this world.

I attacked the Princess Mother on the question of the King leaving his country again so soon after having come to it for almost the first time in his life. I pointed out how lucky it was that he had been recalled by the Regent and the underground movement, since in Yugoslavia, Belgium and Greece they had so far refused to have their King back. I pointed out the obvious danger of His Majesty leaving his country so soon to return to his studies, but was unable to shake HRH.

After a full hour's talk, I drove back once more to the Royal Grand Palace, where a room had been set aside for me to change into khaki, as I had no fancy to parade round Bangkok in full dress; also I was anxious to avoid any chance of photographs being published, since I realized that it would be premature for European countries to see full dress photographs, whereas any lesser dress would have been almost out of the question at a State Audience, and the King had telegraphed his special directions from London that I should comply with the customs of the country and wear full dress.

I had decided to hold an all British Inter-service Parade and Victory March for the King of Siam as our contribution to the peace celebrations. I went to the parade ground for a rehearsal of what I was to do with the King the following day, and then we went to the saluting base for a similar rehearsal. After that we had a meeting to settle details of the next three days' programme. I did not get back to the Udorn Palace until 1850, and within an hour had to leave again for the

Boromphiman Palace, in white mess undress. Here a state banquet was given by the King. I was received with the utmost ceremony and shown into the room which contained all the assembled guests by at least half a dozen bowing court officials, who then left me to find my way round the guests and introduce myself in turn. The Siamese notables had the advantage of me, since presumably they knew who I was, but as I was unable to catch their Siamese names and they did not give their titles in English, I was thoroughly bewildered. To add to the confusion, everyone wore white tunics with gold shoulder straps and medal ribbons. I knew that among them was the ex-Regent (whom I had corresponded with so frequently as 'Ruth'), the Prime Minister, the Cabinet and Commanders-in-Chief, and all the high-court officials, but it was not only impossible to distinguish them from each other, but it was not even possible to distinguish them from the Court servants, who wore identical uniforms, though I later discovered that they had rather less gold on their shoulder straps. Even so, the Assistant Butler, who had been sent to run the Udorn Palace, ranked as a Captain in the army, and no doubt the King's 'Page' holds field rank.

No sooner had I completed introducing myself than the doors at the other end of the room were flung open and the Royal Family entered, accompanied by a cohort of court officials, who remained bowing respectfully in the doorway whilst the unfortunate King was left blinking through his spectacles, obviously bewildered. Everyone bowed, and then an awkward pause ensued; so I came over towards him and shook hands and took him round the twenty or so senior British and American officers and presented them to him. After a further awkward pause, the King made a little gesture to me and then to my great surprise took me in to dinner in front of the Princess Mother.

Mike Goodenough discovered the explanation of the complete disorganization of the state banquet, as he found himself sitting next to the Aide de Camp General, who told him that he had only that morning taken over the job without an opportunity of getting a turnover from his predecessor. He also explained that all the old court officials had been sacked and replaced by new ones, who were themselves unfamiliar with the protocol, and that none of the other members of the Royal Family who might have known something about the procedure had been invited.

In fact, this had been the King's first State Audience, first Parade and his first State Banquet, and there did not seem to be anybody who could tell him how to do it. I discovered during dinner that he had never seen any Royal procedure, had not read *The Prisoner of Zenda*, and had not even seen Hollywood's version of how to behave as a King. In fact, he hadn't got a clue!

I then told him as tactfully as I could how our King managed these affairs of state, and he took it all in with pathetic gratitude.[1]

After dinner we all trooped into the garden, where there was a lovely open-air theatre. Here there was a command performance of old Siamese plays and dancing, including a Khon, or masked play, based on the old Indian Ramayanas. I can never describe the magnificent stage settings, or the gorgeous and expensive costumes that were worn; but by far the most striking thing was the graceful gestures of the dancers, and the pleasant rhythm of the two native orchestras. The music appears to be more tuneful than any I have heard in the Far East. Four armchairs had been placed in front by themselves for the Royal Family and myself, and throughout the performance footmen dressed as officers served us with orange squash and cigars on their knees.

The dancing took place on a carpeted space in front of our chairs, and the plays on a regular stage behind that. The orchestras flanked the carpet. Halfway through the performance, three very attractive dancing girls approached across the carpet on their knees, with a large gold chalice in which there was a collection of miniature masks such as were worn by the principal actors in the Ramayana. These they handed to the Princess Mother, who in turn presented them to me. The gold bowl, however, was not part of the gift, and this was fortunate, since I was under an obligation to give presents of equal value for all I received.

SATURDAY, 19 JANUARY   We got back from the command perform-ance at 0100, and I then had to start work on the day's telegrams that were coming through the Mercury, which took me until 0300. I was called at 0700, and started work again. At 0940 I drove to the Boromphiman Palace to pick up the King for the British Inter-service parade.

We left the palace at 1000 in a Rolls-Royce with a light blue very dashing Mulliner body. The King and I sat on the back seats and the Aide de Camp General on one of the small occasional seats. The

---

[1] 'The poor King hadn't got a clue,' Mountbatten told his daughter, 'but he has now after your father took him in hand.' Denis O'Connor, the Director of Plans, said Mountbatten's attitude was 'the perfect mixture of respect to the King and a fatherly attitude to the small boy at his side.'

chauffeur and footman were dressed in a uniform indistinguishable from the Russian Guards. We never got out of first gear the whole way, and were surrounded by British and Siamese motor-cycle outriders. The footman had a long silver trumpet, which had a stop to produce two notes. This he sounded every two or three hundred yards. I was gratified to see that colossal crowds had collected round the parade ground, for this was to be a day on which I hoped to build up British prestige, since the protracted negotiations in which America had intervened had not served to improve Anglo-Siamese relations.

The King had no idea what to do, but willingly carried out all the instructions I whispered in his ear. I was however unable to prevent him from carrying out his inspection at much too quick a pace. He looked straight in front of him, very nervously, and never once looked at the men he was inspecting. When the parade was over, we drove in a procession back to the Boromphiman Palace for a gossip, whilst the official spectators moved to the saluting base and the troops moved off to the starting point for the march-past.

After an interesting chat at the palace, the King and I once more drove in procession through the streets to the saluting base in Kingsway, a wonderful wide thoroughfare laid out by the late King. Unfortunately the building contractors were running a racket, and several of the houses collapsed before they could even be finished, which rather destroys the appearance of this lovely avenue.

There were colossal crowds in the streets, anxious to see their King almost for the first time. They were polite and bowed, and a few of them raised a faint cheer. The King sat immobile, looking nervously straight ahead. I finally leant across and said to him: 'May I suggest that you should acknowledge the cheers of your subjects? Why don't you salute and bow to them?' He replied gratefully: 'I'm afraid I am not very accustomed to this sort of thing.' He then started acknowledging the cheers of the crowd, which immediately redoubled in consequence. The march-past was really first class, the prize being taken by the Queen's Guard of Honour, in column of sixes.

After lunch we started a series of calls on the Siamese Royal Family. Luckily I only had to sign the books of the Queen Grandmother and Prince Narisra, but with Prince Rangsit and Prince Vudhijai of Singha I stayed and had quite a long talk. The former was most interesting, for during his studies at Heidelberg University he had got to know all the Hessian family very well. Prince Vudhijai had of course been a midshipman in the old *Implacable* with Papa, and gossiped a great deal over old times, and all the officers he had served with. Luckily I was able to tell him almost without exception what had become of them. 'What became of our young sub Andrew Cunningham?' Reply: 'He is now the First Sea Lord.' The poor old Prince is paralysed from the hips down, and I do not think he is much longer for this world. He gave me a present for Mama and one for myself and sent messages to Alice, Louise and Nona.[1]

I also called on the Senior Statesman, as the ex-Regent is now called, and on the Prime Minister, Seni Pramoj, who had recently spent five years as the Siamese Minister in Washington. He had been reputed to be anti-British, but during this visit showed himself increasingly friendly each day.

After dinner we all went on to the Thai Officers' Club. Here we joined a party of the prettiest and sweetest little Siamese princesses imaginable. Although I danced with at least half a dozen, there wasn't one of them who didn't seem to be princess. They were all about four feet nothing high, tremendously attractive and vivacious, and very good dancers. The senior one was Princess Chambphot, who offered to take me on a shopping and sightseeing expedition; but the sweetest one was known at Ying Wun.

This club is completely open all round, with a swimming pool at one end and a revolving stage for the orchestra, so that a hot jazz band alternated with a native Siamese orchestra. Between the European dances Siamese girl dancers appeared and did some fascinating folk dances of a different style to what we had seen the night before, and if possible more seductive. Having not had much sleep the night before I was very sleepy, and had my leg pulled about this by the little Siamese princesses; finally staggering off to bed well after 0100.

SUNDAY, 20 JANUARY Once more I had to work from 0130 to 0330, and was called again at 0645, after much too little sleep.

We reached the ancient capital, Ayuthia, at 1130, and were received here, as usual, by a Guard of Honour and all the local officials in their full dress. We then visited the ruins. They took care to explain to me that it was the Burmese that had sacked and laid waste the city! The Senior Statesman was our host on this party, and this is his home district.

We embarked at 1240 in the magnificent Royal Barge, which has

[1] Nona Crichton, who as Miss Kerr had been lady-in-waiting to Mountbatten's mother when she was Princess Victoria of Battenberg.

some lovely cabins in it, and a fine promenade deck with a dozen small tables at which lunch and dinner were later served.

At 1300 we stopped at the Panang Cheng Monastery, and went to the temple that contains the world's largest Buddha. It is really a most impressive idol, bigger I am told than the Dai Butsu which I had seen in Japan. The figure is 61 feet high seated, so that the Buddha would be 120 feet high if erect. The little finger was over six feet in length!

We then went on down the river by barge until 1430, when we landed to see over the Barng Pa-in Palace. After half an hour we continued down the river. Small native huts have been built in a sort of ribbon development along the forty miles of river. It was dark by the time we reached the Siamese Fleet, moored on the outskirts of the capital. The fleet appears to be undamaged, and the Senior Statesman complained that we hadn't sunk it and saved them its upkeep.

We finally landed at the Senior Statesman's private landing stage by his house at 2015, and got back to the Udorn Palace just in time to change and leave again for the State Ball at the Ananda Semakhom Hall, which is a great marble building in the same park as the Udorn Palace. I was first told to be there at 2145, then I was asked not to come until 2158, in order to be there two minutes before the King, but the King was twenty minutes late, which just shows that he still hasn't got a clue!

Meanwhile all the notables of Siam were awaiting him in the Great Hall where the State Ball was to take place. At my request full dress was not worn, since so few British officers had it, but those princes who had British decorations wore their stars. We trooped in a great procession to the raised dais in the centre of the ballroom, where chairs had been provided for the senior members of the Royal Family and myself. We then sat down and an awkward silence ensued. After a while the band struck up and played a lively foxtrot, but nobody dared to dance. After an interminable pause, I saw a Chamberlain approach Admiral Morse and whisper in his ear, after which the Admiral got up and invited one of the princesses to dance. My Siamese Military ADC, Chitchanok, told me that I had been told off to dance the first dance with my friend Princess Chambphot, and after leaning over to the King and saying; 'Isn't your Majesty going to dance?' and receiving a negative reply, I went off and danced with her.

When I came back I said to the King: 'All over Europe it has always been the custom for the King to open each State Ball. Do you not think you ought to be dancing?' Reply: 'No, I have not yet taken sufficient dancing lessons.' I spent the next ten minutes trying to persuade the young King to dance. Finally I said: 'Your Majesty reminds me of a small boy sitting on the edge of a bathing pool on a very cold day and trying to make up his mind to jump in. If only you will take the plunge you'll find you will quite enjoy it.' He then took refuge in the answer he so often used: 'Please ask my mother.' The Princess Mother supported the King, and said: 'He is not experienced enough to take the floor.' I drew her attention to some British officers who were dancing nearby: 'Look, Mam, these officers are not keeping time to the music! I'm sure the King could do as well as them without any lessons at all!' She remained adamant and as she had already refused to dance with me herself, I got fed up and said: 'I absolutely insist that one of you two dances. Either the King dances with one of the princesses, or I insist that you dance with me.' She laughed good-naturedly, and said: 'Well, if it has got to be one of us it had better be me,' and to everyone's intense astonishment she took the floor with me. The King however remained miserably shy and alone on his throne until midnight, when we all trooped down in a great procession to supper. After this he left, and as I was feeling very tired I too went home, although the ball continued unabated.

MONDAY, 21 JANUARY   After again working until 0230, I was called at 0700, being by now some eight hours short of my usual sleep over the last three nights, and having only spent long enough in the Udorn Palace by day to change my clothes between items of the programme.

I left at 0850 to pick up Princess Chambphot for the promised shopping and sightseeing expedition. This really was great fun, and I bought all sorts of delightful souvenirs, including a picture of an incident in the Ramayanas.

At 1030 we were billed to start the sightseeing tour, and were shown the various palaces and temples in the Royal enclosure. The most interesting was the famous Emerald Buddha. The figure is only about four feet high, and is carved out of the rarest dark green glistening jade. It was taken some three or four hundred years ago from French Indochina, and the French were stupid enough to claim its return in their proposed peace treaty, which so enraged the Siamese that they broke off all negotiations, which have not yet been resumed. In fact part of the object of my visit was to try and induce them to renew negotiations. During my visit I pointed out to the King, the Senior Statesman and the Prime Minister that they could not possibly expect to hold on to the disputed territories, since the United Nations had decreed there should be no change in territorial boundaries as a result of the war.

The Emerald Buddha had just been dressed by Princess Chambphot's husband in his winter clothing, and a colossal wooden ladder some fifty feet long led up the back of the golden pedestal on which the Buddha was seated. What interested me most was the mural painting, many hundred yards long, of the whole of the Ramayanas, which included the original of the little picture I had bought that morning.

We went on to the Great Swing and visited the Wat Sutaat Temple, finally getting back at 1230 to the Udorn Palace, with barely enough time to wash and brush up before leaving at 1245 for the Prime Minister's magnificent offices and residence. Here an official banquet was given, with 75 guests, at which the Prime Minister and I had to make speeches. When he proposed my health the Siamese band played 'Rule Britannia'. It was disconcerting after a quarter of an hour's speech, which I had thought was going particularly well, to sit down in dead silence. None of the Siamese attempted to clap, and the British thought it would be bad form if they did. As I was complimented on the speech by a number of Siamese later, I realized that they had not meant their silence as an insult.

By this time a telegram had been received from the Foreign Office giving grudging permission for me to accept the highest class of the Order of the White Elephant, which is the principal order of Siam, and also the Santi Mala Medal struck for the Siamese Guerilla Forces. The Foreign Office said that they could be worn on this occasion only, and were thereafter to be treated as war souvenirs. I shall ask the Foreign Office to provide me with an explanation that I can hand to the King of Siam if I ever meet him at a State occasion in London and am not wearing his precious White Elephant. It is certainly quite the most expensive-looking order I have seen, and outshines any European order in magnificence.

I had to change into full dress at the Prime Minister's house for the investiture, which was carried out at the Boromphiman Palace at 1500. Afterwards I was taken up for a talk with the Princess Mother, while the King's younger brother took a series of snapshots of us with his Leica camera.

We left again at 1530, and I did a record change of clothes at the Udorn Palace, arriving five minutes late, at 1550, at our 'A' Mess, where a large garden party was being given in my name.

During tea, in a private room, I tried to persuade the King to come out and go round the guests in the garden. He obviously did not want to: I assumed it was his shyness, so I gave him a list of suitable questions he could ask the British Officers by way of making conversation; but he resolutely refused to budge. Finally I asked him if he played any musical instruments, and he replied: 'The saxophone,' so I suggested he should come out and watch the saxophonists perform in the Royal Marine band in the garden. He obviously wanted to do this, but did not dare to make up his own mind and said to me, as usual: 'Please ask my mother.' So, having persuaded the Princess Mother that this was a good idea, we all traipsed out into the garden and chairs were pulled up right under the bass trombones of the band. Luckily the band made so much noise that further attempts at conversation were not necessary.

In the course of the four days, at the urgent instigation of the Senior Statesman, Prime Minister and older members of the Royal Family, I have been hammering away at the King and the Princess Mother, trying to make them realize that it is crazy to leave the country for another two years' study in Switzerland, but all to little avail.

The King did say that he would like to end up with six months in England for military studies, and this I undertook to enquire about on his behalf, but my attempts to make him substitute this for Switzerland did not succeed.

He was nice enough to say on the last day: 'You know, I have given a great deal of thought to what you have been saying, and I hope, if I do not take your advice, you will not think I do not value it. I hope you will agree that I am taking the right decision.' I replied: 'No, I emphatically disagree. I am sure you are taking the wrong decision. In learning to become a very fine lawyer, you will hardly learn to become a very good King; but you have this consolation: that if your present decision loses you the throne (as many people seem to think it may), you will be able to earn your living as a lawyer in Switzerland.' The King took this crack in very good heart, and said how much he had enjoyed my visit and having somebody to talk to who wasn't always saying: 'Yes, your Majesty.'

I really am sorry for him. He is so hedged about by medieval customs and etiquette. His hair has grown long and untidy but he can't get it cut until the high priest has cast an auspicious day. It will then be done in state in a temple.[1]

We got back to the Udorn Palace at 1930, with 25 minutes to change

---

[1] King Ananda was mysteriously killed the following year.

for the official dinner given by the Minister of Defence. In addition to this I received representatives of the Prime Minister, and Senior Statesman, with gifts. The former had sent me an old Siamese sword in a beautiful niello scabbard; the latter a silver cigarette box with the Prime Minister's official arms on it, in the modern niello style. I sent back to the Prime Minister a really lovely Jaipur plate, which Patricia and I had chosen in Delhi, and decided to give the Senior Statesman a Japanese sword.

An extraordinarily good Siamese Naval band played for dinner, and all the waiters were sailors. They have the ideal organization in Siam of a single Minister for the three services, who is himself a full General, having under him three Commanders-in-Chief, one to run each service. Would that we could be as sensible![1]

TUESDAY, 22 JANUARY I staggered back to the Udorn Palace at 0200, only to be called again at 0645, by now more than ten hours short of sleep.

We got to Don Muang airfield at 0845, where there was practically the whole of Bangkok to see us off. Not only all the Ministers, Commanders-in-Chief and court officials, but most of the princesses, including Princess Chambphot and Ying Wun.

I had been pressed on all sides to come back again for three days' informal visit which they promised me would be less rushed. I said I would bring Edwina and Patricia. The former had made a great impression during her visit and I had many enquiries about her.

At 1000 we took off in Hapgift, landing at 1030 at Kellang airfield, Singapore.

WEDNESDAY, 23 JANUARY to MONDAY, 28 JANUARY On Friday I managed to get away at 1400 with Peter and Charles. We flew up in the Air Commander-in-Chief's Dakota to Kuala Lumpur, where I had an important meeting with the GOC Malaya, Frank Messervy, concerning the remission of a sentence of four years' rigorous imprisonment on a Chinese called Soong Kwong, and on the release of certain editors, imprisoned for printing articles against the British Military

---

[1] This was to be Mountbatten's constant refrain for the rest of his life. He almost achieved his end when Chief of Defence Staff; the task being eventually completed twenty years later.

Administration, consequent on my repealing my proclamation No. 2.[1]

Tuesday, 29 January to Friday, 1 February 1946 [Singapore] I had a very busy day on Tuesday, and was already late for dinner when Brigadier McKerron, the CCASO for Singapore, arrived breathless from a large meeting to discuss the General Strike which had broken out in Singapore that day. It appears that the strike, being purely political and aimed principally at the release of Soong Kwong and the editors, was illegal by an Ordinance published in November 1941, on the eve of the Japanese war. They had laid on a large police raid to arrest all the strike leaders at 0200. Naturally I ordered them to cancel these orders at once, as I could not have imagined anything more disastrous than to make martyrs of these men; but I held up the release of the various men concerned until the strike should end, as I could not accept doing this under duress.

On Wednesday I had a rushed and unexpected meeting with Frank Messervy and Newboult,[2] who phoned up from Kuala Lumpur to say they were flying down to discuss the General Strike situation, which threatened to spread throughout Malaya. We also continued the discussions I had had at Kuala Lumpur about stopping the armed gang robberies which are going on. Whereas for the three years before the war there had only been three such robberies, in the first fortnight in January there had been ninety. They suggested extending the whipping ordinance so that robbery under arms would entail flogging, and also a long prison sentence.

I resisted once more, as I did in the case of Burma, any extension of flogging, but since this violence is becoming a serious matter I startled them by suggesting we should introduce the death penalty for carrying firearms.

At a meeting later that evening with everybody concerned about the General Strike, I authorized the use of the armed forces to the fullest possible extent for maintaining the essential services of Singapore during this 'Political' General Strike, and to stop armed intimidation. I also decided to issue a new proclamation imposing the death sentence for carrying arms.

[1] Mountbatten ordered the release of Soong Kwong on the grounds that his imprisonment would smack of 'preventive arrest, which was contrary to my policy'.
[2] Brigadier Newboult was CCASO, Malaya Union.

Between these two meetings I met Sir Archibald Clark-Kerr at Kellang airfield.[1] He is our Senior Ambassador, and since he has come as the plenipotentiary of the British Government I accorded him viceregal honours and had a Guard of Honour of 100 men drawn up on the airfield.

I had a small dinner party of high-ups for him. He has brought some excellent caviare given by Stalin when he left the Ambassadorship at Moscow and of which he made me a present. Stalin's other gift was his Russian Masseur! (in reality an Embassy footman whom Clark-Kerr wanted an exit visa for, and Stalin granted it rather as though he were making him a present of a serf). I was much amused to hear that Stalin was quite delighted at Clark-Kerr's new peerage, which he took as a direct honour to Soviet Russia.

On Thursday I had a tête-à-tête lunch with Archie Clark-Kerr, and a long talk afterwards at which I put him completely into the picture as I saw it in Java, where he is now going to act as mediator.

SATURDAY, 2 FEBRUARY   I left Government House at 0520, and at 0545 was airborne in Baksheesh II. This is Keith Park's personal aircraft, which is fitted with long-range tanks like the Sister Anne. Since his Air Officer Administration, Victor Goddard, had wrecked my Sister Anne, I had no hesitation in asking Keith Park for his Dakota; and I must say he was very friendly about lending it.

We were met by a Spitfire escort to the south of Hong Kong Island at 1730. It was a glorious day with no clouds, and the sun was just setting. The group of rugged islands with the mountainous hinterland looked indescribably beautiful. The landing at Kai Tak airfield is certainly hair-raising, since one has to approach low over a range of foothills on to a short runway at the other end of which there is a range of much higher hills running out to the sea. We landed at 1745.

We drove in cars to a jetty in Kowloon, which is the town on the mainland opposite Hong Kong Island, where there was a Royal Marine Guard of Honour. We then went in an RAF launch to Queen's Pier, Hong Kong, where Guards of Honour were mounted. The Jaipur Guards, whose minimum height is six feet, and who have been trained by four RSMs from our Brigade of Guards, were especially impressive.

I found my memory of this part of Hong Kong was very good,

[1] Clark-Kerr, later Baron Inverchapel, had been Ambassador in Moscow and was now starting a brief stint as Special Ambassador to the Netherlands East Indies.

although it will be 24 years ago on 6 April that I was there with David.[1] Many new houses, including sky-scrapers, have of course sprung up since, and Government House itself, which we drove to next, has been completely changed by the Japanese. It was originally built on the side of the hill, with built-up foundations, and when the Japanese started to dig air-raid shelters the foundations started to move, and they had virtually to rebuild the house. There is no doubt that they have made a much better job of it than the British. The inside now is like a rather dashing Ritz-Carlton Hotel, but half the upper floor consists of a suite of genuine Japanese rooms, with sliding paper partitions, sprung reed mats on the floor, and as usual practically no furniture. It even includes a little shrine. I hope that the governors who succeed Cecil Harcourt[2] will have enough sense to leave these Japanese rooms, with their wooden baths and all, as they are original and very comfortable to live in.

At 2000 there was a firework display from all sides of the harbour and the men o' war, ending up by a searchlight display by the Allied Fleet, in honour of the Chinese New Year. These New Year celebrations go on for about three days, during which there is a ceaseless rattle of Chinese crackers going off wherever there is a Chinese community, and Hong Kong proved as noisy as Singapore had been in this respect.

SUNDAY, 3 FEBRUARY   At 0930 I and my staff attended a Military Council meeting at Government House, to discuss the administrative problems of Hong Kong, as I am responsible for its maintenance. I provide the troops, the RAF, the stores and food, the Political Liaison Officer and many of the Civil Affairs officers for Hong Kong. It is logically and obviously part of SEAC, but as the First Sea Lord made an issue that it was not to be placed under my operational control, since he wanted it as a base for the British Pacific Fleet, which was also not to be placed under my operational control, we have once more had to deal with one of these difficult set-ups that can only be made to work with the utmost good will on both sides. Fortunately this has been forthcoming, and we found a very happy team working in Hong Kong under Cecil Harcourt, who were most grateful for all we had done and were doing for them.

After this we went off in the barge to the *Duke of York*, where I

---

[1] On a tour with the then Prince of Wales.
[2] Vice Admiral Harcourt was Commander-in-Chief, Hong Kong.

was received by the Commander-in-Chief of the British Pacific Fleet, Admiral Lord Fraser, who gave a luncheon party for me. Bruce Fraser embarrassed me considerably by standing up and proposing my health in a speech of the most flattering possible nature.

In the afternoon Cecil Harcourt and Frankie Festing[1] drove our entire party on a two-hour trip round the island, visiting Stanley gaol, where the wretched internees had been locked up and in many cases tortured, as well as Repulse Bay and the Peak. All the houses on the peak, many of which are quite modern, had been looted by the Chinese after the withdrawal of the Japanese, as happened at Singapore, only much more thoroughly. In Hong Kong they had in many cases removed the roof in order to get at the wooden rafters to burn them for firewood, which is their greatest shortage. Practically all the nice trees in Hong Kong have been cut down. The island reminds me so of an enlarged Gibraltar, lengthened and flattened a bit. The streets of the capital, Victoria, are very gay and colourful with all their Chinese signs, and were particularly full of life on account of the Chinese New Year.

We ended up by driving past the racecourse in Happy Valley, where the 12- to 13-hand little racehorses live in three-storey stables! We went on past Causeway Bay, where I played polo for the *Renown* against Hong Kong in 1922, and on to Limoon Barracks. It was on this polo ground that the incident occurred in 1922 when Hugh Bowlby was playing Back and I was playing One. He hit the ball up to me, hitting my pony fairly and squarely under the tail. The pony clipped its tail down over the ball. I rode between the goal posts and pulled up. The pony lifted its tail and the ball dropped out. Was it a goal? They are still arguing about it!

MONDAY, 4 FEBRUARY   We drove all round the new territories and visited a number of frontier posts from one of which we could see the Headquarters of the 50th Chinese Division, which had fought so well under me in Burma, and which was waiting to embark at Hong Kong for Manchuria.

At 1430 we got to Ping Shan, which is the site of the new airfield to be built to international transcontinental standards. This will give a runway 3000 yards long by 200 yards wide, and will probably be the only one of its type in the whole of this part of China. As there is still

---

[1] Major General Festing was now GOC, Hong Kong.

some 50 years of the lease to run, it seems thoroughly worthwhile building this airfield, although it may eventually fall back to China. It is in a fairly narrow valley open to the sea at each end, and is fortunately in the general direction of the southwest monsoon. Nearby is a hill from which they are quarrying particularly hard granite, and within four miles is a beach that had ideal sand for concrete.[1]

'Shield' Force, who were the original Airfield Construction Engineers who were to build the British airfields on Okinawa to support the final assault on Japan, were diverted to Hong Kong and are now being used to build this airfield. Its construction will bring Hong Kong right back into its original importance as the finest all-round port in South China.

All the richer Chinese, including the Government itself, are most anxious that Hong Kong should remain British, since it is the one stable place in which they can invest their money and put up houses. T.V. Soong was here a week ago to look at his own house, and he sent me a very warm invitation to visit Shanghai and Nanking, which however I shall not have time to accept.

After tea we embarked at Castle Peak in a RAF High Speed Air Sea Rescue Launch. I changed from my thick khaki service dress to a monkey jacket on board the launch, so as to be correctly dressed for my visit to the USS *Los Angeles*. In spite of my having said I wanted the visit to be informal, in order to see all the new gadgets which had been fitted on board, it was highly ceremonial, with a large Marine Guard of Honour. I was astounded to note that when I inspected the Guard, each man ported arms for inspection, opened the bolt of his rifle, and made a little bow. They had part of the ship's company closed up at action stations, so that we could see all the turrets, radar stations, etc., at work. She was only commissioned on VJ Day, and so is probably the latest cruiser in the world. She displaces 17,000 tons, and mounts nine eight-inch and eight five-inch guns, the former having a range of 37,000 yards. What struck me most was the extremely intelligent lay-out of the mess-decks, with bunks in four tiers and the usual excellent American cafeteria system. The ship was spotlessly clean, in marked contrast to the way our own ships have fallen off during the war; altogether a very fine man o' war.

During the course of the day I selected some carpets for Flagstaff House, Singapore, since the Japanese left a whole lot of carpets, most of

---

[1] This project was abandoned in March 1946.

them new, in one of the rooms. The first carpet we brought out had 'Shanghai Hotel' written on it, so we hurriedly put it back again; but the others are rather nice.

TUESDAY, 5 FEBRUARY   We left Government House at 0650, and took off from Kai Tak at 0730. It had been a perfectly delightful visit, and the air had been fresh and invigorating. Cecil Harcourt has got a grand team under him and they are all pulling well together. It was the most encouraging of all the areas I have seen in the course of rehabilitation. We landed back at Kellang airfield at 1730.

WEDNESDAY, 6 FEBRUARY to MONDAY, 11 FEBRUARY   We got news unexpectedly that the outgoing Commander-in-Chief of the Netherlands Indies forces, Admiral Helfrich, and his wife were passing through Singapore on Monday on his giving up his command.

I therefore hurriedly arranged a lunch party of the senior Dutch officers in Singapore for him. Considering he must realize that I have been completely at variance with his die-hard policy, he was very friendly and expressed gratitude for the treatment which he received at my hands during the last two and a half years.

In the evening I had an embarrassing dinner with a very charming American author, Mr Ray Murphy, who has arrived to write my American biography. When he applied to the British Information Services in Washington and they proposed to me that he should come I refused categorically. Some muddle occurred and he turned up. I explained to him that I could not possibly give him any personal facilities to write a biography, but since he is now stuck in Singapore I told him I would not prevent him from trying to see members of my staff to collect what information he could. On his arrival he had written half the book, though heaven knows where he could have got his information from.[1]

TUESDAY, 12 FEBRUARY   At 1030 we landed at Samungli airfield, near Quetta. It is over 5000 feet up in the Central Brahui mountains. It was a lovely cold, clear day, though there was far less snow than is usual

---

[1] Ray Murphy's *The Last Viceroy* finally appeared in 1948, by which time he had accumulated rather more material.

at this time of year. Major General Irwin, who is Commandant of the Staff College, met me, and drove me to Quetta.

My lecture was to be given in the great Wavell Hall. This room is at least twice the area of the lecture hall of the Staff College at Camberley, but whereas Camberley will crowd 450 to 500 students into their hall, Quetta had only about half this number, with the result that there was four times as large a gap between each student as at Camberley. I refused to use the microphone, which they said was necessary to reach the back of the hall. I also checked up from the back of the hall that they could not see the maps which they themselves had provided. I therefore made all the students pick up their chairs and walk forward until I had them all crowded in much less than half the usual space they occupy.

I gave a lecture on the strategy of the South-East Asia campaign, and was told by Irwin that it had been received better than any lecture he could remember; but of course the explanation was not that the lecture was particularly good but that for the first time the audience had been arranged in a manner which would make them react with the psychology of a crowd and thus receive the lecture well.

We left from Samungli at 1500, and got to Palam at 1650.

WEDNESDAY, 13 FEBRUARY to FRIDAY, 15 FEBRUARY   On Wednesday, I worked in my office in the Rear Headquarters during the morning, and also saw the Viceroy.

On Friday, Patricia and I flew in the Viceroy's Dakota to Ambala, where we landed at 1245. We drove to Patiala City, which took another hour, and arrived at 1345 at Motibagh Palace, where we were met by the Maharaja and Maharanee of Patiala. The Maharaja is a most magnificent figure of a man, even finer than his father, being over six feet four inches high.

His Highness had invited me down to inspect the Sikh troops that had been in my Command, and as I had not seen Patiala for 24 years I had accepted.

We lunched immediately, and I met several of the old Patiala polo team I used to know. In the afternoon we went sightseeing and visited the Old Fort, armoury, etc., and later practised throwing Sikh quoits. In the evening he had a party and dance for us.

SATURDAY, 16 FEBRUARY   At 1130 I attended the parade at Yadvindra Olympic Stadium. I inspected all the Sikhs returned from

Burma, including about 50 wounded. They then marched past, and I and the Maharaja addressed them. The State band wore the Sikh quoit in their puggarees.

We lunched on an island in the artificial lake which the Maharaja has constructed near the Palace. All the guests went racing round the lake in about six speed-boats. In the central island he has built a cocktail bar below the level of the lake, and I have advised him to put some windows in so that one can see the fishes!

We got back to Delhi at 1800.

WEDNESDAY, 27 FEBRUARY to FRIDAY, 1 MARCH 1946 (Singapore)   I have only just been told that while John Brabourne was talking to Flags on the phone last Saturday, a Japanese prisoner carrying a sandbag across the roof, fell through the ceiling, missing John by six inches. Flags asked what that noise was, and John replied, 'Just a Japanese falling through the roof!'

On Friday, after the usual lunch party, I went round all the police stations in Singapore and saw all the divisions of the Singapore Police and finally addressed all English-speaking officers and men, to try and impress on them that though I would back them in putting down unlawful assemblies and riots, I would in no circumstances permit any form of unnecessary brutality in the execution of their duties, as I regret to say occurred on 15th February, while I was away in Delhi, when two men were killed by shooting and about 15 injured by being beaten up on the ground with sticks by the police.

SATURDAY, 2 MARCH   We landed at Palam at 0830. I went straight to Viceroy's House, where I met Edwina, who had arrived out three days ago from London. The Viceroy gave a luncheon party for the Tibetan Mission. It had taken them three months to come a shorter distance than we had come overnight. I sat next to a bald-headed, wrinkled man who spoke no English. He asked me through our Minister, who was acting as interpreter, what my age was. In return I asked him for his age, and was staggered when he replied '24'.

At 1445 Edwina and I left in the Hapgift, and at 1600 landed at Jaipur. The Maharaja met us. After a quick tea, we went to the polo club, where Jai tried to persuade me to join in an exhibition polo match; but I refused on the same principle as I have refused to shoot or do anything else of this sort during my present job. I did however consent to umpire, and after the match they lent me some first-class ponies to knock about on, which was great fun. On account of Purdah restrictions, Ayesha was unable to come to the Pavilion, but sat in a purdah car on the side-line.

MONDAY, 4 MARCH   We went to the Amber (pronounced as in French) Palace, not far from the town and looked all round, but we were not able to see the higher fort, since traditionally only the Maharaja is allowed to go there and only once in his life to take out one object from the treasure, which he has to replace by something of equal value.

TUESDAY, 5 MARCH [New Delhi]   Edwina and I attended the reception given by the Maharaja of Patalia at the Chelmsford Club, for Indian VCs of World War II. Although the Viceroy and most of the ruling Princes of India and high representatives attended, none of us actually met the Indian VCs, beyond catching a glimpse of them at the entrance gate. They were not invited up to the dais, or introduced to anybody. Altogether a very curious party.

THURSDAY, 7 MARCH   We attended the great Victory Parade. I arrived at the dais at 1456 and four minutes later the Viceroy arrived. We both stood on the dais for the march-past, which was led by the Commander-in-Chief, Claude Auchinleck, in person, with all his senior service commanders, in armoured cars. Later he came and joined us on the dais for the rest of the march-past. The mechanized column took 40 minutes to go past the saluting base, and the marching columns another hour. They were followed by a fly-past of the Royal Air Force.

After tea we went to Willingdon airfield, where Edwina, Patricia and I took off in the Hapgift at 1725, arriving at 1810 at Rampur, where the Nawab met us, and drove us straight to Khasbagh Palace. It was almost exactly two years ago when I was last there. We visited the Old Palace and saw H.H.'s collection of wireless sets. After dinner there was a small dance, during which we were shown H.H.'s collection of cigarette cases, and clothes, etc.

SATURDAY, 9 MARCH [New Delhi]   We had a very hasty lunch in our own rooms at Viceroy's House, and at 1230 took off from Palam in the Hapgift, with Jai and Ayesha and John Brabourne.

At 1550 we arrived at Swai Madhopur airstrip, which had been specially lengthened to take a Dakota as soon as Jai heard we were coming in the Hapgift, 300 men working for three weeks to complete the job! This is a place nearly 100 miles from Jaipur City, where Jai has got his main shooting camp. We drove straight to the camp.

Edwina and I are the only two in the house, since there are only two bedrooms. We left again immediately for a tiger shoot. Edwina, Patricia and I refused to shoot, but it was quite thrilling to watch. John Brabourne shot the tiger, a few yards from where Patricia and I were sitting.

SUNDAY, 10 MARCH   Jai and John took Patricia out to teach her to shoot with a small .240 rifle. When they got out to the target area they found a nilghai (or blue bull), which Patricia shot instead of the target.

The shikar bandobast had gone awry, for the four tigers which had been marked down to their kills all moved off before the beaters had hemmed them in. Thus we did not leave camp until 1130, and had a beat for general game, in which Patricia and Ayesha, who were in the same portable machan as myself, missed a very fine sambhur.

I always think that the general beats are more interesting than the tiger beats, because once there is a tiger in the beat, all the other animals leave, whereas in a general beat you get monkeys, pig, nilghai, bear and chinkara, etc.

We lunched in a delightful valley, and then went up and inspected an Old Fort. History relates that this fort was only once lost by Jaipur, to the Moghul hordes, in the following circumstances: the Moghul army was investing the fort. The garrison decided to do a sortie and arranged that if it were successful they would hoist their own red flag, whereas if it were defeated, the green Moghul flag would of course be seen. If the green flag were hoisted, all the women were to be burnt. The sortie was successful, but in the excitement they carried back the captured Moghul flag, and on return found that all their women had been burnt, as per instructions. In an access of despair, they blindfolded themselves and went into the Moghul hordes, to be sure of finding death in battle, and thus lost the fort.

In the evening we had another beat, at which a big black bear was shot.

After dinner we went out in a station waggon, with headlamps to try and find game. We spotted two tiger cubs drinking at a pool, but missed seeing the mother. We also picked up a very fine head of sambhur in the headlamps.

TUESDAY, 12 MARCH [Bangkok] We called on the Senior Statesman, Luang Pradit. From his house Edwina left with Jitjanok to visit the Chulalongkorn Hospital and 53 Indian General Hospital. I then called on the new Prime Minister (Khuang Apaiwongse), who startled me by saying, 'I sweat you a welcome.' I had heard that he had spent seven years in France, and so replied in French. He was absolutely delighted as he said his English was indifferent, and we spent the rest of the time talking in French. I had an extremely profitable meeting with him about rice and Franco-Siamese boundaries, etc.

I went straight from the Prime Minister to the Boromphiman Palace, where the three of us lunched with the King, the Princess Mother and the King's brother; just the six of us alone. Poor Patricia was stuck between what the Princess Mother called 'the children', and found some difficulty in making conversation with them. After lunch we stayed in the Palace grounds and looked round the various temples and the great mural paintings.

In the afternoon we went to Prince Rangsit's residence, where he showed us his wonderful collection of old Siamese treasures. We got back just in time for the Prime Minister's return call at the Udorn Palace, where a large dinner party was given, which although not called a State Banquet, contained all the Siamese high-ups, and unlike last time, most of the Royal Family.

After that Prince Bhanu had kindly arranged another Royal Command theatrical performance, this time 'the episode of Hanuman breaking the neck of the false Eravan'. Prince Bhanu had specially selected this as it was the episode of which I had bought the picture during my previous visit.

WEDNESDAY, 13 MARCH We left Udorn Palace at 0650, and at 0700 departed from Chitrlada Station in the Royal Train, with the Senior Statesman and the senior British Officers. We had breakfast on board, and arrived at Ayuthia at 0850. Here we carried out practically the same routine as I did last time, but I was very keen for Edwina and Patricia to have a chance of seeing Ayuthia and the giant Buddha at Wat Panancheong and the Palace at Bang Pa-in.

The Senior Statesman had kindly got us a lot of lotus flowers, so that we could have the fun of eating the seeds. We got back to Ta Chang Wang Na, the Senior Statesman's residence, at 1800.

That night we dined with the Prime Minister at his official residence. At my request he had laid on a Chinese dinner, and afterwards had a special Angkaroong band, which plays exclusively on bamboo instruments. Each man has two instruments, one in each hand, which when shaken gives out one particular note (or rather chord). They play the most melodious music, which is the most attractive I have heard in the Far East.

THURSDAY, 14 MARCH We left at 0910, and went to the Temple of the Reclining Buddha. This Buddha is 150 feet long, but as he was in the process of being re-gilded and was surrounded by scaffolding, he was difficult to make out. At 1130 I joined forces with Edwina and Patricia, and we paid our farewell call on the King and the Royal Family. They gave Edwina and Patricia some very charming little pieces of old Siamese jewellery.

We landed at 1600 local time at Siem Reap airstrip and drove straight to the Grand Hotel where rooms had been reserved for the visit to Angkor Vat. I particularly wanted my brief visit to Angkor Vat to be private to avoid the King of Cambodia coming down and hanging about during our visit. In fact I had offered to pay our own hotel bill and run the show entirely from the British Mission, if they would let the visit be private. The British Mission had done things in grand style; a convoy of 15 vehicles had come up and an Indian guard had been sent up, which made our total party nearly 40 and I was told my hotel bill for one night was going to be £75!

Immediately after tea we drove down to Angkor Vat and spent two hours going over this wonderful old temple. It is undoubtedly the greatest temple in the world and in a remarkable state of repair considering it was constructed in about the 11th century and abandoned nearly 600 years ago. An interesting feature is that the face of Lokesvara appears continuously. It is the last remaining relic of the Khmer civilization which appears to have disappeared almost completely 500 or 600 years ago.

After dinner we drove down to Angkor Vat where about 100 small boys, average age about four years old, stark naked, accompanied us carrying torches which illuminated us across the causeway to the Temple.

On the temple steps a troupe of local Cambodian dancers gave a series of dances. We were assured by the Curator that they were not a particularly good or skilful troupe, but what they lacked in skill was made up for in the romantic background of the ruined temple and the light of the moon and torches.

FRIDAY, 15 MARCH   We had breakfast at 0630, meaning to make a very early start for the ruins; but the Curator did not arrive until 0720 on account of a misunderstanding about the transport. We then set off and visited first of all the site of the great capital, Angkor Thom. This was at one time a walled city of at least half a million inhabitants, but the dwelling houses were all built of wood and were destroyed by fire in the course of the fighting which must have driven the Khmer civilization out, leaving only the great stone temples. We visited in turn the temples of Bayon, Ta Prohm, Ne'ak Pean, Prah Khan, and Rod Leprenu.

At first it was considered sacrilege to try to restore any of the ruins which had fallen down, and the most that was permitted was to shore up and buttress any tower or building that was on the verge of collapse, but no attempt was permitted to restore any leaning walls or arches to the vertical.

Recently, however, they have copied the system introduced by the Dutch in the Netherlands East Indies, whereby any part of a building on the verge of collapse is carefully taken to bits and the stones numbered in such a way that they can be restored in a correct vertical position. The many odd stones lying about are then carefully fitted together like a jigsaw puzzle, and by this means it is possible to restore to their original vertical condition entire sections of temples which were previously in complete ruin. As this does not involve the use of fresh material, but only the replacing of the original stones in their correct positions, the effect is very beautiful and sincere; in fact one does not feel that one is looking at any form of restoration.

There are some temples, like Ta Prohm, where the temple has been preserved with jungle growing wild throughout. The roots of the great trees have wrought inconceivable havoc among the walls and towers. Curiously enough there are cases where, a root having started to prize an arch apart, has thrown out a shoot to support it from underneath, to prevent it falling.

In these temples the only work that has been carried out is that of actually rendering the buildings safe from falling as one passes through them. Personally, I like the wild beauty of the temples which have been left as they were invaded by the jungle far more than those which have been restored and have had the jungle cleared away from them.

It must have been a great thrill to Mouhot, the French naturalist, when by accident he first stumbled on the lost city of Angkor. It is even more curious to think that there are probably more undiscovered cities which the jungle has invaded and overcome and which have not yet been rediscovered.

Ne'ak Pean is completely different from the other temples in that it is a sort of swimming pool, with the shrine of the sacred Naga in the centre, over which a great tree has grown.

We managed to take off at 1303 only 3 minutes late from the airstrip in the Hapgift, and reached Saigon punctually at 1500, where Brigadier Mark Maunsell[1] met us.

Mark Maunsell only discovered at the last moment that they were actually proposing to mount a Guard of Honour consisting entirely of German ex-SS guards; and when he protested that he thought this was most inappropriate, the reply was that they were by far their smartest legionnaries!

The Governor of Cochin China[2] drove me to the High Commissioner's Palace, where we were to stay. After tea Admiral d'Argenlieu called Edwina, Patricia and me into his conference room, in which all the high-level British and French officers in Saigon were gathered, and he then presented me with a beautiful stone Buddha, seated on the Naga, which is a wonderful relic from Angkor Vat. It is one of the very finest examples of the Khmer art that any of us have seen, and far exceeds anything left at Angkor itself. It had a discreet little inscription from the High Commissioner on a tablet, since he must have realized how awkward it would have been for me to accept so valuable a gift in all the circumstances.

After this d'Argenlieu and I held a joint conference at which I formally handed over my last responsibilities for French Indochina to him, including the care of Japanese surrendered personnel. My last remaining responsibility is to arrange for their repatriation to Japan.

Edwina went to No. 51 Indian General Hospital and Patricia went shopping; but we all three met at the Museum Blanchard de la Brosse, where the President of the French Far Eastern Archeological School and

---

[1] Brigadier Maunsell had been Chief of Staff to General Gracey and was now Head of the Inter-Service Mission in French Indochina.
[2] Colonel Cedille.

the Curator of the Museum showed us round. It is fascinating to think that since the war started a completely unknown civilization has been discovered in southern French Indochina, about which the world has not yet been told. We saw fascinating exhibits which had been excavated.

Finally we came to the Khmer Room, and discovered that Admiral d'Argenlieu's gift had literally been a 'museum piece', since it was the finest exhibit in this room of the museum which had been given to us. The Flag Lieutenant, being asked what he thought of this Buddha, replied knowingly, 'It looks rather heavy'!

I was only warned late this afternoon that, in spite of my understanding that there would be no speeches, Admiral d'Argenlieu intended to make a speech at the official banquet that night, and hoped that I would reply. I had an agonizing time trying to compose a speech in French and more or less learn it off by heart during the half an hour which had been left us to change for dinner.

Some 50 people, including I am glad to say, many of the leading Annamites, had been asked to the banquet, and the speeches were politically innocuous and appeared to go off quite well. After this a large reception was given, the first of its kind in Saigon since the war, at which again a number of Annamites were present, which was very satisfactory.

SUNDAY, 17 MARCH to FRIDAY 22 MARCH [Singapore]   Early on Sunday morning I read in the press that detachments from the British/Indian forces proceeding to Japan were being landed from their ships and marched through Singapore. I telephoned ACOS to ask if it was true and said that if so I would take the salute. It was true and I arrived at the saluting base literally 3 minutes before the leading column passed.

On Monday Pandit Jawaharlal Nehru came for a week's visit to Malaya. The Viceroy had particularly asked me if I would let him come to Burma and Malaya. I pointed out that Burma was now under Reggie Dorman-Smith and that he must ask him. I gather he received an indignant refusal. As the Viceroy said it would help his position in India if I would allow Nehru to come and make a success of his visit, I decided to do so. I got Frank Messervy's Chief of Staff, Brigadier Chaudhuri, appointed to run Nehru's visit and laid down that I particularly wanted to avoid clashes with our police and, of course, with troops.

Admission to Kellang airfield was only by ticket and ACOS met

Nehru on my behalf and drove him to Government House, to call on me. Here I gave him tea and told him that I would impose no restrictions on his movements or programme and would give him every assistance. I apologized for the action of the British Military Administration (Malaya) in telegraphing to say that they could not provide him with a car or any form of transport and said that this had been through a misunderstanding of my policy.

I asked him to cancel only one item of his programme; namely, the laying of a wreath on the War Memorial for the Indian National Army, since they had fought not only against us but against the local people of Malaya. He agreed to this. I also asked him to avoid incurring any indiscipline among the Indian troops and this he undertook to do. I found him most reasonable.

Fearing there might be trouble during the procession to his hotel, for which great crowds were expected and for which originally police, troops and armoured cars had been suggested, I surprised him by saying I would drive him in my own open car to the Indian YMCA, which was directly on the route to his hotel. This took him aback and caused consternation among his followers, but he nobly rose to the occasion and we drove back through the cheering crowds composed almost entirely of Indians. They had naturally come to give the Pandit a tremendous welcome but I was extremely gratified to find that they included myself to an unexpected degree, and that I was smartly saluted by most of the Indian soldiers in the crowd.

When we got to the Indian YMCA, Edwina and the lady welfare workers were present. The Pandit advanced into the room with his hands joined in the usual attitude of greeting and a very nice old-world ceremony of introduction had just started when a roar as of a dam bursting fell upon our ears and the crowd burst through every door and window of the YMCA. In no time they were upon us. Edwina was the first to be knocked down and disappear under the mob. The Pandit screaming: 'Your wife; your wife; we must go to her', linked arms with me and together we charged into the crowd in an endeavour to find her. Meanwhile she had crawled between the people's legs and had come out at the far end of the room, got on a table and shouted to us that she was all right.

Now the problem was to get the Pandit out alive. His more devout followers have a maddening habit of throwing themselves violently at his feet, their heads between his legs and their arms round them. A good swift jerk will then topple the old man over, but as this always occurs in a crowd, he merely falls back on to the crowd. It is the most effective form of rugger tackle and I am not surprised he gets fed up with it, and tries to push his tacklers away.

I finally found a door in the side of the building through which I rushed him. This turned out to be a sort of kitchen. We put a table across the door and while the Pandit harangued the crowd from the table I tried to find a way out. We broke down another door and eventually found our way to the main entrance through a passage and by this subterfuge we got him out. At the entrance we separated. Edwina and I drove off first and had a very friendly reception from the crowd. Altogether we must have stolen part of the old boy's thunder, besides publicly linking him up with us; so I don't think that his tour will cause any trouble; in fact I am confident it will have a good effect.

That evening we gave a small dinner for Nehru. We had a very interesting evening with very frank discussions, during which Nehru said he would send me a copy of his new book. He said to Chaudhuri on his way back that he hadn't enjoyed an evening with English people so much since he had come down from Oxford more than 30 years ago.[1]

SATURDAY, 23 MARCH An unusually large party came to see us off at 0930 at Kellang airfield for our tour in Australia and New Zealand.

SUNDAY, 24 MARCH We arrived at Canberra punctually at 0900, where we were met by Senator the Honourable J. S. Collings, on behalf of the Commonwealth Government, and Brigadier Derek Schreiber, on behalf of the Governor General. There was a tremendous crowd of photographers and reporters who even got in the way of my inspecting the Guard of Honour. Collings is the Vice President of the Executive Council, and has been attached to us as Minister for the tour.

We drove straight to Federal Government House, where Harry and Alice Gloucester received us and gave us breakfast right away. I spent the rest of the morning going through the final tour programme, which is going to be very strenuous.

Before lunch all the photographers arrived again to take pictures, and Edwina was bullied into giving a Press Conference. The female

[1] The friendship established between Nehru and the Mountbattens on this occasion was to prove of inestimable importance when Mountbatten became Viceroy of India a year later.

Press correspondents couldn't get over the fact that she had a ladder in her stocking!

After lunch Edwina and I were taken to see the wonderful War Memorial, which is also the War Museum. On the way back I insisted on being taken to Capitol Hill, where David had laid the foundation stone when we were out here in June 1920. The hill is entirely unchanged after 26 years, except that the foundation stone has been removed to a place of safety.

Canberra is in fact a city of temporary buildings, with less than half the accommodation necessary for all the officers and government servants who are ultimately destined to work in Canberra. It is, however, very nicely laid out, in beautiful surroundings rather resembling the Scottish Lowlands.

After this we had a very pleasant picnic party, with Harry and Alice and the eldest son William.

After dinner the Gloucesters took us to a film and lecture on the wonders of the Great Barrier Reef, at the principal cinema in Canberra.

MONDAY, 25 MARCH At 1130 I called on the Prime Minister, Mr Chifley. The first part of the meeting was devoted to the newsreel and cameramen, and after that we moved over to the Prime Minister's study and got down to serious business. We discussed the hold-up that the Unions had imposed on Dutch shipping in Australian ports, and various other questions which affected Australia and South-East Asia.

At 1300 the Commonwealth Government gave me a luncheon at which I had to speak. As I had developed laryngitis a couple of days before the trip, and was desperately inhaling and taking lozenges, I found it very trying having to make a public speech, and spoke in as low a monotone as I could, which could hardly have made the speech very inspiring. I ended up by presenting a Japanese officer's sword to the Prime Minister.

After lunch I joined Edwina for a Press Conference at Parliament House, at which I had to make a long statement to the Press, answer questions (including one as to whether I was to be the next Governor General!),[1] and finally make short statements for the newsreels.

In the evening the first full-scale Viceregal dinner party in the history of Canberra was given, since the dining room has only recently been

---

[1] Both the Duke of Gloucester and Mr Chifley suggested this but Mountbatten was not interested.

Between the Princess Mother and the King of Siam – 'a frightened shortsighted boy' – after receiving the Order of the White Elephant. 21 January 1946.

Lord Brabourne, with gun, proudly stands behind the tiger he has shot. His future wife, Patricia Mountbatten, is on his left, with her parents and the Maharaja and Maharani of Jaipur. 9 March 1946.

In Canberra with the Duke of Gloucester and his eldest son Prince William.
24 March 1946.

With a group of war orphans in the Legacy Club in Sydney.
30 March 1946.

increased to take 50 people instead of 24, and this party was the first ever given on that scale.

Alice was a bit worried, as her cook had recently left after marrying Derek's valet, and the kitchen maid was coping; but it went off very well.

TUESDAY, 26 MARCH   We left Government House Canberra after an early breakfast and motored to Fairbairn airfield. They tried to put us off flying, but we took off at 0915, and after a very bumpy flight through clouds and rainstorms we landed in half a gale at Laverton airfield [Melbourne]. Here a record crowd of notables were gathered, and a very smart RAAF Guard of Honour was mounted. While I was inspecting them, two of John Brabourne's cigarette tins rolled through the band, with him in hot pursuit. We talked to an old sailor who had served with Papa and who I had met 26 years ago.

We had a very cold drive in an open car to the city. It took us half an hour to reach the Town Hall: all along the route there were little knots of one or two dozen people, who cheered and waved, and in places there were gatherings of school children. As we neared the city the crowds became quite dense, until we reached the Town Hall, where an im-promptu open-air reception was staged by the Lord Mayor, in his robes of office.

Edwina and I were called upon to address the crowd, through a microphone, and our talk was also broadcast throughout Australia.

The last part of the drive from the Town Hall to Government House was even more crowded than before. Most hot-making remarks were called out, such as, 'She's a beaut, but he's more beaut!' This part of the drive was in rain, but that didn't seem to put off the crowds.

The Governor of Victoria, Major General Sir Winston Dugan, and Lady Dugan, met us. I had not been in the house since the Munro Fergusons had lived in it when he was Governor General in 1920, before Canberra had been built, but I remembered almost every detail of it. It is a nice comfortable Victorian house, rather resembling Osborne House.

We were only given half an hour at Government House before I had to go to Parliament House for the State Government Luncheon. Edwina went to lunch with the heads of the Australian Red Cross, etc. I was introduced to all the members of the Legislative Assembly and

Legislative Council: in all about a hundred people. A series of speeches was made, by the Premier of Victoria, the Leader of the Opposition, the Speaker, Senator Collings (on behalf of the Commonwealth Government) and others; and I of course had to speak. Luckily it was off the record.

We got back to Government House at 1820, which gave me just enough time to change and go out at 1900 to dine at the Oriental Hotel with the Royal Life-Saving Society. This is a society of which I became National President when Lord Desborough died, and which appears to have branches in every part of the Empire. Representatives from every State were present, and no less than 14 speeches were made, occupying 4½ hours.

Whilst these speeches were going on, a large crowd collected in the street and tried to break into the hotel. The Commissioner of Police, who was at the dinner, called out the reserves, and finally John Brabourne went out and addressed them. It then transpired that the noisy section consisted of a number of Australians who had married English girls and couldn't get their wives out to Australia; and they wanted to send a deputation in to see me. However, John arranged for me to see a small deputation the following morning at Government House.

Then a party of sailors on leave from the Pacific Fleet said they were prepared to wait all night to see me; so I left the dinner and came out to talk to them, only to find they wanted to shake hands and generally say how pleased they were to see me!

When I finally got out of the dinner, there was still an enormous crowd surging round the car, so that we had to fight our way through with a police escort to get into the car, and then I was nearly pulled out of it being driven away.

WEDNESDAY, 27 MARCH   I was called at 0700 in order to start work on the speeches for that day, and at 1000 left Government House with Edwina to see a large gathering of the Returned Sailors, Soldiers and Airmen's Imperial League of Australia at Anzac House.

I had been asked by the Government to include these meetings at each city, even though my programme was already quite full, and I was down to make a speech to the men. Judge therefore of my amazement on arriving to find that instead of several hundred ex-servicemen there were a series of Generals, Admirals and Air Marshals with about an equal number of men in plain clothes who turned out to be delegates from the various branches of the RSS & AIL. They presented me with their badge, and made me a life member. After that they expected me to make a speech. Of course the one I had prepared was quite unsuitable, and I had to extemporize. I am afraid I complained bitterly at being misled.

We left straight from Anzac House through the usual large, cheering crowd for the Town Hall, where the Civic Reception was to be held. I was down to speak 'on the record', and on a nationwide broadcast. After I had finished, the Lord Mayor turned to Edwina, who was not down to speak, and asked her if she would say a few words. In her place, I should have absolutely refused; but with a charming smile she got up and made a perfect speech, which was justly summed up by the Lord Mayor, in his concluding remarks, who said, 'I thought his Lordship's speech was good; but he will be the first to agree that Her Ladyship thoroughly wiped his eye.'

We then went round and shook hands with everybody, after which we were called out to the balcony by the shouts of the crowd in the streets, to whom we had to wave.

We got back to Government House shortly after 1230, where Leading Seaman Solomon, the Coxswain of the *Kipling*'s motor-boat,[1] and his wife, were waiting to see me. I had thought that he and the whole of his crew had been killed when Hugh Beresford and the First Lieutenant of the *Kipling* were killed; but amazing to relate they got away from the wreckage of the motor-boat alive, and swam to Gavdo Island, where they were picked up by some returning Australians later on. This is a great load off my conscience, as I was always rather worried as to what happened to the motor-boat's crew who none of us saw again after she was wrecked.

We left Government House in time to reach the Victoria Barracks at 1500 for a meeting with the Australian Chiefs of Staff and the British Joint Staff Mission. It was an unusual arrival for a Chiefs-of-Staff meeting because it was practically impossible to get into the barracks since the crowd had surged all round and General Sturdee, the CGS and I, had to fight our way through.

The meeting lasted about 1½ hours, and was, I thought, good value.

---

[1] *Kipling* was a sister destroyer to *Kelly* and had picked up survivors when *Kelly* was sunk. Mountbatten was rather disconcerted when Solomon was introduced to him as 'the man who saved your life'.

THURSDAY, 28 MARCH   We left at 0930 to drive out to the Wild Life Sanctuary to see some Koala bears, which were as sweet and ridiculous and stupid as ever. We got back to Government House at 1050 with half an hour to spare to rub up my speeches for the day.

At 1130 we arrived at the Masonic Hall for a reception by the Royal Empire Society, of which it appears I accepted the Vice Presidency in a fit of absent-mindedness. Again Edwina was called upon for an impromptu speech, but this time appeared to have been ready for it.

At 1230 I insisted upon being taken to a private room to read up the notes I had made for my next speech; and got to the Melbourne Club at 1250. Here I was told they had a record gathering, so many members applying for seats that they had to ballot for them. The only occasion that really beat this one in number of applications was for the Prince of Wales in 1920. The speech, being off the record, was a great deal easier for me, and of course went down better with the audience.

We got to the Mural Hall at Myers Department Store by 1930 for dinner with the Overseas League, of which I became the World President in succession to George Kent.[1] They had various other patriotic societies associated with them, and in order to leave room for dancing afterwards in this big hall, had very wrongly, in my opinion, made the members ballot for seats. They expected me to make a speech, with everybody waiting for the dancing to start, so it naturally wasn't very easy. Edwina this time quite firmly and wisely refused to speak.

We had to stay for part of the dance, but on coming out into the street were once more mobbed. When I got back I had to start work again on my telegrams and correspondence.

The great snag about Melbourne has been that I have had to make nine speeches in three days, and on practically every occasion at least two dozen of the most important people were present, such as the Premier and Ministers, the Lord Mayor, Chiefs of Staff, etc.; so that I always had to try and find something different to say, which is extremely wearying.

FRIDAY, 29 MARCH   We left Government House at 0850, and were airborne from Laverton airfield by 0930. We arrived punctually at 1150 at Mascot airfield, Sydney, where I was met by the Premier[2] and all the senior service officers, etc., and the usual Guard of Honour.

---

[1] The Duke of Kent had been killed on active service in an air accident in 1942.
[2] Mr J. McKell.

It took us half an hour to drive in an open car to Admiralty House, and the crowds along the route exceeded Melbourne, both in density and in the loudness of their cheers. In fact, in the centre of the city they broke through the police cordons and practically brought the car to a standstill. When I later congratulated the Premier on having made arrangements to produce so big a crowd, he replied: 'No arrangements whatever were made; your route was not even advertised. We were all taken completely by surprise.'

The Gloucesters were still at Norfolk Island, so we just went and brushed up at Admiralty House and then I left for the State Government luncheon at the Australia Hotel, whilst Edwina, who apparently hasn't found her programme strenuous enough, rang up and volunteered to go and look at a hospital instead of having lunch!

The speech at the State Government luncheon was luckily off the record, and fairly hilarious, recalling old times. The present Premier, who was in 1920 regarded as a very rabid Socialist, reminded the company that he had been seated between Claud Hamilton[1] and myself at the similar function held for the Prince of Wales in 1920. Mr Holman, a noted humorist, sent him a poem written on the back of the menu, which he had got, and which read as follows:

> What freak of fortune could impel
>   two noble Lords to isolate McKell;
> And, Oh, what mystery unexplored
>   could make McKell rub shoulders with a Lord?

We went straight from the State Government luncheon to Parliament House for an Editors' Conference at 1450. I left there again at 1530 to go to the General Post Office and meet the Trade Union Leaders at the invitation of the Commonwealth Prime Minister, Mr Chifley. Edwina waited with the head of the Post Office. I had a good barging match with the leaders about releasing Dutch shipping tied up in the harbours by the Unions. As this meeting had not been put on the programme, no police arrangements had been made, and by the time we got out the crowd was so enormous that it was a real hand-to-hand fight to get into the car; and it took ten minutes to get the car to advance 100 yards.

The result was that we arrived 20 minutes late at the Town Hall for the Civic Reception. Here barriers had been put up to keep the crowd at

---

[1] Lord Claud Hamilton had been one of the Prince of Wales's equerries on the tour of Australasia in 1920.

a distance; which made it easier to move about, but destroyed the friendly atmosphere of the previous crowds.

Although I was down to make a speech on the record, I discovered to my absolute amazement there was to be no speech. My relief at this was somewhat tempered with annoyance at having wasted time preparing one!

After this I met Edwina again as we had got involved in going to the Legacy Club, which was not on the programme. Here there were 100 boys orphaned by the war. All their orphans are looked after by ex-servicemen's organizations: a really admirable idea. Edwina and I were called upon to address these children, whose average age could not have been more than seven, and found this even more trying than usual. However, we finally sat on the floor with them and they all gathered round for a photograph, falling all over us in great glee.

We arrived back at Admiralty House just after 1900, to find that Harry and Alice Gloucester had returned. We naturally wanted to see something of them. The result was that, although we changed as quickly as we could, we arrived late for the Lieutenant Governor's dinner at Government House.

SATURDAY, 30 MARCH   We had hoped to go riding in the morning but there was so much to do in the way of preparing speeches etc. that we had to cancel it although we were called at 0700.

We left Admiralty House steps at 1030 by barge and went straight to the Captain Cook Dock. The *Implacable* was in the dock, which is the finest in this part of the world and big enough to take the *Queen Mary*. We also looked round the machine shop etc. and drove round the Naval Base and Garden Island, which is being modernized. Garden Island has now been joined up to the mainland by reclaiming the channel with the material out of the dock.

We got back to Admiralty House in time to leave for our respective engagements. I had to go to the Union Club for lunch. The speeches had to be hurried as I had to meet Edwina at 1430 to drive to the races at Canterbury Park.

We drove down the course escorted by 12 mounted police and it was reported to me afterwards that the unprecedented spectacle could be seen of all the bookies leaving their stands to watch our arrival, except one who laid 10 to 1 that Edwina would get out of the car first (and was taken up by several people who did not appear to realize what a gentleman I was!). Edwina lost £1 on the Mountbatten Cup but won £3 on the HMS *Kelly* Handicap.

Afterwards we had to leave again in state to get to Anzac House by 1630. In spite of having asked to meet the greatest possible crowd of returned servicemen and in spite of a message to that effect having been sent, only the Committee and very few representatives were present. When I asked the Chairman why this was, he said he had been told not to have any one around and had had to turn away hundreds of applicants. This continued muddle is really maddening. I absolutely refused to make a speech on the lines I had prepared for this occasion, as it was quite unsuitable for those who were present.

MONDAY, 1 APRIL 1946   We arrived at 0800 at Ohakea airfield in the rain. Although this is nearly 2½ hours by car from Wellington, the Minister of Defence, the Honourable F. Jones, who is the Minister for our New Zealand tour, and his staff, as well as the three New Zealand Chiefs of Staff and Sir Patrick Duff, the UK High Commissioner, etc., had come up the night before to meet us.

I was led to believe that I should have to give an off-the-record talk at the New Zealand Government lunch that day and that an on-the-record talk would be broadcast at the Civic Reception that night.

We left by car at 0930 and reached Wellington at 1120. On the way up I was preparing an off-the-record speech in my mind for the Government lunch. Imagine, therefore, my consternation on being told at 1130 at the Wellington Hotel, where we were staying, that the speech was to be on the record and broadcast. This meant recasting it at a moment's notice and having more or less to write it out since it would be on the record. I am afraid I became temperamental and was about to throw in my hand when a solution presented itself in cutting out most of my interview with the Prime Minister[1] and by doing this I just had time in which to prepare the new speech. At 1130 I went to the State lunch, whilst Edwina lunched with all the wives of the Ministers.

There must have been about 300 at the luncheon, which included all the members of Parliament as well as all the High Commissioners and Consul Generals, etc. Mr Fraser stressed the great interest New Zealand was taking in post-war affairs in South-East Asia. Therefore, after paying a tribute to the New Zealand war effort, I talked about the

[1] Mr Peter Fraser, who had been Labour Prime Minister of New Zealand since 1943.

post-war affairs of South-East Asia instead of the Burma Campaign, as I had intended to do, so I really need not have taken so much time in preparing the speech!

TUESDAY, 2 APRIL   We were airborne in the Chief of the Air Staff's Lodestar by 0900, and arrived at 1145 at Taieri airfield. The weather was lovely and we had a good view of the Sound and flew past Kaikoura and Looker-on Mountains.

The Mayor of Dunedin and other notables met us, and we were driven to Wain's Hotel, Dunedin, in a 19-year-old car; when we started down a very steep hill, the driver missed his change, the brakes wouldn't work, and we were saved from destruction by running hard into the back of the police car.

We arrived at 1230 at the Wain's Hotel, which is a funny old-fashioned one, rather like one gets in an English provincial town. The town itself is a Scottish settlement based on Edinburgh, the main street being Princes Street.

After a private dinner at the hotel, we went at 2000 to a Civic Reception at the Town Hall. The hall is very fine and large, and was filled to overflowing with about 2000 people. As usual, we found ourselves down in the programme among various musical numbers, such as The Dunedin Pipe Band, an organ voluntary, and singers. The proceedings were broadcast, so I had of course to change my speech again. Edwina was on the programme, and spoke very nicely.

From here we went on to one of the principal restaurants in the town, where the Mayor held a reception of about 400 high-ups, with whom we shook hands. As we sat down to our tea and buns, the Mayor said, 'I hope you won't mind if we don't have any more speeches.' But I might have guessed that this was only a prelude to more, for practically everybody at our table, including myself, was eventually called on to make further speeches.

As we were leaving, Mr Heenan[1] sidled up and with a knowing wink whispered in my ear, 'I want you to come to the house of a great friend of mine, Mr Smith, because he has the most amazing piece of furniture in Dunedin, and you mustn't miss it on any account.'

We drove off all agog to see the startling furniture, and were driven

---

[1] Mr Joe Heenan, Under Secretary of the Interior, who was responsible for organizing the tour.

to an office block. In the lobby there was a marble bust of a very naughty-looking young Italian girl, which raised my hopes as to what the amazing furniture might be.

When we got inside, the amazing piece of furniture turned out to be a very ordinary cupboard, with whisky bottles and glasses; and with many a knowing wink and references to this being better than tea, we were served out with brandy and ginger ale.

WEDNESDAY, 3 APRIL   We left Wain's Hotel, Dunedin, at 0930, and took off from Taieri airfield at 1000. We flew in the Lodestar inland to fly over the Southern Alps and the cold water lakes. We had a lovely view of Mount Cook in the distance, which rises to 12,349 ft, and landed at Wigram airfield, Christchurch, at 1200.

Here we were met by the Mayor of Christchurch. We drove to Warners Hotel where our party lunched privately.

THURSDAY, 4 APRIL [Wellington]   I spent the afternoon going through the telegrams that had arrived from the Mercury, while I was in the South Island, and in catching up with my correspondence.

At 1700 we attended a cocktail party given by the Minister of Defence and the New Zealand Chiefs of Staff in the Waterloo Hotel.

The Chief of the Naval Staff, said: 'I would like you to meet my Wren driver afterwards as her brother was picked up when the *Kelly* was sunk at Crete.' I surprised myself by being able to say: 'Is her name Raymond?', which turned out to be the case. Actually I only had two New Zealanders in the *Kelly*, Urquhart, who was killed, and Raymond, who was picked up so it wasn't very difficult.

FRIDAY, 5 APRIL   We had a complicated journey to Auckland: John Brabourne left in one Lodestar with our luggage in the early morning from Paraparauma; another Lodester left with the Press party, and the rest of us left from Rongotai in three Dominie aircraft at 0830. This is a minute airstrip, placed on the edge of Wellington harbour between hills, and even in a small Dominie aircraft is rather a frightening airfield to use.

We flew to Ohakea, where we changed to the York, and went on in her to Whenuapai, where we arrived at 1110. Here we were met by the

Mayor of Auckland and the usual officials, and drove straight into the town reaching the Grand Hotel at 1200. We had to go on at 1230 to the Civic Reception, which was about the biggest of the tour and went extremely well. By a misunderstanding, they had failed to provide a jeep for driving away from the Civic Reception, and so we went for about half a mile through dense enthusiastic crowds in a closed car, which was most unsatisfactory.

We lunched at the Grand Hotel, and at 1445 Edwina and I left for a weekend's fishing holiday. We left from Mechanics Bay in a Catalina flying boat at 1550, landing in perfect weather conditions at the Bay of Islands at 1640.

We spent the evening being shown the various challenge cups which one could win, and photographs of the colossal fish that they had been catching.

The season was rather later than usual, and during the past week some good swordfish had been killed, and no less than six had been sighted on Wednesday. Unfortunately there was a bad weather forecast which worried us all. As usual in New Zealand, there was an enormous menu, which I understand was not laid on specially for us, but is always the case here. We retired to bed early.

SATURDAY, 6 APRIL During the night a northerly gale had sprung up, which had lashed the ocean into a fury and made it quite impossible to go outside the bay to the fishing grounds. We finally decided to go round inside the bay trolling for Kahawai. I used my little trout rod and it was quite fun playing them. They averaged about six pounds apiece, which is the normal size that they use as bait for swordfish.

Since the weather forecast indicated that the first day one could reasonably expect to fish would be Monday, we rang through to Joe Heenan and got him to cancel our visit to the Glow-worm caves at Waitomo, although Edwina told me it was one of the world's greatest wonders; but I was mad keen to try and land a 400-pound Blue Marlin or 600-pound Black Marlin, which everyone says is the greatest thrill in the world.

SUNDAY, 7 APRIL Although the wind had gone down the swell was enormous. However, they very kindly took us out to the fishing grounds, although it was clear that the chance of getting a swordfish was small, and had we hooked one the motion on the boat was so terrific that it would have been extremely difficult to play it. In the evening I listened to my farewell broadcast to New Zealand, which I had recorded at Wellington before leaving.

MONDAY, 8 APRIL   The weather forecast had been wrong, and it started to blow again, so that we could not get out to the proper fishing grounds; but we did troll in waters where they occasionally get swordfish, without luck. We all left by the Catalina at 1350, landing at Hobsonville (at the head of Auckland Harbour) at 1500. We took off in a Lodestar from Whenuapai at 1515, landing at Hamilton at 1550. Here we picked up the rest of the party and motored to Ngaruwahia, where Princess Te Puea, the great Maori woman leader, had arranged a reception for us headed by her nephew King Koroki, who turned out to be a complete nonentity.

Twenty-six years ago we had learned by heart the words of the Maori welcome Haka, and I recognized it as the Maoris chanted it on our arrival. When my turn came to speak, through an interpreter, I ended up by repeating the words of the welcome Haka to them, which went very well. We left at 1730 and got back to Auckland at 1915.

We went by car and barge across to the Naval Base. Captain Bingley met us and took us straight to the canteen, where it was evident that most of the 'watch ashore' had stayed 'on board'. I gave them a somewhat light-hearted and informal talk. After this I went on to the wardroom, where I was made a Buzzard with the Honorary Title of Acting Probationary Temporary New Zealander (second class fourth grade) (unpaid).

Afterwards we dined in the Captain's quarters. They had never had so many stripes at one dinner in their mess, as we succeeded in producing one Admiral, one Rear Admiral, two Captains and a Commander.

After dinner I did a tour of the Naval Base, which has been wonderfully developed during the war and is capable of refitting and docking cruisers and destroyers.

We got back to the hotel at 2240 for the off-the-record Press Conference. I said goodbye to Edwina, who now starts her separate tour of New Zealand and Australia. We left at 2315, and got to Whenuapai just before midnight, where we said goodbye to all our New Zealand friends, and then took off.

TUESDAY, 9 APRIL   We arrived at Brisbane at 0800, after an 8½ hour flight, landing at Eagle Cliffe Farm airfield, and were met by our old friend Senator Collings. By some extraordinary muddle everybody in Brisbane had thought we were landing at Archerfield airfield, and they only discovered the change in the small hours of the morning.

The Premier of Queensland[1] drove me to the hotel, the road being spasmodically lined with enthusiastic knots of people. He explained to me that the route from the other airfield would have been much more thickly lined, as people did not know of the change of programme.

We arrived at Lennon's Hotel at 0830, and I was shown straight up to the MacArthur suite, where my colleague in the South West Pacific lived while he had his Headquarters in Brisbane. I got to work straight away on preparing the day's speeches and readjusting my mind to Australia's war effort as opposed to New Zealand's.

A large luncheon was given by the State Government. H.E.[2] made some very touching references to Papa, with whom he had served as a young subaltern.

Before leaving, the Premier kindly gave me ten minutes in his own study to run through my speech for the Civic Reception, and at 1445 I left in an open car to drive along a pre-arranged route. We drove at about 10 miles an hour through densely packed streets of wildly enthusiastic and cheering people, to the square outside the Town Hall, where stands had been erected. The Civic Reception took place in the open, the speeches being relayed by loudspeakers. After this was over, we were taken into the main concert chamber of the Town Hall, where about a thousand people had been invited. The Lord Mayor led me straight to the top table, at which 50 of us were to sit in state, whilst the others stood around drinking tea. He had made no arrangements and had contemplated none, for meeting anybody or shaking hands with them, so I insisted on standing at the door with him and shaking hands with everybody as they came in, much to his distress and their surprise. He kept saying to John, 'It isn't fair, it isn't fair!' – though whether he was referring to the strain on me or to the strain on himself trying to introduce a lot of people whose names he didn't know, was not apparent.

We got back to the hotel at 1625 and left again at 1640, giving me a bare quarter hour to run through my evening speeches.

At 1700 we attended a cocktail party given at Government House.

[1]   Mr Frank Cooper.
[2]   The Governor of Queensland, Sir Leslie Wilson.

What a funny thing memory is: I was introduced to the Mayor of Toowoomba and was able to say to him, 'How is Mary Grant?' She fortunately turned out to be a friend of his. As I had only met her in the course of a single evening at Toowoomba in 1920, and had not heard her name since, I was surprised at the subconscious process that produced it.

At 1900 we went to the dinner given by the committee and leading members of the Returned Sailors, Soldiers and Airmen's Imperial League of Australia. I had only prepared one speech for the evening and found to my horror that I was down to make two! The Chairman made a very foolish speech in which he appealed to everyone present to forget all about the horrors of war and to remember only the bright side of it – the comradeship, and the pleasant adventures.

This was more than I could take, so I stood up and disagreed violently with him, asking everyone to remember the lousy side of war, so that there should be no fear of the real horrors of war being forgotten and conditions being created again when another war would be possible. This, as might be expected, caused considerable consternation. However, we all moved on to the local cinema which had been taken for the rest of the members, and I made up for it by making a very light-hearted impromptu speech to them.

We got back to the hotel at 2215, to find an enormous quantity of correspondence to be dealt with before we left. After about half an hour, a loud commotion took place in my flat, outside my sitting room door. It appears that two extremely inebriated Australian girls, who had married Americans, wished to see me, and were assaulting the various members of my staff that were trying to prevent them from getting through. When Brian and Mike[1] turned up and tried to help the ADCs, they were set on and physically assaulted. This surprised me when I first heard it, until I discovered that they had both met these girls in a night-club in Sydney, so I reckon they deserve what they got! Brian had his general's cap badge pinched by one of them, and they had to call in the police to get it back.

We finally got to the airfield at midnight, where we said goodbye to all our Australian friends and took off soon afterwards.

WEDNESDAY, 10 APRIL We arrived at 0740 at Darwin after an 8-hour flight, where we were met by the Administrator of the

---

[1] Brigadier Michael Wardell, the Assistant Deputy Chief of Staff (Information).

Northern Territories, Mr Abbott, who drove us to his house for breakfast.

An elaborate table plan had been arranged, and we were all invited to autograph the original. The junior member of the party, John Brabourne, was put on the hostess's left, in spite of our having an Admiral and a General in the party, nor would anything induce Mrs Abbott to place a Lord below them.

During the tour I made 44 speeches, including broadcasts in 17 days – most exhausting. Poor Edwina has another 25 days to do. The reception we had everywhere was quite overwhelming, which buoyed us up; a great experience but not one I want to repeat.

THURSDAY, 11 APRIL to WEDNESDAY, 17 APRIL [Singapore]
On Saturday I had a formal meeting with the Raja of Sarawak (Sir Charles Vyner Brooke) and his staff to arrange for the handing over of territory to him. Afterwards the Ranee and the Killearns[1] joined us for lunch, Lady Killearn having arrived the night before. The Brookes very kindly invited me to visit them with Patricia.

On Sunday the representatives of the great Singapore Food Conference began to arrive. Patricia, Peter and I had a quiet dinner. Peter left the house at 0430 on Monday to fly home and be demobilized after practically four years' faithful and invaluable service on my staff at COHQ and SEAC. At 1000 I attended the opening meeting of the Food Conference which was attended in person by the Governors of Burma, Malaya, Singapore and Ceylon, the C.-in-C. (as Military Governor) of Hong Kong, a British delegation from Siam, FIC, and NEI, as well as representatives from India, Australia and Borneo. It is more than clear that the warnings I have given of there being famine in Asia for a long time past are coming true in spite of every effort that has been made. Considering that I have now turned over my responsibility to Lord Killearn I fear I spoke rather a lot at this meeting; but I felt very strongly about the impending famine.

At 0830 the next morning we all said goodbye to Bimbo Dempsey on his giving up the command of ALFSEA. He is going to relieve Paget as C.-in-C., Middle East, and is in turn being relieved by Monty Stopford. He will be a very great loss. Of the 20 Cs-in-C. I have had (5 Fleet, 5 Land Forces, 5 Air Forces, and 5 US Forces), I put him at the top of the list.

---

[1] Lord Killearn had been appointed Special Commissioner in South-East Asia.

THURSDAY, 18 APRIL to SUNDAY, 21 APRIL   On Thursday I gave a luncheon party for the King of Cambodia, who was passing through on board the French cruiser *Gloire*. The hostess of Flagstaff House[1] is certainly no snob or respecter of rank: at the dinner last night she arrived between Excellency No. 5 and Excellency No. 6, and at lunch today Thursday she arrived long after his Majesty and all the other guests. She puts on a disarming smile and explains how busy she is kept at the Signal Office!

MONDAY, 22 APRIL   Patricia and I left Flagstaff House at 0830. The party took off shortly after 0900, in a Sunderland of 209 Squadron, to visit Sarawak.

My original intention had been to go over with the Raja and read my own proclamation ending my military administration and handing the government back to him; but as the date of his visit had been altered and unfortunately coincided with the great South-East Asia Food Conference, I sent Brigadier Gibbons over to read it, but I still felt it necessary to accept H.H.'s invitation to pay a courtesy call.

We landed in the Kuching River at 1230. An Australian Catalina landed at the same time which rather complicated matters. At 1300 we arrived at Pangkalan Batu steps, in front of the Secretariat Buildings, where I inspected Guards of Honour provided by the 9/14 Punjab Regiment and the Sarawak Constabulary, who also had their band on parade. The band had hidden their instruments during the Japanese occupation, but the mouthpieces had had to be re-made.

We then crossed the river in the Raja's barge, which was paddled by men squatting cross-legged. At the steps of the Astana we were met by the Raja, who conducted us up to the house itself, where the Ranee was waiting for us.

During luncheon the Raja and Ranee told us more of the troubles that they had had with their nephew Anthony (known as Peter) Brooke. He is a young man of 32 who was on my Intelligence Staff, and who appeared to all of us to be somewhat unbalanced. The Raja said he had given him three shots at running the State, and had had to supersede him on each occasion. The climax was reached when he refused to accept an official British adviser after the war. The Raja then decided that it would be in the interests of Sarawak to turn it over to the British Empire and

---

[1] i.e., his daughter Patricia, who was now working in the Singapore HQ.

have a decent Government, but Peter Brooke and his father, the Tuan Mudah, and his brother-in-law, Arthur Bryant,[1] immediately made the most frightful scenes, which have resulted in a Parliamentary Delegation being appointed to try and find out the will of the people of Sarawak. There is one thing there is no doubt about, and that is their genuine affection for Sir Charles Brooke, the present Raja; and if he were 41 instead of 71, or if his brother were young enough, I am sure they would never agree to cession. As it is, it seems the only reasonable solution.[2]

Patricia admired a large, flamboyant, wooden bird which stood in the main room of the Astana. The Raja, with true Oriental munificence, promptly gave it to her; rather to her embarrassment!

During lunch it came on to rain very heavily, which spoilt the afternoon's programme of sightseeing, but finally at teatime we went to the museum, which was quite interesting.

After dinner we were paddled up in two barges to Fort Margaret, where a tattoo was held. The Dayak dancing was particularly interesting as they brought in some genuine head-hunters from the hills.

After the tattoo we had drinks in the Constabulary Mess. The Dayaks rushed forward and greeted Patricia and me very warmly. One old boy pointed to a wrist-watch which he was incongruously wearing, with great glee, and I was then told that he had taken it off the Japanese District Commissioner, having first dined with him and then cut his head off.

Sarawak was of course the home of the head-hunters until the Raja made it illegal; but early in 1942 he opened the season for Japanese head-hunting. The Dayaks explained that the Japanese heads were particularly satisfactory, being the right shape and many of them having gold teeth, which they prized very highly.

THURSDAY, 25 APRIL [Singapore]   I left for Kellang at 0900. We landed at 1245 at Batavia, where I was met by Lieutenant General Bob Mansergh, who is Acting Commander of Allied Forces, Netherlands East Indies, between Monty Stopford leaving and Douglas Gracey taking over.

I drove straight to the Governor General's Palace, to call on the

---

[1] The popular historian.
[2] Sarawak became a colony in July 1946.

In Katmandu in May 1946. The King of Nepal is instructing his C.-in-C. to enquire after Mountbatten's health. Mountbatten is with the Maharaja.

Malcolm MacDonald, Governor General of the Malayan Union, says goodbye to the Mountbattens at Kellang Airfield, Singapore.

General Juin invests Mountbatten with the Grand Cross of the Legion of Honour. 3 June 1946.

Acting Lieutenant Governor General, Dr Blum. Van Mook and Archie Clark-Kerr (now Lord Inverchapel) are at home for meetings with the Dutch Government.

Blum asked me to see that a fair share of rice was passed from Central Java into the Allied perimeters, since there was likely to be a shortage in Batavia soon. I told him that this was a matter I would take up with Dr Sjahrir when I saw him that afternoon.[1] On the mere mention that I was going to see any Indonesian leaders, Blum practically had apoplexy. It appears that he had protested violently at meetings yesterday afternoon and this morning to General Mansergh.

As a result, the latter had sent a most immediate telegram yesterday saying that the Governor General could not agree to my seeing Dr Sjahrir. Luckily I had not had this telegram, and Mansergh did not warn me, so I was able to say in all innocence that I had not received the telegram, and that if I had I should not have come to Batavia, since I had no intention of coming here and failing to see the leaders of both sides, the more so as Sir Archibald Clark-Kerr, Bimbo Dempsey, Monty Stopford, and in fact all other British personalities, invariably saw Sjahrir, and Van Mook used even to go to his house.

I made it very clear that it was not for the Governor General but for me to decide, and that I considered it would be out of the question my coming to Batavia, even if I hadn't got military subjects to discuss with Sjahrir, without my seeing him. Actually, I had the question of rice and also the question of the attacks on our convoys to discuss with him.

When we drove away from the Palace, Mansergh told me that Blum was so excited this morning that he had said that if I intended to see Dr Sjahrir, he hoped I wouldn't come and call on him at the Palace! Fortunately Mansergh, thinking I had had the telegram, did not deliver this message to me, as otherwise it would have made it very awkward. As it is, I had the good luck to get off my call on Blum without having to give up seeing Sjahrir.

At 1600 I visited the Harmony Club, which is an excellent club run for the BORs. The Club was crammed full of BORs, playing billiards, reading, writing letters, having tea, etc. They tried to make me do the usual thing of going round which I refused to do. I explained to Brigadier Mitchell, who met us here, that I was sure he would object very much if the Archbishop of Canterbury came round the Rag while Brigadier Mitchell was reading his *Times* over his afternoon coffee, and

[1] Dr Sjahrir had temporarily replaced the more abrasive Sukarno in command of the nationalists, but he was not emollient enough to satisfy the Dutch.

patronizingly enquired whether he was having a good time. We finally compromised, and I went into the Library, which was practically empty, and then passed the word round that anybody who wanted to come in and hear me talk, could come; and a most gratifying number turned up.

At 1700 we left the airfield and drove on down to the port of Batavia, Tanjong Priok. We left the port at 1815, and drove straight to Lieutenant-Colonel Van der Post's house.[1] He is a South African of Dutch extraction in the British Army, who was interned in Java and is now G.1, Intelligence. He was the officer I sent to The Hague to try and explain to the Dutch Government what the situation was in Java in the early days. He had arranged to ask in for drinks the Indonesian Prime Minister, Dr Sjahrir. We discussed purely military matters, in a very friendly atmosphere. I took a great fancy to Sjahrir, who has got a charming personality. Archie Kerr's description of him as '. . . a spaniel whom one expects to jump on one's lap and lick one's face if petted', cannot be bettered.

FRIDAY, 26 APRIL   I left Mansergh's house at 0800, and arrived at the airfield at 0820. At 0830 we were airborne in the Hapgift, and at 0905 arrived at Bandoeng. At 0930 we left for a drive round the town. This is divided by the railway, and until some three or four weeks ago the Indonesians held the southern half and we held the northern. As they mortared the RAPWI camps we decided to take over their half as well, and negotiated this with Sjahrir, who ordered them to withdraw. Before withdrawing, however, they set fire to most of their part of the town, which was destroyed.

Most of the Chinese are back and about 10 per cent of the Indonesians have drifted back so far; but it takes courage for an Indonesian to come back, since he may well be scuppered by the extremists.

We ended up at 23 Divisional Headquarters in the great Secretarial Buildings, which were put up when it was intended to shift the seat of Government to Bandoeng. Actually there was never enough money to complete the project.

We next went to 49 Brigade Headquarters, finally reaching the famous Isola Hotel at 1200 to see the 1/10 Royal Gurkha Rifles. The

---

[1] Laurens Van der Post, writer, savant, mystic and authority on Bushmen.

hotel is a very dashing, small modern hotel, with a glorious view and lovely gardens, and was full before the war with honeymooners, both official and unofficial.

Alongside the hotel the Japs have put up a large basha hall, which they have used as a Japanese propaganda war exhibition. It has in it captured British Naval guns, British tanks, and an almost complete Flying Fortress. As the Isola Hotel was practically unused during the war, I cannot imagine why they went to the trouble to start up an exhibition at this point. The British officers were so amused by this Jap exhibition that they were foolishly proposing to leave it intact when they withdrew; but I gave orders for the whole thing to be destroyed.

We took off from the airfield at 1330. On leaving Bandoeng, I told the pilot to fly over Krakatoa. This meant a diversion over territory held by the extremists, and I found we had been briefed to fly around the edge of the sea, as they apparently preferred that I should be ditched in the sea rather than parachute into the hands of the extremists!

I had always wanted to see Krakatoa, as I had been so fascinated by its history, particularly its final and greatest eruption in August 1943. The most violent eruption known to nature took place from this volcano, which before the eruption measured five miles by three, but afterwards all that part north of the highest peak completely disappeared. During the 1883 eruption, the steam from the volcano reached a height of more than twelve miles, and the rain of ashes fell over most of Sumatra and Malaya and Java, and as far southwest as the Cocos Islands. The finer particles of dust floating in the upper atmosphere enveloped the earth, and caused brilliant sunsets for the rest of the year. The sound of the explosions was heard as far apart as Western Australia and Mauritius.

The tidal waves swept the shores of the Sunda Straits, utterly destroying four towns, and afterwards crossing the oceans as far as South Africa and Karachi, at a speed of 400 miles an hour. At Merak, the tidal wave reached a height of 120 feet, and every object on the shore as far inlaid as the first range of hills was levelled to the ground; and where the land was low the wave penetrated five miles inward. At Teluk Betung the water rose to the square of the Resident's House, 118 feet above normal high water. Over 36,000 people perished in the disaster.

Almost more interesting than Krakatoa was the disappearing island. It first appeared in 1929, in a place where formerly there had been a depth of 15 fathoms. It then disappeared again, but came up again in 1930, and in 1933 increased its size. One of our submarines on patrol during the war reported seeing an island appear out of the sea, but I am not sure if it was this one.

Altogether the Sunda Straits have always fascinated me, and I was glad to have this chance of a good look round from the air.

We had left time in hand for this trip, but unfortunately we found the dreaded Black 'Cu Nimb' clouds over the land, and had to make a diversion over the sea to miss them; and thus arrived 20 minutes late, at Palambang at 1620.

I of course knew that we had been forced to keep Japanese troops under arms to protect our lines of communication and vital areas in Sumatra for which the British/Indian troops did not suffice; but it was nevertheless a great shock to me to find over a thousand Japanese troops guarding the nine miles of road from the airfield to the town, and to find them drawn up in parties of twenty, presenting arms, the officers saluting with swords which long since should have been our war souvenirs.

I recognized my old friend the smiling Sikh, whom I had seen the Viceroy decorate at Imphal and who had then come to me to be decorated a week later; I told his CO I wasn't prepared to decorate him a third time!

I had drinks in their mess to meet the senior Dutch Naval and Military officers, and then went to the Brigadier's house, which he has kindly turned over to me, and had a meeting with him and the General.

WEDNESDAY, 1 MAY to TUESDAY, 7 MAY 1946 [Singapore]   On Friday I had a terrific meeting which was attended by all the Service Commanders from Java and Sumatra and their staffs to enable me to put up final proposals for the NEI to the Chiefs of Staff. I gave a large luncheon party for them and for my Dutch Liaison Staff who are leaving me.

On Saturday, the 4th, I left Kellang in the Sister Anne at 0800. This is the first trip Sister Anne has made since her forced landing on Sado Island, from which the Americans had done a miracle of recovery for us.

We arrived at Kuala Lumpur at 0930 and we were met by the GOC, Malaya, Sir Frank Messervy. We went straight to Frank's house for talks. It was raining which was unfortunate as the 1st (King George V's Own) Battalion the Sikh Regiment were celebrating their centenary by a big parade today. However, the rain gradually eased off and stopped shortly after the parade started.

The Governor of the Malayan Union arrived three minutes late with the result that I very nearly arrived at the same time as him and had to wait until he had taken his place. I actually arrived at the dais at 1050 and was received by 'Rule Britannia' and then carried out an inspection of the four guards. After this I was to have delivered a specially lengthened address in Urdu through a microphone, but as it had broken down through the wet I had to bellow it out for the parade was drawn up about 200 yards away. They then carried out the full ceremonial trooping of the colour and did it as well as I have ever seen the footguards do it for the King's birthday in London.

I left the parade exactly one hour after I had arrived to call on the Governor at the King's House. I drove with H.E. to the GOC's house for a fork luncheon party and after lunch we drove to the grounds of the King's House and planted a Lager Stroemia tree. Although there were not more than two or three dozen Malays and just our own party gathered round the tree, H.E. startled us by stepping forward and making a speech to which I found myself quite unable to reply, particularly as three cheers were called for, first for me and then for him, which made the whole thing very 'Noel Cowardish'.

We spent a hectic afternoon packing and saying goodbye to those members of my staff who will not be here when I get back from the next tour. Edwina, Patricia, John and I left in the York from the newly opened airfield at Changi after dinner for the tour to Nepal and Kashmir.

WEDNESDAY, 8 MAY   We arrived at Allahabad at 0910, where we transferred to the dear old Sister Anne, who had preceded us. After half an hour we took off, arriving at 1100 at Simra, which is the only airfield in Nepal and a very doubtful one at that. It is on the extreme edge of the Nepalese Terai, and short and bumpy and often very wet. The advance party Dakota had crashed on landing, but can fairly easily be salved. Another Dakota had gone in to prepare the field for us. As our wheels touched Patricia said, 'Well, we're down all right' – upon which the aircraft promptly leapt about six feet in the air as it hit a bump.

On alighting we were met by the new Maharaja's brother, General Sir Hiranya Shumshere Jung Bahadur Rana (who reminded me he had first met me at the Prince of Wales's shoot at Bikna Thori in the Nepalese Terai in 1921). He had a couple of station cars to meet us and drove us to Amlekganj, where we had lunch. We had hoped to be allowed to go in the toy railway (about a two-foot gauge), but they actually took us by car as it is quicker and takes only 50 mintues.

After lunch we changed into trousers or jodhpurs, and left again at 1310 by car. We went over a very rough and twisting road, and finally reached Bimphedi at 1440, where the road stops altogether and an incredibly rough mountain track begins. We all transferred to tiny little Tibetan ponies, standing about 12 hands. The Maharaja had sent two ADCs and a 'Master of the Horse'. There were twelve ponies altogether in the procession. Each pony had a groom. In addition there were two dandies (carrying chairs) carried by six men each, intended for the two ladies, who scornfully rejected them; they took our light luggage instead. There were about another half dozen porters carrying suitcases, etc., on their backs, so that our total party exceeded 40.

The heavy luggage went up by the ropeway. This is a fine engineering feat, as it stretches the whole way from Bimphedi to Katmandu, spanning valleys up to three quarters of a mile in length with single spans. The ropeway handles eight tons a day inwards and four tons a day outwards.

Bimphedi itself is slightly less than 5000 feet, and we climbed to a small village called Sisigarhi, at an altitude of some 7000 feet, which we reached just after 1600.

On arrival a rather ragtime Guard of Honour turned out, who defeated all attempts at being inspected by standing at ease each time I tried to approach them. Meanwhile an ancient battery of muzzle-loaders fired a 17-gun salute. It was most dramatic to see the man with the quick-match running from touch-hole to touch-hole! We spent the night at the Rest House, the food having been sent up from Calcutta.

THURSDAY, 9 MAY At 0800 the same procession left Sisigarhi. We soon reached the top of the pass and started the descent into the first valley, which was so steep that we had to walk, or rather clamber down nearly the whole way on foot. It also rained, which prevented John's rubber crepe-soled shoes from holding, so that he constantly fell down without warning. When we got to the bottom of the valley we followed the river for several miles and then struck off to cross the next range, arriving at Chitlang at 1320 for lunch.

After lunch we all put on collars and ties to look a bit smarter on arrival, and spent a busy time trying to get rid of leeches.

One of the most fascinating parts of this trip has been that we have passed a constant stream of delightful little Gurkha soldiers on their way back home on leave or to be demobilized. They all grinned broadly and saluted smartly as we passed, and each was accompanied by one or two porters carrying their worldly belongings by means of a strap passing over the head and under the inevitable tin box.

The next climb was considerably tougher than the first one. Being hampered by the presence of the President of our Dumb Friends' League,[1] most of us were made to get off and walk much earlier than we thought was necessary, though later on it was clear that the ponies could not possibly have got up with anyone on their backs, and it is still a mystery to me how they climbed up almost vertical precipices by themselves. This pass was also over 7000 feet high, and then began the difficult descent into the valley of Katmandu. It had been raining, but presently the clouds lifted and we got a glorious sunlit view of this fertile and lovely valley with the city gleaming in the distance.

Whenever we passed through a village we noticed that every house had a brass water-urn placed in the street, filled with flowers. It turned out that this had been specially arranged in our honour. We arrived at the foot of the pass at Thankote at 1600. Magnificent tents had been specially erected for us to tidy up, and the ladies changed from trousers into skirts.

We were surprised to find large modern motor-cars to meet us and enquired how they had got there. General Krishna[2] explained that they were carried in by coolies, 105 coolies to a car. It takes them a fortnight, and I cannot even begin to imagine how they lift them up that terrible precipitous mountain track.

On arrival at Kalimati, on the outskirts of the capital, a large Guard of Honour of the Kali Bahadur Regiment was drawn up, with colours, band and bugles. The band played a complete verse of 'Rule Britannia', whilst the bugles did their best to drown it with a different tune. The guns on the ancient fort thundered a 17-gun salute whilst I inspected the guard.

I addressed one man in my best Nepali, upon which he took three paces smartly to the rear. After this I gave up trying to talk to them.

We arrived at Bahadur Bhawan, the residence of Commanding General Sir Bahadur Shumshere Jung Bahadur Rana. We were embarrassed to find that the General had turned over his magnificent residence

---

[1] Edwina Mountbatten.
[2] General Krishna Shumshere Jung Bahadur Rana, who had been Nepalese Liaison Officer in Delhi.

completely to us and had moved to the great Singha Durbar, until we discovered, later on, that the new Maharaja had ordered him three months previously to move into the Singha Durbar, for no special reason that anyone could discover.

Within ten minutes of our arrival His Highness Sir Padma Shumshere Jung Bahadur Rana, the Maharaja, and the Prime Minister of Nepal, called. He only succeeded his brother Joodha three months ago, and is a comparatively poor man by Nepalese standards. For instance, the eight sons of Joodha each inherited £5,000,000 sterling, and are reputed to be better off than the Maharaja.

The Maharaja was very friendly and spoke volubly in a language which one gradually got to realize was meant to be English. It required great concentration and skilful guesswork to follow him at all. Unlike the rest of the family, he has practically never left Nepal, which presumably accounts for his being the only one whose English is difficult to follow.

As soon as the Maharaja left, the Acting Senior Commanding General, Sir Kaiser Shumshere, etc., called. Kaiser was my especial buddy in 1921, when he had a big moustache and plenty of hair. He is now clean-shaven and bald, but has retained his encyclopaedic knowledge which had so staggered me in 1921, and again when we met him at the Coronation.

He began by saying to Edwina: 'Let me see, Lady Patricia Ramsay is your daughter's godmother, isn't she: and your Patricia must be just 22 years old now!' Later he said to me: 'Do you mind if I examine your salad bowl?' and then peered over and went through my medal ribbons one by one. He then exclaimed: 'Insufficient recognition, as I thought. I suppose a mixture of the King's fear of being accused of nepotism and the jealousy of the Commanders older than you.' It was difficult to explain to him how highly the KCB and DSO are valued by us.

FRIDAY, 10 MAY At 0930 Macleod[1] called and took the male members of our party down to the Durbar Hall for a rehearsal of the afternoon's ceremony. We had hoped to do a sightseeing tour later, but it came on to rain heavily when we got back to Bahadur Bhawan, so we spent the morning at work.

After lunch I got into blue full dress uniform, which Claude Auchinleck said was essential for the State Durbar, and which the King

[1] Lieutenant-Colonel Macleod, HM Chargé d'Affaires.

had given me authority to wear. At 1505 we collected in the Throne Room to meet the various Nepalese Generals, who had come to conduct us to the Durbar.

At 1515 the rest of us drove off in an open State Coach. A large guard and band of the Kali Bahadur Regiment, in scarlet full dress, was drawn up in the Palace grounds, and we had a mounted escort of 22 Lancers, also in scarlet full dress. As we drove past the parade ground, we saw a procession of motor-cars with flags flying driving across it at very high speed with the horns screwed down, racing to get ahead of us. This was the King of Nepal, who had started rather late, and was let in through one of the French windows, sliding on to his throne a few moments before we arrived.

Considerable crowds lined the route, and gave us a friendly reception. The Durbar square was lined with Infantry, Cavalry and bands in full dress in every direction.

A thunderstorm which had been gathering broke just as we arrived, only about two or three drops of rain actually falling on us before we got out of the coach; but then it came down properly. Edwina and Patricia, who were watching our arrival from the balcony, reported that a buffalo got loose in the square and was chased by Lancers in full dress to make way for our coach.

General Kaiser met me at the carriage step, and conducted me to the top of the stairs where the Maharaja was awaiting us. The Maharaja clasped hands with me in the traditional Nepalese manner, all fingers interlocked and the forearms held horizontally.

We then advanced down the length of the Durbar Hall, which presented a magnificent scene, being lined on one side by a great many Nepalese Generals and a few Nepalese Colonels in full dress. Down the other side were high court officials (Mir Munshis) and priests.

The Nepalese Generals' full dress uniform closely resembles that of our own Generals, but is even more magnificent. Their headdress consists of a helmet studded with pearls and diamonds, and hung with a fringe of uncut emeralds, the whole surmounted by a magnificent and enormous plume of bird-of-paradise feathers. I was credibly informed that the headdresses of the Generals who were present at the Durbar were valued in the aggregate at over £100,000.

In spite of meticulous rehearsal and our own party thus knowing exactly what to do, the Maharaja led me off in the wrong direction after I had shaken hands with the King, and I had to tell him what we ought to do next! We then sat down on sofas whilst the Commander-in-Chief went backwards and forwards between the King and myself, exchanging enquiries about our health, etc.

After this two Generals and a Colonel received His Majesty's permission to withdraw. They returned with the Colonel carrying a large purple cushion glittering with insignia, and escorted by the two Generals.

They advanced by short rushes, stopping to bow every ten yards, until finally they reached the Presence. I was then called forward and the King started to invest me with the Most Refulgent Order of the Star of Nepal. However, as this was against the agreed procedure in the rehearsal, I murmured that I thought the King's speech should come before the investiture, to which everyone agreed, and General Bahadur then read out the King's speech.[1]

I then stepped forward and the King not only pinned the biggest star I have ever seen on to me, but after hanging the broad ribbon over my right shoulder he also hung the collar of the Order round my neck.

After the investiture and before I was allowed to start my speech, a salute of 17 guns was fired. Then I stepped back and made my reply, after which I presented H.M. with a Japanese samurai sword. We then sat down again whilst a procession of Mir Munshis came in carrying itr and pan. The whole of our party then came up in turn with white handkerchiefs on which the itr (attar of roses) was sprinkled and in which the pan (betel-nut wrapped in gold leaf) was placed.

Here I made my first mistake, for I should have shaken hands with the King and said goodbye; but having forgotten to do this, the whole of our party had to go by a second time to say goodbye, first to His Majesty and then to all the Court officials and Generals. Great care was taken to avoid our shaking hands with any mere Colonels. This is because the members of the Maharaja's family are born Colonels and become Generals at an early age.

As we withdrew, the rain stopped as if by magic. I gather that the behaviour of the weather on this occasion was regarded as a good omen. On our departure this time we were escorted by the King's own Bodyguard, who were somewhat similarly dressed to the Lancers except that they wore gold spurs instead of silver ones.

SATURDAY, 11 MAY We left the house at 0800 for the magnificent parade ground. General Kaiser joined my car halfway as he was in

---

[1] He had probably written it too; in 1946 the King was a cipher and all power rested with the Bahadur Ranas.

overall command of the arrangements. On the parade ground between 3000 and 4000 men were drawn up. Every man on the parade ground had served under my orders in the Burma campaign. I was much touched by the trouble the Maharaja had taken to arrange this parade.

After receiving the general salute, to my great astonishment we went round the parade in an open motor-car escorted by a cavalry escort. The parade then marched past in extremely good order, after which they advanced in review order. Since I had asked that they should come as near as possible, instead of advancing a mere hundred yards they advanced about three hundred yards, in very good line. This still meant that the far flank was four or five hundred yards from where I was standing, which meant that I had to shout like a Sergeant Major to make my speech in Nepali heard. I had rehearsed this carefully with General Bahadur, and it appears that the men both heard and understood what I said. I had not had time to learn it by heart, and had to keep glancing at a little card in my hand.

After this General Kaiser read a reply in an inaudible voice, but full of knowing references to 'the young tri-phibian', etc.

After this the Nepalese artillery on the parade ground fired a 17-gun salute, and we left the parade.

It was very aggravating to note that the parade ground, which is nearly a mile long, would have taken the York without much difficulty; but as they have a theory that aeroplanes would cut the spirits departing from the dead on their way to Heaven, this has been forbidden. This is of course a very convenient myth to preserve the feudal system from the encroachment of civilization and democracy.

SUNDAY, 12 MAY   General Krishna came and fetched us again for sightseeing, and we drove off in the opposite direction to the town of Bhatong. After this we went to a fascinating holy burning ghat at Pashupati Nath. The sacred monkeys all collected round to be fed, and were very tame and amusing and cheeky.

We then drove to the new Nepalese Museum and were completely tired out walking round it. On the way back we were taken to see a recumbent Buddha, lying half-immersed in a water tank. General Krishna explained that this was not the original, but a copy made specially for the King to look at, since tradition forbade him to look at the original and he was naturally interested to see what the forbidden figure looked like. Next door there was a tank with large marseer fish, which we fed.

We had a small luncheon party for the six British residents in Nepal, the Macleods and their two sons, and the Smythies.[1] They told us that in the 131 years since Nepal has been theoretically open to Europeans only a very few hundred have ever been allowed into the country. Since there is no means of getting in except by the Maharaja's invitation and arrangement, and the trip is extremely difficult, this is not surprising.

The Singha Durbar is a most magnificent building, so great that to go from one part to another one drives in a motor-car. The usual scarlet guard and band were in evidence at both parts of the palace, and the Kali Bahadurs gave a performance of native dancing which enlivened the otherwise rather tedious process of a party at which neither drinks nor eats are served.

Next we were conducted up to meet the ladies of the family. The others tried to follow but were turned back on the grounds of Purdah, though I was for some curious reason allowed to come. All the ladies were dressed in their very best, with colossal diamond tiaras and jewels, which appeared to be rather wasted since they are usually seen by practically nobody but the other ladies.

On returning to the Durbar Hall, the Maharaja read a speech. Having seen it before, I succeeded in more or less recognizing it. I then had to reply, and after this we departed and the Generals trooped out into the courtyard and the Maharaja came across to shake hands with me in the open car and holding my hand firmly he made me a loud speech of loyalty and devotion to his Ally our King, ending up with the message, 'Please tell His Majesty he can always count on Nepal.'

We then drove to the British Legation, where the six members of the British community gave a supper, at the end of which the Chargé d'Affaires proposed the health of the King and then the Maharaja. We assumed that the King was the King of England, and that the King of Nepal was omitted: but we didn't like to ask.

After our own health had been drunk in champagne supplied by the Maharaja we retired to bed.

MONDAY, 13 MAY We presented swords and framed photographs to all the Generals, in accordance with the regular custom, and

[1] The Forestry Officer and his wife.

at 0900 were seen off from Bahadur Bhawan by General Bahadur himself.

When we got to Malimati on the outskirts of the city there was the usual large guard and band drawn up. The car slowed down but showed no signs of stopping, and when I protested Colonel Mukunda[1] said that he had been told that it was unnecessary for me to waste my time getting out to take the salute. Being unable to make the driver stop, I leapt out of the car, which was going fairly slowly and thus brought it to a full stop. Meanwhile the old business of bugles and band took place, whilst another 17-gun salute was fired from the fort. The great thing in Nepal is to take no notice of the Guards of Honour.

We arrived at Thankote at 0930, and then started the reverse procession back to civilization.

Actually we took a slightly different route between the first and second mountain ranges, going to a perfectly delightful place called Markhu for lunch. Here to our intense astonishment the khitmagars who had served us breakfast at Bahadur Bhawan, had arrived ahead of us to lay lunch. As we thought we had gone as fast as it was possible to go over that treacherous ground, it is still a miracle how they arrived ahead of us with the whole of lunch.

At 1730 we got to Sisigarhi, where we sat down and wrote our bread and butter letters and tried to dry off our wet clothes, for it had rained hard part of the way.

TUESDAY, 14 MAY   I made another abortive attempt to inspect the guard, but was once more frustrated by their being stood at ease as soon as I got anywhere near them. As we proceeded to mount the ponies a 17-gun salute was fired, which almost stampeded them. This is the sixth salute in our short stay, which has involved the Nepalese Army in expending 102 rounds.

We left Sisigarhi at 0720, and changed back to cars at Bimphedi, reaching Simra airfield at 1020. We had been very worried by reports on account of rain, for the problem of getting ourselves to the next airfield would have been a very difficult one to solve. Fortunately, however, it was dry enough for us to take off with a light load of petrol. We therefore had to land at Cawnpore to refuel, and then made straight for Jammu.

[1] Colonel Mukunda Bahadur was the engineer in charge of the ropeway to Katmandu.

When we got to Jammu we found that clouds had filled the pass into the Vale of Kashmir, rising from 10,000 feet to about 16,000 feet. We eventually had to climb to 17,000 feet to get over the mountains and clouds. There was no oxygen on board. The second pilot blacked out, and John struggled like a fish out of water against passing out completely. We finally landed at 1820.

SUNDAY, 19 MAY   Just before we were due to take off a Most Immediate telegram came from Flying Control at Delhi telling us that all grounds were unserviceable on account of a dust storm at Delhi, and that they regretted it would be impossible for our trip to take place that day. I'm afraid I didn't believe Flying Control at Delhi, and as it is by no means certain that one can get out of the Vale of Srinagar on any day and cumulus nimbus clouds had already begun to form over the hills, we took off and raced for the pass, getting by about five minutes before the clouds closed in. The weather on the other side appeared to be perfect, so I sent a message saying that I particularly wanted to get through to Delhi to meet the Cabinet Mission;[1] only to receive a curt order to land at Lahore.

On landing at Lahore I rang up the Air C.-in-C. in India (Sir Roderick Carr), and he undertook to go down to Palam airfield and open it himself. When we got there we found visibility was at least two miles, and that an inexperienced young officer, without reference to higher authority, had taken it upon himself to close all airfields and turn us back. We landed successfully at 1910.

There was a message from the Viceroy asking if I could come and see him at once. He wished to discuss the offer of rice made by the Indonesian Prime Minister Sjahrir to Nehru. He asked me whether I would meet Nehru with him after dinner, to which I agreed.

We went to a small party given by Claude Auchinleck at which I was able to have long talks with Lord Pethick-Lawrence, the Secretary of State for India and Burma, and A. V. Alexander, First Lord of the Admiralty. I asked the latter if he would be prepared to give me a command afloat when I had finished writing my despatches, and had had my full share of leave. He was very friendly about this and suggested an aircraft-carrier squadron.

---

[1] An abortive mission consisting of Stafford Cripps, A. V. Alexander and Pethwick-Lawrence, trying to establish a basis for a transfer of power in India.

At 2215 I attended the meeting with the Viceroy and Nehru, and we took off from Palam in the York at 2330.

MONDAY, 20 MAY to SATURDAY, 25 MAY   We arrived at Kellang airfield at 1400, and drove to Flagstaff House with Boy Browning, with whom I immediately started work. After he had gone Miles Killearn came to see me to discuss the rice situation, etc.

On Tuesday we drove out together in the afternoon to meet the new Governor General, Malcolm MacDonald,[1] at Changi, and in the evening attended a farewell cocktail party given to us by the Australian Mission in the Assistant Secretary's house in the Government House grounds, which Edwina had originally occupied during the surrender.

So many people wanted to give farewell lunches, dinners and cocktail parties during our last few days in Singapore that the Assistant Chief of Staff had had to have a Staff 'plan' made!

On Wednesday Edwina and I attended the swearing-in ceremony of the new Governor General, and immediately after this I had my first interview with him at Government House, which was very satisfactory.[2]

We attended the big official dinner for the Governor General at Government House, which was a proper muddle as none of the ADCs had a clue. This was combined with the Governor's farewell dinner for us.

My SAC meeting was attended not only by the Special Commissioner, as usual, but by the Governor General and the Governors of Singapore and Malaya.

I had a small luncheon party for Malcolm MacDonald and Miles Killearn, at which we talked very valuable shop.

On Saturday I had a SAC meeting at 1000, and at 1100 all the Dutch representatives came in for a two-hour meeting, which I thought was going to be terribly stormy but passed off better than any we have ever had with them.

After this I had a large lunch party for all the Dutch which included Vice Admiral Edelsten, who is here representing C.-in-C. British Pacific

---

[1] Malcolm MacDonald was to remain Governor General of the Malayan Union and Singapore only until July, at which point he became Governor General of the whole of British South-East Asia.
[2] Malcolm MacDonald and Mountbatten were at one in their views about the future of Malaya, or indeed any other colony.

Fleet, as they take over the areas to the east of the straits of Malacca from the East Indies Fleet at the end of the month.

Edwina arrived back at teatime and came with me to a cocktail party given by the signal officers of all three services for me in my capacity as an ex-signal officer. Rear Admiral Egerton gave a farewell dinner to which he invited the two dozen senior Naval officers at present in Singapore. Without a word of warning he stood up at the end of dinner and made a carefully prepared speech with a sheaf of notes in front of him. It could not have been more friendly or pleasant but as I had not thought of one word to say in reply, I found the situation very difficult. Great applause was evoked when he referred to Edwina as the Florence Nightingale of Burma.

SUNDAY, 26 MAY   At 1900 we went to the farewell cocktail party given by the American Liaison Staff in the Tanglin Club. After that we drove out to Johore Bahru to attend the farewell dinner given by Miles and Jacqueline Killearn at Bukit Serene.

Miles embarrassed me very much by standing up and making an excessively flattering speech without any warning, to which of course I had to reply. He could not possibly have said nicer things about the whole of SEAC and the way we have turned over to him. In particular he regretted the removal of the 'umbrella' under which all of them, including himself, had sheltered for so long!

After dinner they had a dance which was attended by a baby elephant carrying an illuminated sign, 'Goodbye, Supremo'. After this there was an exhibition of Malay dancing, at which Miles and I were suddenly called upon to take part.

WEDNESDAY, 29 MAY   People are being really extraordinarily kind about my departure. Apart from Van Mook and his Commanders-in-Chief coming over, partly to say goodbye but mainly for the meetings, the High Commissioner, Military and Naval Commanders-in-Chief in French Indochina have today sent down their three Chiefs of Staff (all old friends of mine) with letters of farewell, and to represent them at my departure.

At 1700 there was a very fine ceremony which was in the nature of my farewell to Singapore, at which I presented a captured 105 mm high-velocity Japanese gun to the Governor for the people of Singapore, and a Union Jack which was used at both the British and Japanese surrenders of Singapore, to the Singapore Municipal Council. Guards of Honour from the three services were drawn up, and subsequently did a very smart march-past. I read a short address, which was followed by addresses by the President of the Municipal Council and by the Governor. Wild (now a full Colonel), who had carried the Union Jack at our surrender, carried it into the Municipal Building, where it was hoisted in the very room in which the Japanese surrender was signed. I unveiled a silver tablet commemorating the surrender.

It all passed off very well, with quite a large crowd watching.

THURSDAY, 30 MAY   I went to my office for special meetings with the Governor General, Special Commissioner, Monty Stopford (in his capacity as Acting SAC Designate), and COS. Although this was virtually a meeting of the Defence Committee, of which the Governor General is Chairman and the Special Commissioner Deputy Chairman, they both waved me into the chair, which was a very generous gesture on their part and means that I have taken the chair at every meeting convened since the restoration of civil government.

We discussed my final telegram in which I am recommending a British Supreme Commander for South-East Asia for the future, together with all the details of how I feel the command should be set up.[1] I was most gratified to receive wholehearted and enthusiastic support from Malcolm MacDonald and Miles Killearn.

We got back to our own farewell cocktail party at 1815, to find, to my intense astonishment and annoyance, that no less than 50 of the guests had already arrived, a quarter of an hour before they were asked. Altogether over 400 people came, and the party appeared to go very well.

The last guest left at 2030, and then we both sat down to sign letters and photographs, whilst eating fish and chips between signatures.

We left the house at 2230, in a procession with police outriders, and stopped at the entrance to Kellang airfield where Jack McKerron, the Chief Secretary of Singapore, met us with a small deputation to show us the new signs which had been put up for 'Mountbatten Road', the by-pass road which is shortly to be re-opened.

---

[1] Little attention was paid to his views; the system of Supreme Command was not reintroduced until 1962, when he was Chief of Defence Staff.

When we got to the airfield a surprise was in store of us, for without my having been consulted they had arranged to lay on a Guard of Honour and band, which were floodlit (a most unusual performance, reminiscent of the Aldershot Tattoo). Two or three hundred people had come to see us off, and we went round shaking hands with everybody. Both the Governor General and Governor, as well as the Special Commissioner, Commanders-in-Chief and all the other high-ups had come.

FRIDAY, 31 MAY   We landed at Dum Dum airfield, Calcutta, at 0715, after a 9-hour flight. The Governor's Military Secretary met us, and drove us to Government House where we had breakfast with the new Governor, Sir Frederick Burrows. He is a railway trade union official, and used to be a Sergeant Major in the Grenadiers, and everyone tells me that he is making an outstanding success of his present job. He certainly is a most charming and intelligent man, and we had a very interesting conversation.

We were airborne at 0930 and after a 4-hour flight arrived at Palam at 1230. We were met by the Air C.-in-C., Sir Roderick Carr, and others, and drove straight to the Viceroy's House. I had final talks with the Viceroy and Claude Auchinleck, whom we are all delighted to hear has been made a Field Marshal. This is the very least recognition that could be accorded to him for the grand part he played in supporting our operations in South-East Asia.

SATURDAY, 1 JUNE 1946   An official farewell had been arranged by India Command and two very smart Guards of Honour from the Royal Scots Fusiliers and the Rajputana Rifles were mounted on Palam airfield. All the senior officers of all Services, including various members of the Government of India, had come down to the airfield, headed by Claude Auchinleck, to see us off. We were airborne at 0810.

We landed at Habbaniya at 1710, after an 11½-hour flight. Edwina, Patricia, John and I flew on to Baghdad in an Anson, whilst the remainder of the party remained in Habbaniya and bathed etc.

In the absence of Stewart Perowne (on leave), Richmond, who is the Oriental Minister, took us round the various sights of Baghdad, and we had a fascinating time in the museum. I believe it is easily the best collection of antiquities in the world, and they have recently opened up a room with their new discoveries dating back to the sixth millennium before Christ.

The Director insisted on having a group taken in the Babylonian Room. After six misfires with the flashlight, the photographer doubled the dose.[1] He then had a hang-fire and we started to move away, when a terrific explosion took place, which appeared to both blind and burn the photographer! We went to the Embassy to change and had dinner.

We flew back at 2300 and took off in the York from Habbaniya at midnight.

SUNDAY, 2 JUNE We landed at Orly, Paris, punctually at 1230. Here I was met by a great gathering of notables. A large Guard of Honour with band and colours was provided by the Garde Republicaine in their pre-war full dress.

Eric Duncannon, who was representing the Ambassador, drove us to the Embassy, where we are staying, and where we were met by the Ambassador (Duff) and Diana Cooper. There was only a small luncheon which included the service attachés.

MONDAY, 3 JUNE Admiral du Vignaux, who used to be the Captain of the *Richelieu*, has been appointed as Chief of my honorary French staff, and he drove with me from the Embassy at 1055 to the Invalides. Here I was met by General Juin (the French CGS) and General Legentilhomme (the Governor of Paris). Inside the courtyard large Guards of Honour (about 150 men apiece) were provided by the infantry of the Garde Republicaine, by the cavalry of the Garde Republicaine (both in full dress), by a detachment from the *Richelieu* sent specially from the ship, and by a detachment from the French Air Force.

After inspecting the guards, I was invested by General Juin with the Grand Cross of the Legion of Honour and the Croix de Guerre. John Brabourne let the side down by smirking visibly when the General was kissing me on both cheeks.

After the investiture there was a march-past at which I took the salute.

The Governor of the Invalides then showed us round the museum

[1] Of magnesium powder.

and church of the Invalides which now includes the tomb and body of Napoleon's son, the Duke of Reichstadt, which was returned from Vienna by Hitler as a gesture during the war.

Next I was driven in an open car by General Juin with outriders in a procession up the Champs Elysées, where Guards of Honour were drawn up, which I inspected. After this I laid a wreath on the tomb of the Unknown Warrior, and signed the book. The crowd gave us a very friendly reception.

We were given a lunch party by General Juin in his suite in the Ministry of War. In the evening I went with the Ambassador to call on the present Head of the French Republic, M. Gouin, and had a very interesting talk. There was a dinner party at the British Embassy, after which they had a singer in, who we were told afterwards had been a collaborator, though this may be a libel.[1]

TUESDAY, 4 JUNE   At 1055 I left with General Juin in an open car with outriders for the Hotel de Ville, driving down the Rue de Rivoli. We were received by M. le Troquer, Minister of the Interior, and led to the great hall, where there was a large and distinguished gathering who M. le Troquer proceeded to address, delivering a typically flattering French eulogy of what I had achieved in the war and for France.

I had only had 24 hours in which to prepare a reply which I had luckily very nearly learned by heart, since there was no pulpit or table on which to lay any notes. It was a great ordeal making a fairly lengthy speech to such a distinguished gathering in French.

After this there was a reception, and Edwina and I both signed the famous *Livre d'or*, she being, I believe, one of the first, if not the first, woman to do so.

We were given an official lunch by M. Michelet, the Minister of the Armed Forces, who had returned from the country specially to give this. Afterwards he (who had spent so long in a German concentration camp) and M. Bidault, the Foreign Minister, got me aside and drew attention to the fact that we had all been born in the same year – 'a good vintage year', they said.

We left from Orly airport, being seen off by the same notables who received us, and with the same large guard and band. We landed in the rain at Northolt airfield at 1730 and were met by representatives from

[1] It was.

the three service ministries, as well as the CCO, Bob Laycock, and Lomax, who used to command 26th Indian Division and now is the District Commander, and others. Last but by no means least was Pamela, and members of my personal staff who had either been demobilized or preceded me to London.

At 1830 we left for London, calling in to see Mama at Kensington Palace *en route*. The family dined quietly at our new house, 16 Chester Street, which is next door to our old one, No.15.

It is lovely to be home again. I am looking forward to taking part in the Victory Parade and to a series of festivities such as receiving the Sword of Honour and Honorary Freedom of the City of London, the Freedom of Romsey, honorary degrees at Oxford and Cambridge, besides innumerable public luncheons and dinners given by various livery companies, clubs and societies, with which I am connected or about to become connected. In fact the next two months look as though they will be fully occupied, but as my job is nominally over now that I have landed in England, except for writing my despatches, the diary will end here.

APPENDIX I

Abbreviations used in text

ACOS	Assistant Chief of Staff
ADCOS	Assistant Deputy Chief of Staff
ALFSEA	Allied Land Forces, South-East Asia
AOC	Air Officer Commanding
BNA	Burmese National Army
BOR	British Other Ranks
CCASO	Chief Civil Affairs Security Officer
CCO	Chief of Combined Operations
CIGS	Chief of the Imperial General Staff
COHQ	Combined Operations Headquarters
COJP	Combined Operations Joint Planners
COS	Chief of Staff
DCOS	Deputy Chief of Staff
DMS	Director of Medical Services
DDMS	Deputy Director of Medical Services
D. of I. or DI	Director of Intelligence
DSAC	Deputy Supreme Allied Commander
ENSA	Entertainments National Service Association
FIC	French Indochina
GHQ	General Headquarters
IBGH	Indian British General Hospital
INA	Indian National Army
KP	King's Pavilion (at Kandy)
LCP	Landing Craft, Personnel
LST	Landing Ship, Tanks
MOI	Ministry of Information

NEI	Netherlands East Indies
PAO	Principal Administrative Officer
PMO	Principal Medical Officer
QMG	Quarter Master General
RAPWI	Returned Association of Prisoners of War, India
SAC	Supreme Allied Commander
SEAC	South-East Asia Command
SHAEF	Supreme Headquarters Allied Expeditionary Force
WAAF	Women's Auxiliary Air Force
WAC	Women's Army Corps
WRNS	Women's Royal Naval Service

APPENDIX II

Christian names and nicknames used in text

Al	General Albert C. Wedemeyer
Alex	General Sir Harold Alexander
Bob	Major General Sir Robert Laycock
Boy	Major General Frederick Browning
Brian	Major General Brian Kimmins
Bunnie	H. H. Phillips
Charles	Squadron Leader Charles St John
Claude	General Sir Claude Auchinleck
D.I.	Lieutenant General D. I. Sultan
Edwina	Lady Louis Mountbatten
Flags	Lieutenant Commander Arthur Leveson
Frankie	Major General Francis Festing
Gimo	Generalissimo Chiang Kai-shek
Henry	Lieutenant General Sir Henry Pownall
Janey	Mrs Peter Lindsay
Micky	Commander Michael Hodges
Pamela	Miss Pamela Mountbatten
Patricia	3rd Officer Patricia Mountbatten
Peter	Peter Murphy
Philip	Prince Philip of Greece
Ronnie	Paymaster Captain Ronald Brockman
Speck	Lieutenant General Raymond Wheeler
T.V.	T. V. Soong

INDEX

A comma rather than a semi-colon between entries denotes that both entries are covered by the preceding sub-heading.

Leese, Lieutenant General Sir Oliver, 150;
154–6; 160; 165; 187–8; 194–6;
disagreements with Mountbatten 199;
202; and dismissal of Slim 205, 207;
209; dismissed 220, 234
Legentilhomme, General, 341
Leigh-Mallory, Air Chief Marshal Sir
Trafford, 124; 147; 154; 189
Lentaigne, Major General Walter, 82;
88–9; 111; 114; 131
Letellier, Yola, 70n
Le Troquer, André, 342
Leveson, Arthur, 'Flags', 3; 6–8; 21; 59;
69; 75; 101; 109; 120; 165–6; 182;
leaves 270
Liao, General, 78
Lincoln, Colonel A., 103–4
Lindsay, Janey, 102–4; 163
Lindsay, Peter, 102–4
Linnell, Air Marshal Sir John, 5
Lomax, Major General Cyril, 46n; 76;
94; 204; 343
Lothian, Sir Arthur, 140
Lovink, Dr, 25–6; 103
Lowther, Brigadier, A. W., 94
Lumsden, Lieutenant General H., 23
Lutze, Captain Betty, 103–4

MacArthur, Arthur, 222
MacArthur, General Douglas, 23; 40;
148; Mountbatten visits 221–5; 232;
235; 238; 241n; 248; 254
MacClure, Major General Robert, 193
MacDonald, Lieutenant Colonel, 180; 191
MacDonald, Malcolm, 337; 339–40
McGeary, Sister, 22–3; 64; 90–1
McKell, J., 310–11
Mackenzie, Colin, 263
McKerron, Brigadier Patrick, 289
Macleod, Brigadier M. W. M., 31; 59
Macleod, Lieutenant Colonel N. M., 330;
334
MacMichael, Sir Harold, 272
McMullen, Major General Donald, 190
Maisey, Lieutenant Colonel, 256
Makassar, 269
Malaya, xiii; 241; 243–5; 256; 271–3;
public order in 288–90; 303–4; 325;
327

Maltby, Air Vice Marshal Paul, 240
Mandalay, 121n; 165n; 175; 180; 188;
190; captured 196, 199; 275
Manila, 221–5
Mansergh, Major General R., 194; 322–4
Marshall, General George, 34–5; 50;
111; 150–1; 185; 212; tells
Mountbatten about atom bomb
229–30; 241
Martin, Rear Admiral B. C. S., 244
Mary, Queen, 237
Mason-MacFarlane, Sir Noel, 3
Maunsell, Brigadier Mark, 302
Melbourne, 307–11
Messervy, General Sir Frank, 45; in the
Arakan 66–7, 94–5; 181; 204; as
GOC Malaya 271, 288–9; 303; 326
Michelet, Edmond, 342
Milford, Major General E. J., 269
Milford-Haven, Dowager Marchioness
of, 122; 234; 283; 343
Mogaung, 131–2
Montgomery, General Sir Bernard (later
Field Marshal Viscount) 124–5; 235;
270n
Moody, Vice Admiral C., 104; 111; 214
Moore, Petty Officer Steward, 20; 53;
127
Moore, Sir Henry and Lady, 197; 199;
210
Mountbatten, Edwina Lady Louis (later
Countess Mountbatten of Burma),
15–16; 45; 49; 55; 71; 122–3; 125; to
visit South-East Asia 132; 144; 157; in
South-East Asia 168, 170–2, 177–8,
186, 188–90; in Chungking 191–4;
198–202; 210; 233–7; returns to
South-East Asia 238; 242–3; 245; and
prisoners of war 250–1, 253, 255–6;
259–65; 269–70; 288; 296–300; 302;
and Nehru 304–5; in Australia
305–13; in New Zealand 313–14,
316–17; 320; in Nepal 327–31;
337–40; 342–3
MOUNTBATTEN, ADMIRAL LORD LOUIS
(later ADMIRAL OF THE FLEET EARL
MOUNTBATTEN OF BURMA), appointed
xi; staff xii; task xii–xiv; journey out
3–6; arrives Delhi 7; opens HQ 7–8;

of Rangoon 211, 214; succeeds Sultan 217; 219; 237; at surrender ceremony, Singapore 245–6, 250; 254
Whitehead, Major General Ennis, 225
Whitworth Jones, Air Vice Marshal J., 26–7; 206
Wild, Major, 255; 339
Wildman-Lushington, Major General G. E., 82–3; 89; 102; 112; 151; 198–9
Williams, Air Vice Marshal, 18
Williams, Lieutenant Colonel J. H., 'Elephant Bill', 60–1
Williams, Thomas (later Baron), 236
Willingdon, Marchioness of, 23
Wilson, Squadron Leader, Douglas, 8; 18; 102; 106; 138

Wilson-Haffenden, Brigadier, 82
Wilson, General Sir Henry Maitland (later Field Marshal Baron), 5; 31; 35; 100
Wilson, Leonard, Bishop of Singapore, 247; 251–2
Wingate, Major General Orde, 7–8; illness of 22–3, 27–8; 45; 50; 55–6; 64–5; killed 82, 88, 90–1; 86; 92; 114; 130
Winterton, Major General T. J. W., 45; 66
Wise, Sir John, 111
Wood, Major General Samuel, 161–2

Yount, Colonel, 26

Zipper, xiv; 221n; 244